AF413342

CHESS
PLAYERS

FROM   WU-TANG CLAN
CHARLIE CHAPLIN   TO

CHESS PLAYERS

FUEL

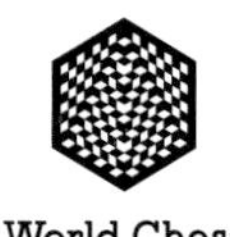

World Chess

What is chess? The answer is obvious, right? It's a game.

But throughout its history, it has often represented more than that, even taking on metaphorical meanings. In the latter half of the 13th century, Jacobus de Cessolis, a Dominican friar, wrote a series of sermons using chess to explain morality and the place of people in society. They were collected and published in a 1472 book called *Libor de moribus hominum et officiis nobilium super ludo scacchorum* (*Book of the customs of men and the duties of nobles, or the Book of Chess*). The book was among the most popular in Europe in the Middle Ages.

Peter Alfonsi, a 12th-century Jewish Spanish physician, writer and astronomer (among many other trades), wrote in *Disciplina Clericalis* that mastering chess was one of the seven skills any good knight must acquire. In other words, it was an essential part of the chivalric code.

For some, chess has never been simply a game. Marcel Duchamp, one of the most influential artists of the 20th century, said, 'All artists are not chess players – all chess players are artists.'

Then there are those who have devoted themselves to mastering chess's intricacies. Anatoly Karpov, the reigning world champion from 1975 to 1985, opined that 'Chess is everything: art, science and sport,' while Bobby Fischer, who preceded Karpov as champion, stated even more succinctly, 'Chess is life'.

A Great and Long History

Fischer's statement is obviously an exaggeration and for anyone who has not deeply immersed themselves in the game, the remark might suggest that the person who said it was obsessive, at the least, if not psychologically unstable. That Fischer spent the latter part of his life as a recluse spouting conspiracy theories and antisemitic vitriol adds to the sense that his comment is hyperbole.

It has more than a grain of truth, however, when chess's development is examined against the arc of human evolution and achievement.

The exact origins of chess are not known, but its precursor, called chaturanga, a Sanskrit word meaning 'four-limbed' or 'four arms', came from what is modern-day India and seems to have originated about the fifth century AD, though some information suggests it is older. The name chaturanga was a reference to the ancient army divisions on which the game was based: infantry (today's pawns), cavalry (knights), elephants (bishops), and chariots (rooks). As in modern chess, there was a king (raja), but instead of a queen, there was a counsellor or vizier. In addition, the object was also to corner, or checkmate, the king.

From South Asia, the game spread along trade routes (particularly the legendary silk road) and, as it did, the rules evolved. Heading east, it became xiangqi in China (commonly known as Chinese chess), and in Japan, it morphed into shogi.

To the west, the game became popular in Persia (modern-day Iran) before spreading through North Africa and eventually up into Europe through the Iberian Peninsula and Italy.

By the eighth century, it had conquered most of the ancient world, east and west.

But the rules of the game were still not fixed. Despite Jacobus de Cessolis's use of chess to teach probity and social order, in some parts of Europe, playing chess was seen as evidence of moral decay because it was played with dice (to determine the moves) and so became associated with gambling. Furthermore, the moves of some pieces, notably the pawns and the vizier, which had now become the queen, often varied.

It was not until 1497, following the publication in Salamanca, Spain, of the *Repeticion de Amores y Arte de Ajedrez con CL 150 Juegos de Partido* (*Discourse on Love and the Art of Chess with 150 Games*) by Luis Ramírez de Lucena, that the modern rules of the game were first codified.

Once the rules were set, chess strategy evolved. The game and the quest for its perfection were perceived as a worthy pursuit in their own right. Some philosophers of the Enlightenment (a 17th- and 18th-century European intellectual movement) enjoyed chess, elevating its status in their writings. It soon became widely accepted and revered, not only in elite social and political circles, but also among the general population.

Across Europe, cafés and clubs opened their doors for people to watch and play the game. One of the most famous was the Café de la Régence in Paris, where people from all walks of life gathered to play. Among them were noted philosophers and writers such as Diderot and Rousseau, as well as political figures, including the American polymath Benjamin Franklin and even Napoleon shortly before he became emperor.

Early Innovators and Champions

The first great practitioner of the game was François-André Danican Philidor (1726–1795), a prominent French opéra comique composer, his bust is enshrined on the exterior of the Opéra Garnier in Paris. He was the first player to appreciate the importance of the organisation of pawns (which he called the 'soul of chess') on the board during a game. His ideas remain influential today.

In 1834, the first legitimate 'great' chess match took place. It was actually a series of six matches played at the Westminster Chess Club in London between the players widely acknowledged as the best of their day: Louis Charles Mahé de La Bourdonnais of France and Alexander McDonnell of Ireland. Over a period of four months, the men played a total of 85 games, with La Bourdonnais coming out on top by a score of 45 wins to 27 losses with 13 draws.

The next innovation arrived in 1851 with the first international chess tournament. It was organised in London by Howard Staunton, an English player who for the previous decade had been considered the best in the world. Staunton clearly expected to win, but the champion turned out to be Adolf Anderssen, a German mathematics instructor. Thanks to this victory, he would wear the mantle of world's best player until the end of the decade, when he was beaten and surpassed by Paul Morphy, an American master who is still considered one of the greatest players ever.

During the London tournament, Anderssen also played a casual game with another participant, a fellow German named Lionel Kieseritzky. After Anderssen won with one of the greatest sacrificial attacks in history, it became known as the Immortal Game. A year later, Anderssen authored another brilliant win against Jean Dufresne, another German, which became known as the Evergreen Game. Anderssen's manner of play was typical of the era – a period called romantic for its stunning, swashbuckling style and the lack of defensive capabilities of the players.

After Staunton failed to win his signature event, he quickly faded from the scene, but he left one other permanent mark on the game. In 1849, a designer named Nathaniel Cooke created a new set that he patented. Staunton agreed to lend his name to the design to promote it. It has been known as the Staunton design ever since and following that first tournament in 1851, was adopted as the official design for pieces used in all tournaments worldwide.

As the 19th century drew to a close, there was one more important evolution to the game. In 1886, a match was organised between Wilhelm Steinitz, an Austrian, later American, player, and Johannes Zukertort, who was born in Poland but later lived in Britain. By general acclaim, the match was acknowledged to be for the world championship. Steinitz won decisively thus becoming the first official world champion and marking the beginning of the modern era of chess.

Why People Like Chess

The popularity of chess has exploded in recent years. On World Chess Day 2023 (20 July), the United Nations estimated that more than 600 million people regularly play the game. One factor that has contributed to its growth was the onset of the Covid-19 pandemic in early 2020 – people who were confined at home wanted something to do and chess is ideal to play online, day or night. The mini-series *The Queen's Gambit* aired on Netflix in late 2020 and within weeks of its release had been viewed by more than 60 million people, giving the game a huge boost.

Even without those events, however, chess has features that help it flourish.

It is accessible and easily portable. There are sets made of expensive precious materials, but simple plastic or wooden sets can cost as little as a few dollars, making it an affordable leisure that from the very beginning could be taken anywhere – even into space, as when the cosmonauts played a game against ground control in 1970 (page 127) a scenario that was repeated in 2008 with Greg Chamitoff, an astronaut aboard the International Space Station.

For musicians who can be on the road for months at a time, chess is an engaging pastime that is easily carried on trips between gigs (for example, Ray Charles on page 47 and Dizzy Gillespie on page 49). It can also be played anytime, as by showgirls waiting to go on stage (pages 30–31).

Despite the glamour of the movies, film sets can be boring places. It might take hours to set up a take, then shoot it over and over from different angles, until the director is satisfied. For decades on the sets of films, chess has been a way for actors, such as John Wayne (pages 20–21 and 28) and Marlon Brando (pages 13–14 and 29), to while away the time between shots. Before he became an A-list star, Humphrey Bogart (pages 8–11) often supported himself as a chess hustler on the streets of New York City. He also taught the game to the actress Lauren Bacall, his last wife, and they would play at home.

Though it might seem a bit paradoxical because it is a war game, chess is a fixture among those in the military, whether waiting for action (pages 113–121) or as prisoners-of-war (page 112).

Chess has long been a solace for another group of people with a lot of time on their hands: prisoners (pages 128–129). In recent years, a number of prisons have partnered with chess federations to use the game as part of the rehabilitation process. Chess is used to develop memory, logical thinking and inspire self-motivation.

We are (mostly) social animals and chess encourages social contact because anyone who wants to play needs an opponent. If played in public, such as in parks (pages 131–135, 139–143, 154–155), on beaches (pages 156–157, 160–161, 165, 167) or even the thermal baths of Budapest, Hungary (pages 163–164), the players may attract an audience, even if the weather is inclement (pages 136–138). Some of those people may even participate by offering their own (sometimes unwanted) opinions about the moves of the players – an activity called kibitzing – making the game the basis for even more social activity.

As Duchamp said, playing chess requires creativity because the players must imagine a goal and then invent a path to reach it. Duchamp, who gave up his career as an artist for many years to be a full-time chess player, was hardly alone among artists for his appreciation for the game. Among those who shared his passion were Man Ray (pages 62–63) and Max Ernst (pages 58–59 and 61). A seminal exhibition in New York City in 1944–45 called *The Imagery of Chess* included those three artists as well as others (i.e., Alexander Calder, Yves Tanguy, Isamu Noguchi, as well as the composer John Cage), who each designed a set or a piece of art around the theme of chess.

Great writers, including Vladimir Nabokov (pages 72–73) and Leo Tolstoy (pages 106–107), alongside revolutionaries like Lenin (page 109), Castro and Che Guevara (pages 122–123), and philosophers too, such as Nobel laureate Bertrand Russell (page 74), have all been drawn to chess.

Some musicians, in addition to playing the game, have incorporated ideas and themes of chess into their music. For the Wu-Tang Clan (pages 188–189), who revolutionised hip-hop music in the 1990s, chess is one of the three legs of the group's ethos (along with martial arts and music). RZA, the group's architect, wrote in *The Wu-Tang Manual* (2004), 'Another reason that chess is part of the Wu-Tang essence is because it's a game of war – it's about a battle. And Wu-Tang was formed in battles, from challenging each other. In MCing, the Wu-Tang Clan was always powerful because we were challenging each other all the time.'

Perhaps because many people find chess so difficult to master, playing the game has always been associated with intelligence, so when movies or television series want to show that a character is formidable, that character is often portrayed as a chess expert, as with Mr Spock (page 43) in *Star Trek* (1966–1969).

Sometimes mastery of chess and the intelligence it represents signifies evil or evil intent, as with Kronsteen, the SPECTRE agent in *From Russia with Love* (1963), who is also a grandmaster. Or in *Blade Runner* (1982),

when Roy Batty, the replicant, helps J.F. Sebastian beat Eldon Tyrell, the designer of the replicants, thereby tricking Tyrell into letting them into his residence, where Batty murders him.

From the dawn of the computer era, building a computer that could play better than the best person was a benchmark for artificial intelligence. Even after a computer beat the world champion, chess has continued to be a rich resource for testing the problem-solving capabilities of these machines. As recently as 2023, a chess problem that was apparently impossible for computers to understand was finally solved by using artificial intelligence systems working in parallel like microprocessors – a new way of configuring them.

In many sports, differences in strength, speed, or size create inequality. As a coach once said about basketball, 'You can't coach height,' meaning you can't make people taller than they already are. Chess holds out the promise that if people work hard enough, they can be as good, or better, than anyone else. Moreover, since everyone plays by the same rules and with the same number of pieces, theoretically chess is a level playing board.

Or it should be. For reasons that no one understands perfectly, women have, in general, underperformed in comparison to men. There have only been two women – Judit Polgár of Hungary and Hou Yifan of China – who have ever been ranked within the top 60 players in the world. But if one day a woman is to triumph in a sport or game in which men usually excel, it is perhaps more likely to be chess than anything else.

The Essence of Chess Is...

While the above explains somewhat the fascination that chess holds for many people, it does not explain it all. Some regard it as more than a pastime: they eat, breathe and live the game. Why? One clue is in what Karpov said about chess: it is art, science and sport – a combination of activities, sometimes overlapping, that people value and enjoy.

Chess undeniably has sporting elements in that it is a competitive game, even for casual fans. When you play chess, it can sometimes feel as if time itself has stopped and the only thing that matters is the board in front of you. Note the look of concentration on the faces of Humphrey Bogart (page 9), Paul Newman (page 37) and Bob Dylan (page 45).

The level of competitiveness among professional players can reach stratospheric heights. The ferocious stare of Mikhail Tal (page 83), one of the most formidable opponents in history, could be unnerving and the same was true for Garry Kasparov (page 97). The same look is equally evident on the face of Nona Gaprindashvili (pages 92–93).

While it is clearly a sport, chess is also artistic. Sometimes when discussing a game, great players will describe a move or series of moves as 'beautiful' just as someone might describe a goal in football (soccer). Vasily Smyslov (page 80), who won the world championship in 1957, was almost as much an artist as a chess player – a bass singer, he had auditioned for the Bolshoi Opera and at the time he won the title his profession was listed as 'music student'.

World-class musicians also appreciate chess for its artistic tendencies. In 1937, a 10-game match was organised at the Master of Arts Club in Moscow between Sergey Prokofiev, one of the 20th century's greatest composers, and David Oistrakh, one of the world's preeminent violinists. Only seven games of the match were completed before Oistrakh conceded, but the club was packed with spectators who had come to watch the great musicians play chess.

Unlike some artistic endeavours, chess is not usually a solo act. (The exception is in the creation of chess problems, of which the great writer Vladimir Nabokov was a passionate originator, describing the results as 'worthwhile art'.) The back and forth of a game is like counterpointe in ballet – it takes both players to create something artistic, even if they are not intentionally working together to do so. In that respect, chess is not, or at least does not have to be, purely adversarial. Such a possibility is suggested in Yoko Ono's 1966 work, *Play It By Trust, aka White Chess Set* (pages 178–179), which depends on collaboration between opponents because they are required to work together to remember whose pieces are whose.

(Unfortunately, collaboration also occasionally happens in competitive chess when it should not. In these cases, for reasons of their standing in a tournament, or their friendship away from the board, players agree to not really play a game. This act is called a grandmaster draw and is frowned upon by fans and purists.)

The intellectual connection between science and chess goes back centuries – to the 1770s to be exact. This was when a Hungarian inventor named Wolfgang von Kempelen created the Mechanical Turk, a chess-playing automaton. Although it was a fraud (a chess player was concealed inside, working the machine), it captivated people in Europe and the United States for decades, playing games against notable statesmen, including Napoleon and Benjamin Franklin.

On a more credible level, Mikhail Botvinnik (pages 80–81), Smyslov's adversary in his three world championship matches, embodied the sense of chess as a science. Indeed, his preparation and approach to the game were guided entirely by scientific reasoning, as he explained in his writings.

Whether or not Botvinnik was right, chess clearly has a mathematical basis as there are only a finite number of possible moves in a game – though estimates of that number is anywhere from 10 to the 50th power to 10 to the 120th power, which is more than the number of atoms in the observable universe.

It also explains why preparation and study are so essential to becoming a good or even great player. Like scientists, chess players are constantly searching for answers and 'truths' – trying moves and discarding them if they do not hold up to scrutiny in the crucible of competition, just as scientists discard theories that do not explain the data gleaned from experiments.

More Than a Game

As Jacobus de Cessolis demonstrated, chess lends itself to metaphor and over the centuries the ideas of the game have become part of everyday language. When Bob Dylan wrote the song 'Only a Pawn in Their Game', the meaning was understood. Indeed, there are numerous examples of how chess references have worked their way into common terminology.

Someone can be put in checkmate, or in check. A person may be stalemated, or try a risky gambit, or an operation in business may reach the endgame. In politics, there is often a comparison between one person or side playing chequers (the less complicated and therefore less sophisticated game) while the protagonist is playing chess, denoting a large superiority in strategy and/or intelligence. Even some of the more technical terms, like zugzwang (meaning that any move or action will result in catastrophe) sometimes crop up in common use.

Chess is clearly many things to many people, which makes it more than a game. On the pages that follow, there are photographs of people famous and unknown playing chess in competitions and in the streets. Some of the images are by world-famous photographers, including Henri Cartier-Bresson and Gordon Parks. There are images of the best players who ever lived and of people who were casual fans but perhaps loved the game almost as passionately. These photographs demonstrate the beauty and complexity of the human condition through the prism of the 'game of kings'.

Humphrey Bogart might have been the best chess player ever among Hollywood's A-List stars. How good was he? In the 1920s, as a struggling New York City actor, he was able to survive by hustling chess in arcades against all comers for dimes and quarters. After he became a star, Bogart remained dedicated to the game, becoming a tournament director for the United States Chess Federation and serving as the head of the California State Chess Association. He also taught Lauren Bacall, his fourth wife, how to play and the couple often played at home (see overleaf, 1955).

Right: Lew Snowden, John Loder (who was visiting the set), Humphrey Bogart, and Lizabeth Scott between scenes filming *Dead Reckoning* (1947).

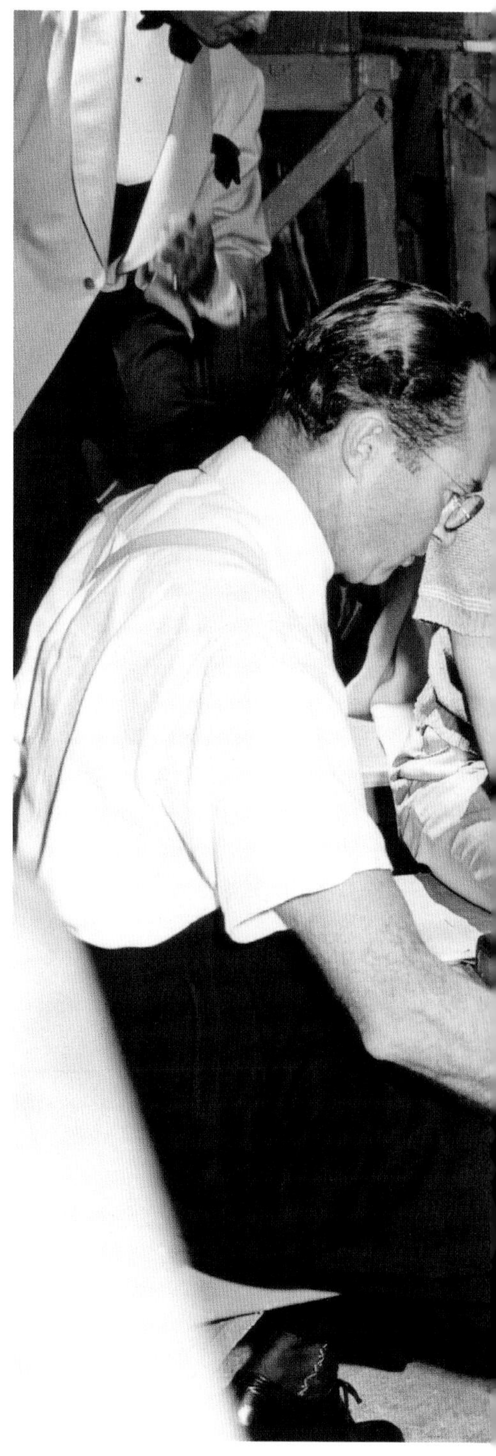

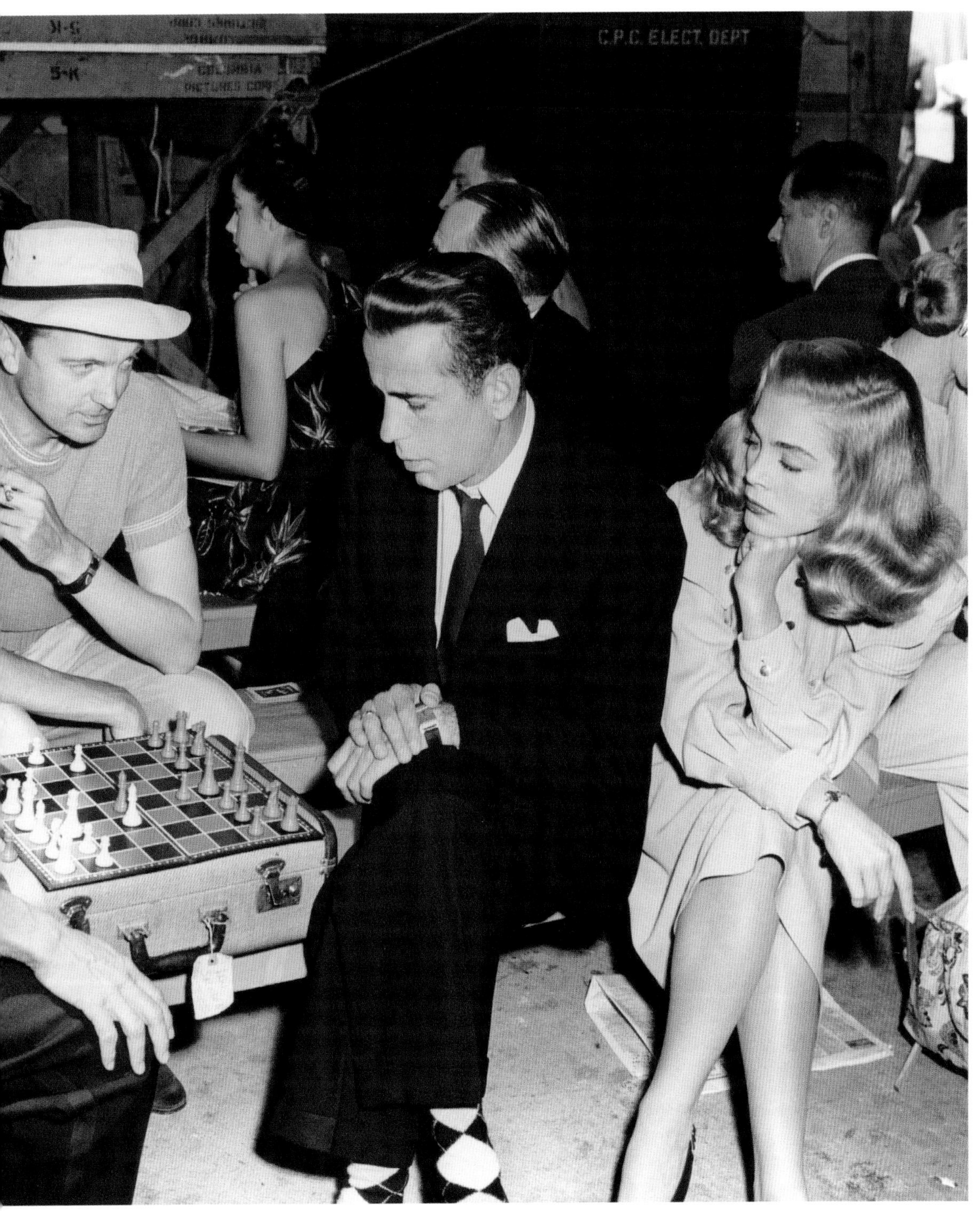
C.P.C. ELECT. DEPT
COLUMBIA
PICTURES CORP

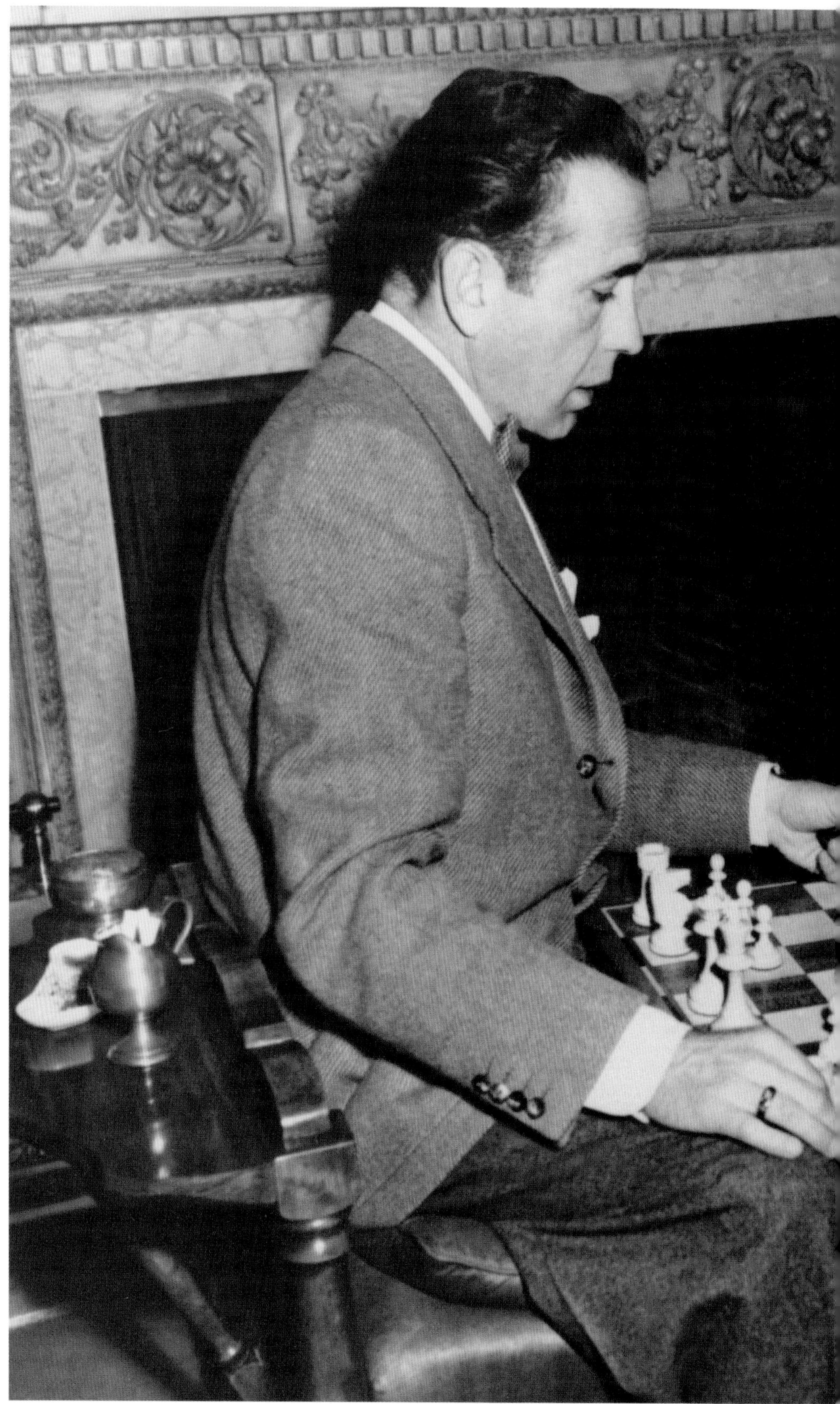

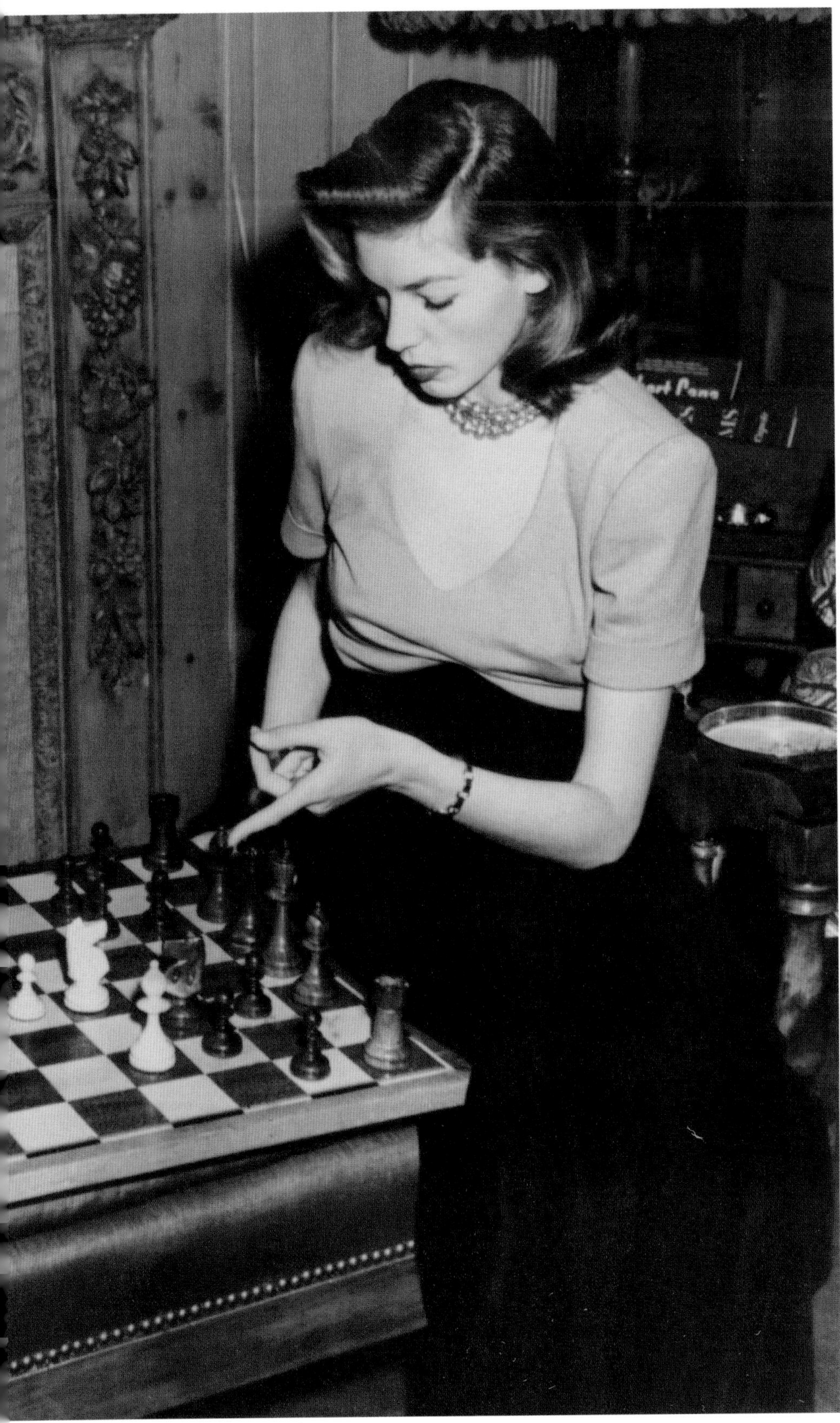

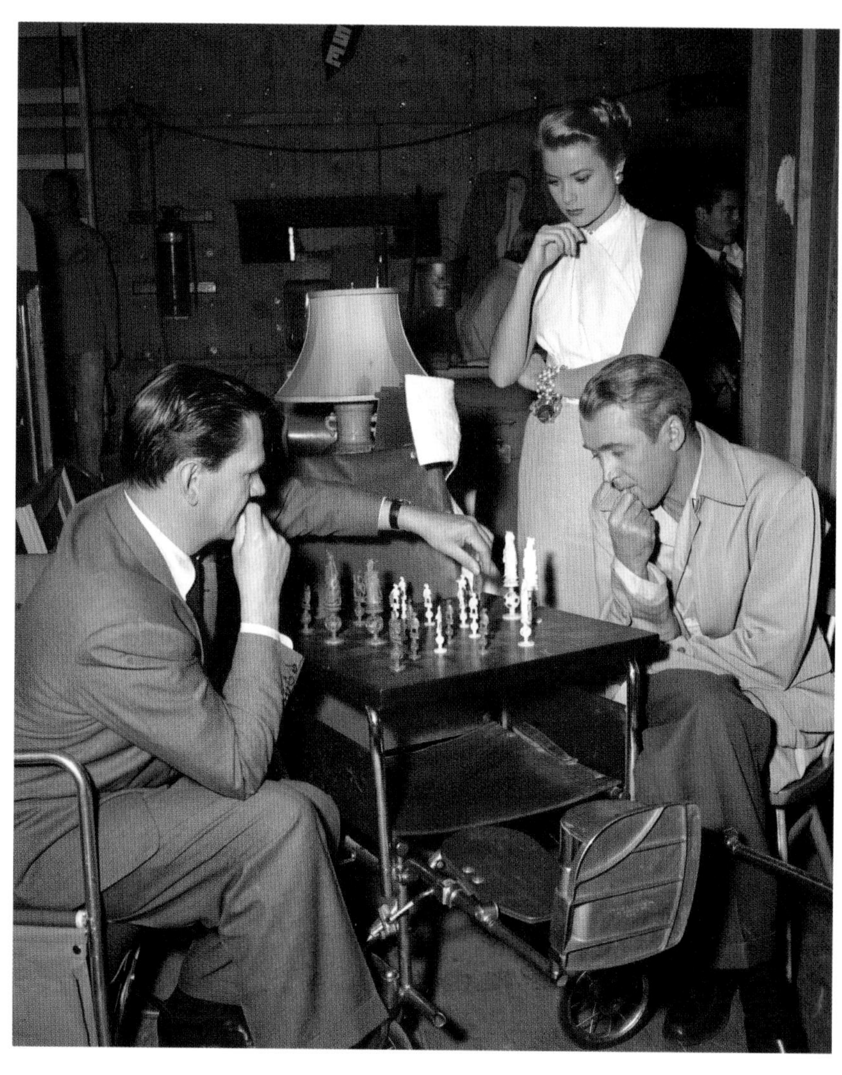

Wendell Corey and Jimmy Stewart
playing on the set of *Rear Window*,
with Grace Kelly watching, 1954.

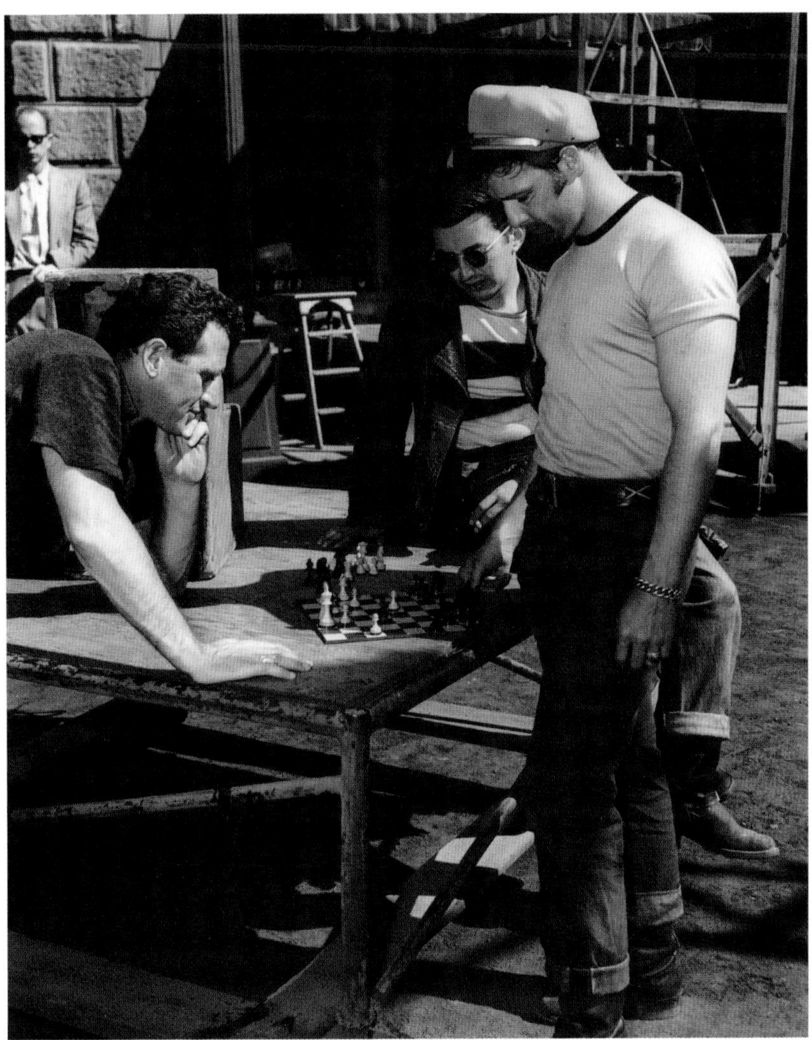

Marlon Brando was an avid chess player and there are many photos of him playing on movie sets, including *The Wild One* (1953) with Sam Gilman (above), and *Julius Caesar* (1953). Despite Brando's passion for the game, rumour has it that he may not have been very good. There are stories, including one from a former girlfriend, of him losing often and being a sore loser.

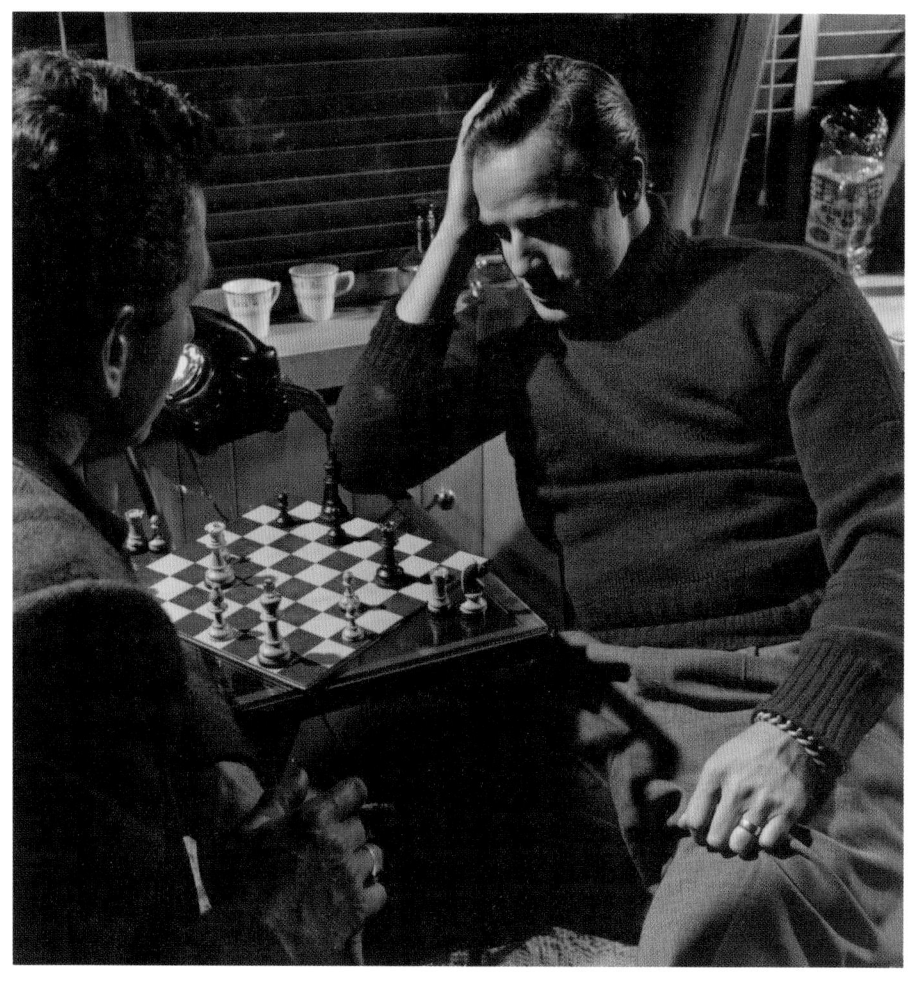

Brando playing in his Los Angeles home in Beverly Glen, 1953. Note that the board is oriented incorrectly as a white square should always be on lower right for both players.

Right: James Dean plays against Perry Lopez on the set of *Rebel Without a Cause* (1955).

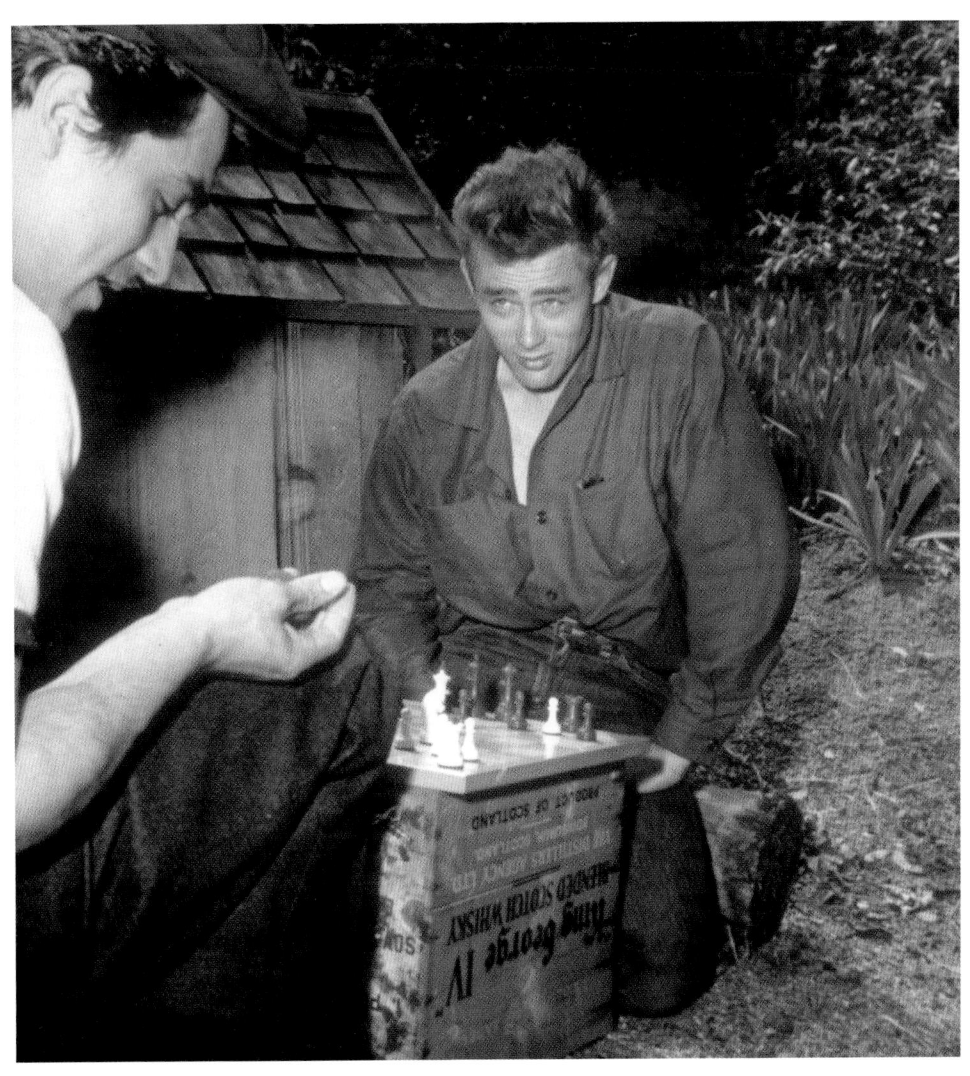
King George IV
BLENDED SCOTCH WHISKY
PRODUCT OF SCOTLAND

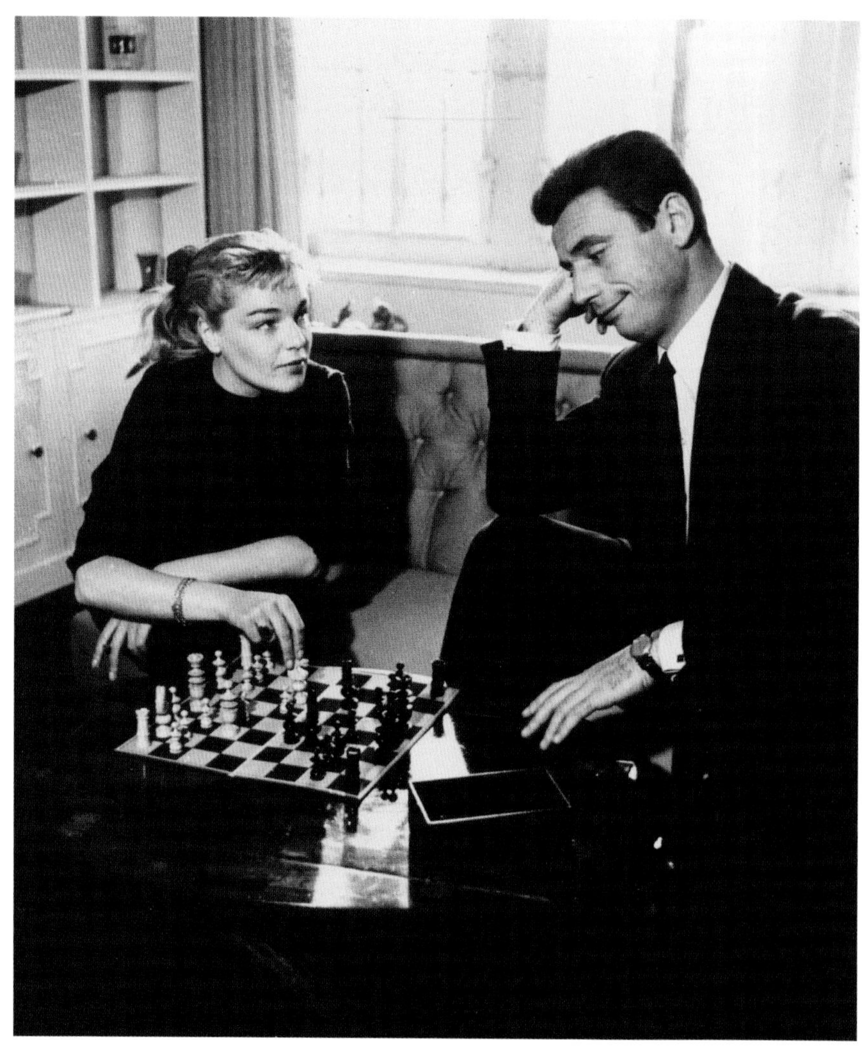

Simone Signoret and Yves Montand in their
Paris apartment in Place Dauphine, 1954.

Right: On the set of *To Kill a Mockingbird*
(1962). Gregory Peck plays Phillip Alford
(who was cast as Jem in the movie), while
Mary Badham (Scout) watches.

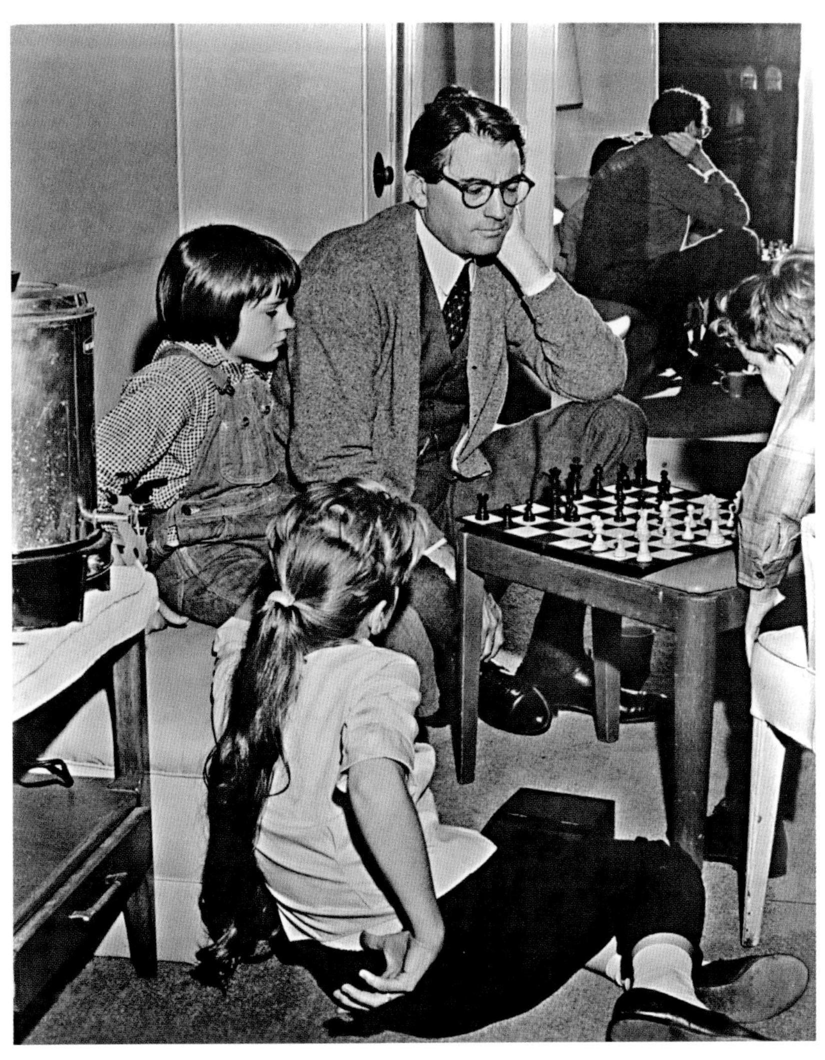

A central element to the plot of *The Seventh Seal* (1957), written and directed by Ingmar Bergman and considered one of the greatest movies of all time, is an allegorical match between a knight, played by Max von Sydow (right), and Death, played by Bengt Ekerot. Though the knight is destined to lose, he plays the game so that he may live long enough to perform one meaningful deed. In this scene, they are choosing colours by the age-old tradition of one player holding out his hands with a different colour pawn in each. Death has just chosen black. 'It becomes me well,' he says.

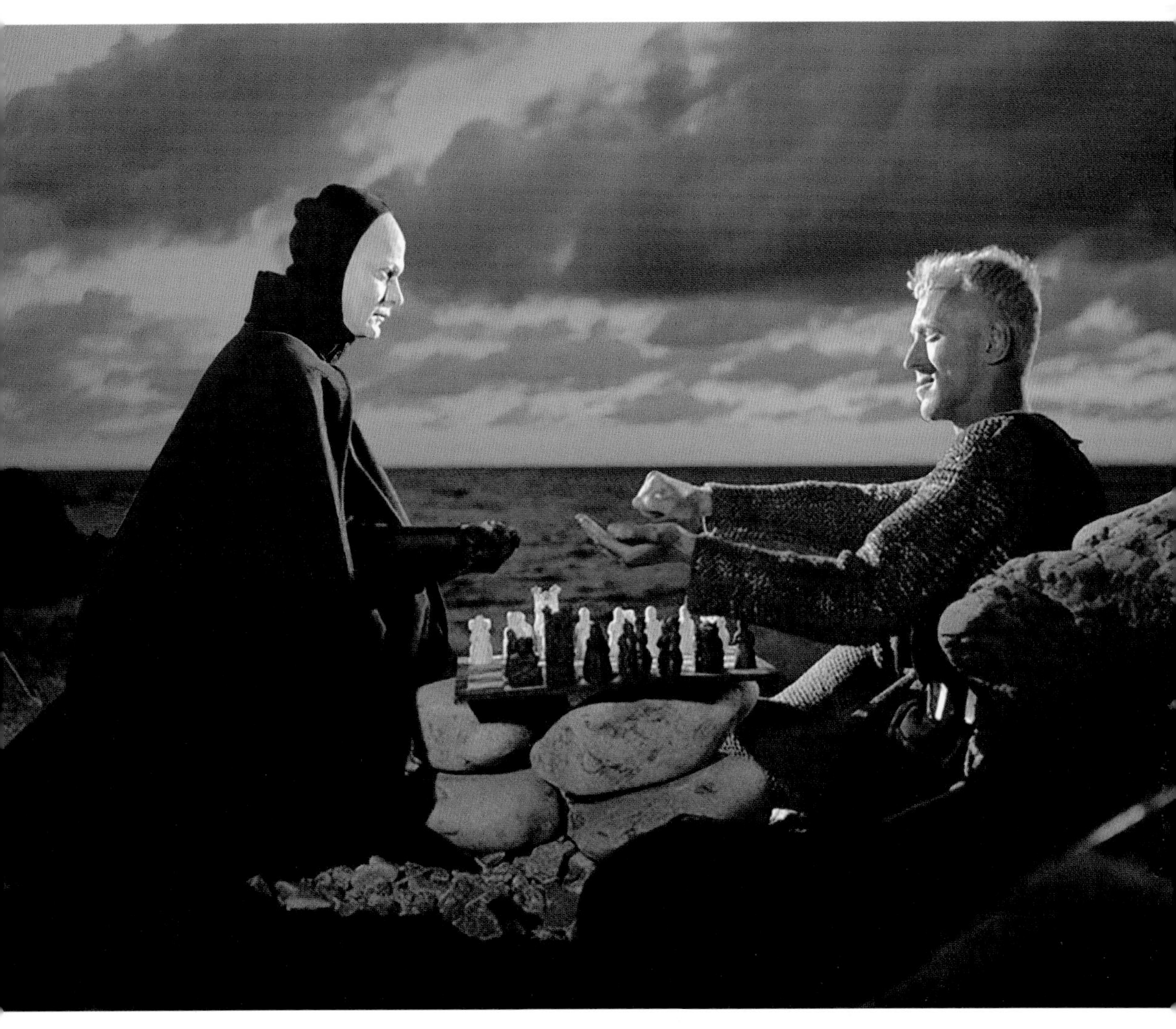

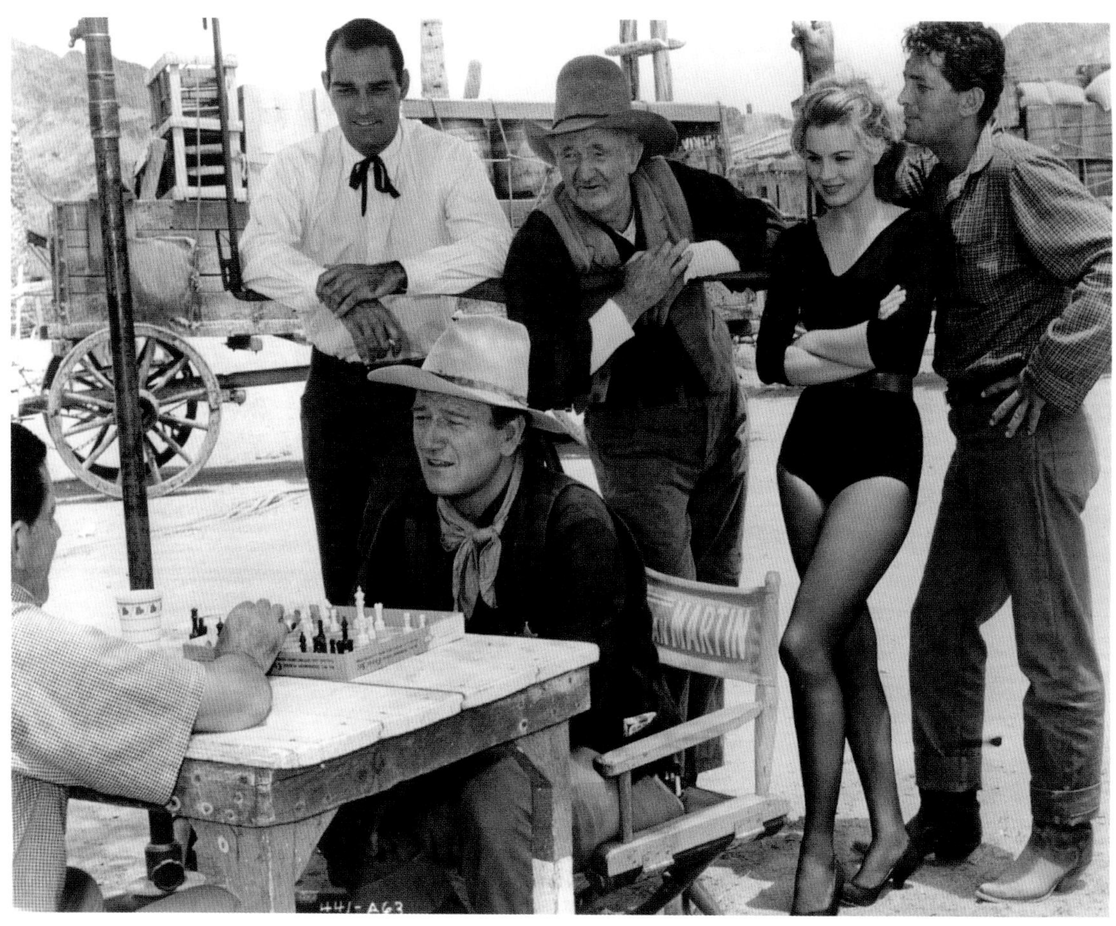

The Duke, a.k.a. John Wayne, was another Hollywood legend who loved chess. One of his California high school teachers noted that Wayne was an aggressive and accomplished chess player. Before he became a star, he would often bring a set to movie shoots, and once he was a star, he liked the game so much that he would challenge fans and anyone else who could play. He reportedly played thousands of games against the noted photographer David Sutton while filming.

Wayne's socially conservative views did not apply when it came to chess. He once said of Rock Hudson, 'Who the hell cares if he's a queer? The man plays great chess.'

Above: John Russell, John Wayne, Walter Brennan, Angie Dickinson and Dean Martin on the set of *Rio Bravo* (1959).

Right: John Wayne in Madrid on the set of *Circus World* (1963).

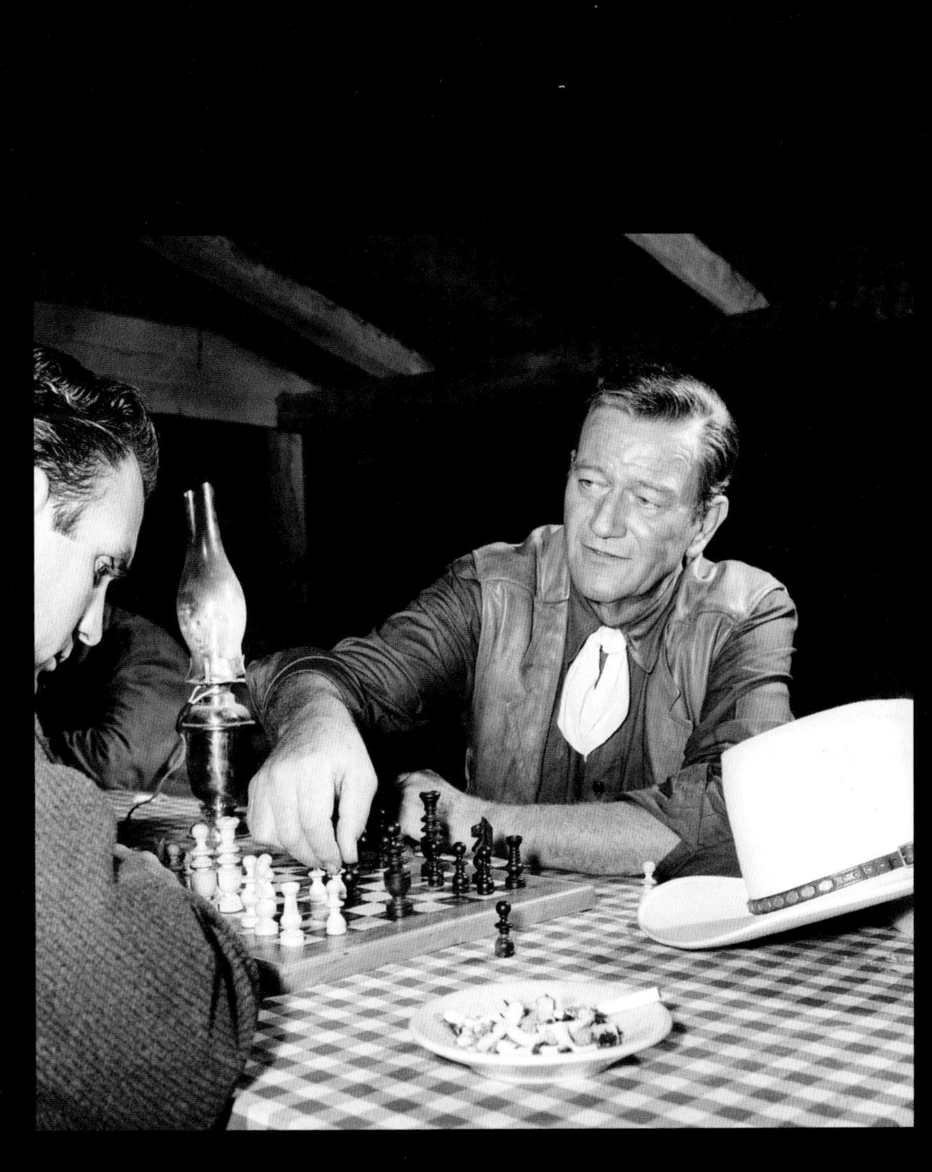

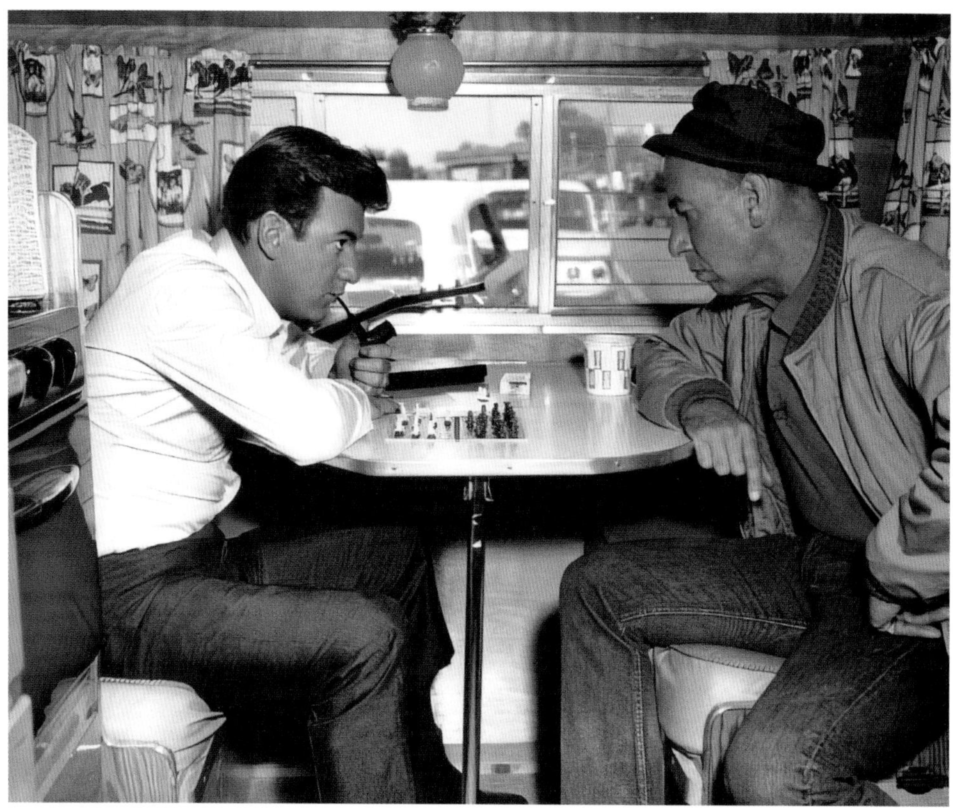

The photograph above from 1963 shows a game between Bobby Darin, the silky-smooth singing star of the 1950s and 1960s (with hits including 'Mack the Knife', 'Beyond the Sea' and 'Dream Lover') and José Ferrer, the Oscar-winning actor and director. Both players loved chess.

In 1973, Darin offered to sponsor a tournament in the United States featuring 16 of the world's top players competing for $25,000 – the largest prize money for a tournament up to that point. Unfortunately, the event had to be postponed because of a scheduling conflict with the Soviet Championship (the organisers wanted at least two or three of the strongest Soviet players to compete). Sadly, in December of the same year Darin died of a heart condition and the tournament never materialised.

Ferrer was the master of ceremonies for the Los Angeles leg of the ill-fated 1961 match between Samuel Reshevsky and Bobby Fischer, a match that never finished because Fischer quit with the score tied at 5.5 points apiece.

Right: Hollywood has long had a fascination for chess, and not just because so many of its stars play the game. Playing chess is often a shorthand for the idea that actors, or the characters they play, are intelligent and even cunning. As such, the game has often been used as a prop in movies, including *The Talk of the Town* (1942) starring Cary Grant.

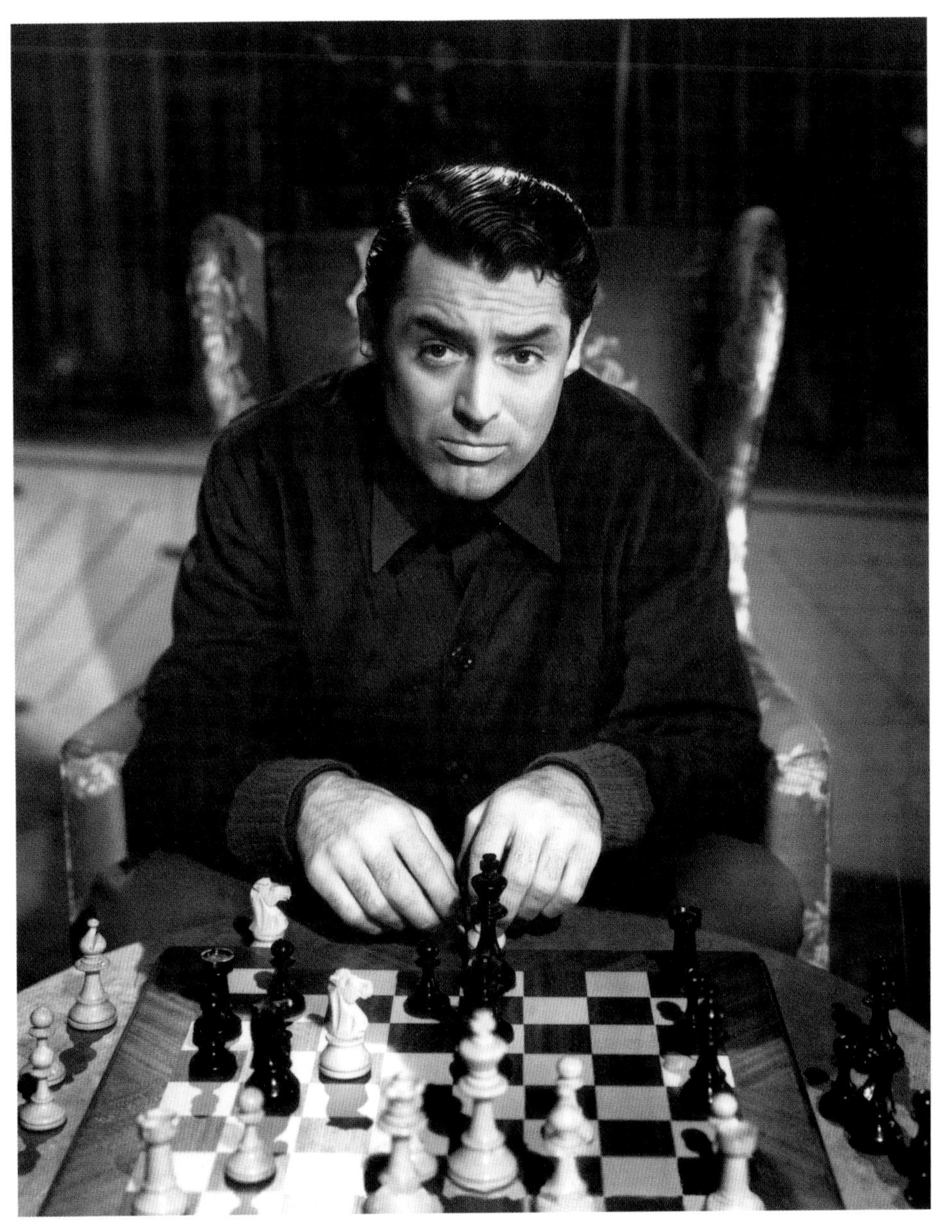

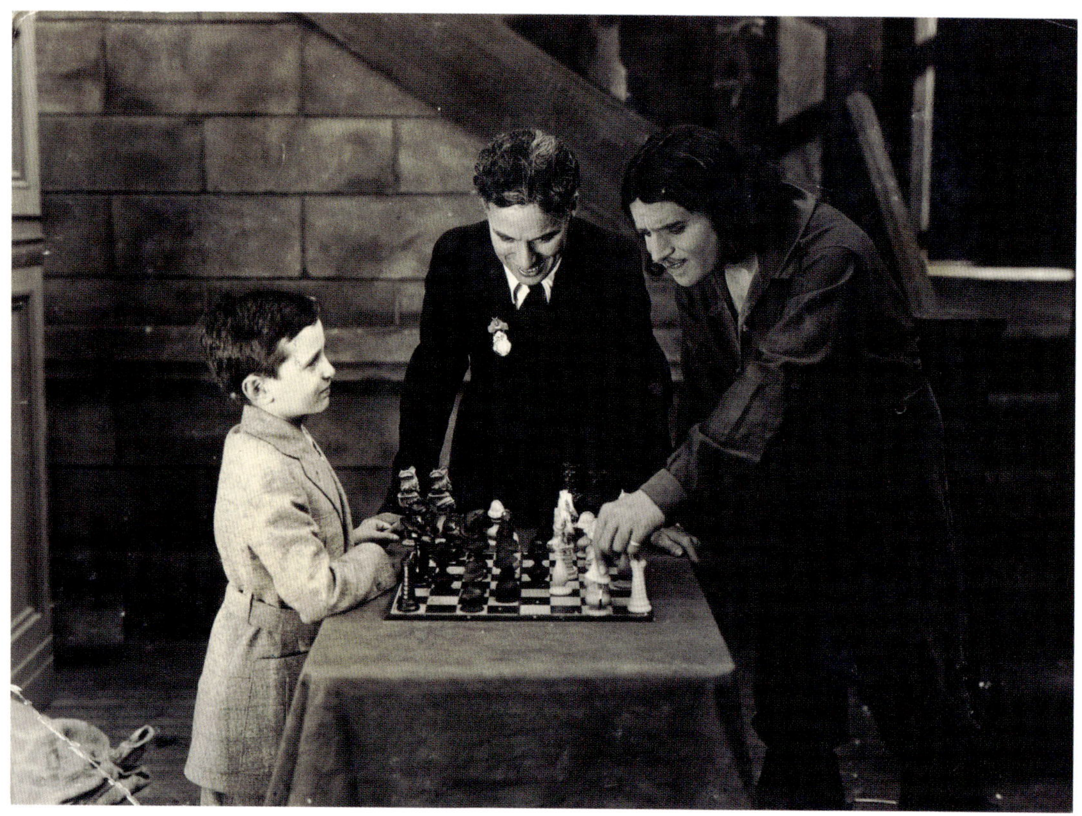

Samuel Reshevsky, who was born in Poland in 1911, was one of chess's greatest prodigies. By the age of eight, he was astounding people by playing simultaneous exhibition matches and beating all-comers. Unsurprisingly, Hollywood royalty fell in love with the little boy. In this 1921 photograph, he poses with the stars Charlie Chaplin and Douglas Fairbanks: neither were accomplished players.

Reshevsky spent most of his life in America, winning eight United States Championship (a number only equalled by his arch-rival Bobby Fischer). Despite his early promise, he fell just short of becoming world champion.

Right: Alastair Sim, seen here in 1955, was a noted Scottish actor. He appeared in more than fifty British films, including the 1951 adaptation of Charles Dickens's *A Christmas Carol* playing the lead character Ebenezer Scrooge.

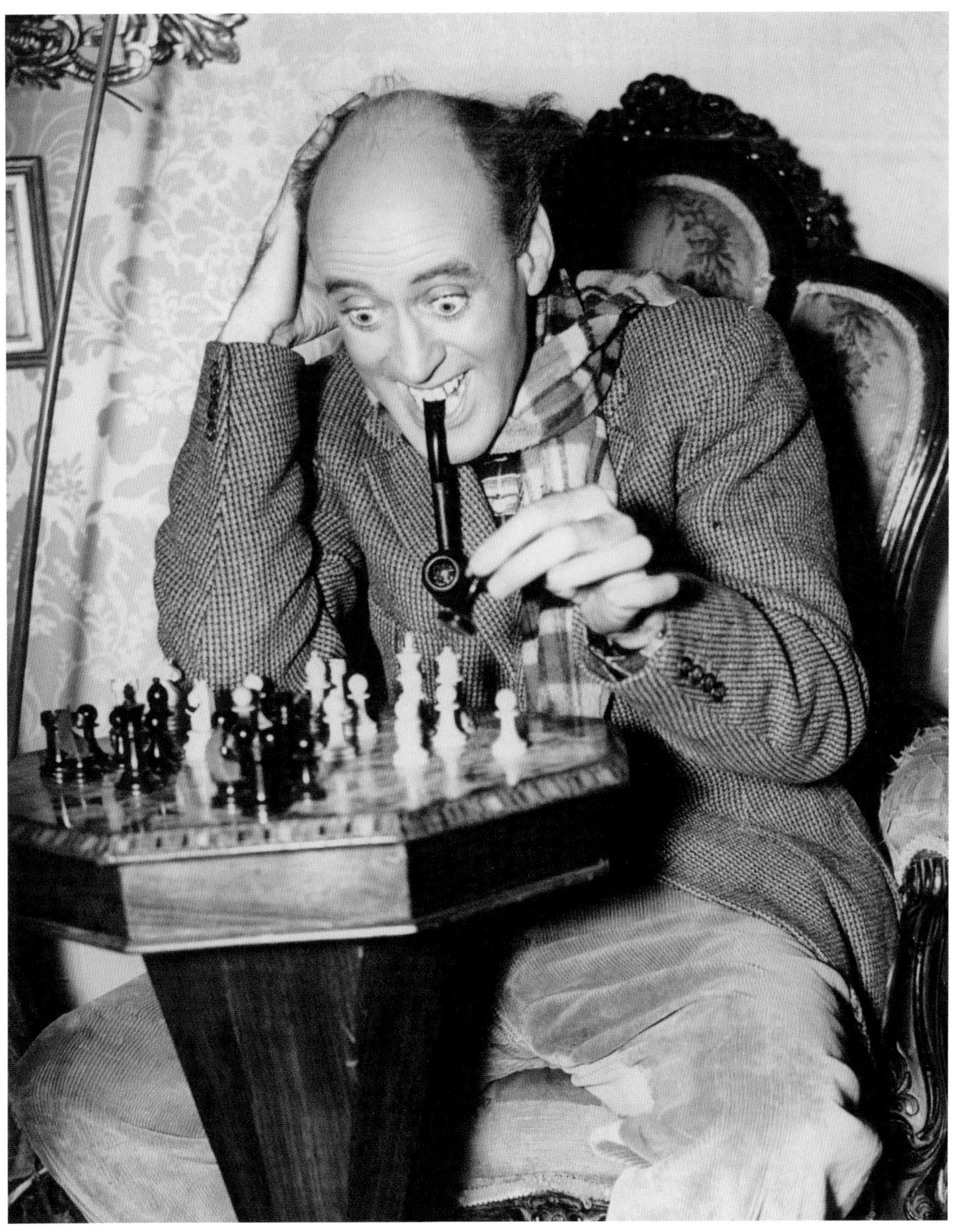

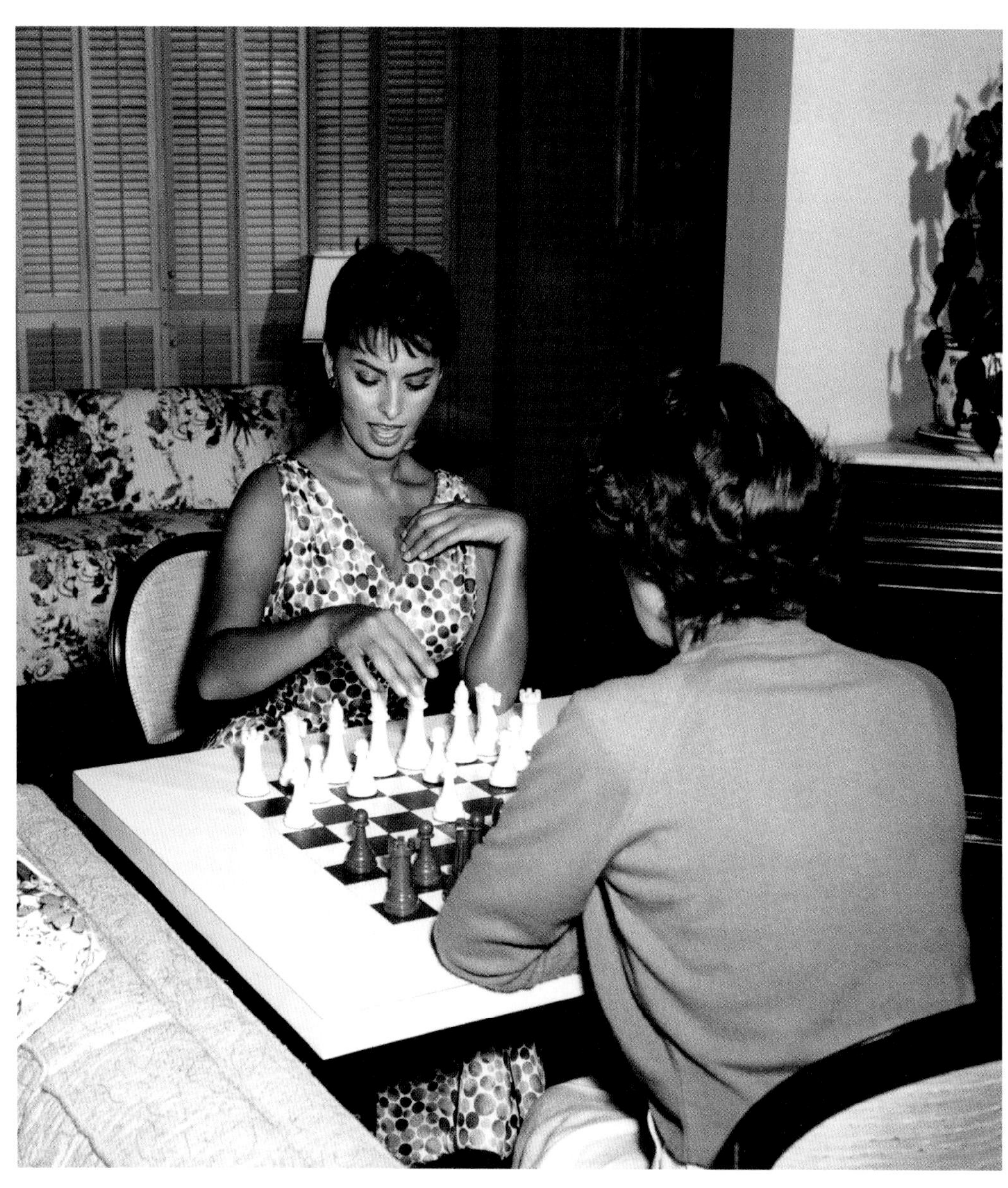

Sophia Loren, Hollywood, 1950s.

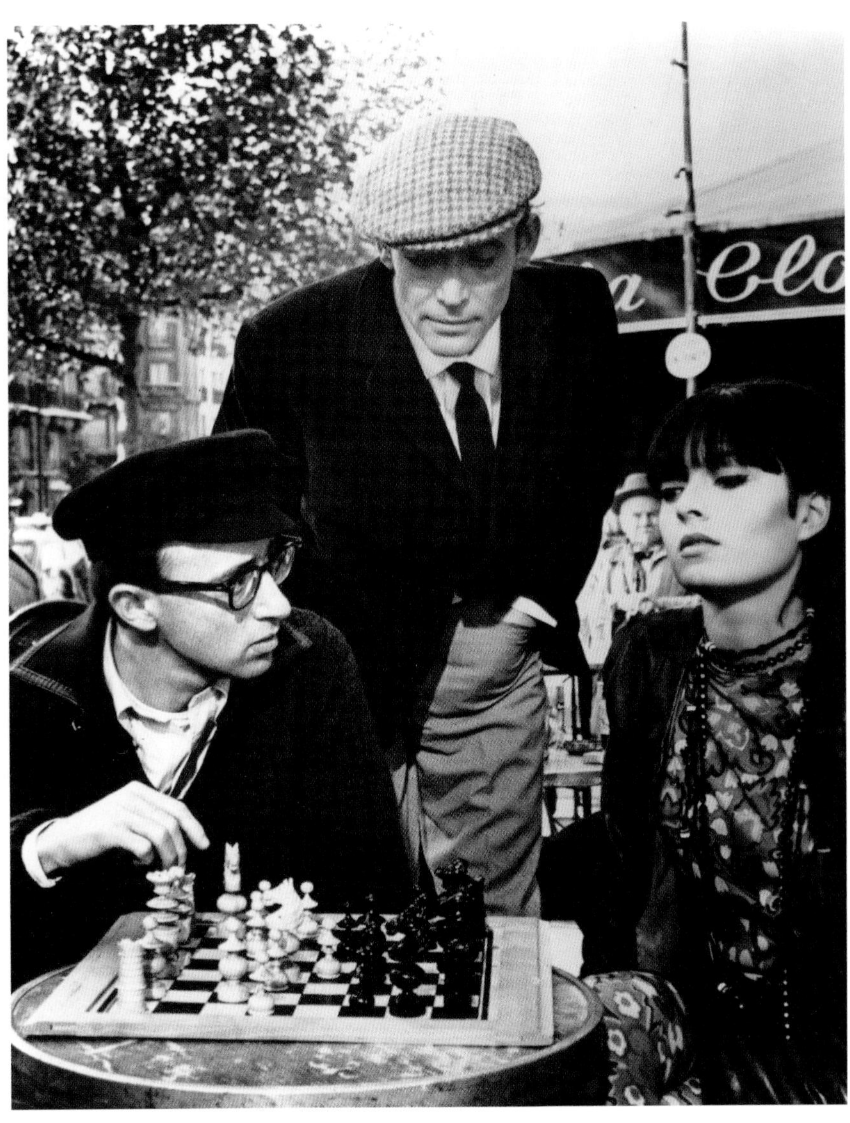

A scene from *What's New Pussycat?* (1965), with (left to right) Woody Allen, Peter O'Toole and Nicole Karen. Allen's character, Victor Shakapopulis is cheating against Tempest O'Brien (Karen), by distracting her while he takes her pieces off the board – before getting caught.

Allen again explored the theme of dishonorable behaviour when it comes to chess in a hilarious short piece of fiction published in the *New Yorker* magazine on 14 January 1966. The story, called 'The Gossage-Vardebedian Papers', recounts part of a correspondence game of chess in which the two players accuse the other of having lost track of the moves, culminating in each announcing that he has checkmated the other.

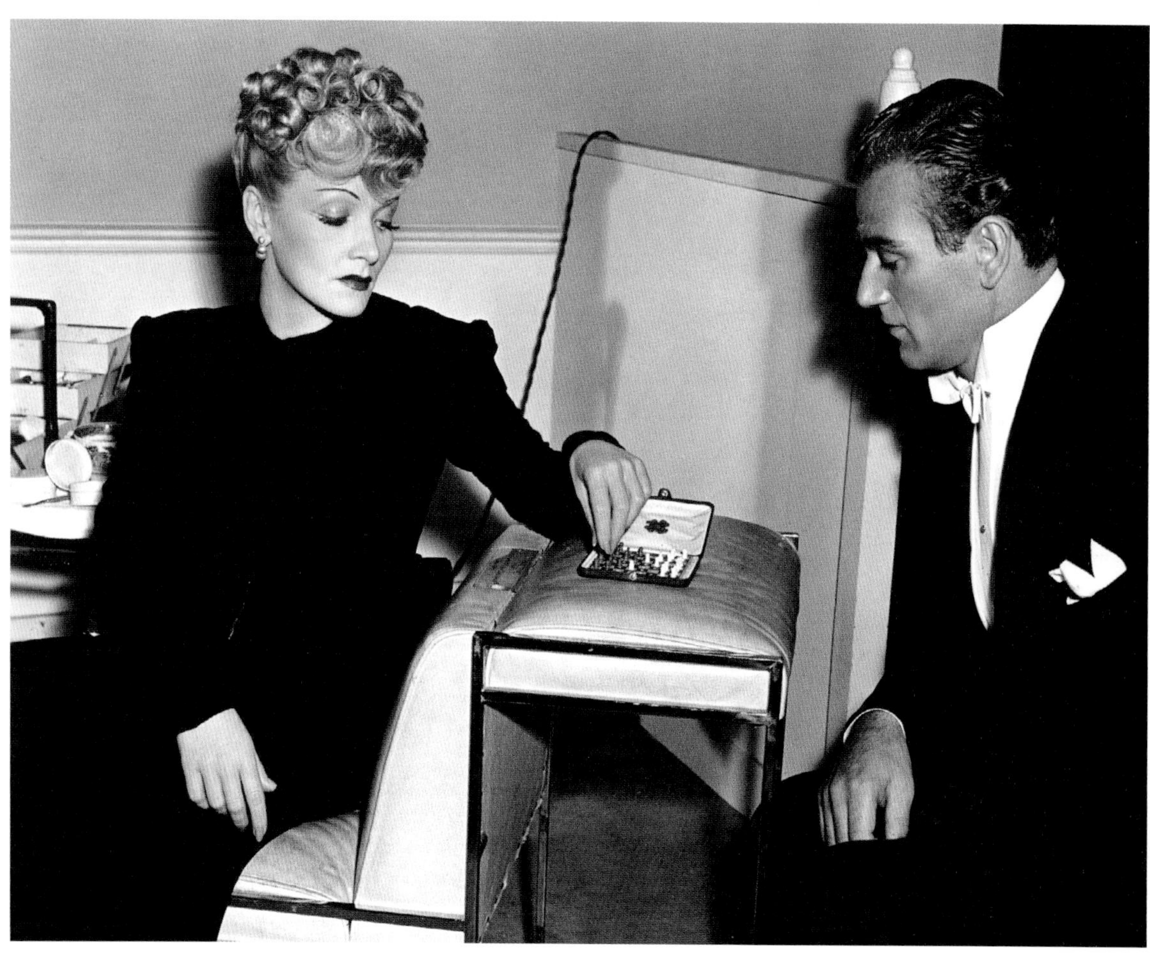

Marlene Dietrich and John Wayne playing
chess on set in Pittsburgh, 1942.

Right: Marlon Brando, Charlie Chaplin and
Sophia Loren, from the April 1966 issue of
Life magazine promoting the film *A Countess
from Hong Kong* (1967), which was written
and directed by Chaplin.

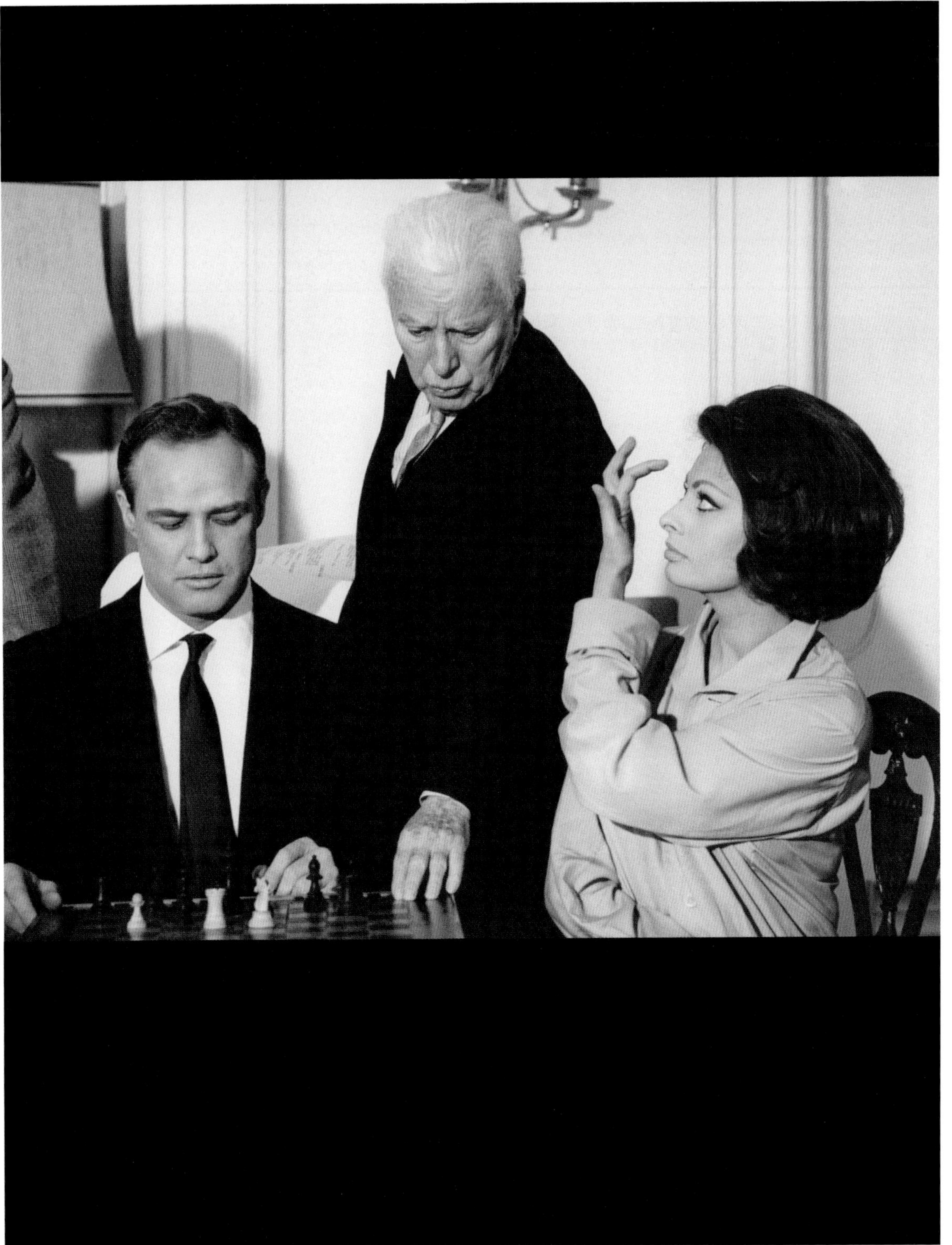

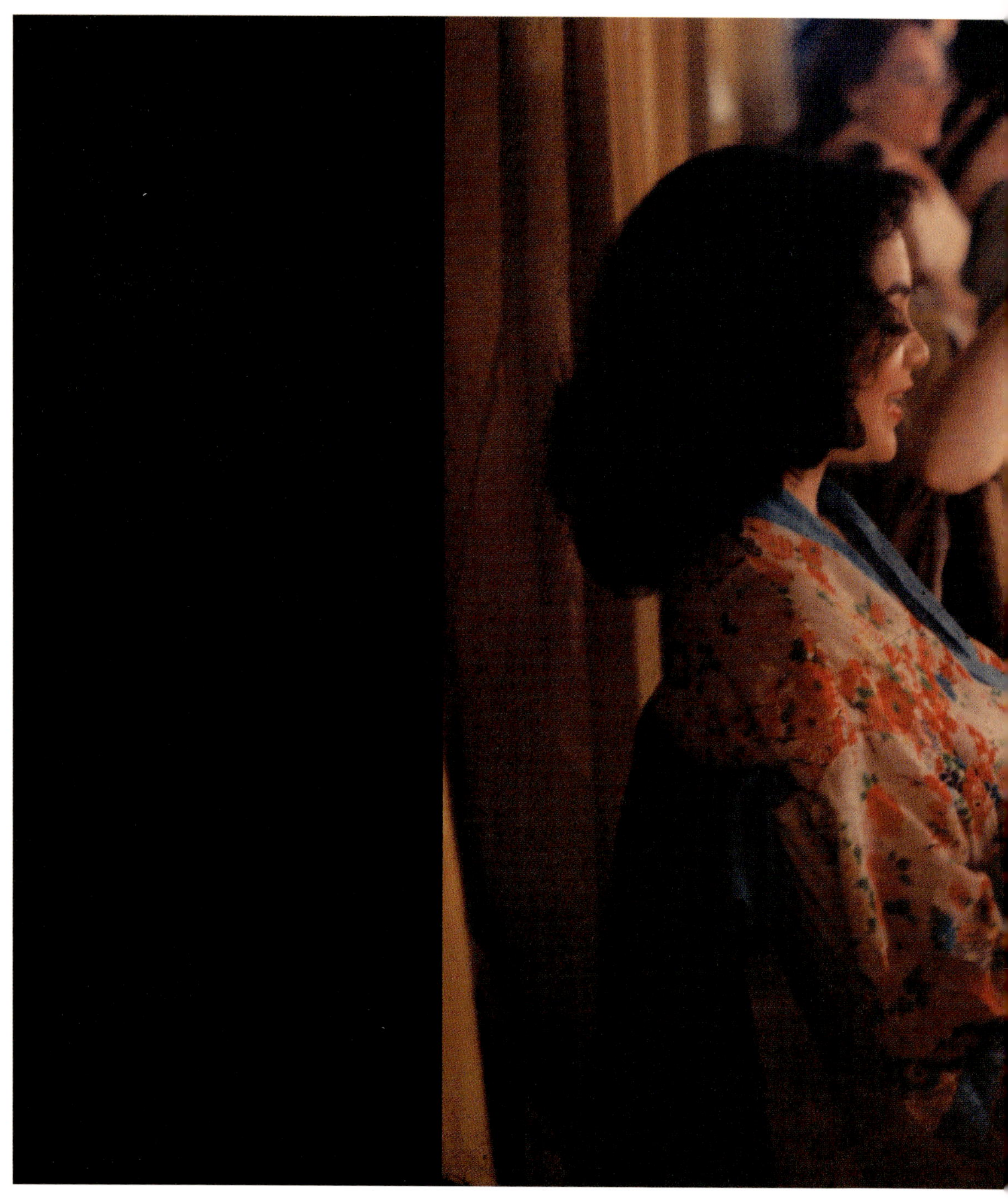

Backstage at the Latin Quarter nightclub on West 48th Street, just off Times Square in New York, 1958. Along with chorus girls, the club featured big name acts, including Frank Sinatra, Ella Fitzgerald, Patti Page, Diahann Carroll and Frankie Laine.

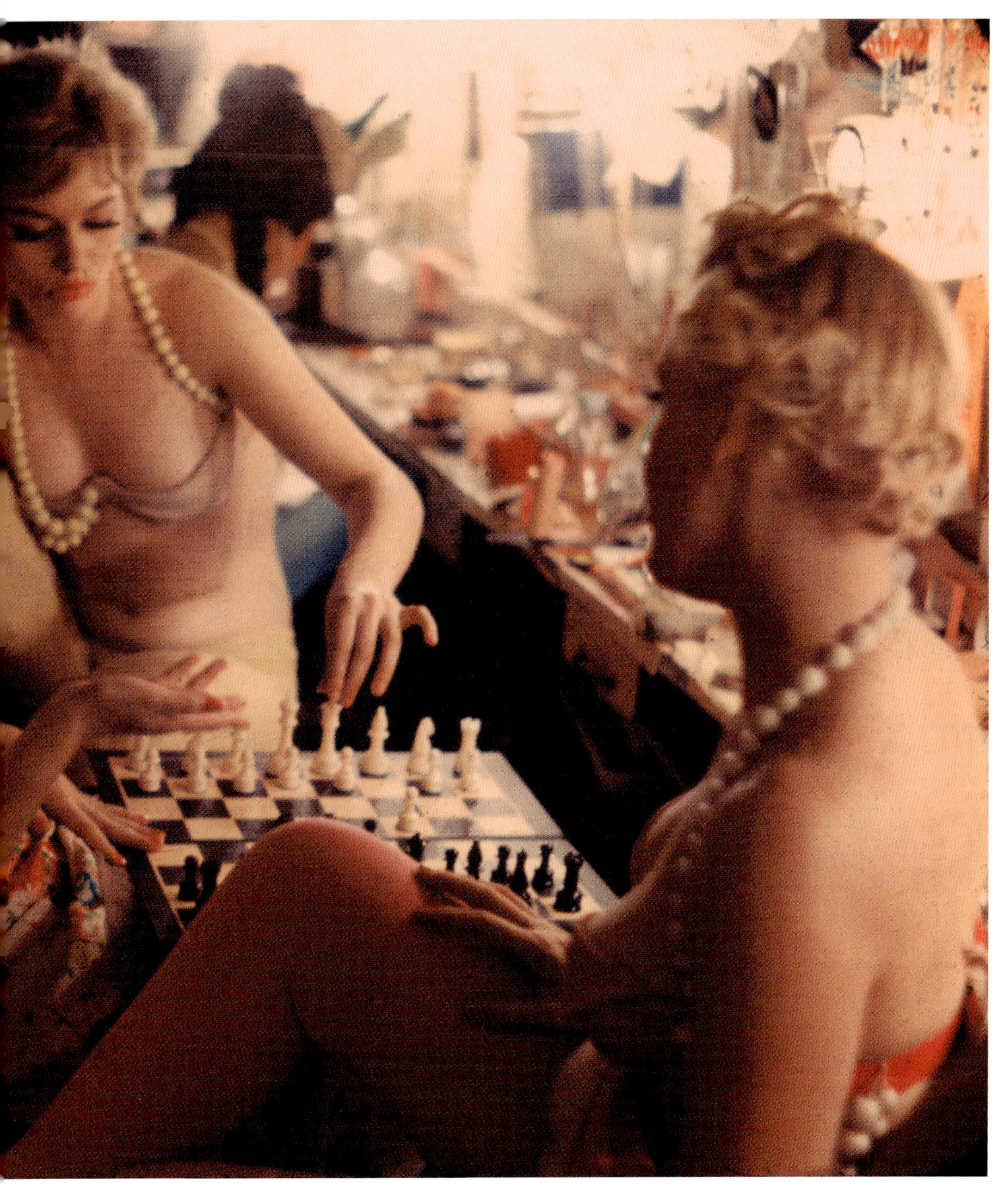

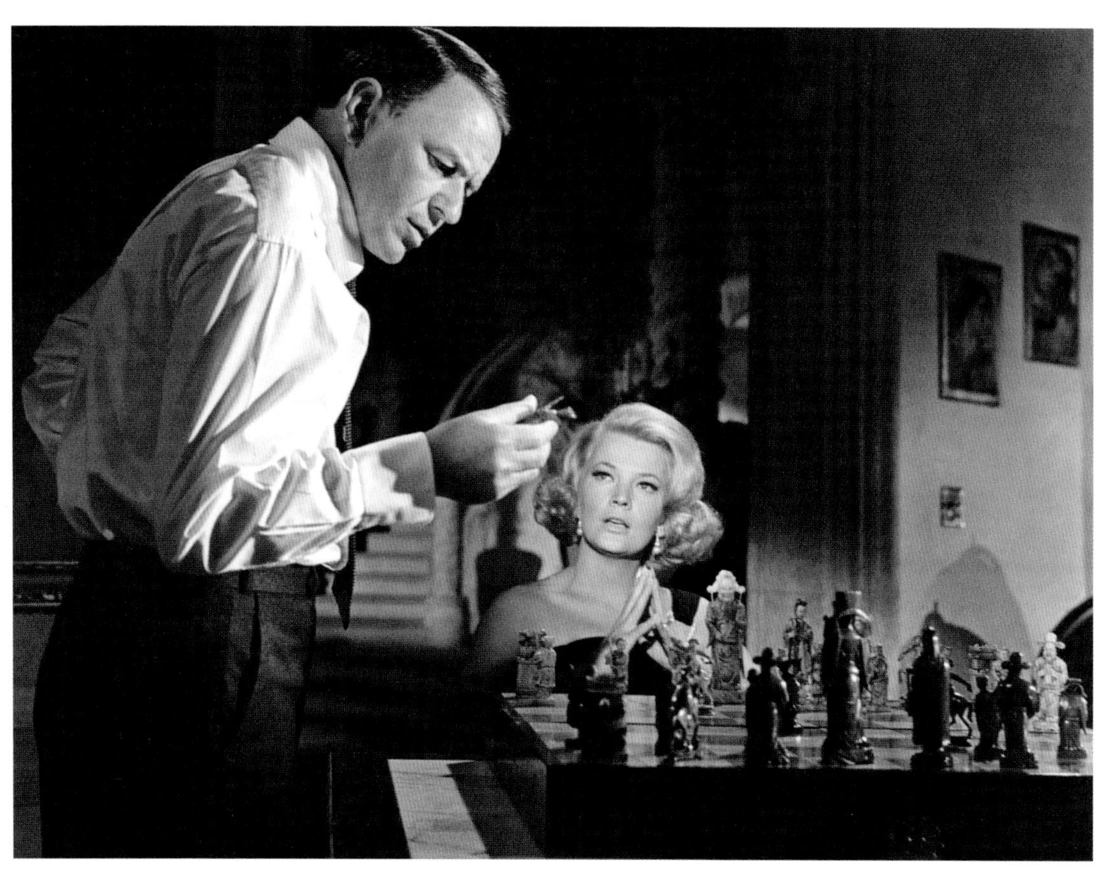

Hollywood isn't the only place fascinated by chess. The people of the West African country of Guinea are evidently great fans of the game. The country has a series of stamps featuring great players, and a 1998 collectible set is printed with the above photograph of Frank Sinatra in the neo-noir crime thriller *Tony Rome* (1967) with Gena Rowlands.

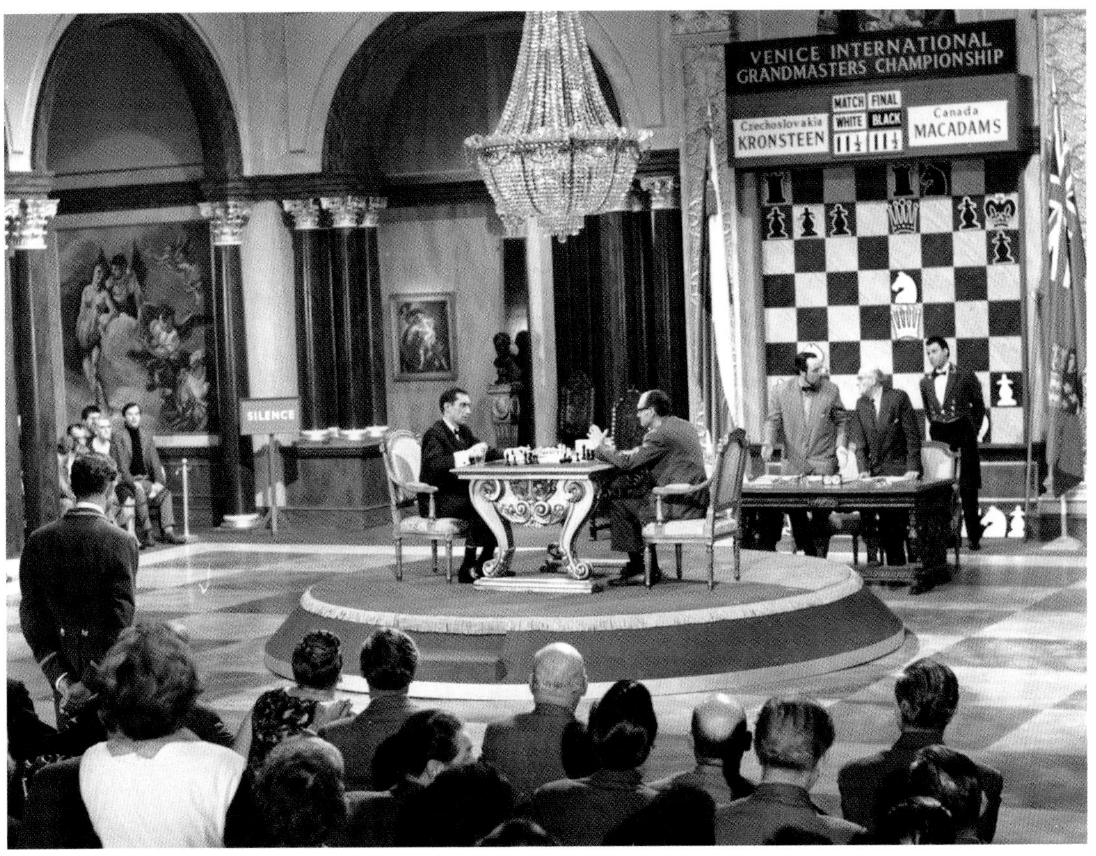

From Russia with Love (1963), the second James Bond film, opens with a chess match at the Venice International Grandmasters Championship between Kronsteen, a Czechoslavkian, who is also an agent for SPECTRE, the secret evil organisation, and MacAdams, a Canadian. In the scene, Kronsteen finishes off MacAdams with a beautiful attack. Though the movie is fictional, the game was not. It was played in the 1960 Soviet Championship between Boris Spassky, the future world champion, who had white, and David Bronstein, who had narrowly lost a match for the world championship in 1951.

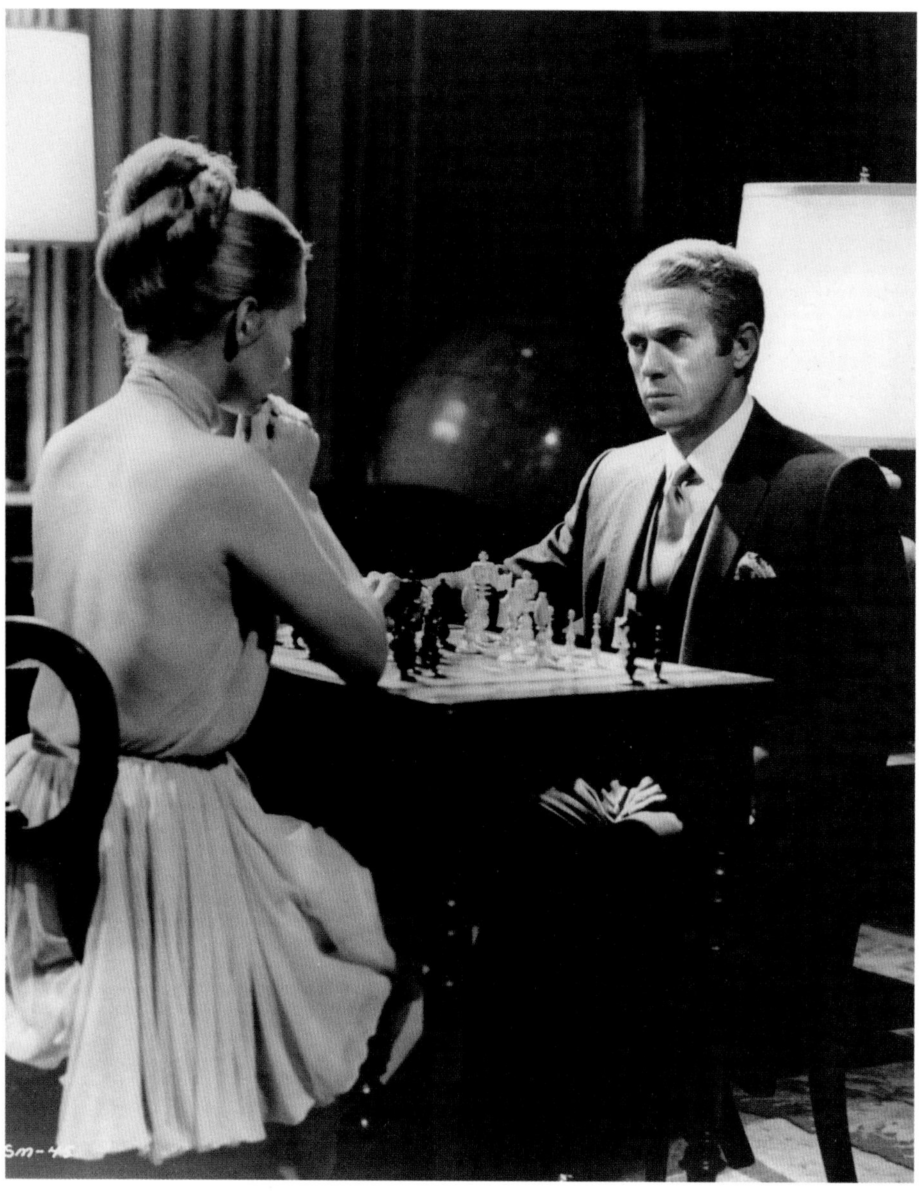

Chess has been used as a metaphor for many things, but one of the most memorable is as a game of seduction in the famous scene from *The Thomas Crown Affair* (1968). Hardly a word is spoken between Faye Dunaway and Steve McQueen. The erotic tension builds until McQueen can't take it anymore and grabs Dunaway for a passionate kiss, saying, 'Let's play something else.'

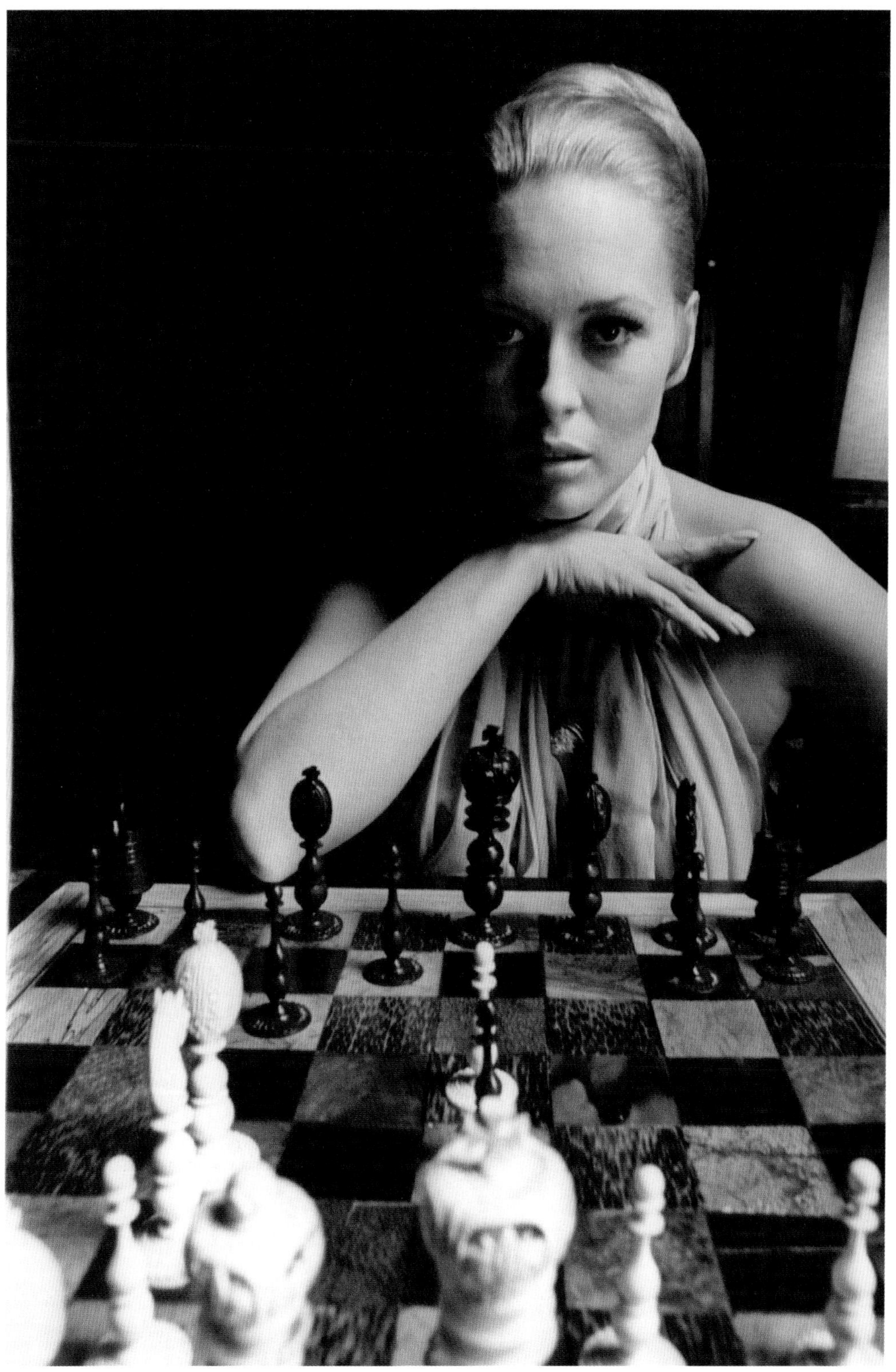

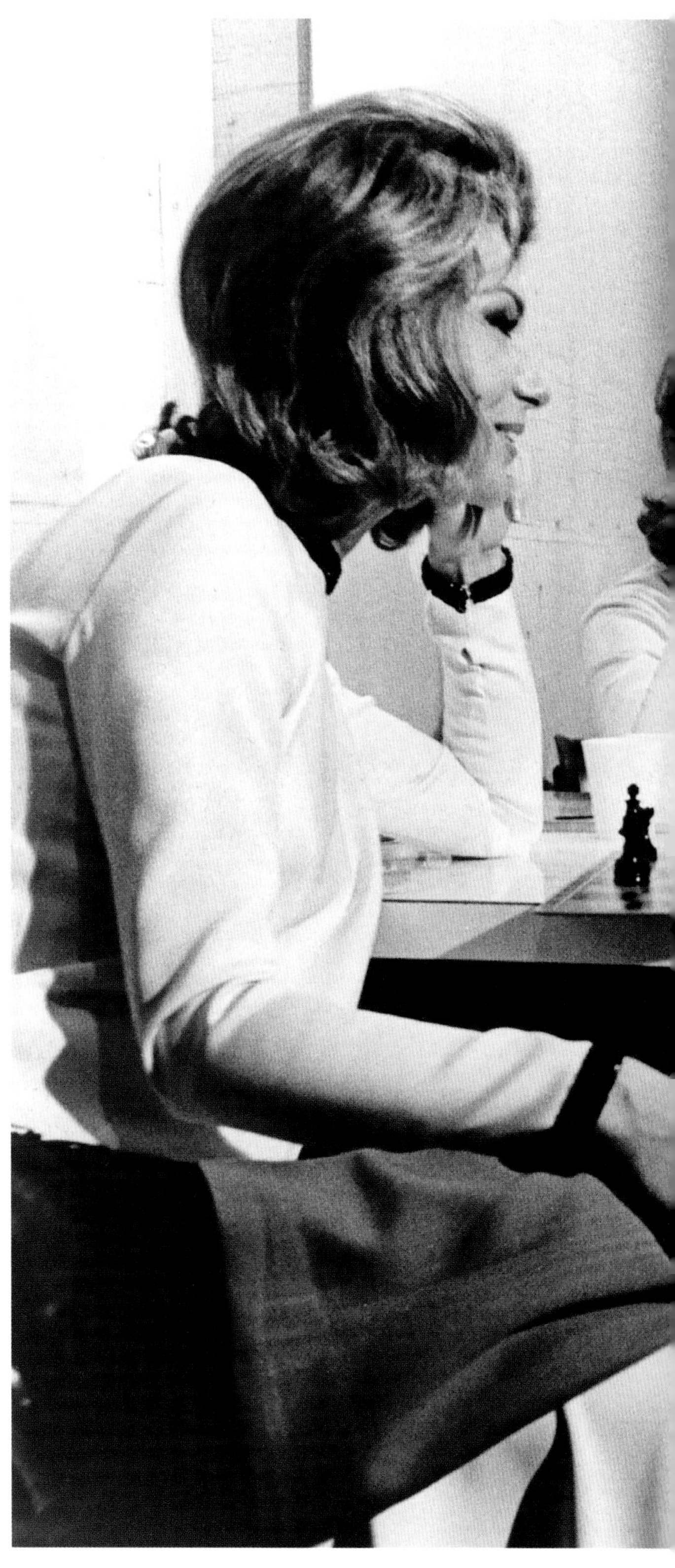

Sylva Koscina and Paul Newman in *The Secret War of Harry Frigg* (1968).

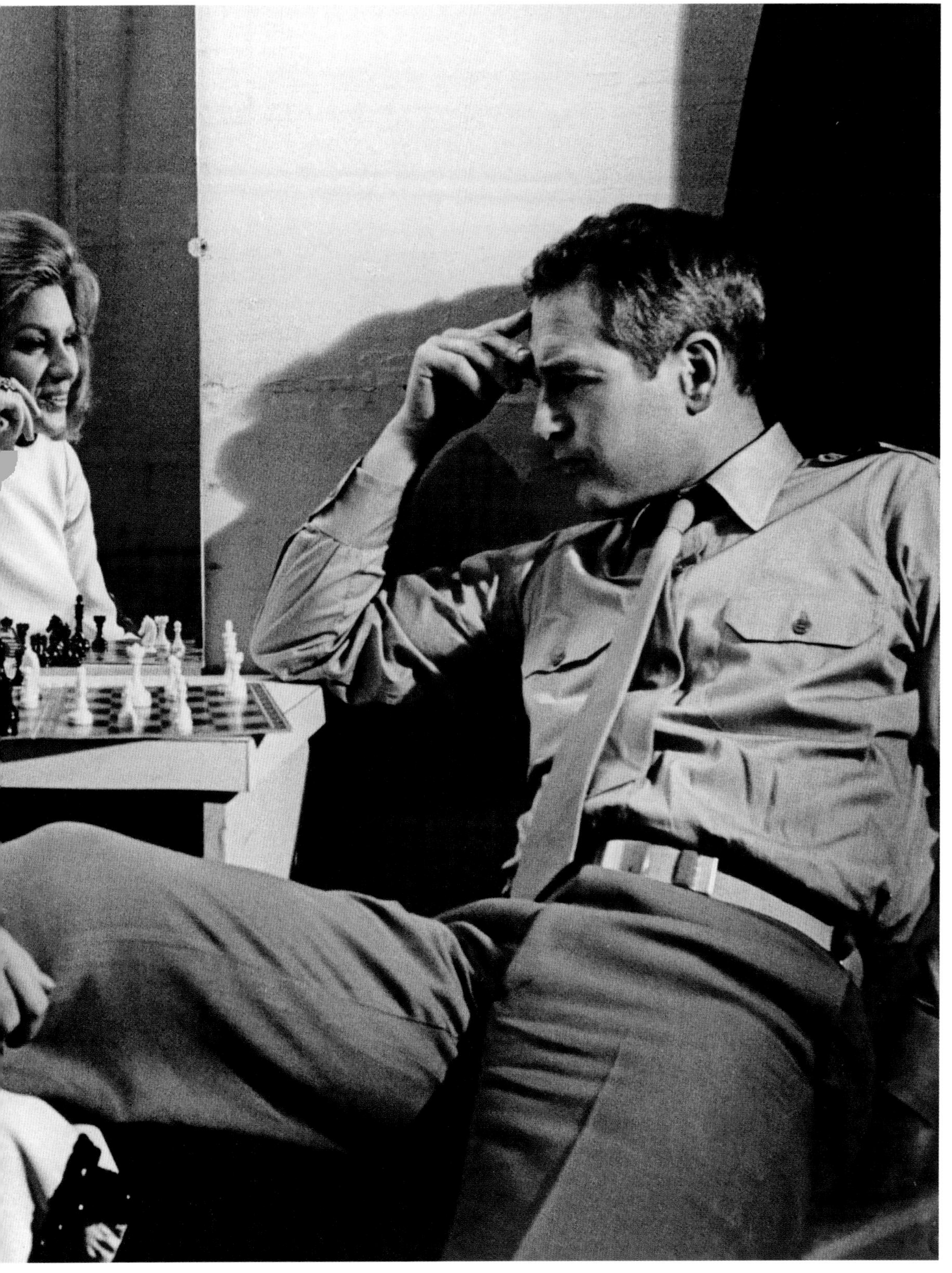

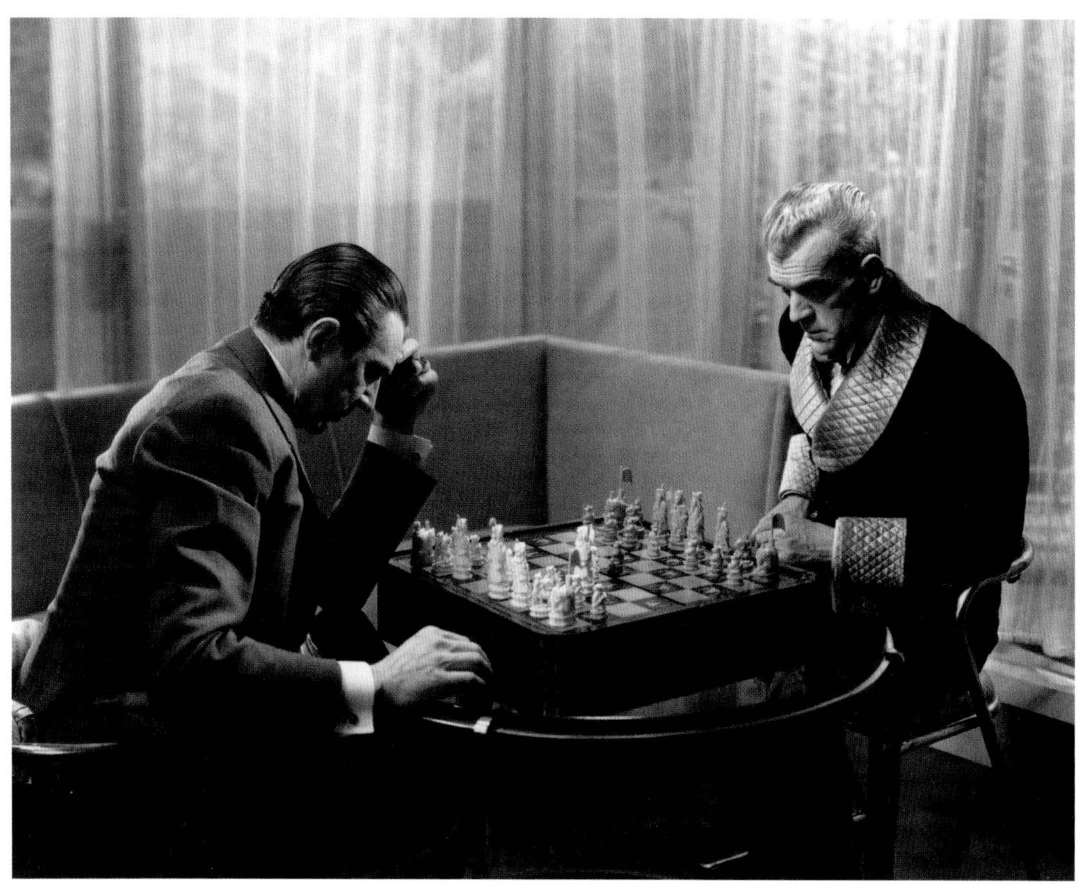

The Black Cat (1934) featured Béla Lugosi and Boris Karloff and was the first of eight films that the two actors, best known for their portrayals of Dracula and Frankenstein respectively, made together. In *The Black Cat*, Lugosi and Karloff play a game of chess to decide the fortune of a young couple staying in the mansion where the film takes place. Lugosi loses, apparently sealing the couple's fate at the hands of Karloff's character.

Right: Usually, when you take a new wife home to meet the parents, you don't bring a photographer. But if the wife is the screen star Ginger Rogers and the person taking the pictures is Philippe Le Tellier, a noted French post-war photographer, different rules might apply. Rogers, above left on the couch, is talking with her mother-in-law, Alice Bergerac, while her father-in-law, Charles, left, plays chess against his son, and Roger's new husband, Jacques. The photograph was taken at the Bergerac's home in Biarritz, France, in April 1954. Rogers and Bergerac, who was 16 years her junior, had met and married the year before. Evidently, the Bergeracs were not great chess players as the board is oriented in the wrong direction. (There should always be a light square in the lower right for each player.) The marriage only lasted four years.

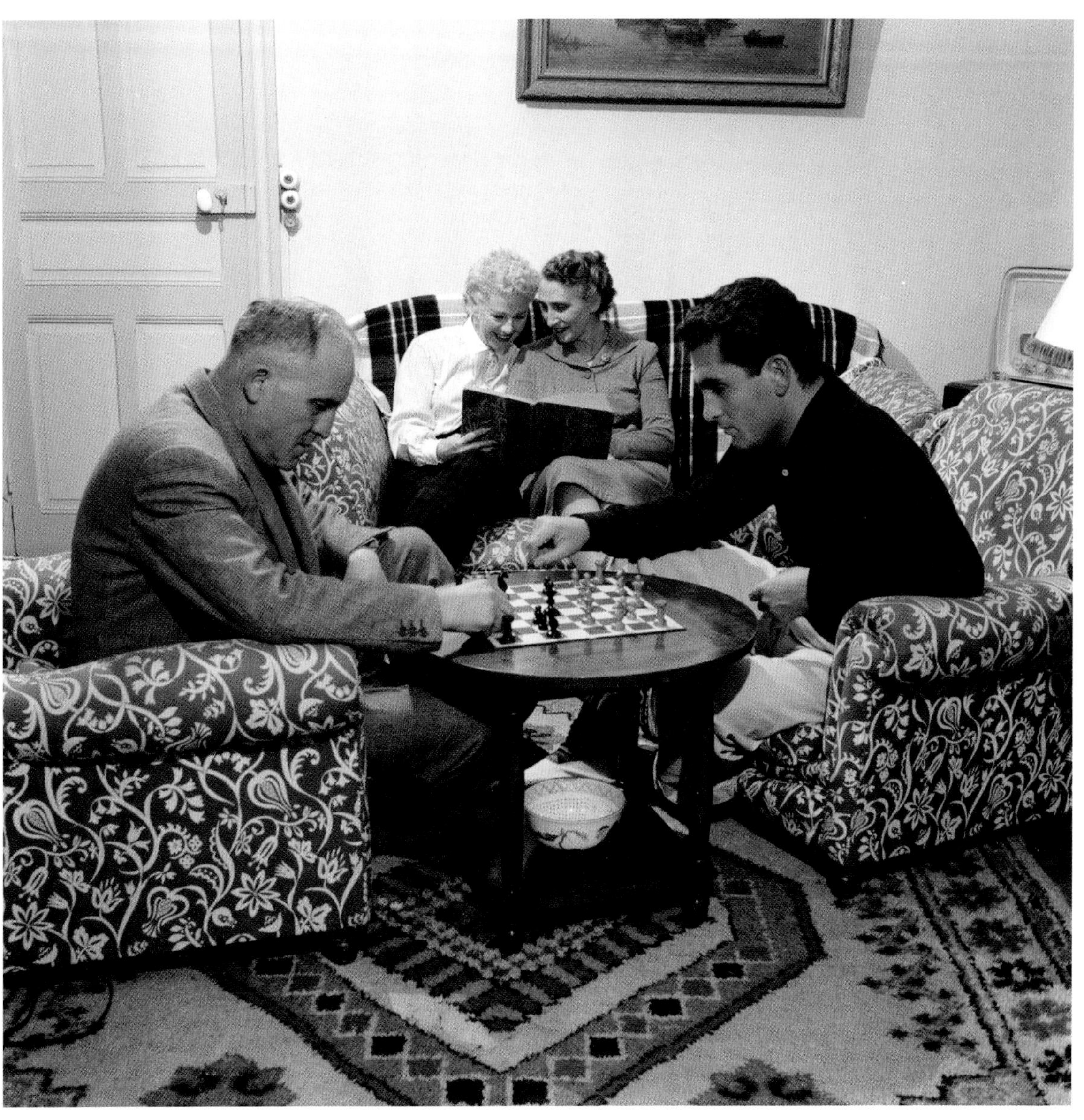

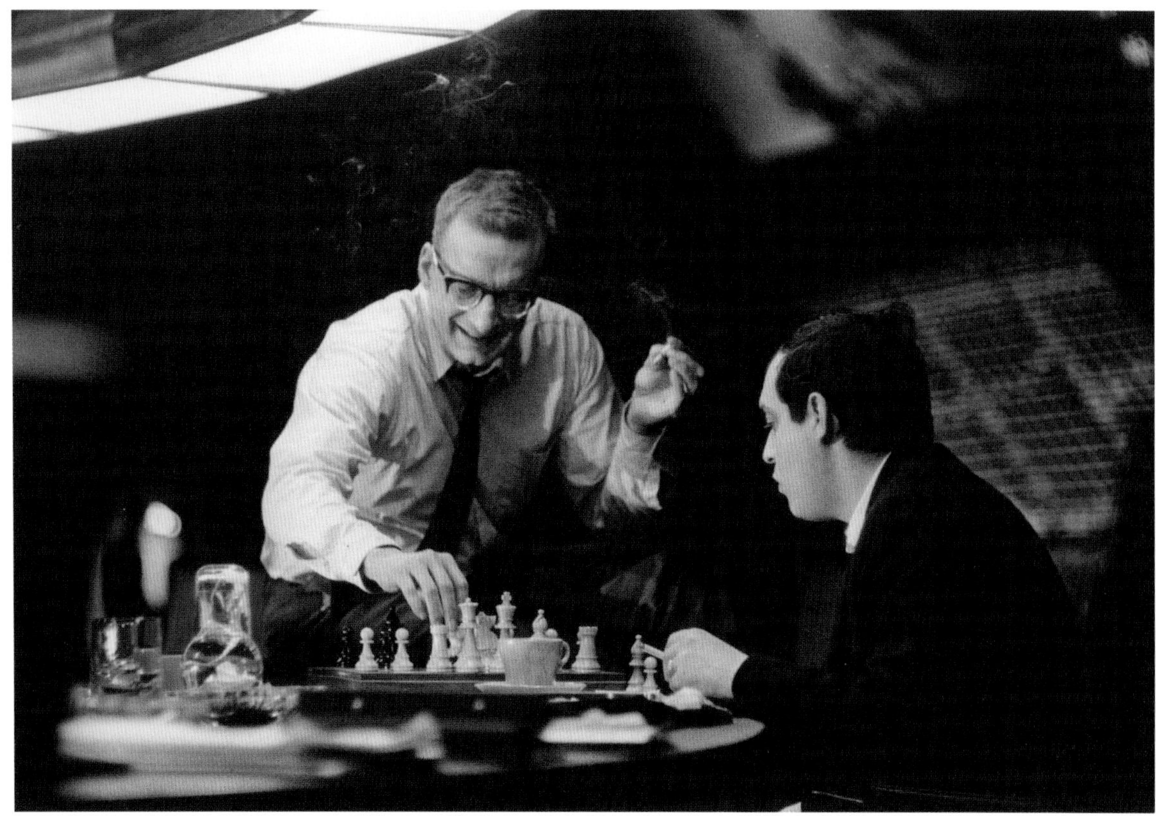

The film director Stanley Kubrick loved chess. He incorporated the game as part of the plot in a couple of his movies – *The Killing* (1956) and most memorably in *2001: A Space Odyssey* (1968). He also played frequently on set. The photograph above shows him with George C. Scott during the filming of *Dr Strangelove* (1964) and right, with Tony Burton while making *The Shining* (1980).

Kubrick said that some of the principles he learned in chess helped with his movies. It was the game itself that got him into filmmaking. He joined the Marshall Chess Club in New York when he was young and learned about the film industry from a fellow member who was a newspaper film critic.

He also said that for many years, while he was waiting for approval for some of his projects, he would go to Washington Square Park and hustle chess for dimes and quarters from noon to midnight, making about $20 a week.

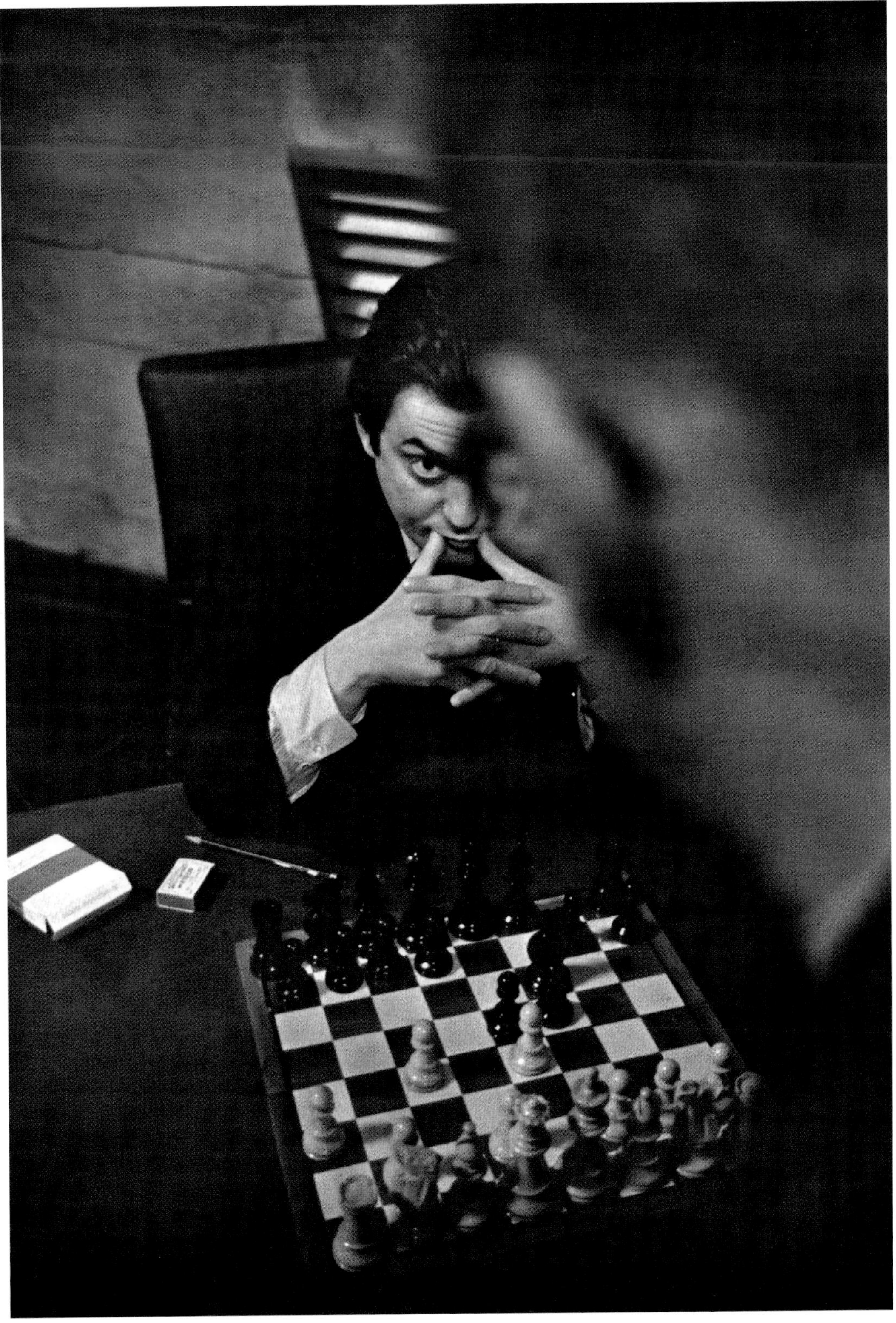

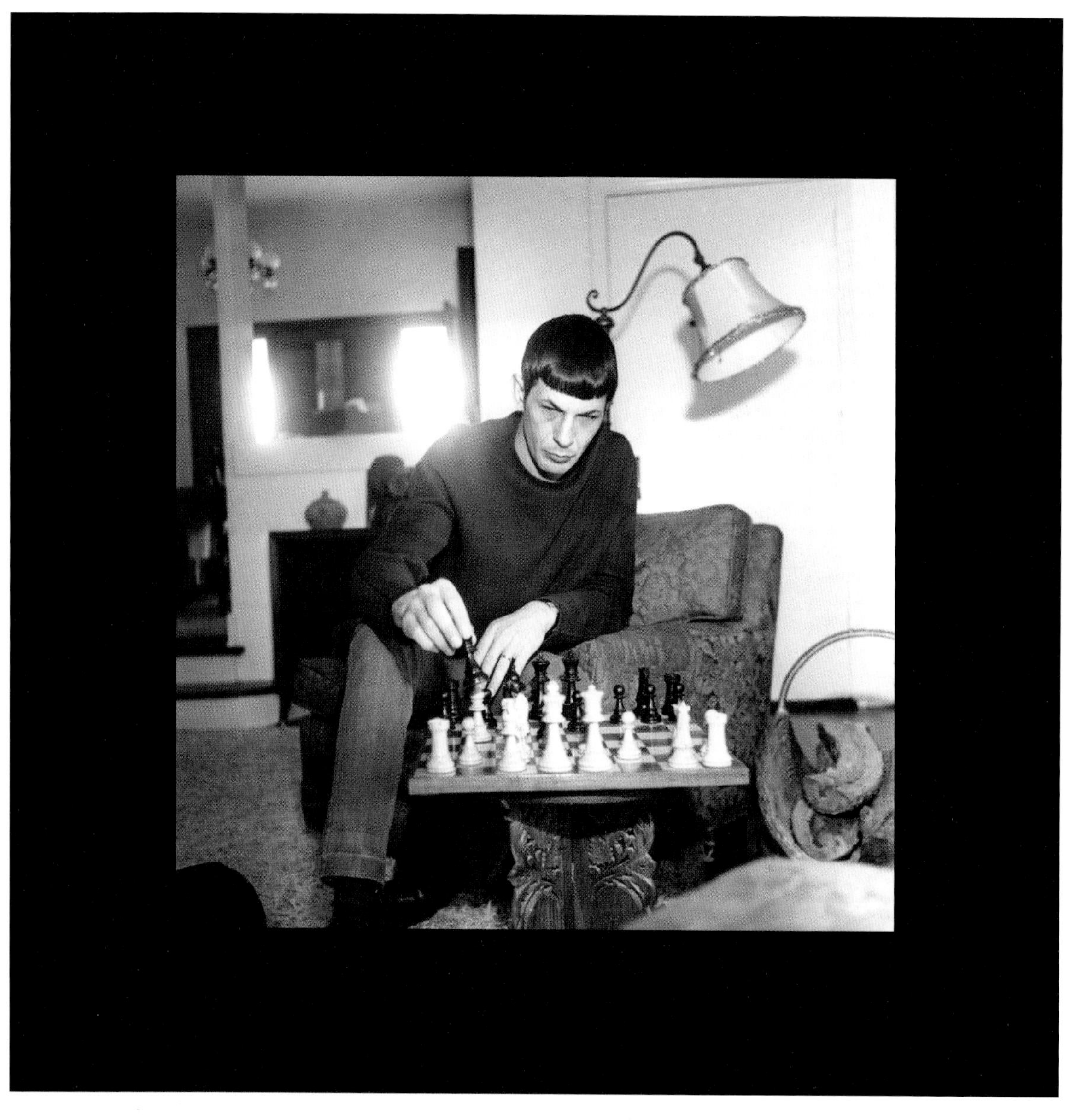

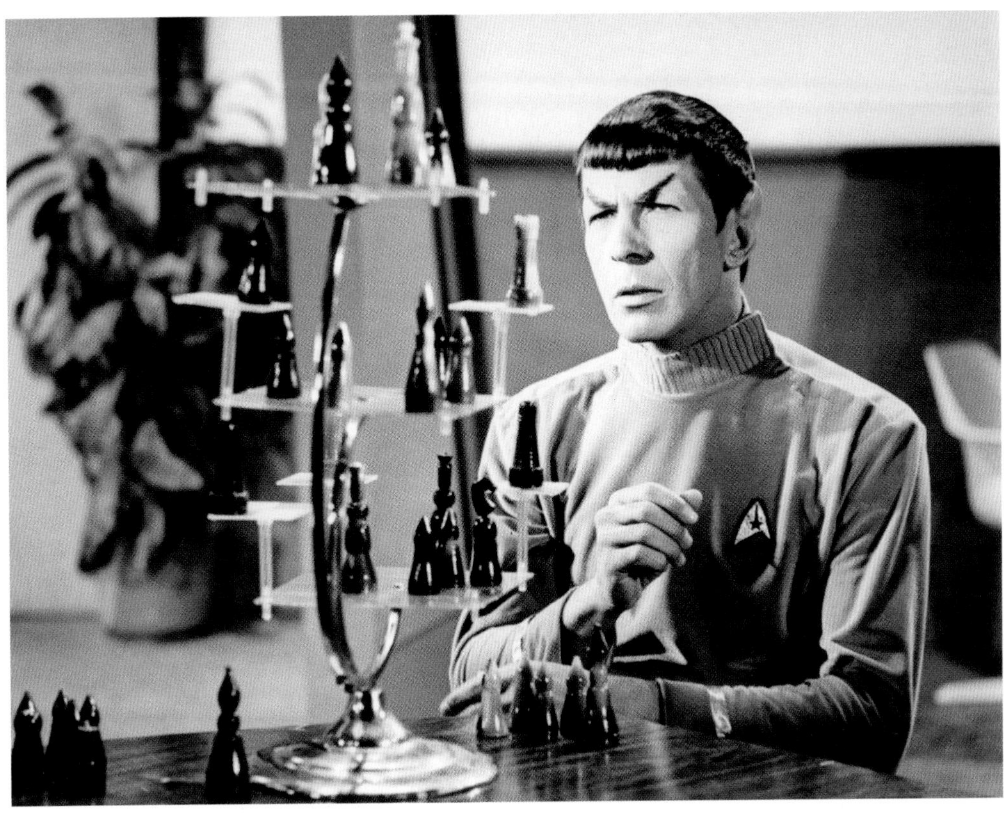

When the creators of the science fiction television series *Star Trek* (1966–1969) wanted to demonstrate that Mr Spock, the iconic half-Vulcan, half-human character, was a paragon of logic, they decided to have him play chess. As *Star Trek* takes place in the future, it was reasonable to assume that the game had evolved, so the series creators invented a 3-D version called tridimensional chess.

In episode two of season one, 'Charlie X' (1966), Spock plays and beats Charlie, a 17-year-old castaway with terrifying powers. Spock also plays Captain Kirk in the beginning of episode three, 'Where No Man Has Gone Before' (1966). In 'Court Martial' (1967), the 20th episode of the first season, Spock even helps to clear Kirk's name through chess by beating the computer five times, thereby proving the machine has been tampered with and its testimony against Kirk is unreliable. Tridimensional chess continued to appear throughout the series.

The set was made from parts of 3-D chequers and Tic-Tac-Toe games, with pieces designed by Peter Ganine. Collectively, the boards had the same number of squares, 64, but arranged on different levels. As tridimensional chess did not really exist, there were no rules for the game.

Enter the Trekkies (the rabid fans of the series), one of whom, Andrew Bartmess, wrote a set of rules for the tridimensional game. He was quickly followed by others. At least one Trekkie has created variants of tridimensional chess using transporter pads, warp factors, and even a Borg queen – a familiar reference for those who have watched *Star Trek, The Next Generation* (1987–1994).

Leonard Nimoy, the actor who played Spock, was evidently less accomplished at the game than his character. The picture opposite shows him playing at his home in Westwood, California, in 1967, but the board is oriented incorrectly.

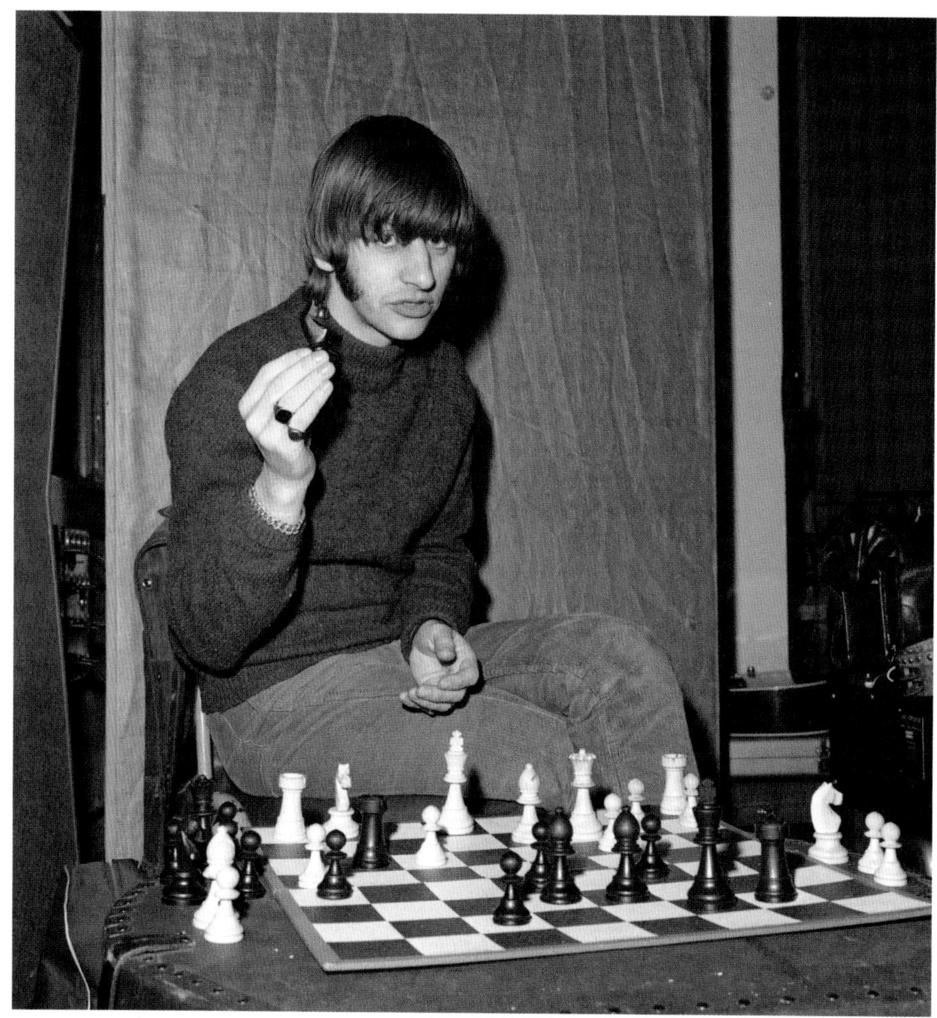

Ringo Starr, the Beatles drummer, at EMI Studios in 1966 during the recording of 'Paperback Writer'. In 1973, a gold and silver set with pieces modelled from castings of the drummer's hands was made by Asprey, a London-based luxury goods designer.

Right: Chess has long been part of the life of Bob Dylan, the Nobel Prize-winning singer-songwriter, shown here playing at a restaurant in Woodstock, in 1964. He used the game as a motif in the title of 'Only a Pawn in Their Game', a song about the assassination of Medgar Evers, the civil rights activist, as well as in the lyrics of 'Love Minus Zero/No Limit', with the line, 'In ceremonies of the horsemen, Even a pawn must hold a grudge.'

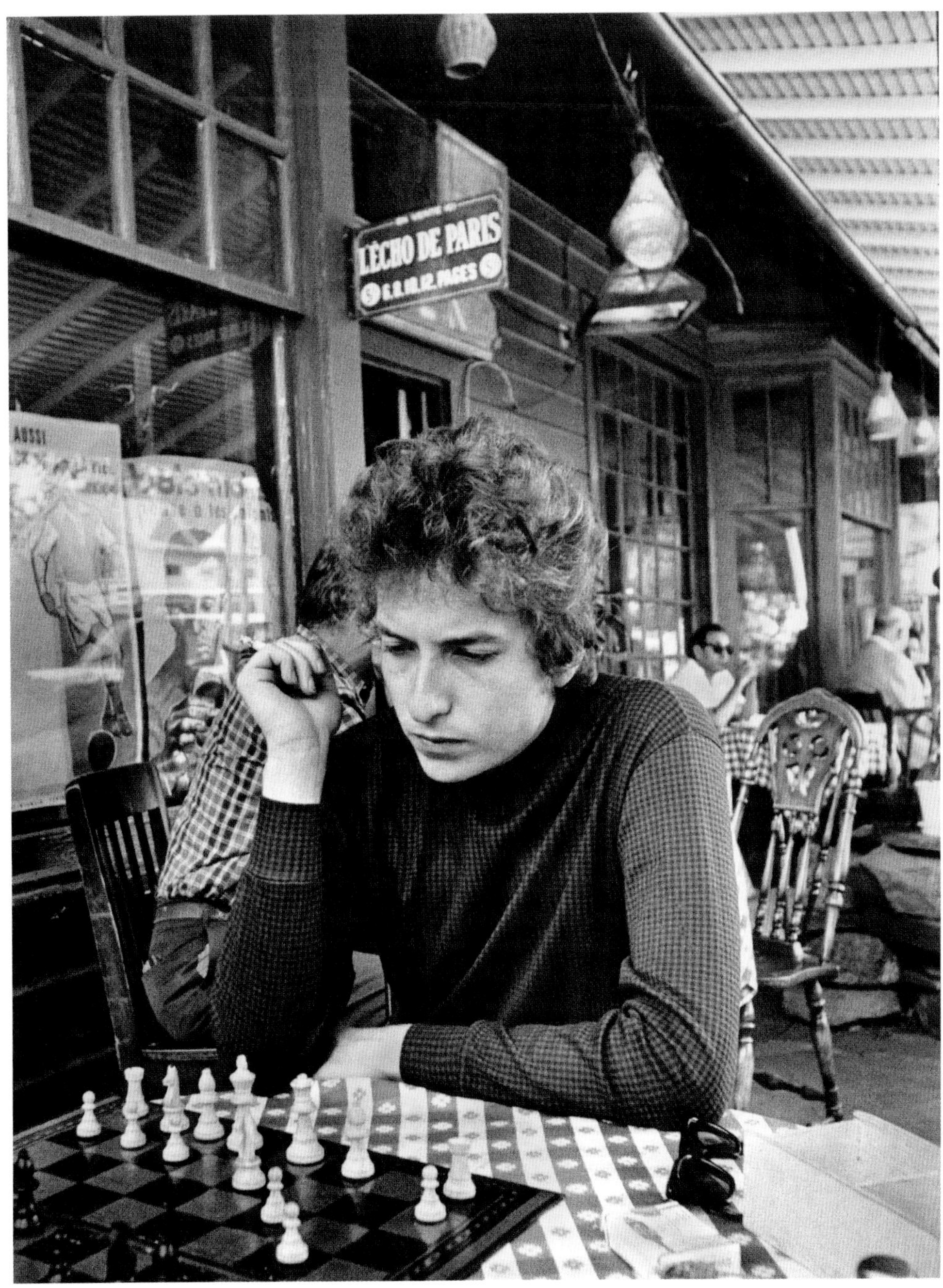
L'ÉCHO DE PARIS
6, 8, 10, 12, PAGES

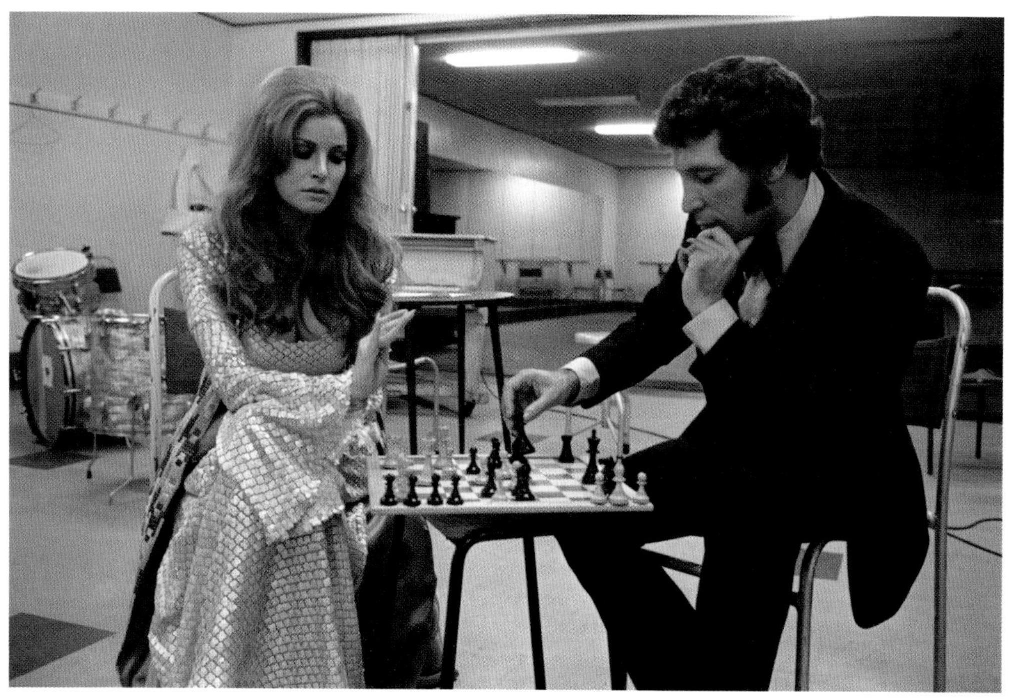

The actress and model Raquel Welch, whose films included *One Million Years B.C.*, is shown in the photograph above playing with Tom Jones, the Welsh singer, whose hits include 'She's a Lady' and 'It's Not Unusual', during a break in the filming of a television special in 1970.

Right: Ray Charles, the blind musician and composer, learned to play chess in 1965, while in a rehabilitation programme to kick his heroin habit. After he learned, he played all the time with fellow band members and other performers, including the singer Willie Nelson, whom Charles called his 'chess partner'.

Charles's specially made board had raised and lowered squares, enabling him to distinguish between light and dark squares. Similarly, the white pieces had rounded tops, while the black ones were sharpened. Charles's set is held in the collection of the Smithsonian Institution's National Museum of American History in Washington, D.C.

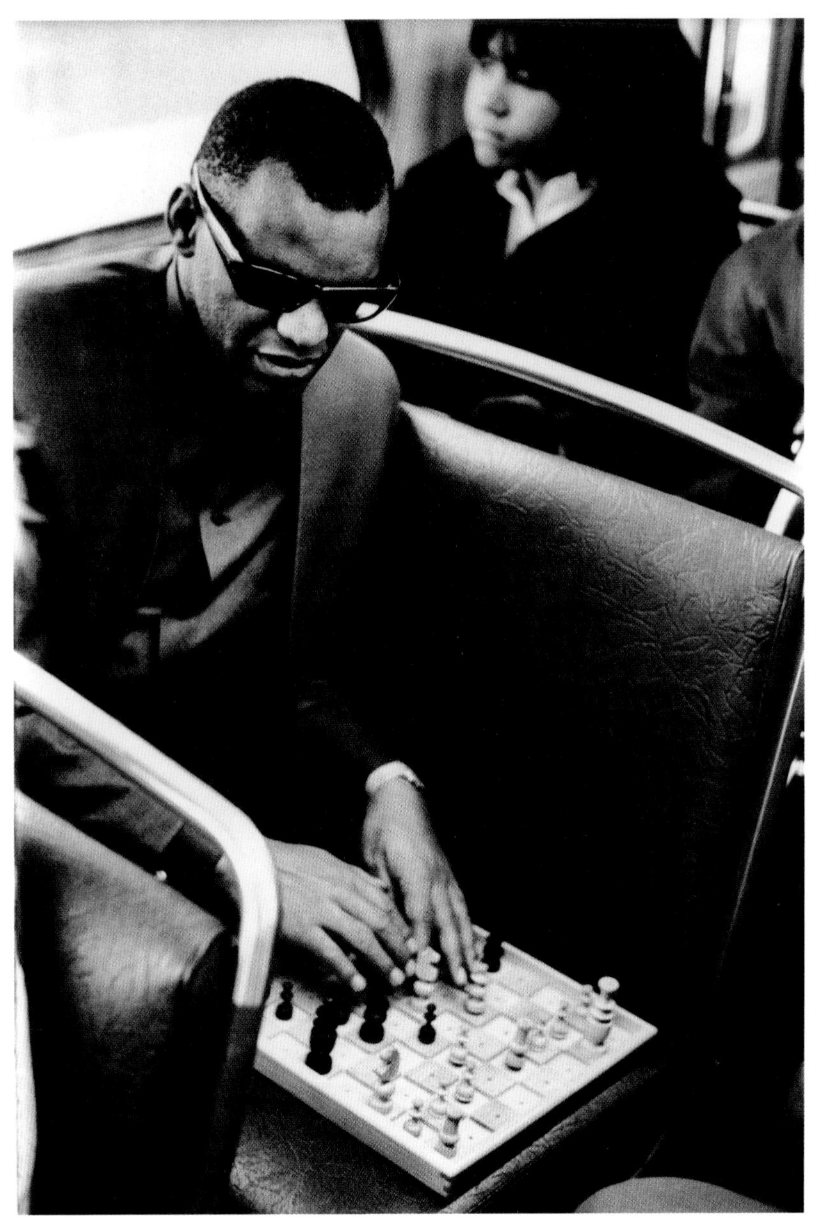

The great jazz trumpeter Dizzy Gillespie loved
chess. There are many photos of him playing
backstage and with friends while he was on the
road. He even played a correspondence game
(long distance) with the English jazz pianist
Ronnie Aldrich. He is seen here playing with
Harold Keith in Pittsburgh, Pennsylvania, in 1958.

Overleaf: Eddie Vartan, the French musician and
bandleader, playing chess with his younger sister,
the singer and actress Sylvie Vartan, 1963.

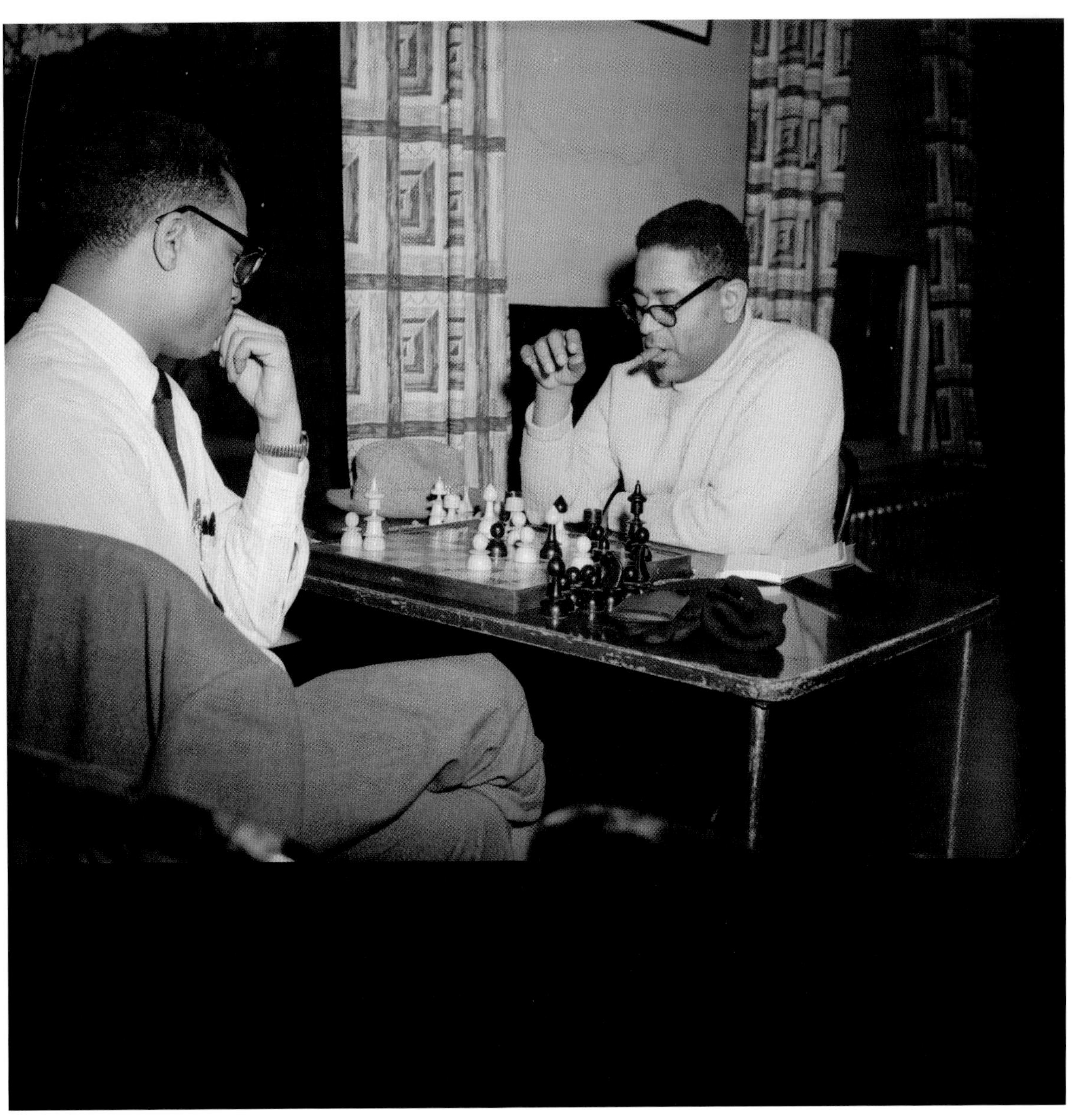

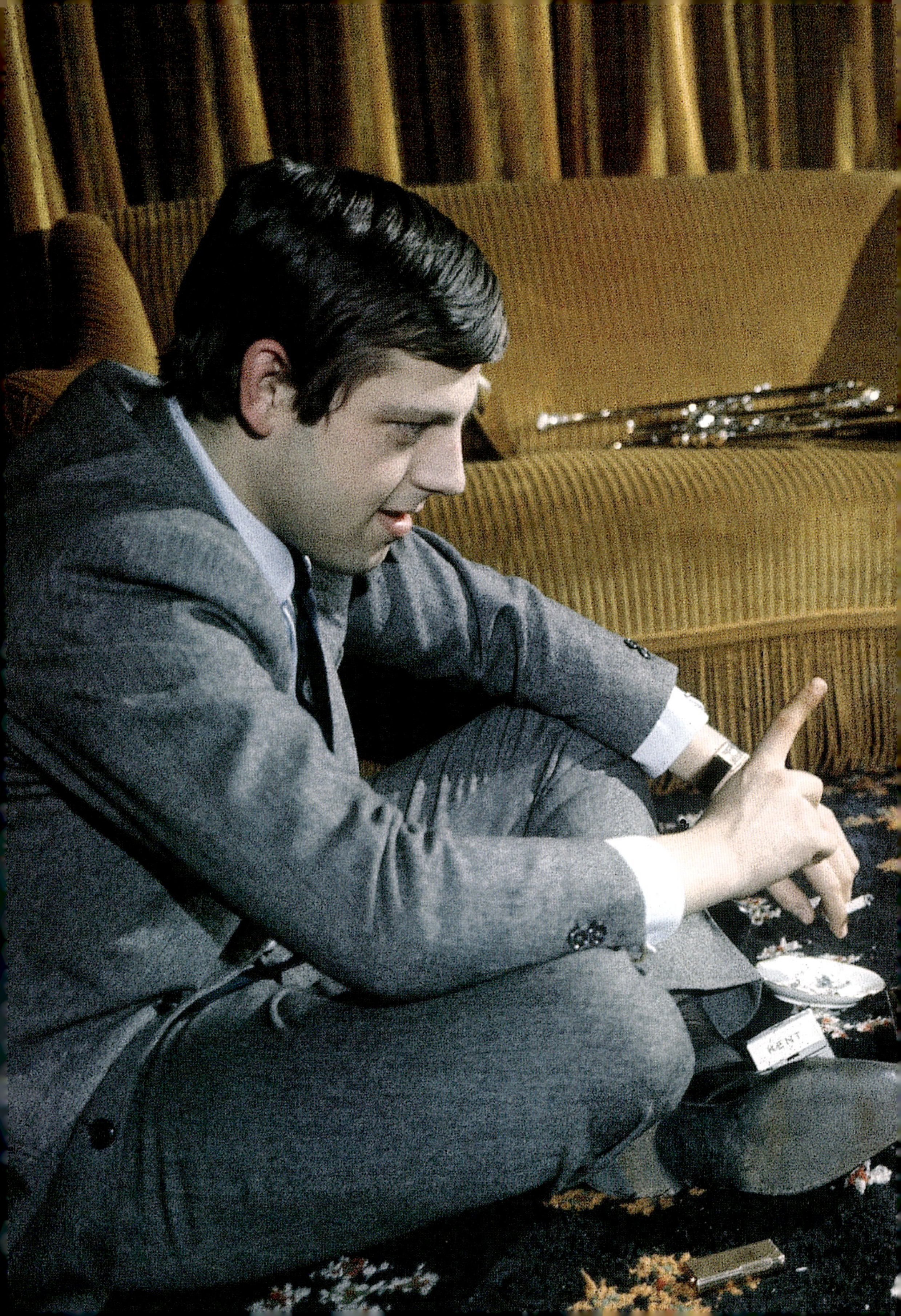

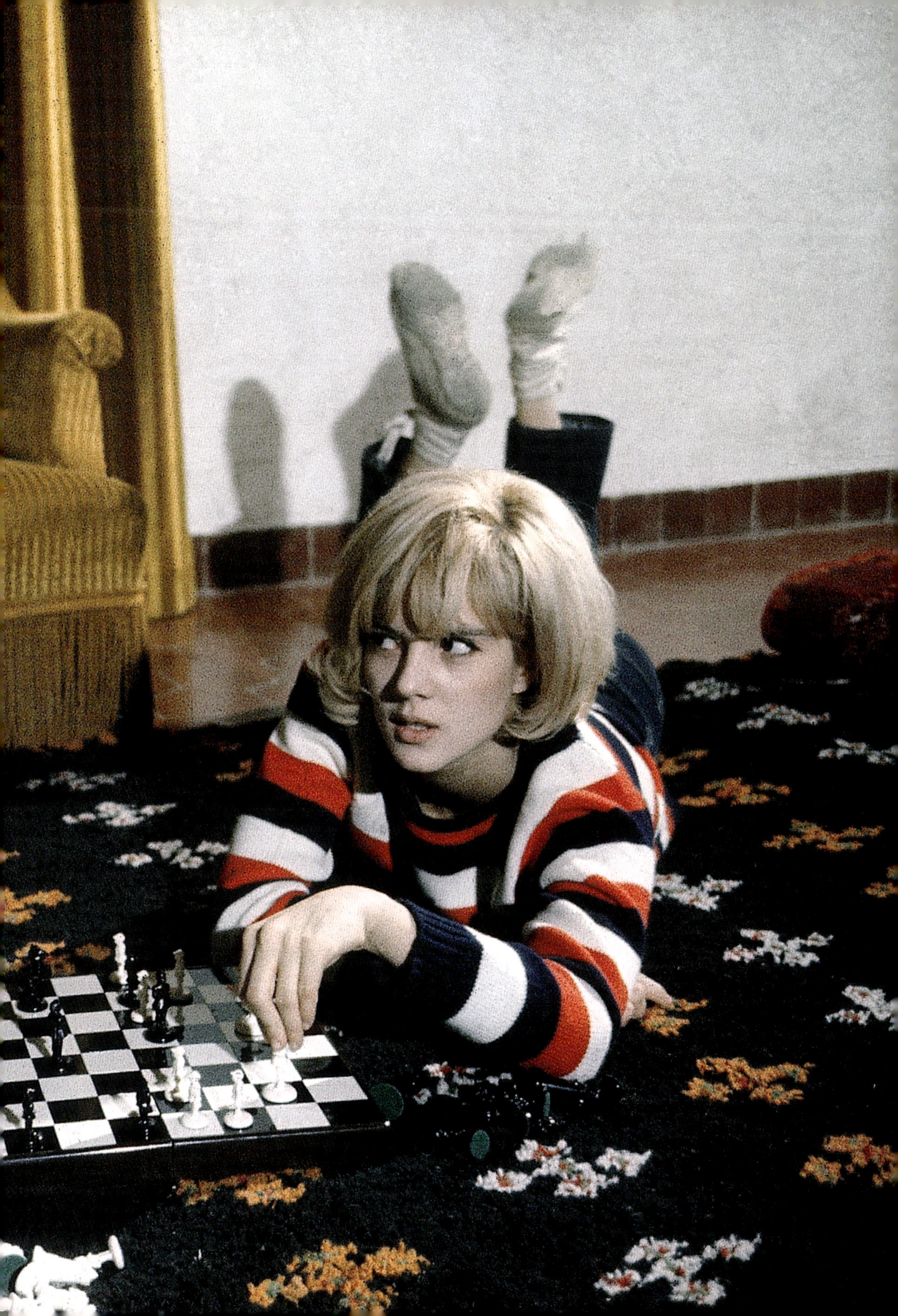

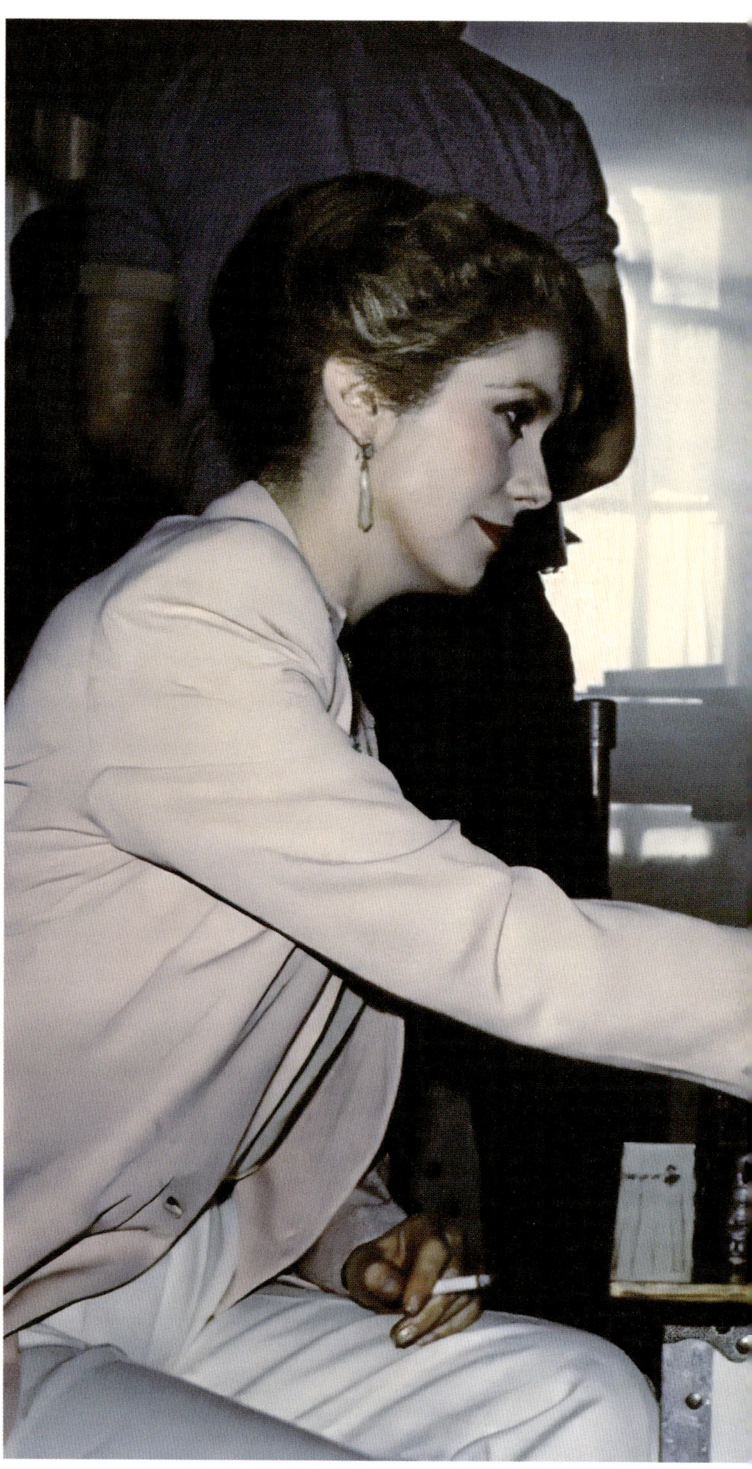

Catherine Deneuve and David Bowie, co-stars of the 1983 cult vampire film *The Hunger*, play chess on set.

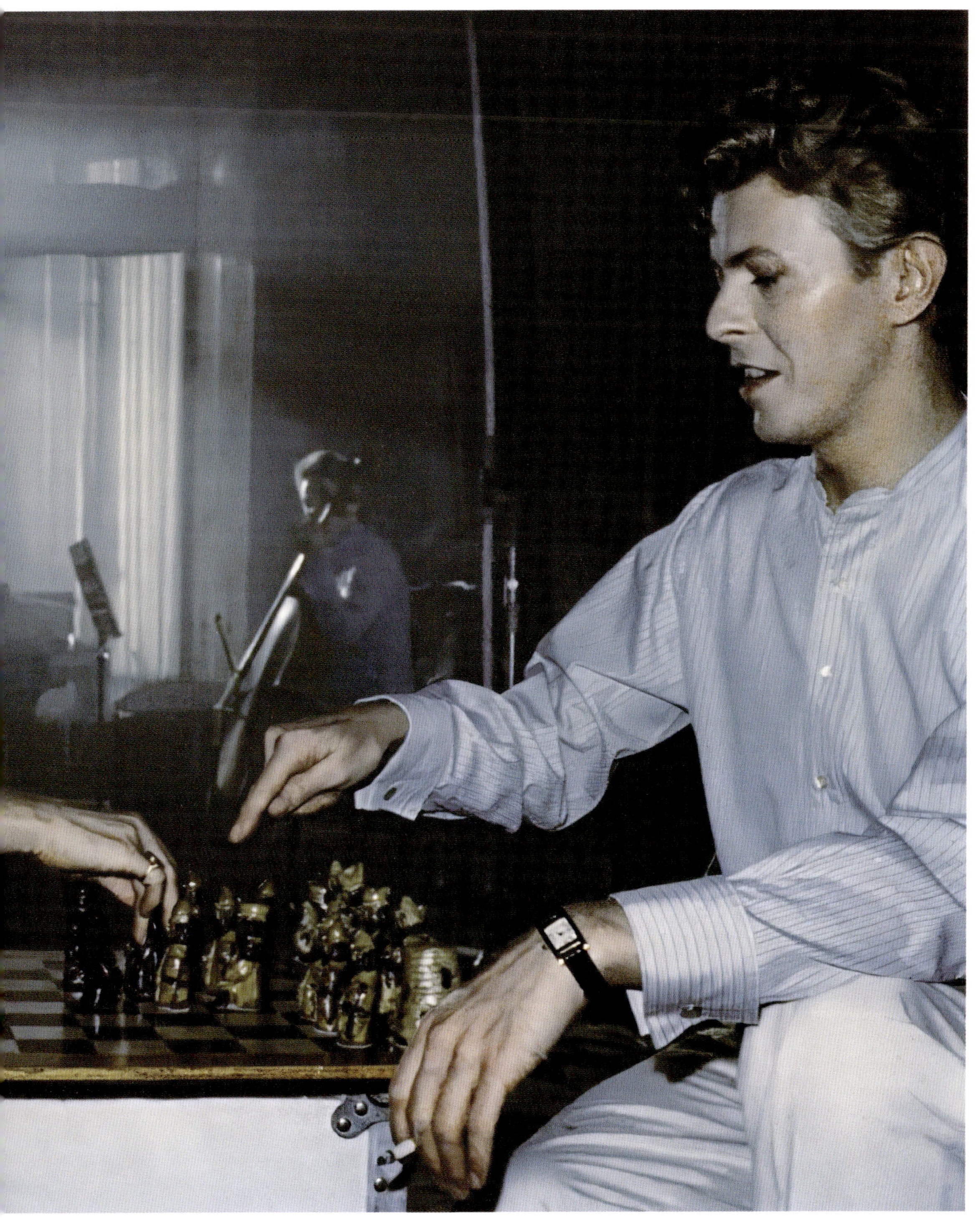

Brassaï, the pseudonym of Gyula Halász, was born in what is today called Brasov, Romania. He was one of the greatest street photographers of the 20th century. Emigrating to Paris just after World War I, he wandered the metropolis and made a name for himself photographing the nightlife of the 'city of light'. This image from 1934 is called *Papillon à la lampe* (*Butterfly in the lamp*), but it also captures a chess player lost in thought – the type of voyeuristic photograph of which Brassaï was a master.

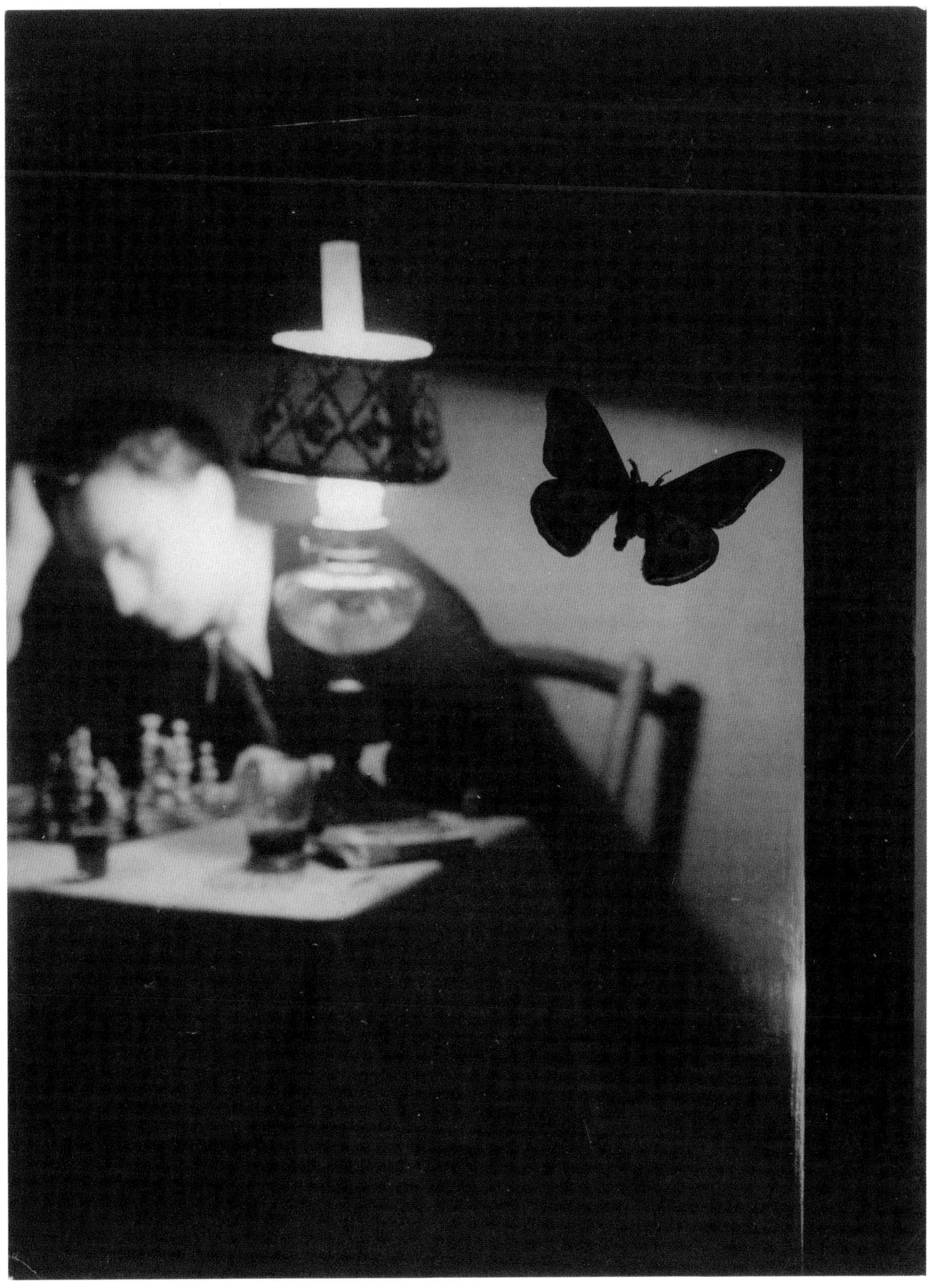

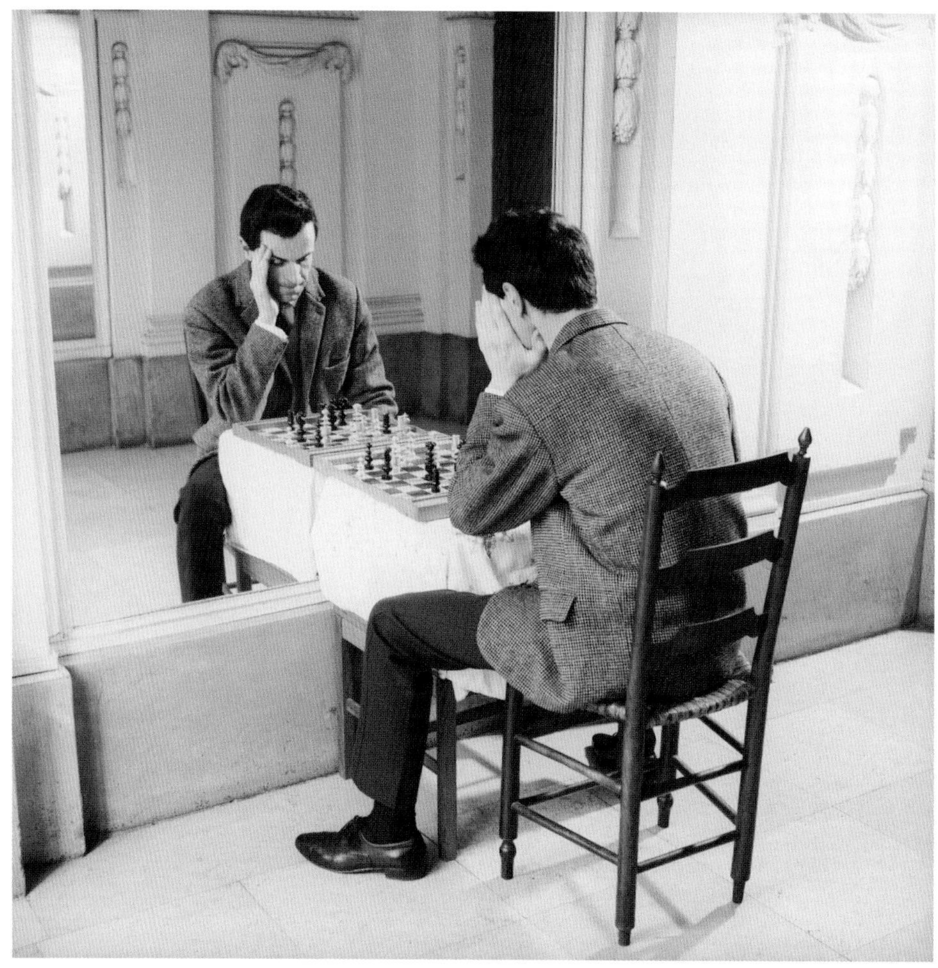

René Maltête (1930–2000), was a French photographer known for his humorous compositions. Some were based on visual puns (a herd of sheep walking past a sign saying, 'You are the majority'), others on incongruous juxtapositions. Still others were staged, as in this image of a man playing chess sitting in front of a mirror, so it appears he is playing against himself. The photograph appears in a book of his work published posthumously called *Des Yeux plein les poches* (*Pocket Full of Eyes*).

Right: René Magritte was one of the giants of the surrealist art movement that emerged in Europe after World War I. Enamoured with chess, he used its imagery in a number of his works, including *The Encounter* (1926) and *The Annunciation* (1930). In this photo from 1937, he poses with a chessboard in place of his head. It evokes what would become one of his best-known works, a 1964 self-portrait called *The Son of Man*, in which a green apple hovers in front of his face.

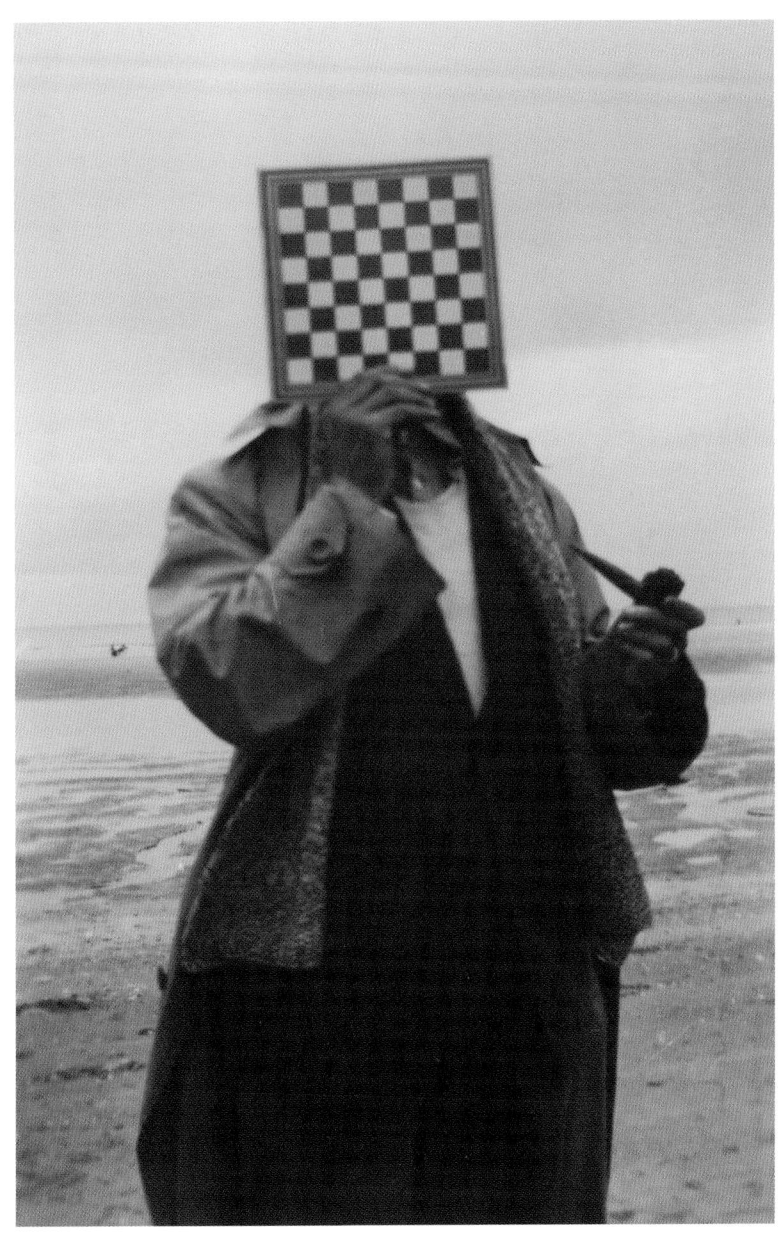

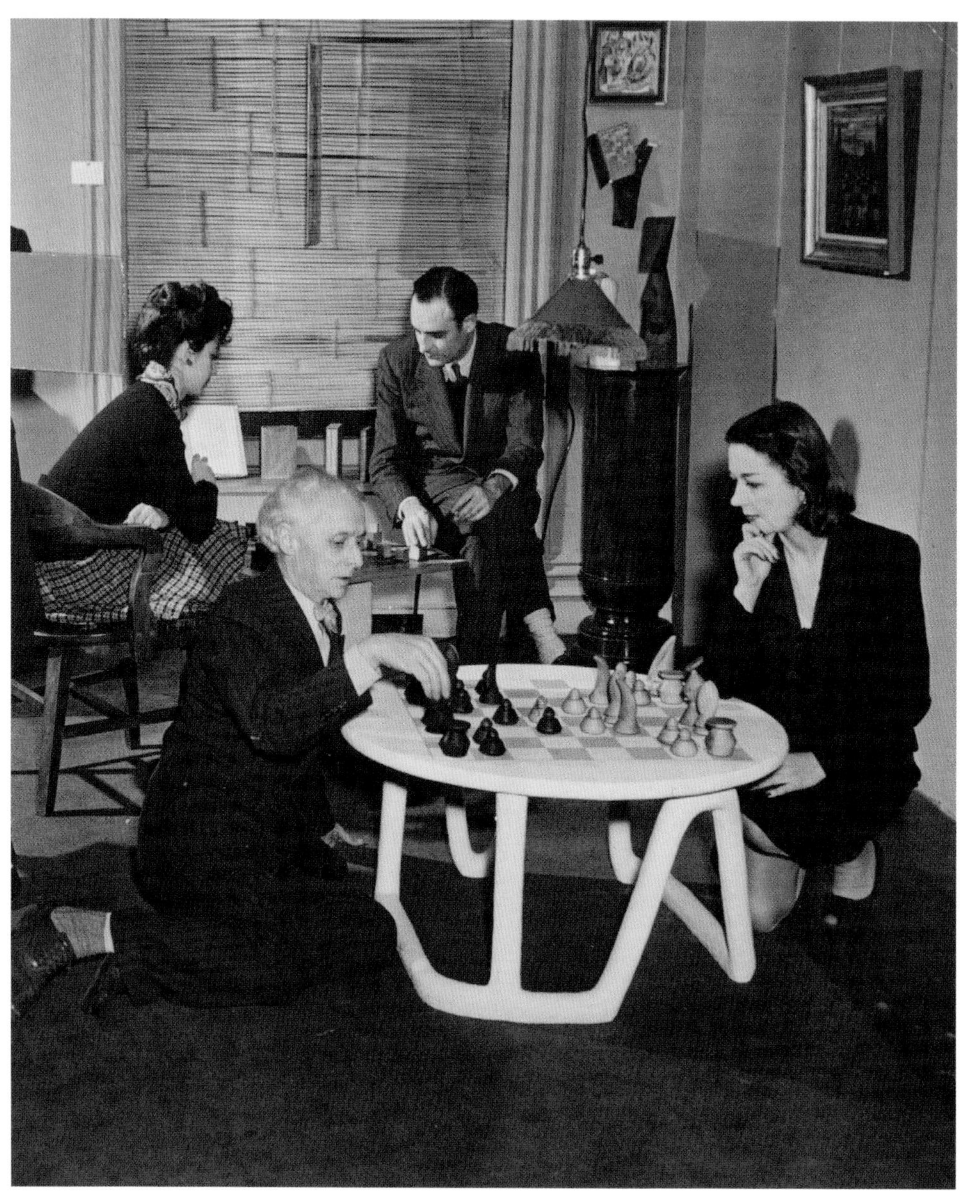

In late 1944 and early 1945, Julien Levy, one of the most important art gallery owners in New York, organised an exhibition of surrealist and avant-garde art called *The Imagery of Chess*. The exhibition included many of the most important artists of the time, all of whom designed sets for the show. In the background of the photograph are Muriel and Julien Levy, in the foreground Max Ernst and Dorothea Tanning, (his wife), playing on a set designed by Ernst.

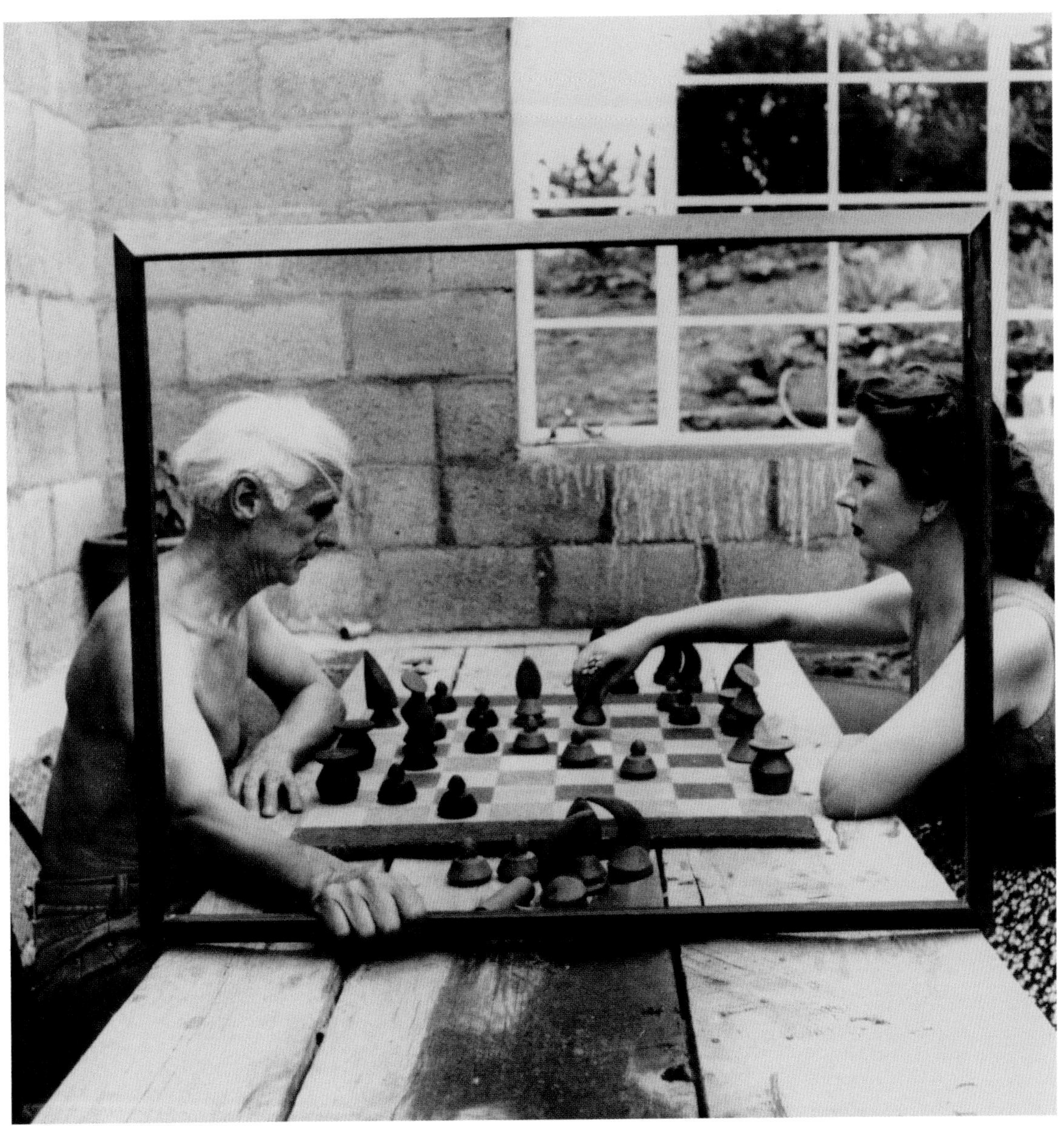

A 1948 photograph, showing Max Ernst and his wife Dorothea Tanning using the set designed by Ernst, in the house they built in Sedona, Arizona. They met at a party in 1942 and shortly afterwards Ernst visited her studio (Tanning was a noted artist in her own right), where they played a game of chess. A week later he moved in with her.

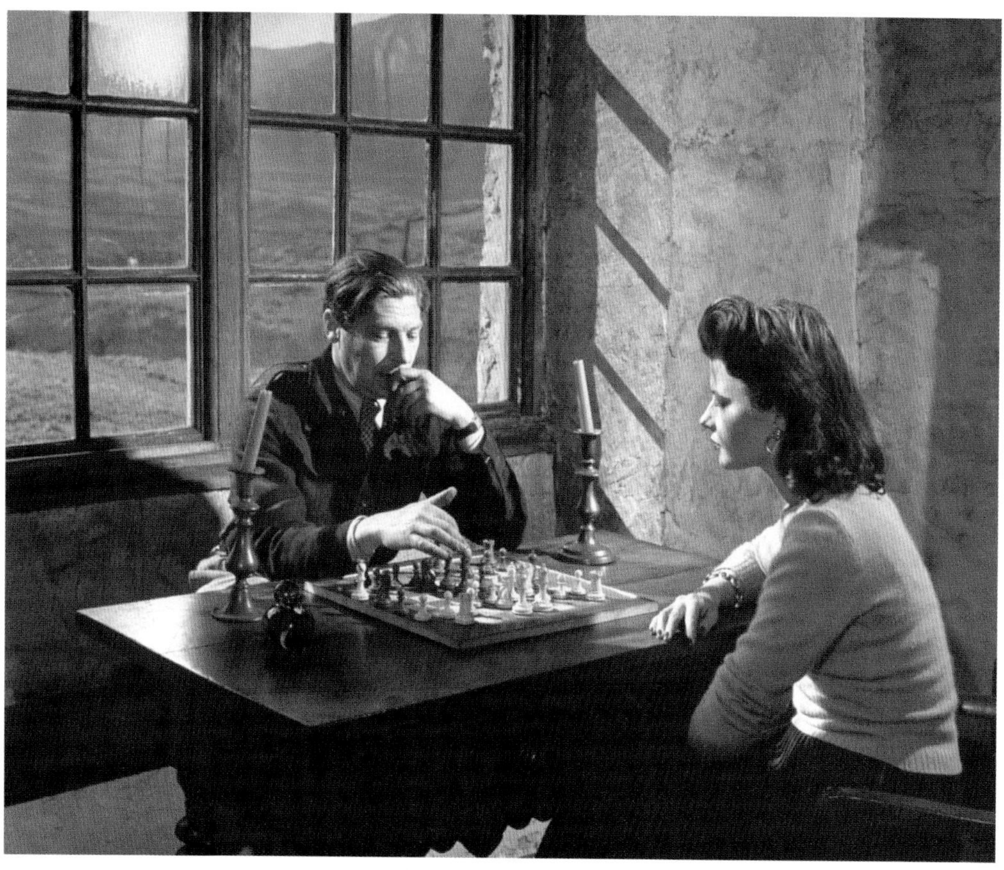

Arthur Koestler, an award-winning Hungarian-born writer and journalist, playing chess with the British socialite Mamaine Paget in 1947. They married in 1950.

Right: This 1944 photograph taken in Amagansett, New York, shows the surrealist artist Max Ernst (with his back to the camera) and his friend the abstract expressionist, Robert Motherwell. That year, Ernst made a plaster cast of a sculpture based on chess called *The King Playing with the Queen*. The cast was not well received by critics, but Motherwell loved it, so Ernst gave it to him. Nine years later, two collectors arranged to have several copies of the work cast in bronze and Ernst presented one to Motherwell for having safeguarded the plaster cast. The work is now considered one of Ernst's most important sculptures.

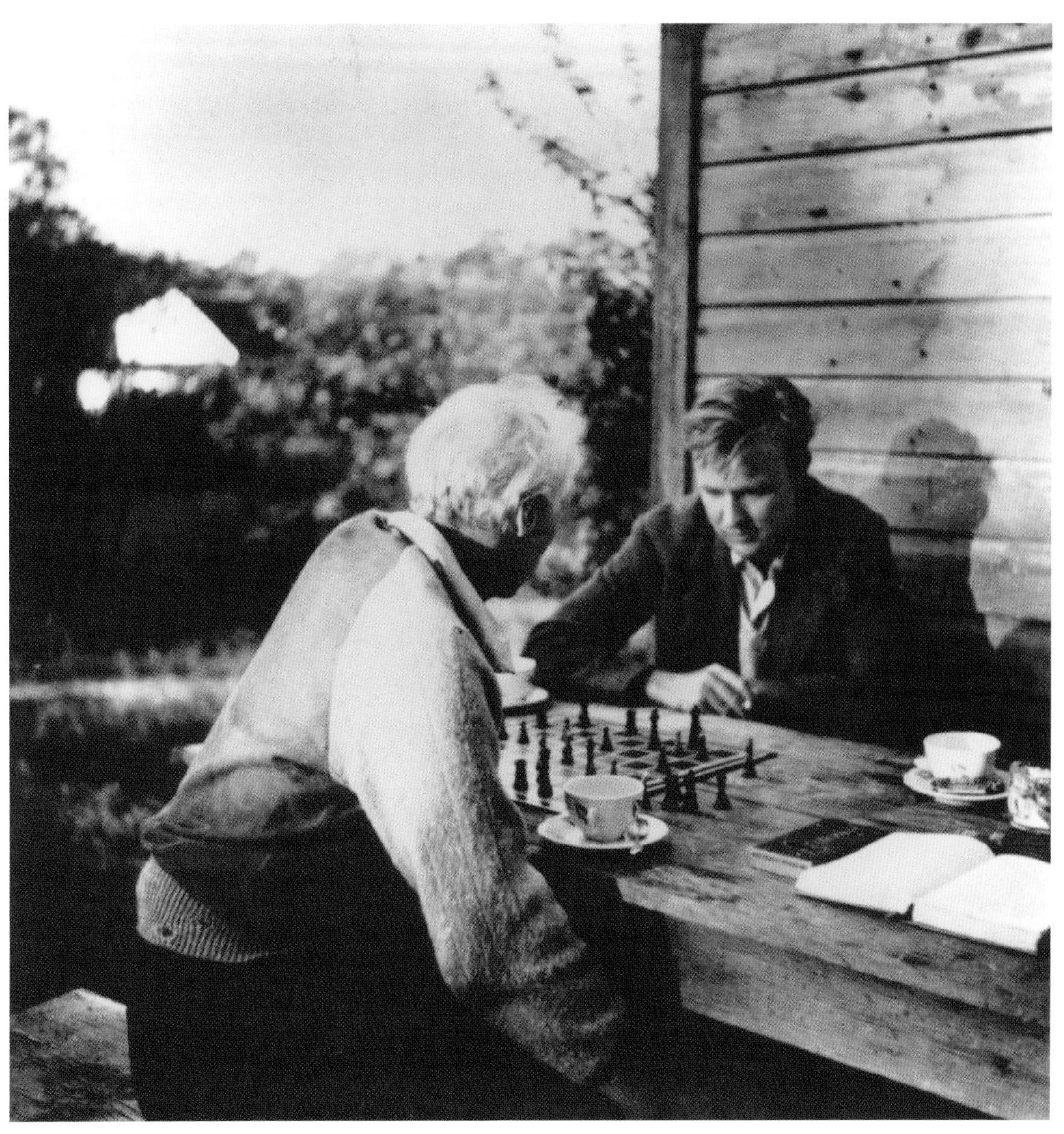

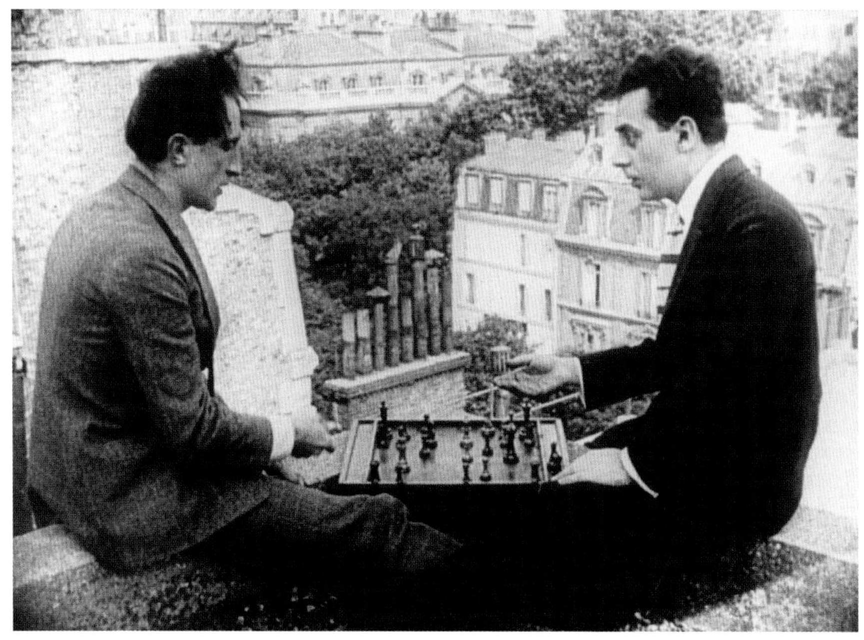

Marcel Duchamp, a leading artist of the early 20th century, was smitten by chess. In 1923, at the height of his career, he essentially stopped producing art to focus on the game. He was quite successful at it: the French Chess Federation awarded him the title of 'master' in 1925 and he played for the French national team in the Chess Olympiads from 1928 to 1933, accumulating an overall score of four wins, 22 draws and 26 loses.

Above: Duchamp (left) and the American visual artist Man Ray bonded over chess. They are seen here playing on the roof of the Théatre des Champs Elysées, Paris, in the 20-minute experimental film *Entr'acte* (*Intermission*), by René Clair, 1924.

Right: Man Ray (left) and Duchamp, playing on a copy of the set based on simple geometric forms designed by Man Ray in 1920.

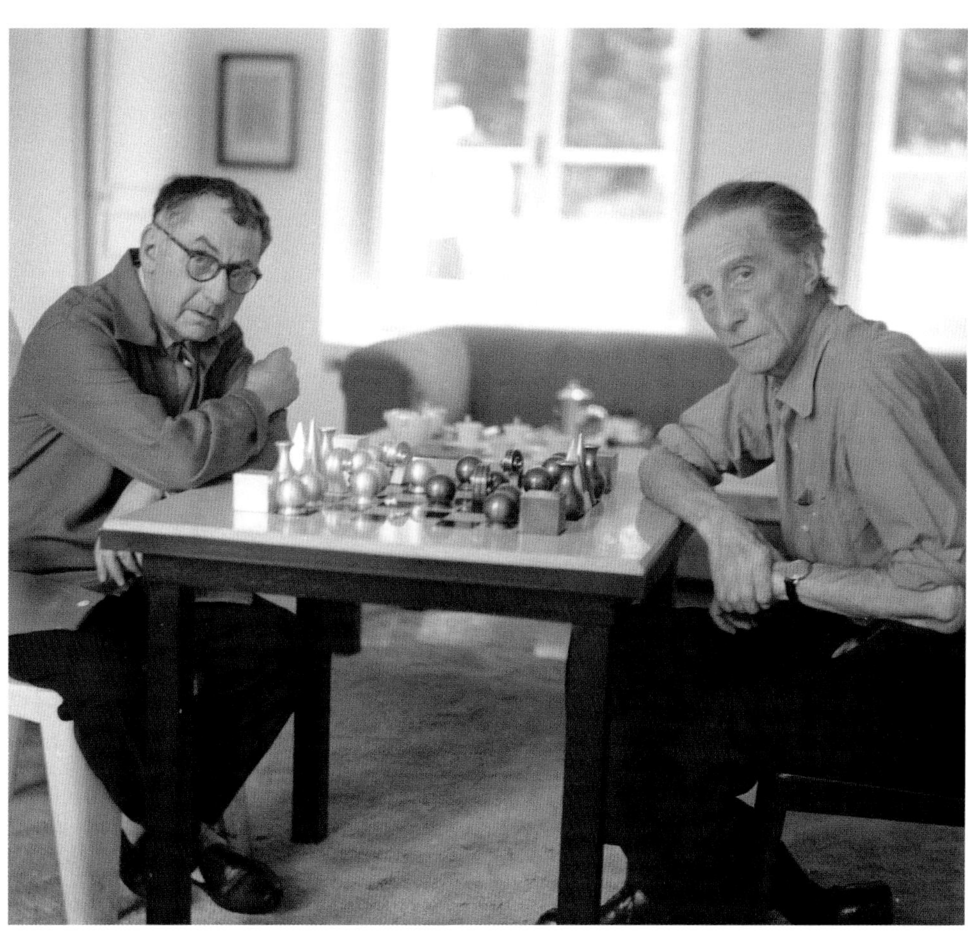

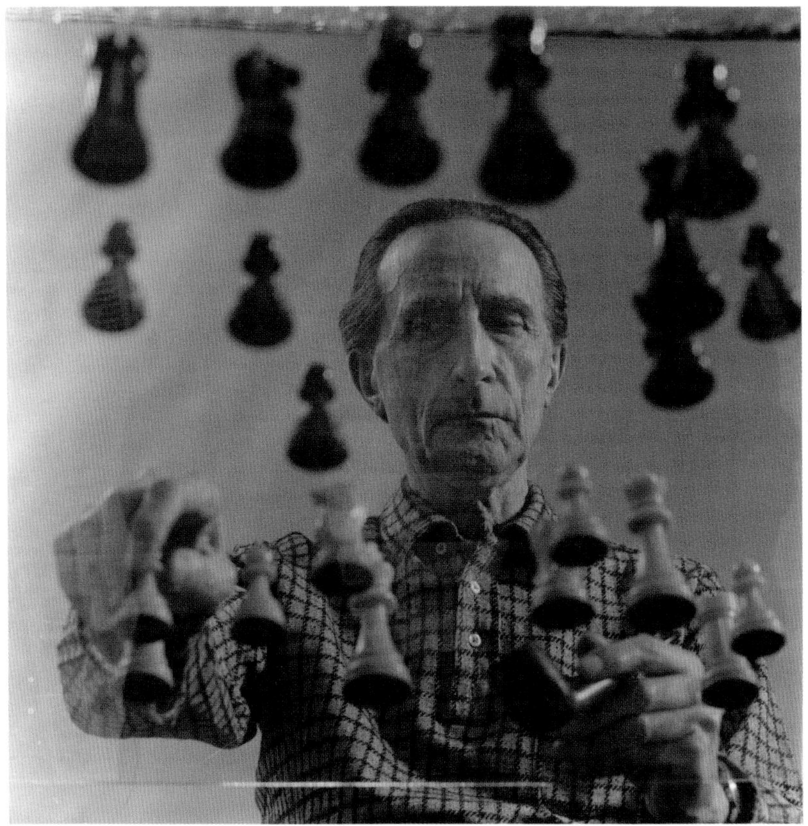

Above: Marcel Duchamp plays chess on a sheet of glass, 1958.

Right: Duchamp, sitting in the tree in the background, and Hans Richter, the avant-garde artist and film director (back to camera), play a game using live pieces on the lawn of Richter's house in Southbury, Connecticut. The photograph was taken during the filming of Richter's *8 x 8: A Chess Sonata in 8 Movements* (1956).

Overleaf: The 1963 photographs of a naked Eve Babitz, a buxom 19-year-old ingénue, playing chess against Duchamp at the Pasadena Museum of Art, caused a sensation – partly because both players seemed completely indifferent to her nudity. The occasion was a retrospective of Duchamp's art, but there was a backstory to the image.

The museum curator, Walter Hopps, was having an affair with Babitz, but she was not invited to the opening of the retrospective, because Hopp's wife was going to be there. An additional insult was that Babitz's younger sister, Mirandi, had been invited. Knowing what was going on, Julian Wasser, a *Time* magazine photographer, suggested the shoot as a means of revenge and Babitz agreed. When Hopps walked in during the shoot, he literally spat out the gum he was chewing.

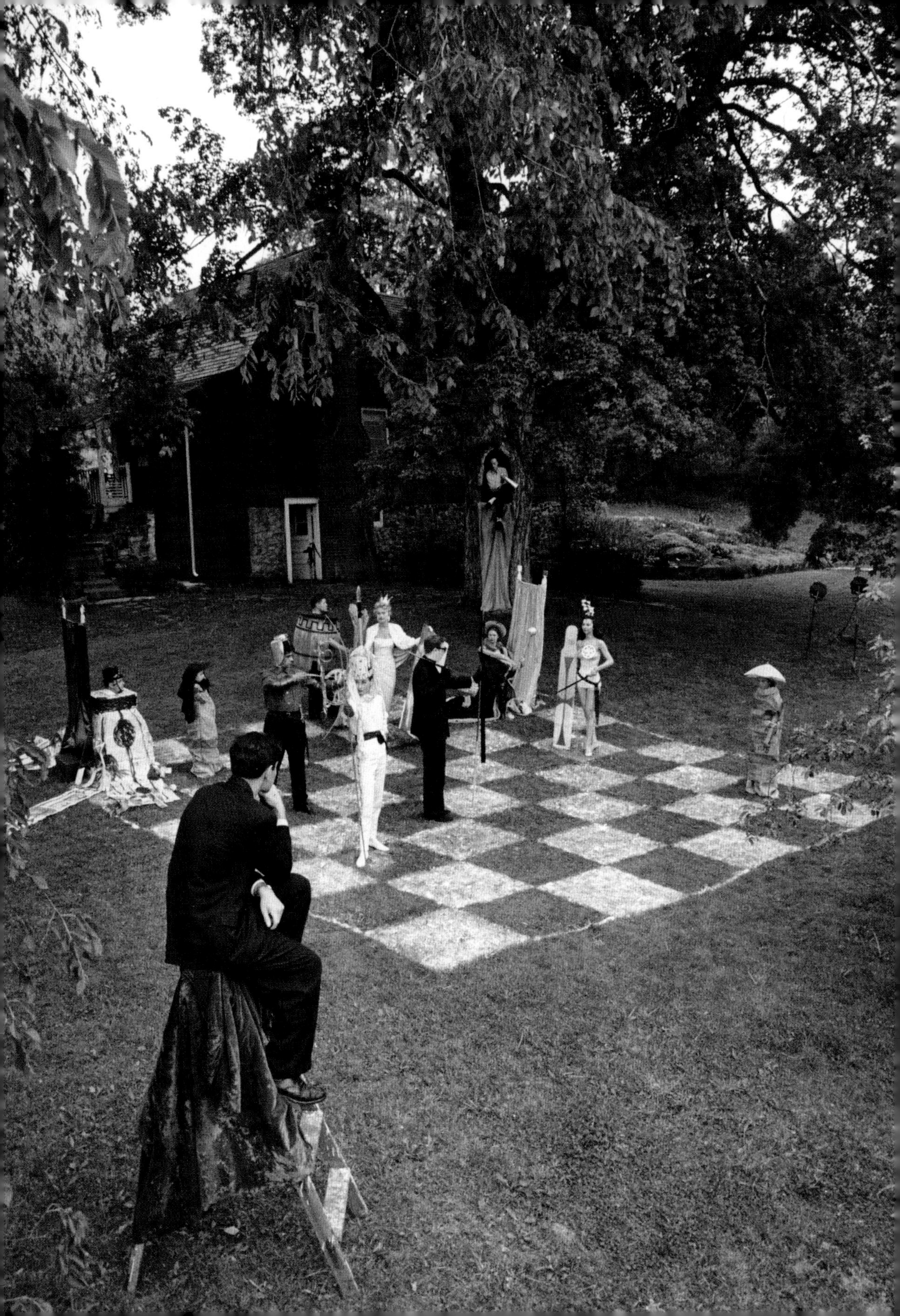

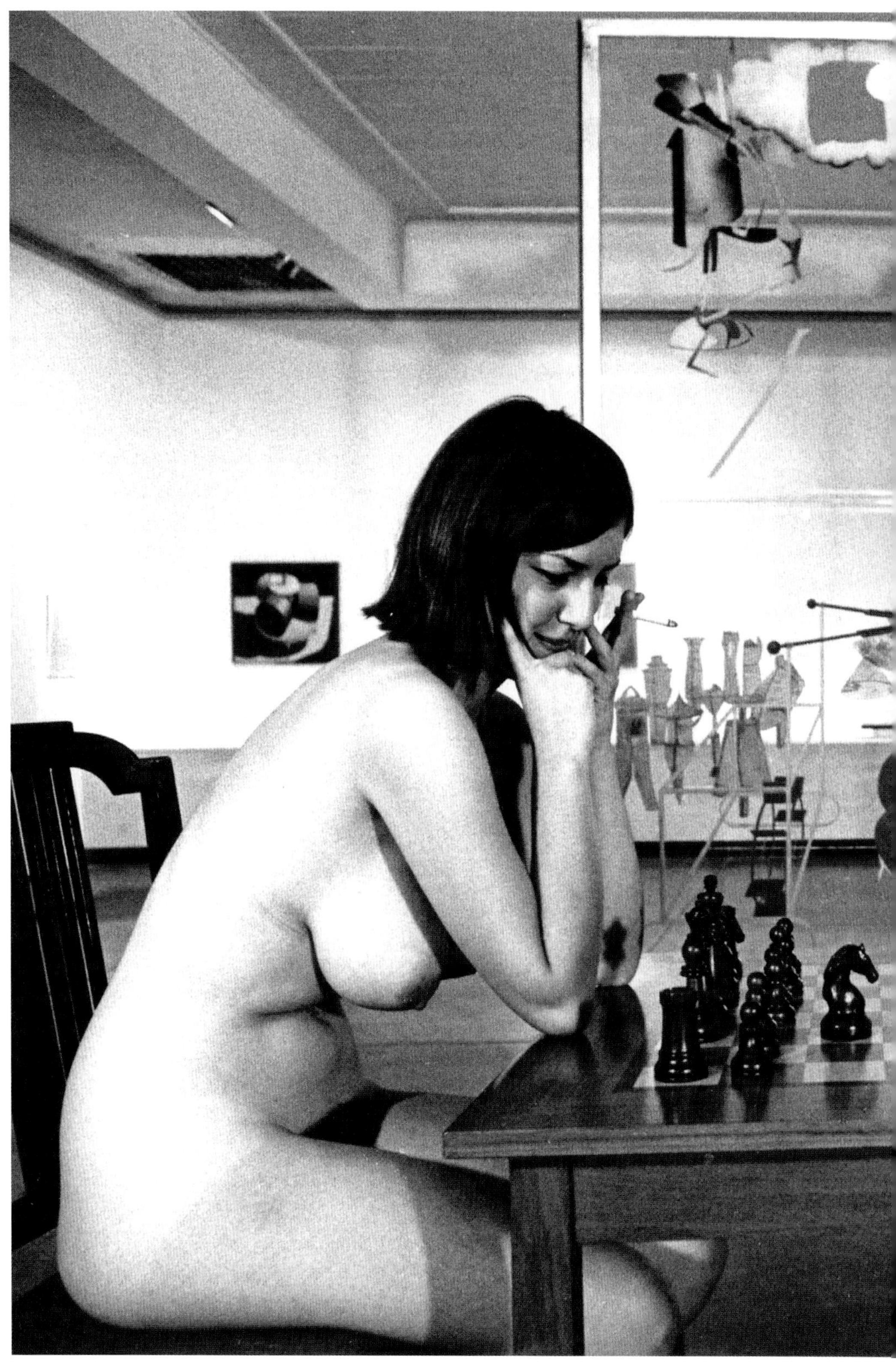

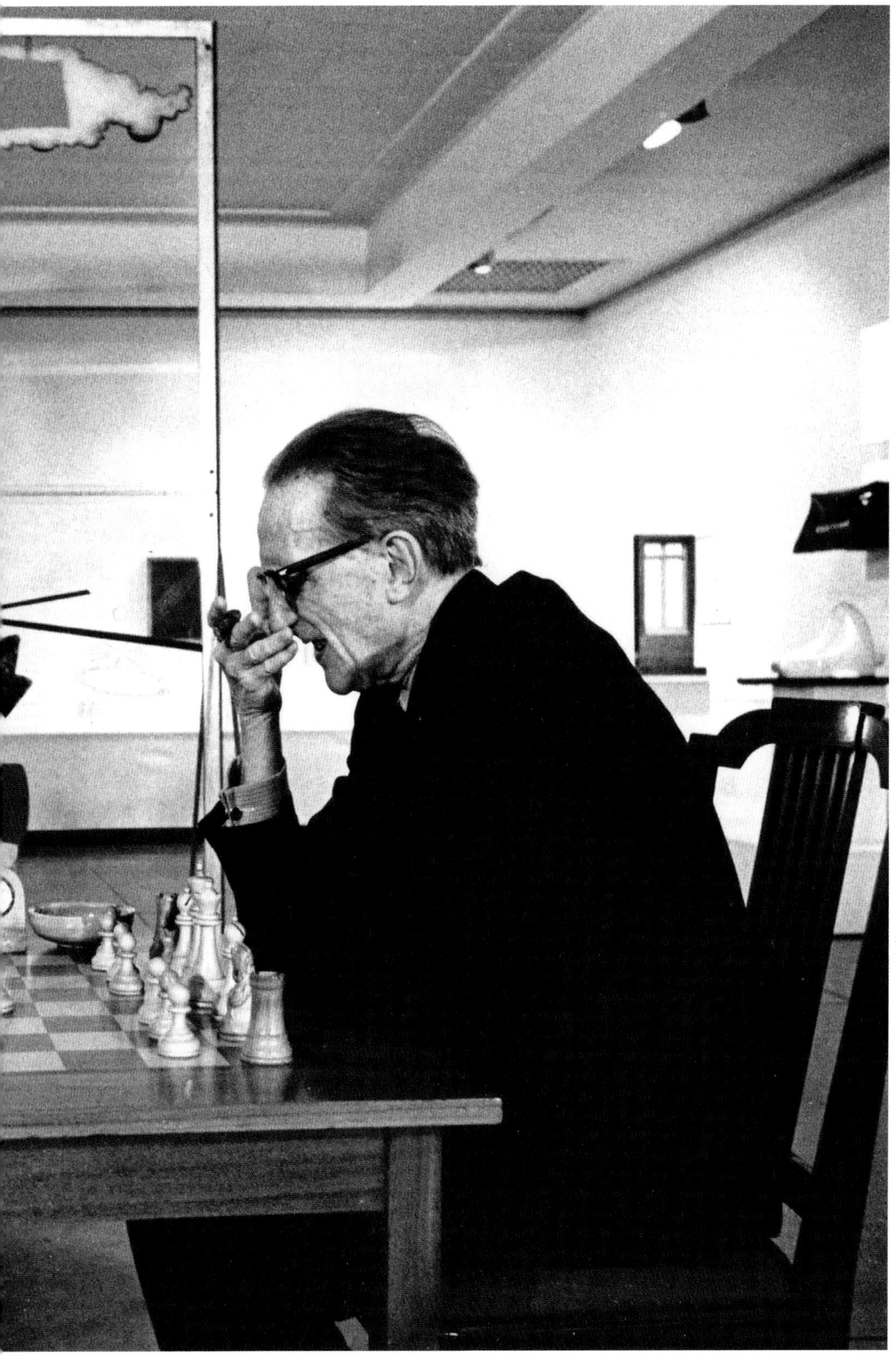

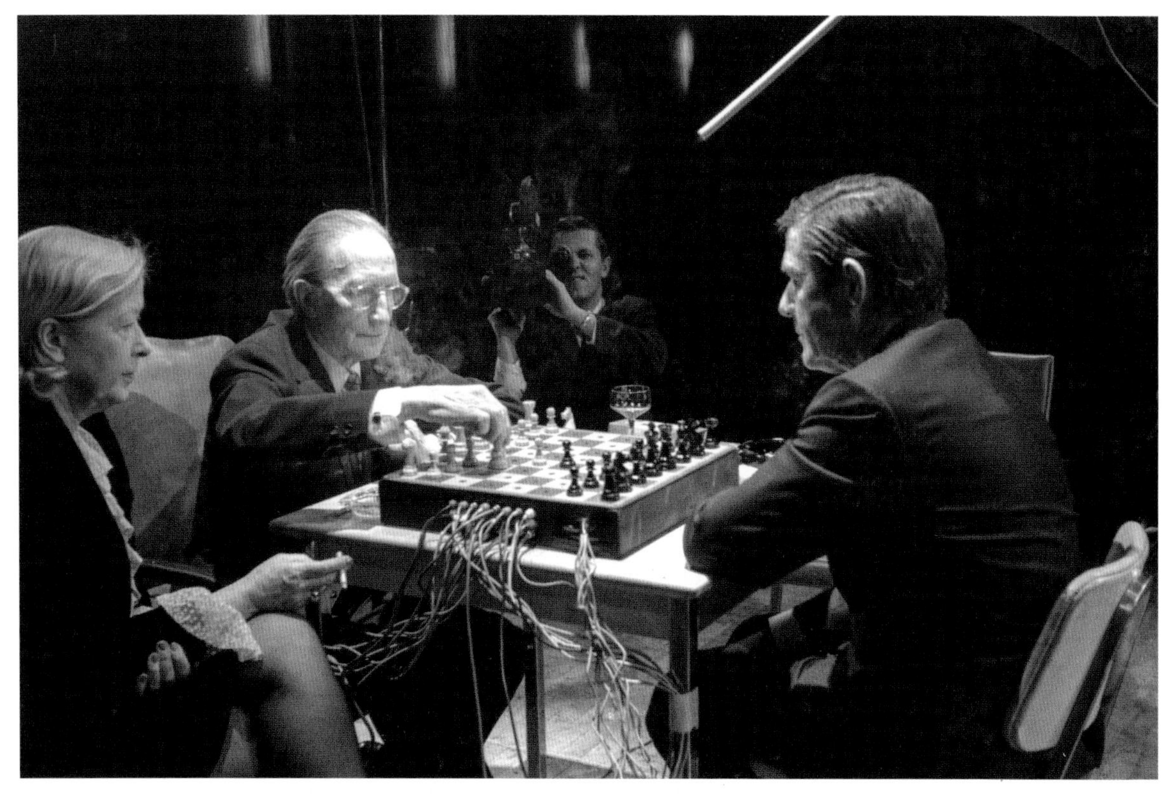

Marcel Duchamp and John Cage, the American composer, playing chess during *Reunion* (1968), a work of performance art in which moves on a chessboard were turned into electronic music. Alexina 'Teeny' Duchamp, Duchamp's second wife, is watching. After Duchamp had won the first game, Teeny played Cage in a second game. She also won.

'All artists are not chess players
– all chess players are artists.'
Marcel Duchamp

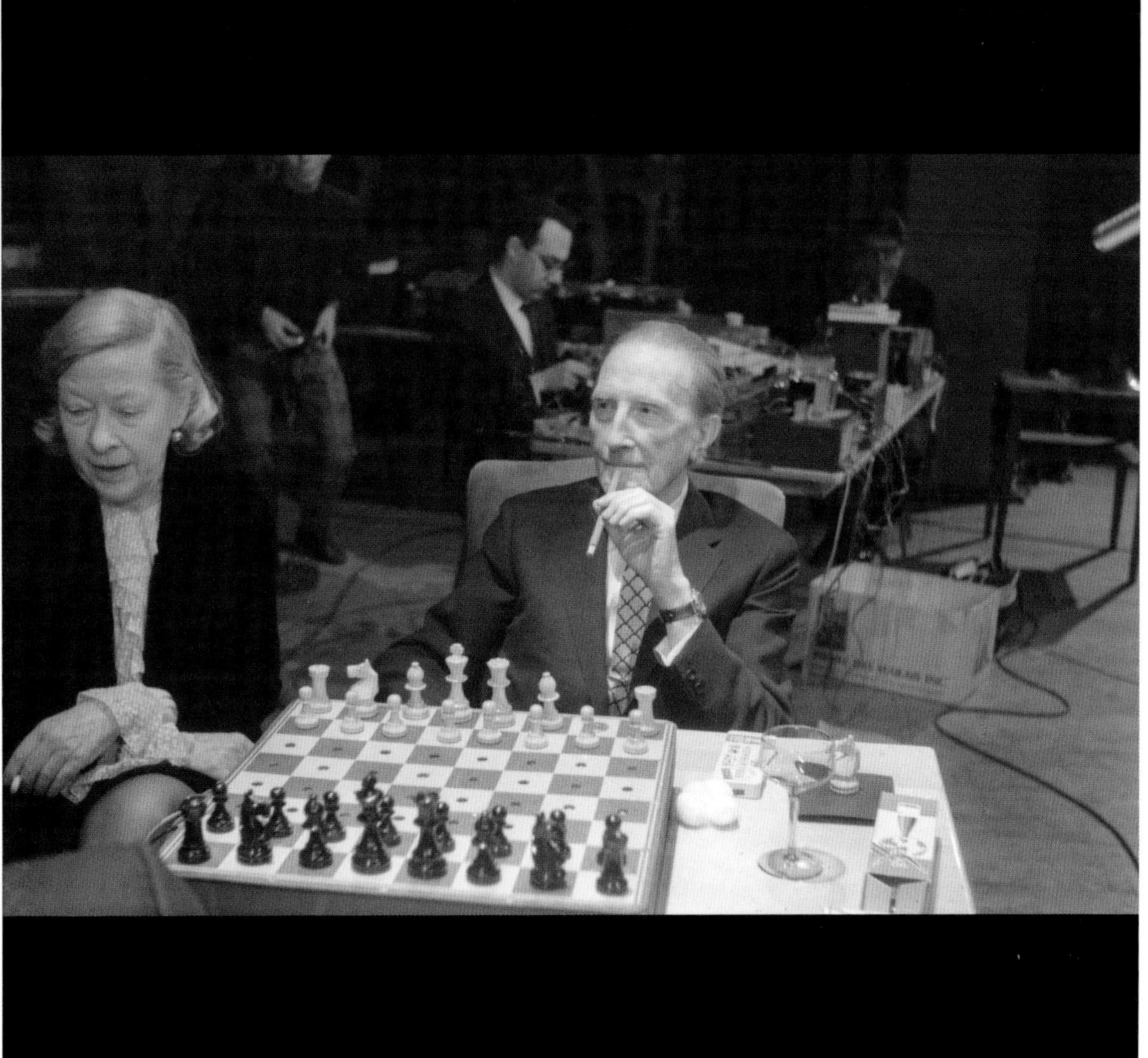

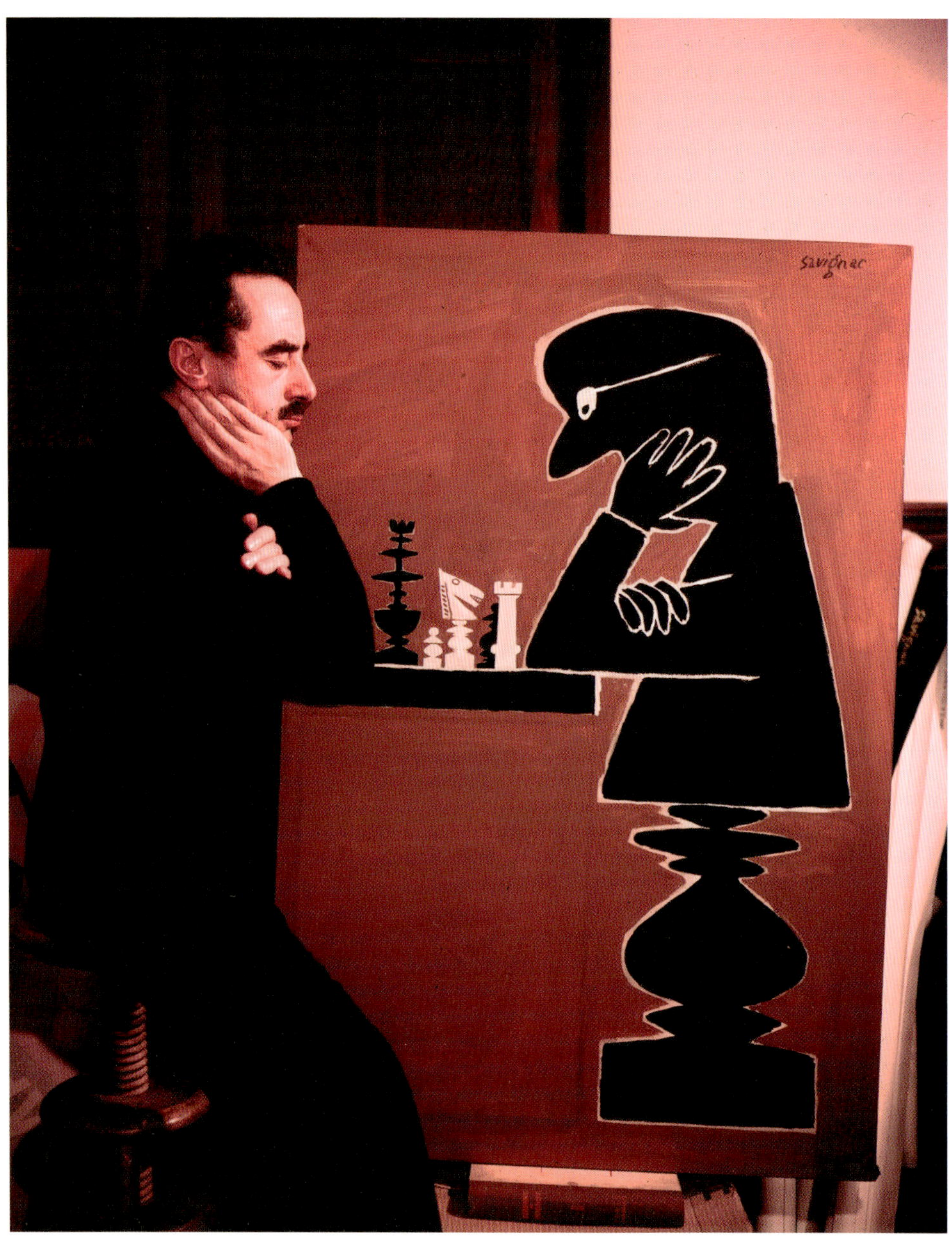

Savignac

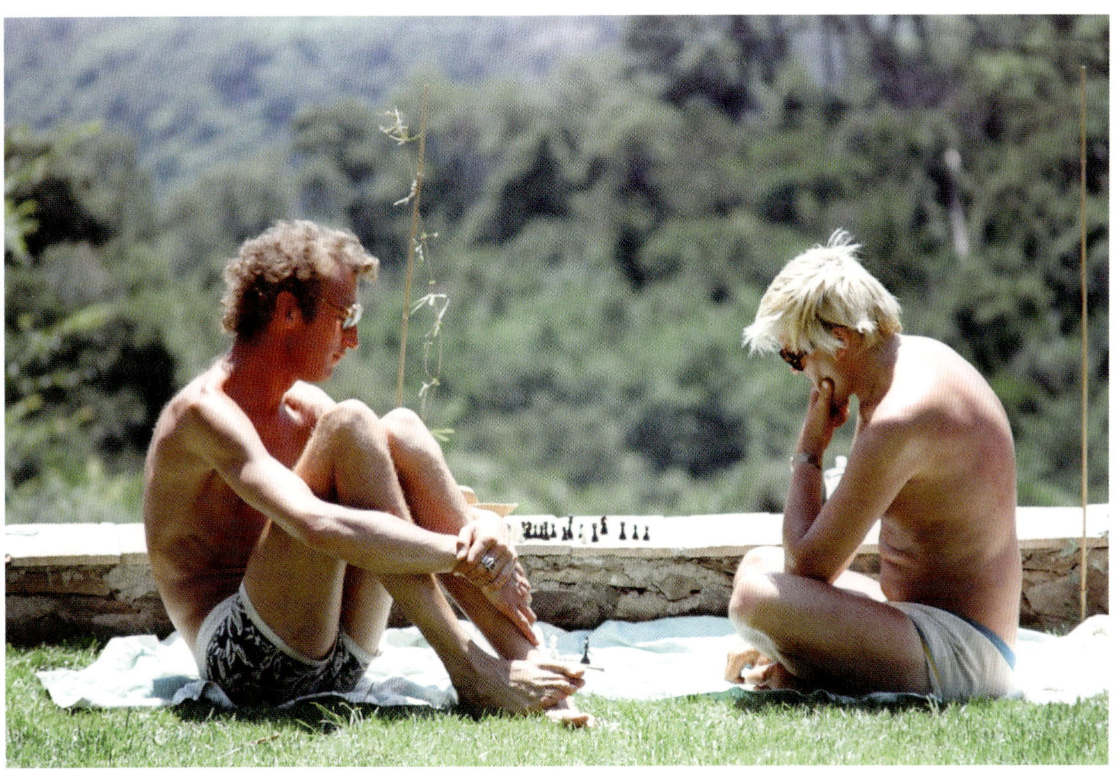

The artists Patrick Procktor (left) and
David Hockney, playing chess at the
home of the film director Tony Richardson
near St Tropez, France, 1969.

'Drawing is rather like playing chess: your
mind races ahead of the moves that you
eventually make.' David Hockney

Left: Graphic artist Raymond Savignac
with a poster he designed for a chess
tournament in France, 1950.

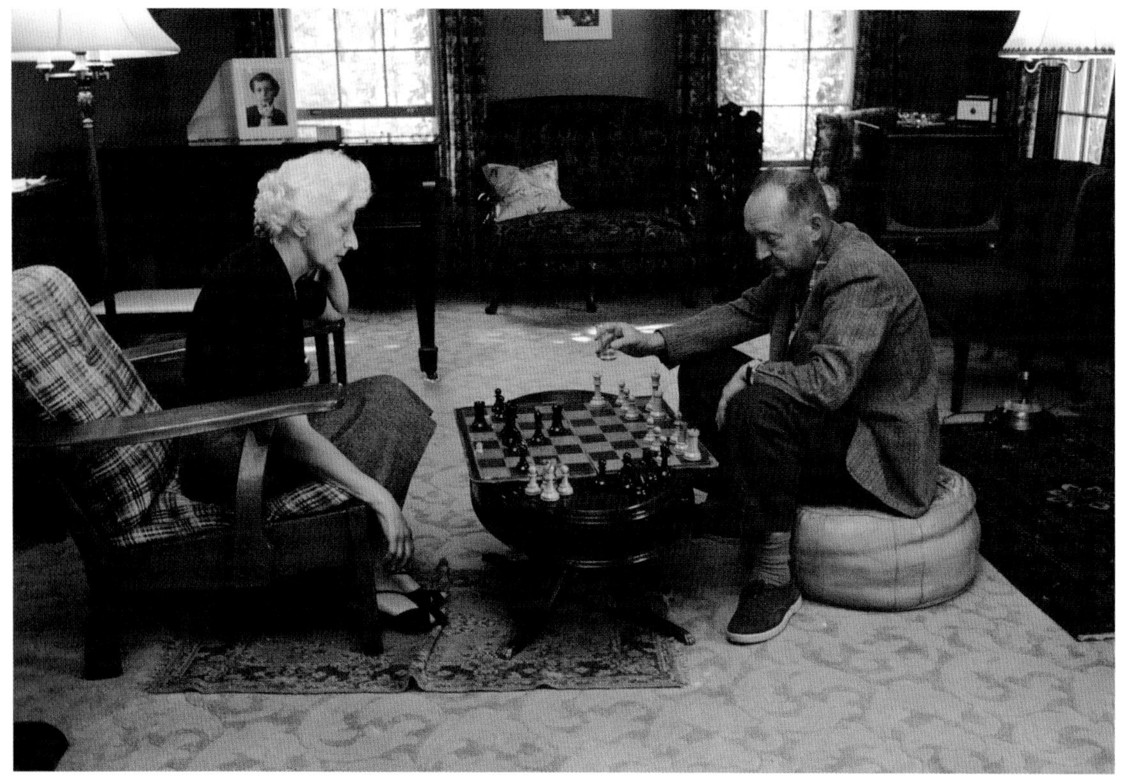

These photographs from 1958 (above) and 1968
(right) show Vladimir Nabokov playing chess with
his wife Vera, at their home in Ithaca, New York.
One of the greatest writers of the 20th century,
he also had a passion for chess, in particular for
composing problems – mostly mates in two or
three moves. He wrote, 'Chess problems demand
from the composer the same virtues that
characterise all worthwhile art: originality,
invention, conciseness, harmony, complexity,
and splendid insincerity.'

One of Nabokov's books, *The Defence* (1930),
is centred around chess and was adapted for a
film called *The Luzhin Defence* (2000), starring
John Turturro.

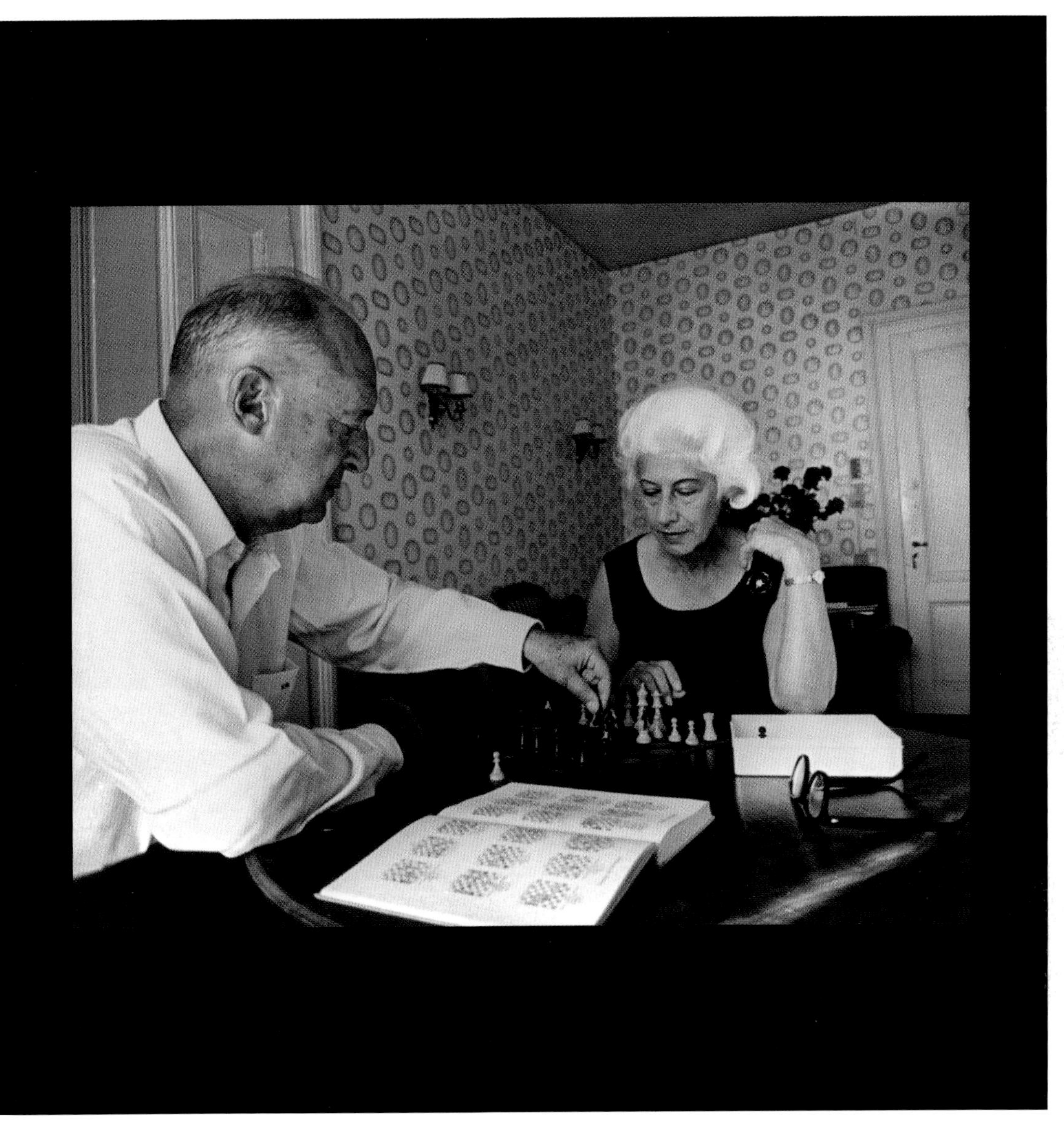

In *The Conquest of Happiness* (1930), the philosopher and mathematician Bertrand Russell wrote, 'The man who likes chess sufficiently to look forward throughout his working day to the game that he will play in the evening is fortunate, but the man who gives up work in order to play chess all day has lost the virtue of moderation.'

Below, Bertrand Russell playing chess with his oldest son, John Conrad Russell, at home in Los Angeles, 1940.

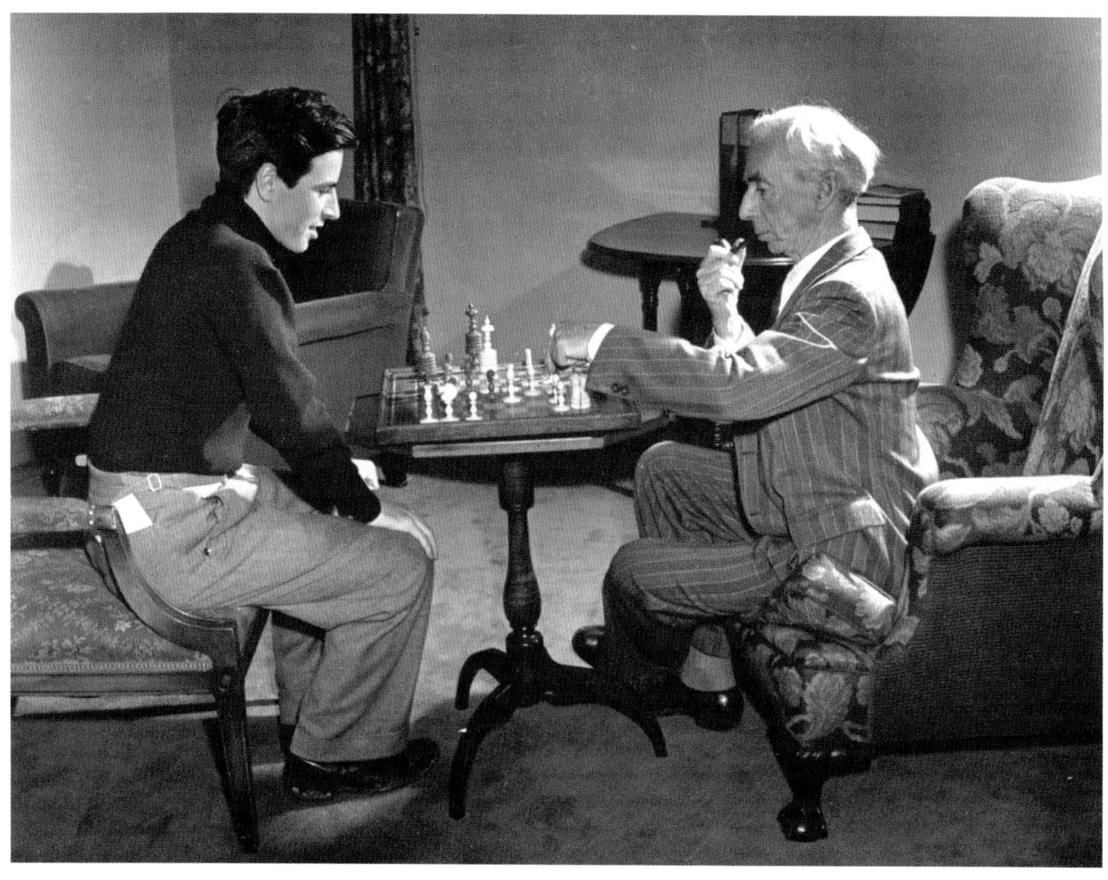

Right: Sir Kingsley Amis, one of the most popular British authors of the second half of the 20th century, plays chess at home with his sons Martin and Philip, London, 1961.

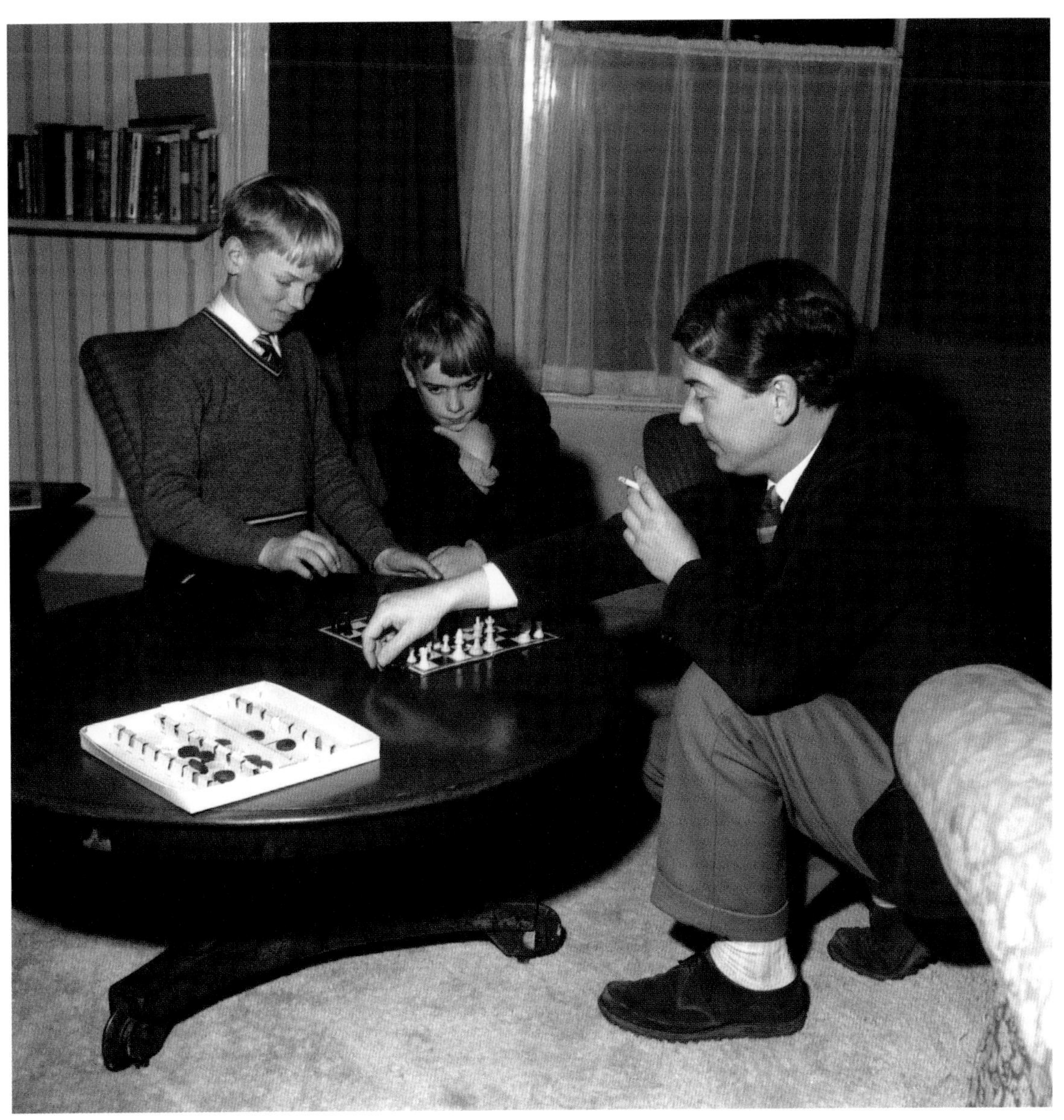

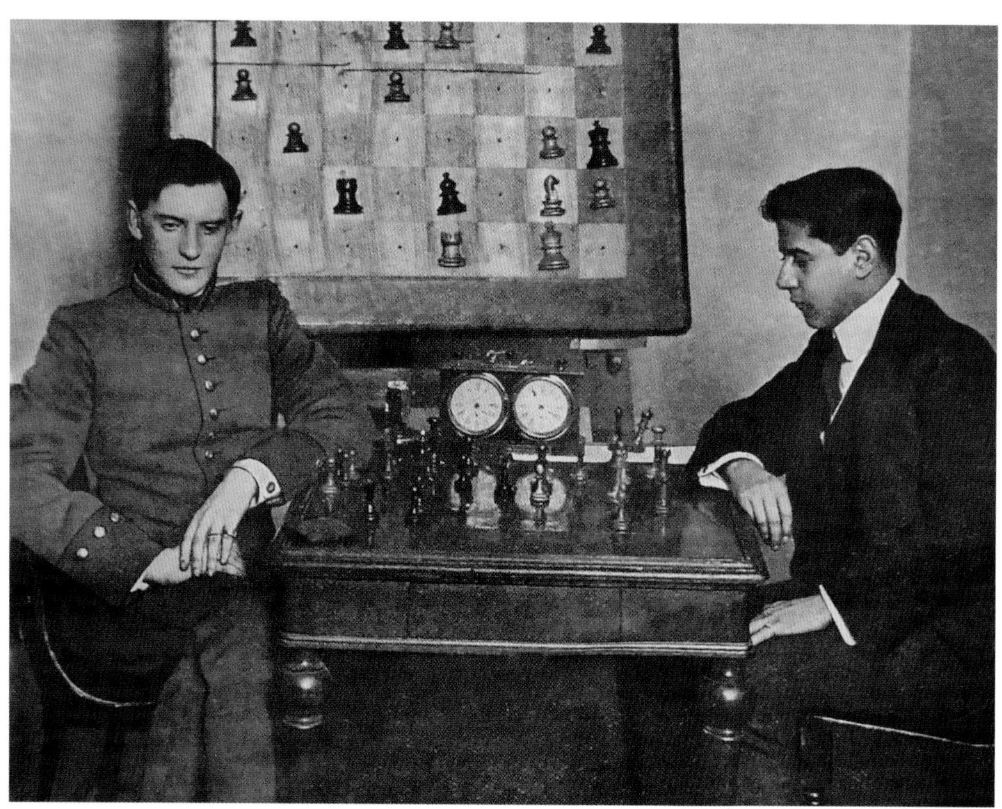

Alexander Alekhine (left) was world champion from 1927 to 1935 and 1937 to 1946. José Raúl Capablanca was world champion from 1921 to 1927 (until Alekhine dethroned him). This photograph shows them playing in a tournament in St Petersburg, Russia, in 1914.

Right: Emanuel Lasker (left), the second world chess champion, who reigned from 1894 to 1921, and Akiba Kiwelowicz Rubinstein, in a tournament in St Petersburg, Russia, in 1909. Rubinstein is considered one of the greatest players never to become world champion. In this game, their first meeting, Lasker won.

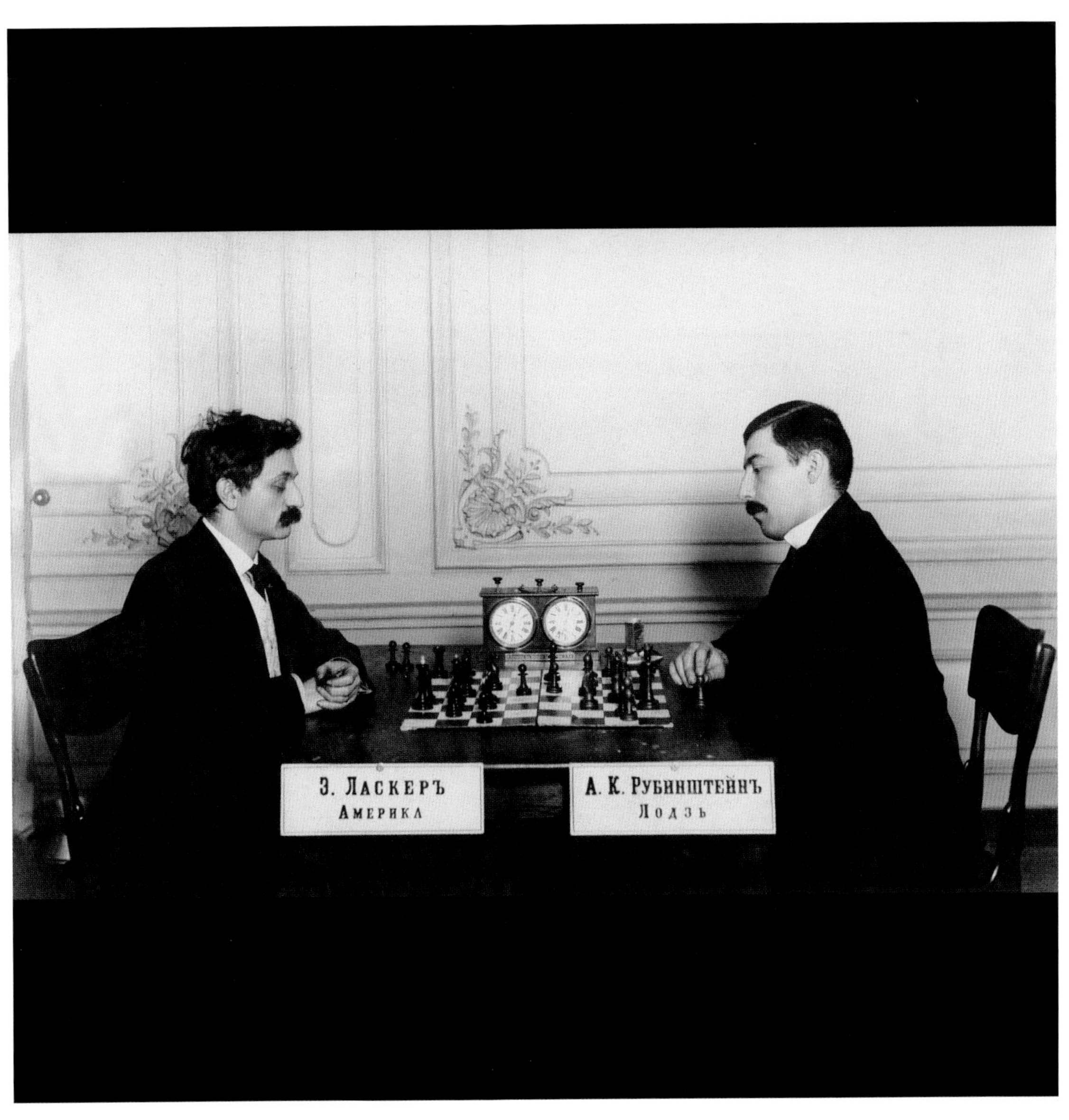

З. ЛАСКЕРЪ
Америка
А. К. Рубинштейнъ
Лодзь

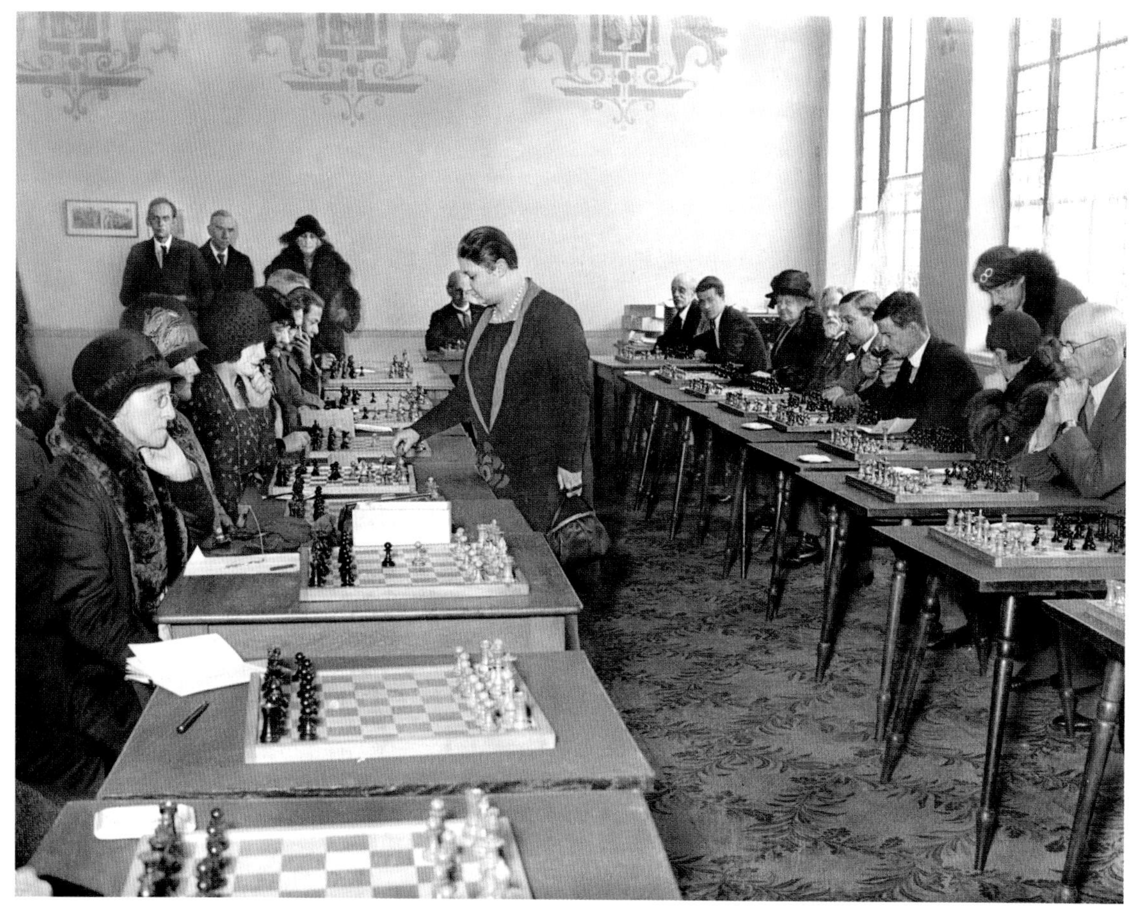

Vera Menchik was the first women's world chess champion and also the first woman to regularly compete against men in elite tournaments. She was killed, alongside her sister and mother, by a V-1 flying bomb in south London in 1944. Above: Menchik gives a simultaneous exhibition in 1939.

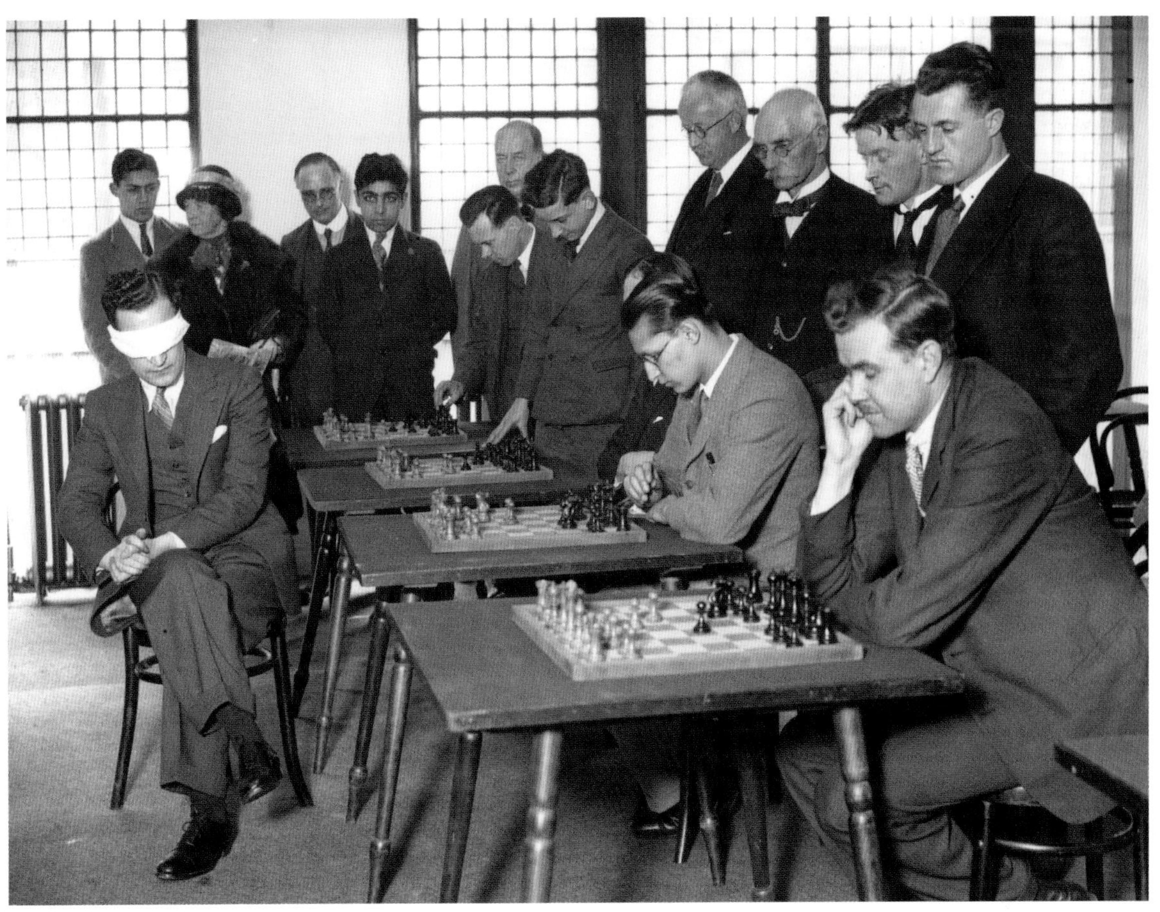

Blindfold chess – having a player who cannot see the board or boards call out the moves of the game and having the opponents' moves relayed to the player – has amazed spectators since it was first played over 1,000 years ago.

Of all the people who performed blindfold exhibitions, one of the best was George Koltanowski, pictured above playing 10 opponents simultaneously, at the Empire Chess Club in London in 1937. That same year, he set the then world record by playing 34 simultaneous blindfold games.

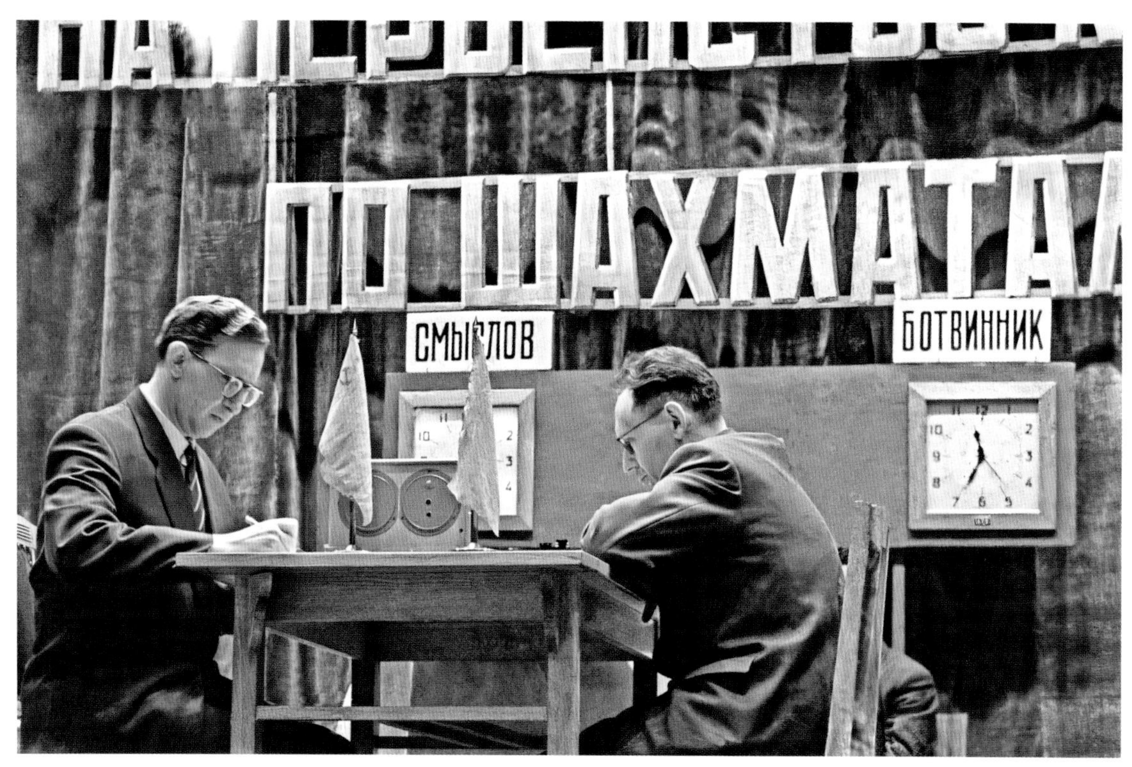

Soviet grandmasters Vasily Smyslov (left)
and Mikhail Botvinnik, during their 1958
world championship match. Smyslov had
dethroned Botvinnik the year before,
but under the rules of the time, Botvinnik
was entitled to a rematch. He won and
regained the title.

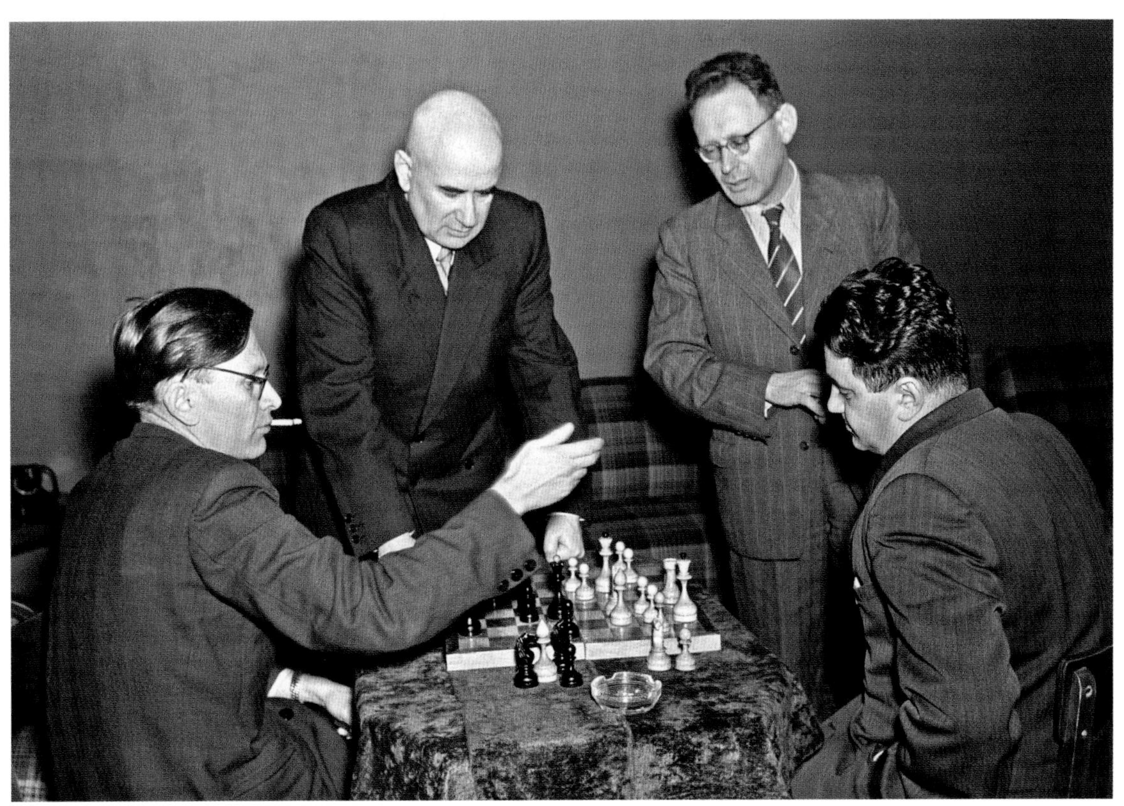

Vladimir Simagin, Ilya Kan, Mikhail Botvinnik (the world champion) and Georgy Borisenko, analysing moves during the 22nd Soviet Chess Championship in Moscow, 1955.

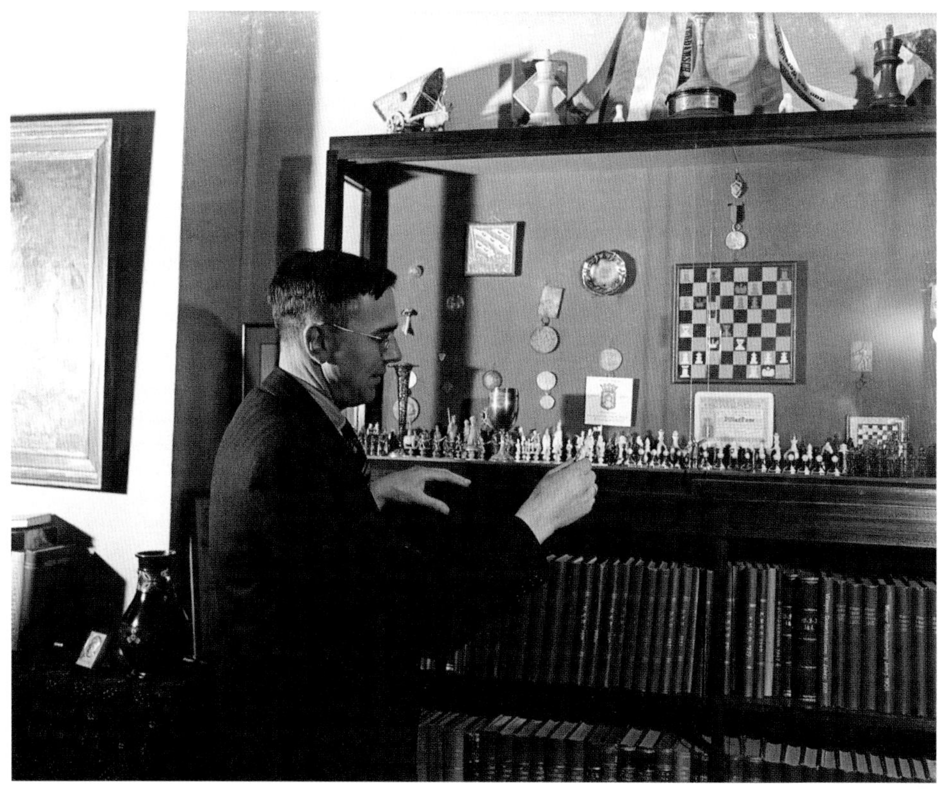

Above: Max Euwe, from the Netherlands, was the fifth world chess champion, a title he held from 1935–37.

Top right: Tigran Vartanovich Petrosian, a Soviet-Armenian, was world chess champion from 1963–69. He was nicknamed 'Iron Tigran' because of his almost impenetrable defensive playing style.

Bottom right: Mikhail Nekhemyevich Tal, a Soviet-Latvian who was known as the 'magician from Riga', was world chess champion from 1960–61. He is considered one of the greatest attacking players of all time.

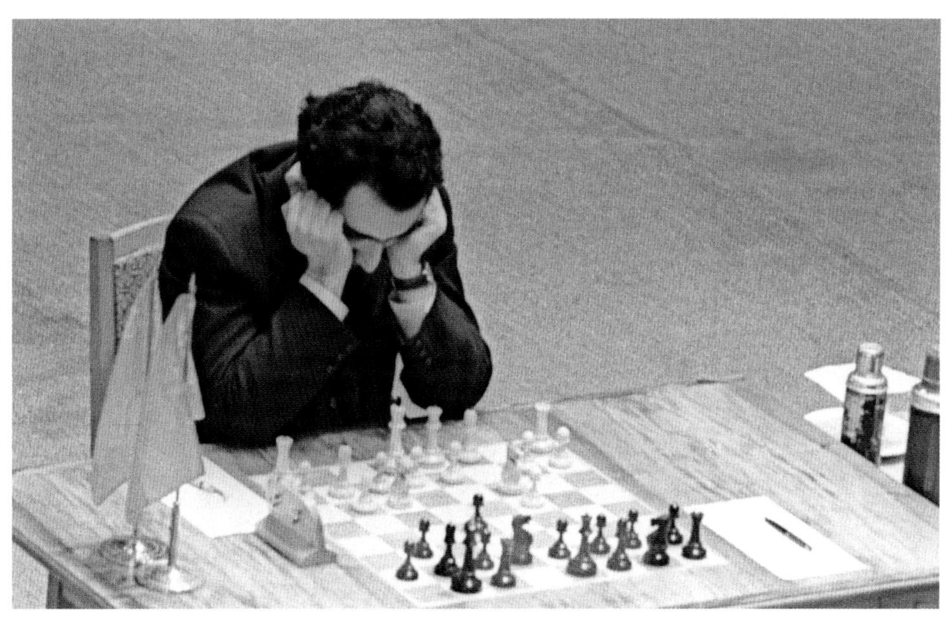

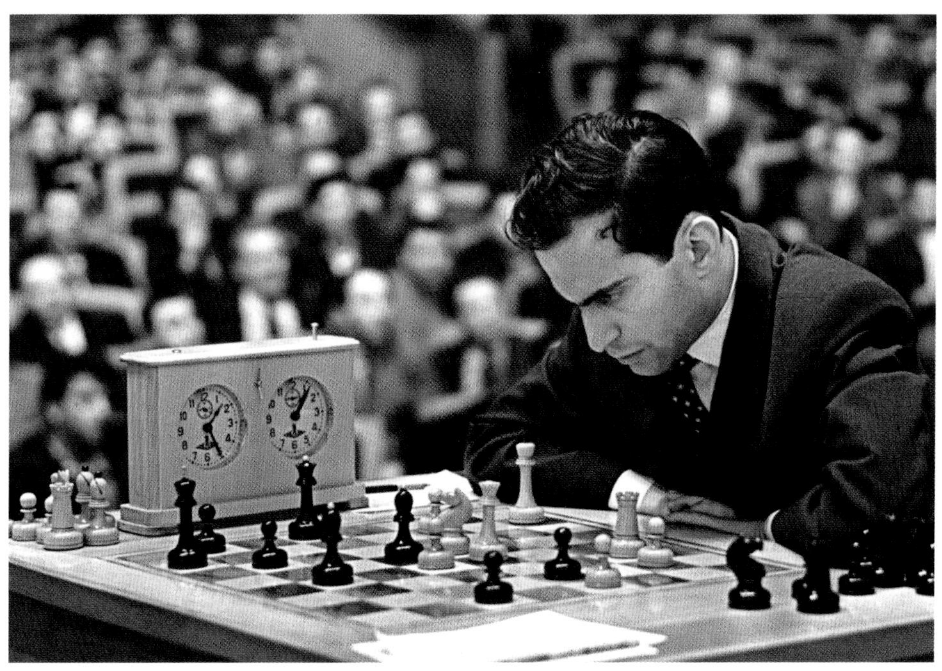

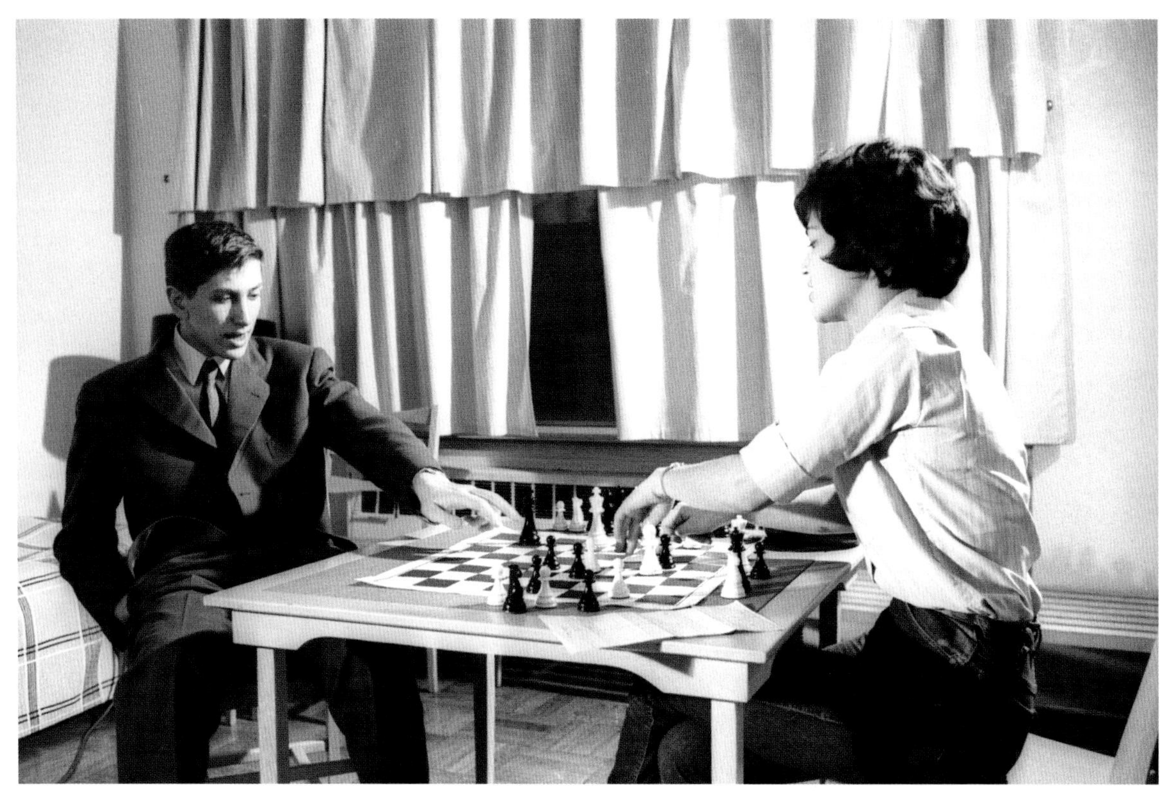

Bobby Fischer and Lisa Lane, the United
States women's chess champion in 1959
and 1966 (tied with Gisela Kahn Gresser),
New York, 1961.

Right: Lisa Lane, New York, 1961. That year
she became the first American chess player
to appear on the cover of *Sports Illustrated*.

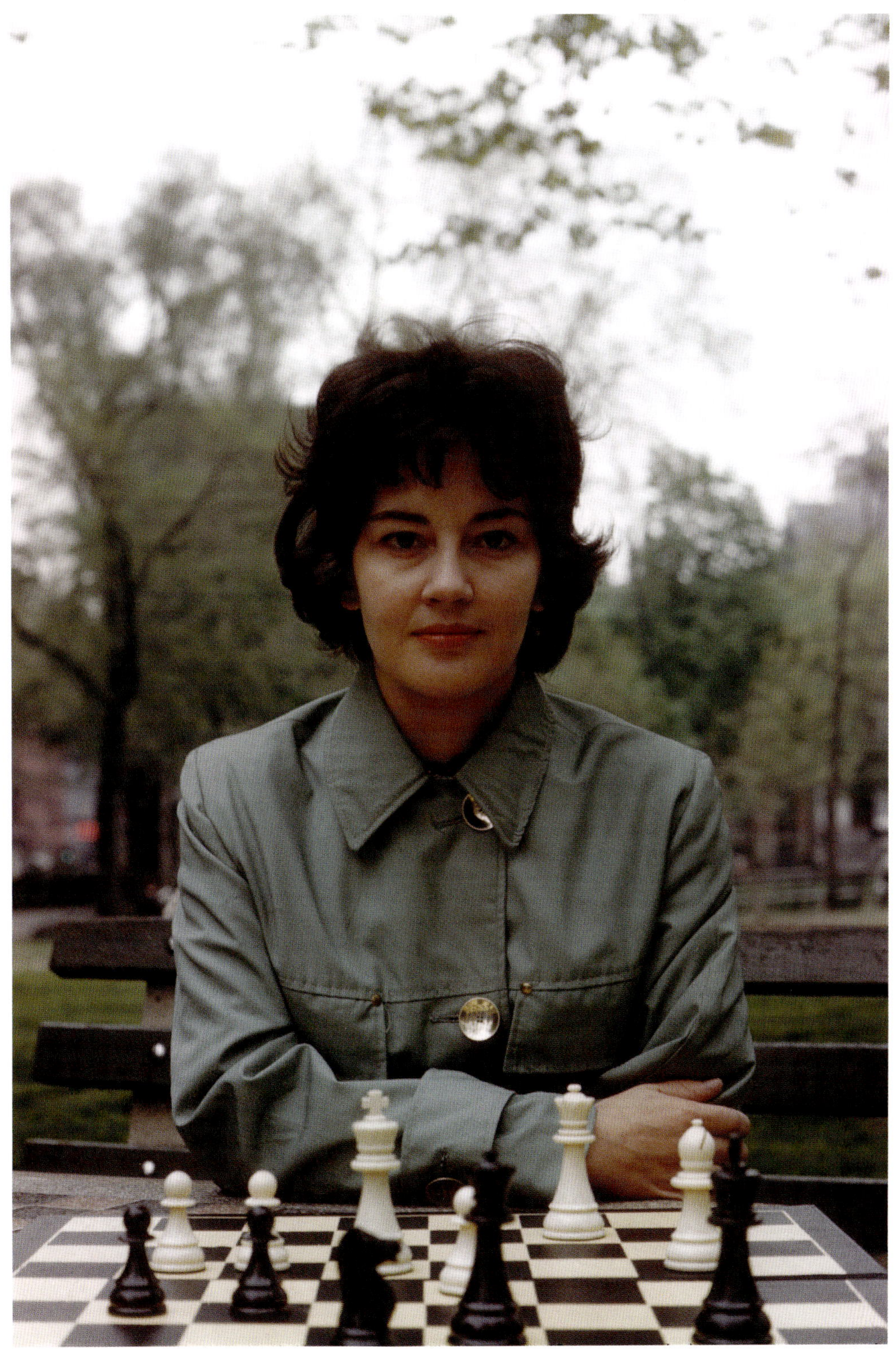

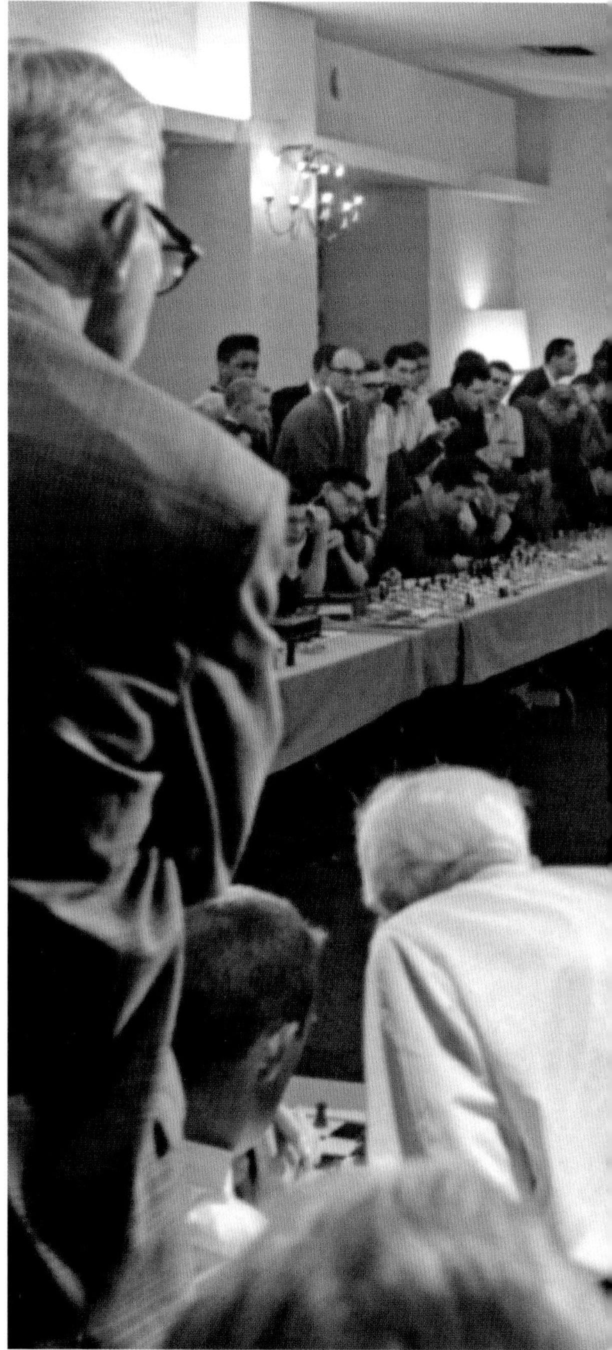

In 1964, following his record-breaking performance at the United States Championship, in which he won every game (a feat that has still not been equalled), Bobby Fischer went on a tour of the United States and Canada, giving simultaneous exhibitions. In all, he played in 34 cities, from Montreal to Little Rock to San Francisco and many places in between. Everywhere he went, crowds came out to see the young champion.

The *Los Angeles Times* wrote of Fischer's exhibition at the Knickerbocker Hotel in Hollywood (right): 'Fischer (21-year-old U.S. chess champion) moved constantly from board to board, sizing up each position, rarely pausing more than a few seconds before making his move. He won a total of 47 games, lost one, and drew two.'

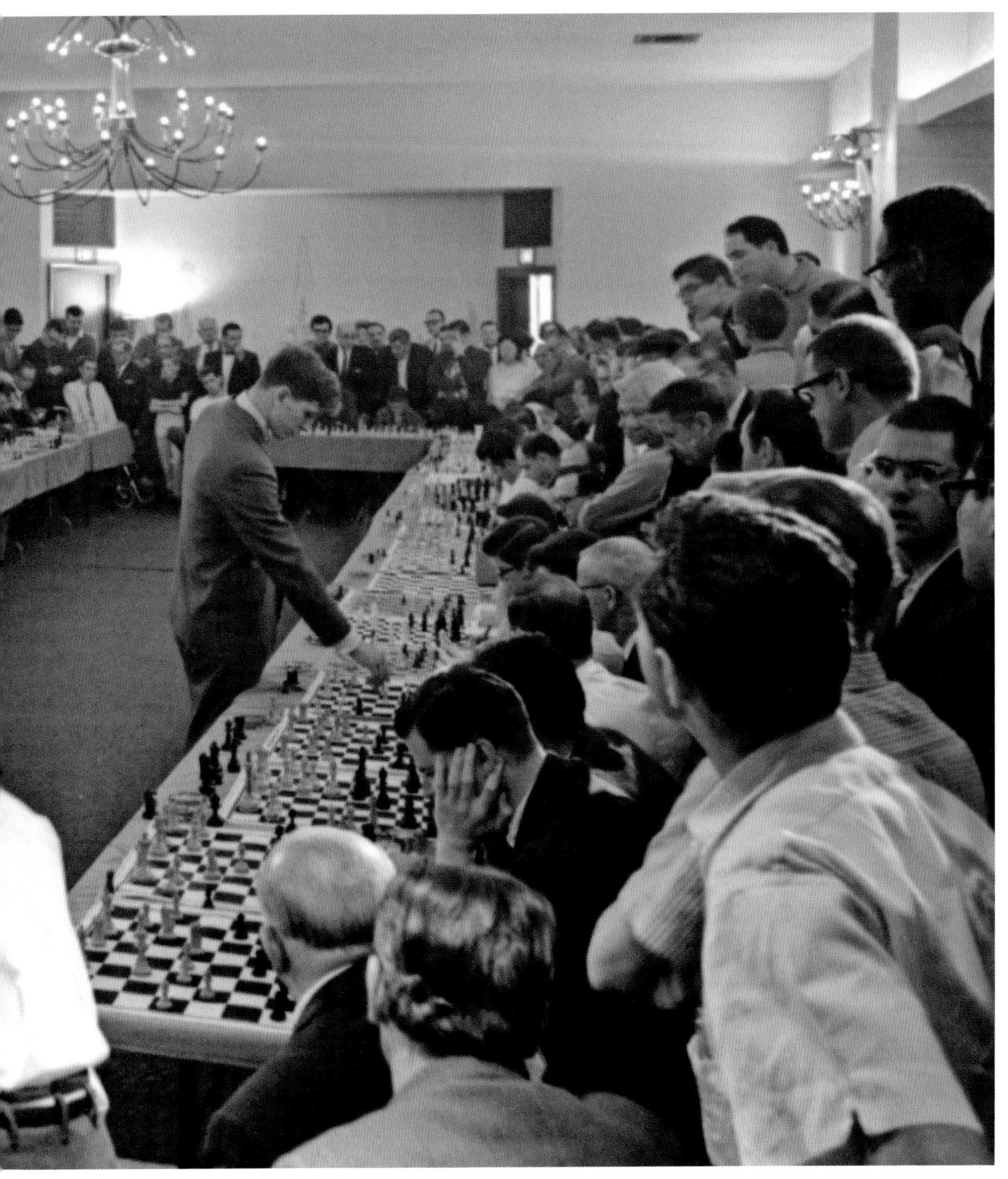

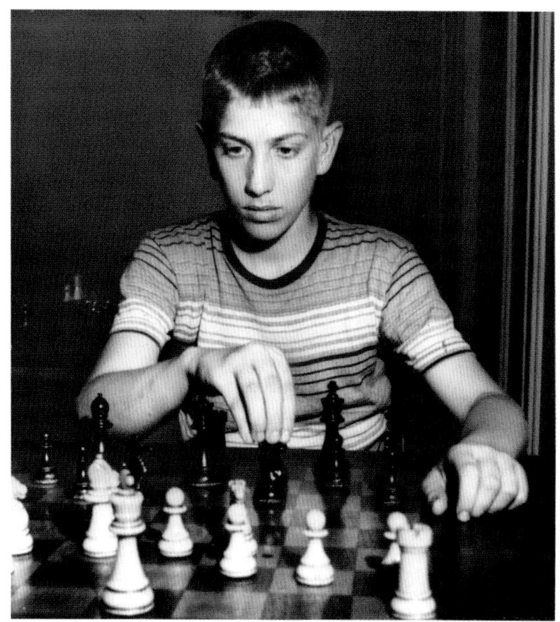

Above: Bobby Fischer, aged 14, around the time that he won his first United States Championship. New York, 1957.

Overleaf: Bobby Fischer and Andrew Soltis playing a speed chess game at the Manhattan Chess Club, New York, 1971. Soltis managed to win Fischer's queen for a rook, but still lost the game.

'Chess is war over the board. The object is to crush the opponent's mind.'
Bobby Fischer

Right: Bobby Fischer and Larry Evans in the pool at the Grossinger Hotel in the Catskill Mountains, New York, 1971. Fischer was there to train for the world championship and Evans, who won five United States Championships, assisted him until they had a falling out.

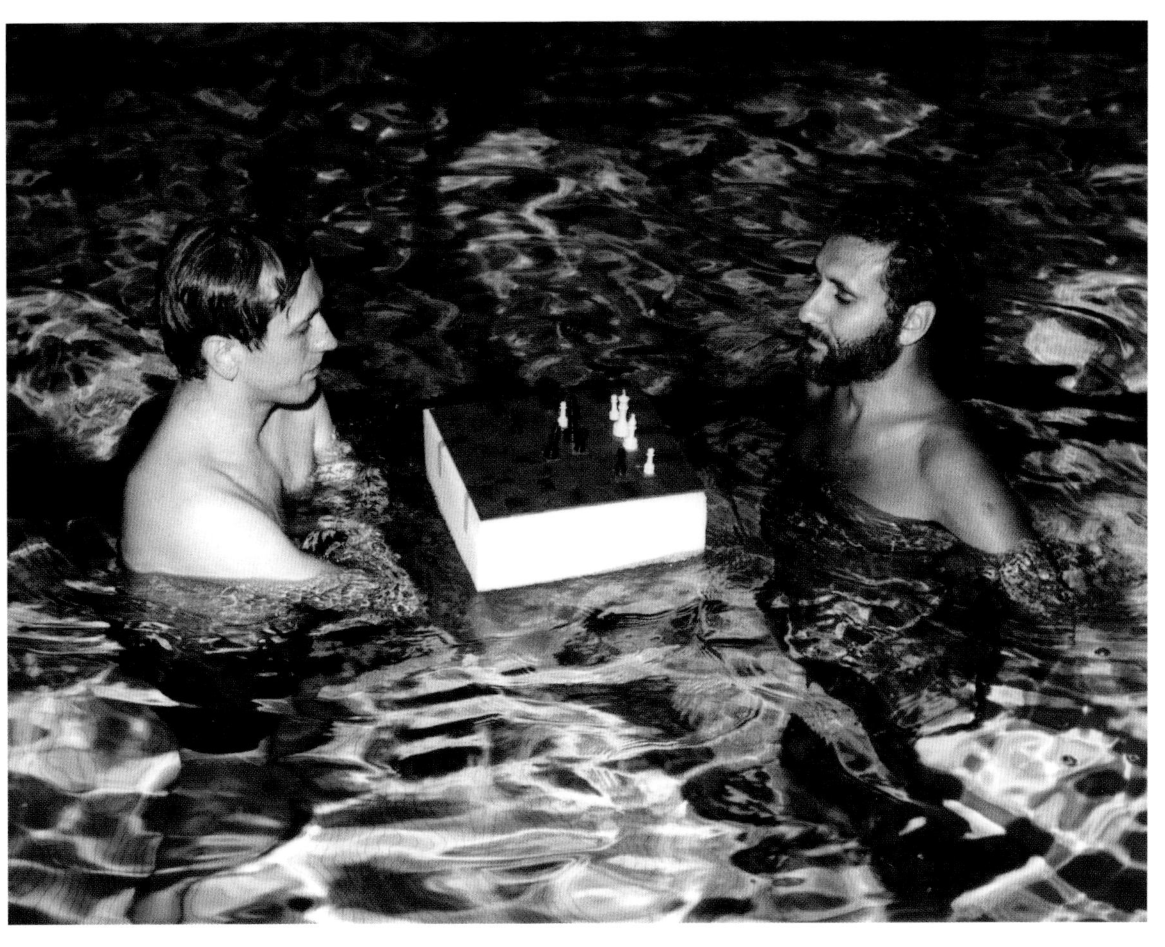

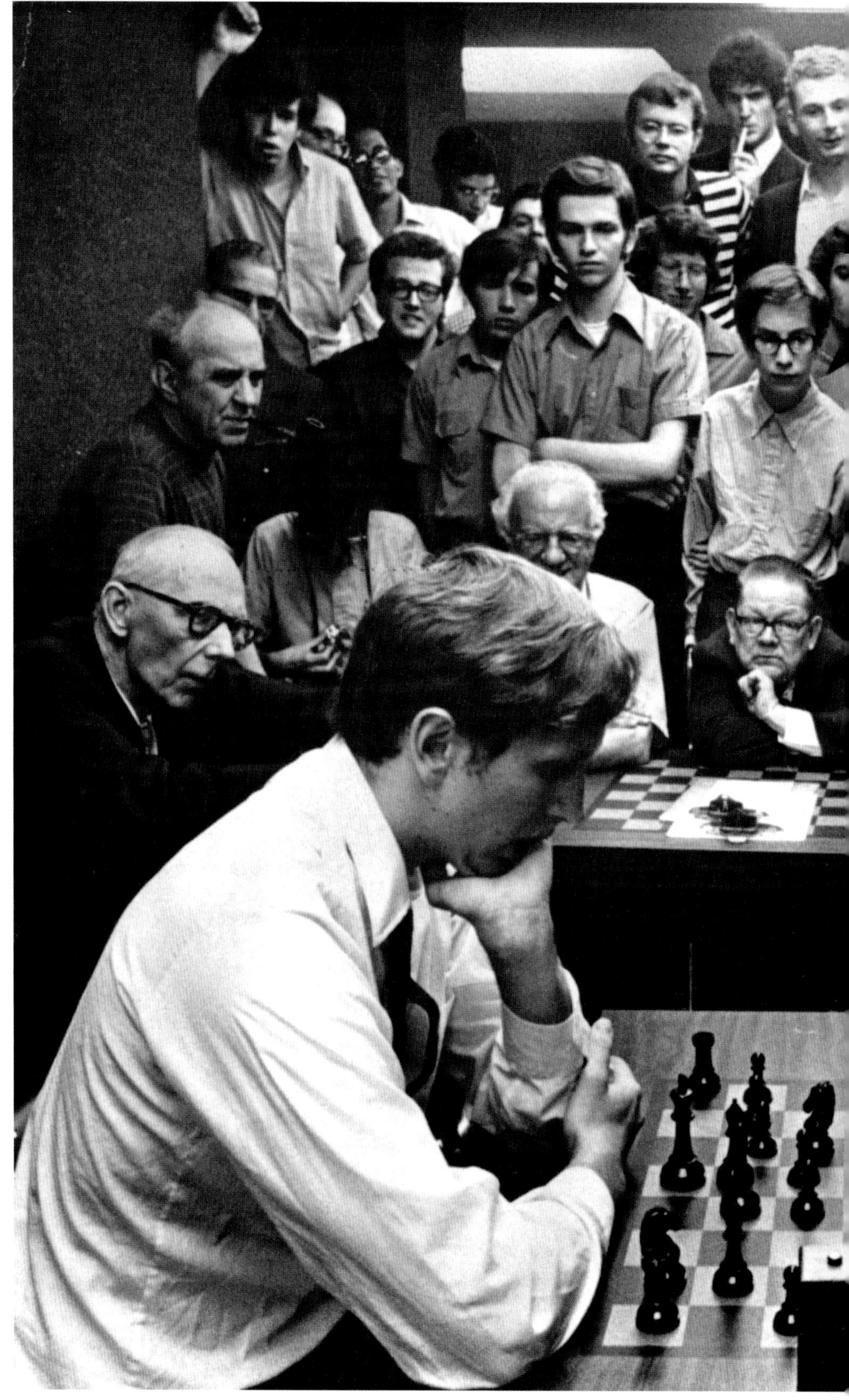

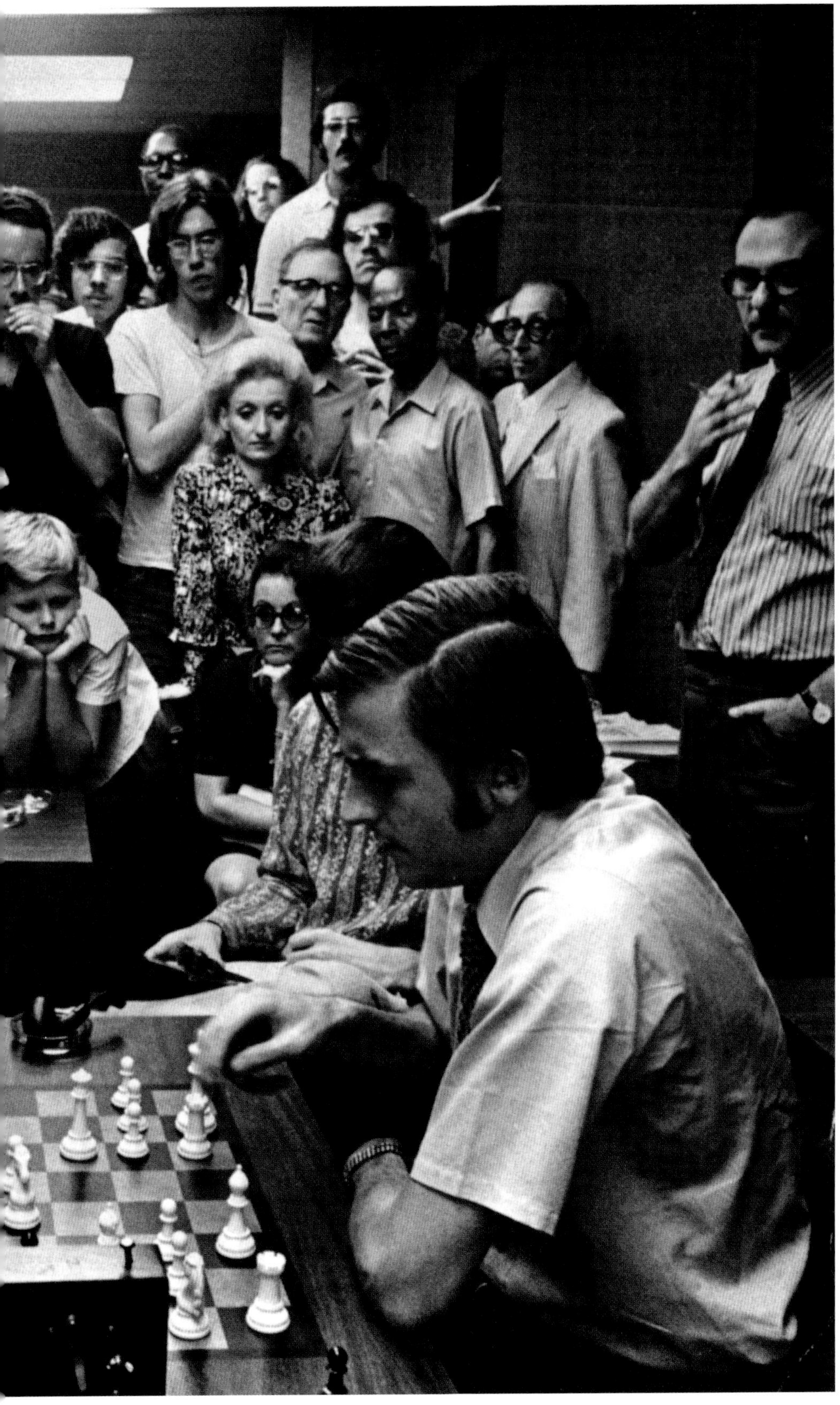

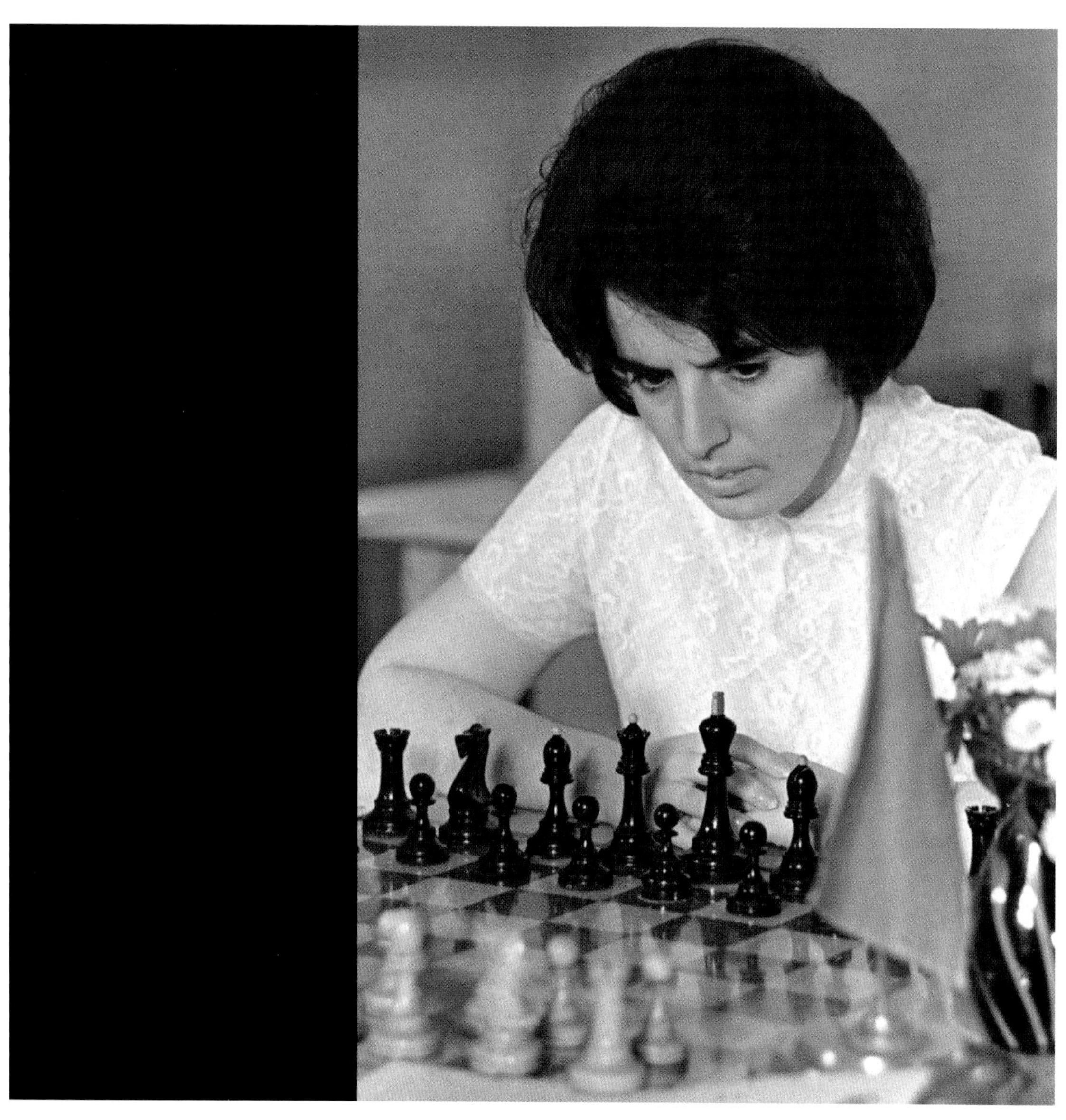

Nona Gaprindashvili, a Georgian chess player who was the women's world champion from 1962 to 1978. In 1978, she became the first woman to be awarded the title of grandmaster.

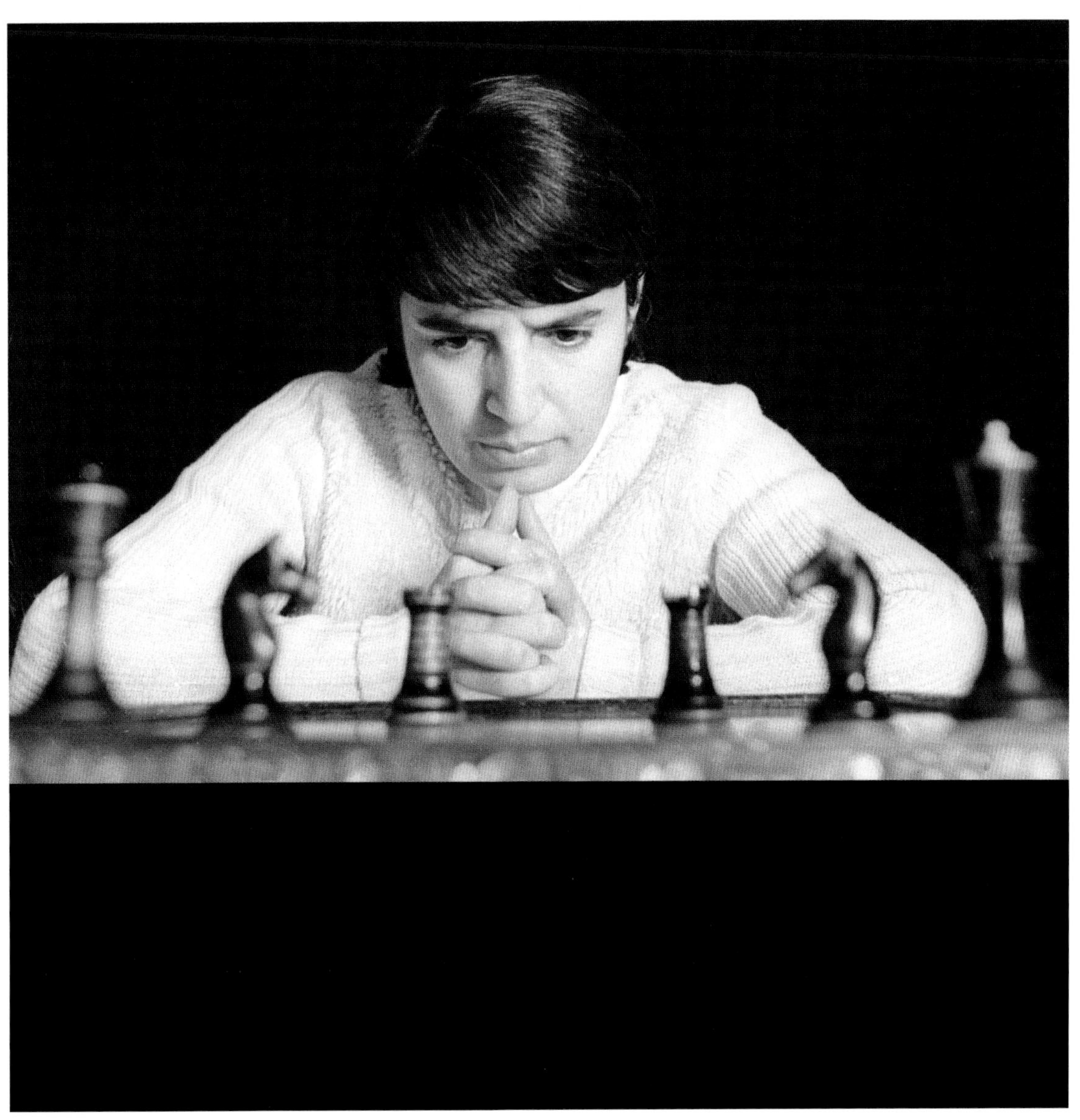

MARTIN AMIS: KASPAROV v. KARPOV

The World Chess Championship opens tomorrow [28 July 1986] in the usual atmosphere of vendetta, scurrility, machination and counterploy. Unquestionably chess is 'the most beautiful game'. Why, then, does it always turn ugly? The principals have been in town for some time. They enjoy the trappings of movie-stars yet they live like ascetics. Hungrily the young Champion works out in the gym and on the football field – even his seconds have been off alcohol for weeks – and continues his campaign against 'the chess mafia'. Meanwhile the Challenger broods and meditates, rebuilding his game, his confidence, and his tattered image. On paper, or on smudged photoprint, it looks like Diego Maradona versus Alex Higgins. Grimly they square up for their strange board meeting. What, exactly, are these characters up to? What are they playing at?

To begin with, Kasparov and Karpov are playing the foremost game of pure skill yet devised by the human mind, a game that is in fact beyond the scope of the human mind, well beyond it, an unmasterable game. Monitored by millions, they are playing this game at a level that they alone can comprehend. Towards the end of some of the games in their last match, world-famous Grandmasters had no idea who was winning. Only in the slow motion of analysis do the lines become clear. To take an analogy from another sport (of which we will need plenty), it is as if Becker and Courier are hitting so hard that not even Connors, craning forward in the front row, can see the ball.

Let us take an average experience of chess. You master the moves, start to play frequently, buy a book or two, learn some ground-rules, some openings, develop a little 'vocabulary', a bit of 'pattern recognition' ... After a while you notice that you have stopped improving. Your progress, so far, has felt like a slow ascent along rising ground; then you pause, look up, and see a cliff face almost beyond the dimensions of the globe, whose crest is merely a false summit, itself the first of many.

Quickly you relapse into the kind of player who knows one opening to a depth of three moves, who flounders into the middle game hoping for errors more egregious than his own. That is the amateur game: an uninterrupted exchange of howlers. You aren't any good. And the man who always beats you in the pub or the cafe isn't any good. And the man who always beats him in the clubhouse isn't any good. And the man who always beats the man who always beats the man who always beats *him* may just be starting to get somewhere.

Nowhere in sport, perhaps nowhere in human activity, is the gap between the tryer and the expert so astronomical. Oh, I have thrown 180 at darts – twice in a lifetime. On the snooker table I have brought off violent pots that would have jerked them to their feet in the Sheffield Crucible. As for tennis, I need hardly hype my crosscourt backhand 'dink', which is so widely feared in the parks of North Kensington. But my chances of a chess brilliancy are the 'chances' of a lab chimp and a typewriter producing *King Lear*. Even at the most rarefied level, though, chess has a robust universality. The two Ks start a tournament tomorrow, but they will also be starting something else: scores are to be settled, grudges are to be purged. Openly and avowedly, noisily and pridefully, they will be hunting each other's blood. That we *can* understand.

Until 1972 the triennial World Championships were quiet affairs – or at any rate Soviet affairs. Then Bobby Fischer emerged, and the fortress of Soviet supremacy felt the challenge of American 'brashness': the histrionic gamesmanship of the stand-off and stalk-out, the tantrum and the sulk. Fischer himself seemed to sense a decline, an air of *ubi sunt*? 'When it was a game played by aristocrats it had more like you know dignity to it.' In retrospect, shaded from the glare of his chess, we can see Fischer as the classic *idiot savant*; he resembles the mental-home chronic who, by some twist of the circuitry, can do cube roots in his head. Fischer had the highest Elo rating – this is the chess computer – of all time. With his contempt for women, his glorification of expensive clothes and what he called 'class' (as in 'he doesn't have any class'), his antisemitism, and his cornball paranoia, Fischer shows that supreme chess genius can ally itself with the paltriest human material.

By 1975 Fischer had gone mad, or gone madder; he was, in any event, too mad to face the defence of his title. (It is said that he suffered a 'panic-fright' at his own achievement.) Anatoly Karpov was thus promoted by default; and the next two Championships took their tenor from the situation and temperament of the challenger, Viktor Korchnoi: Viktor the Terrible, the Leningrad Lip. Disciplined for unsoundness – i.e., near-pauperised for sins of candour – Korchnoi had defected in 1976. He was then boycotted by Soviet players, and his wife and son were refused permission to emigrate. Both these actions were designed not just to punish Korchnoi's treachery but to weaken his game. In his two Championship matches with Karpov – 1978 and 1981 – Korchnoi showed symptoms of what might be called *displaced* paranoia: he *was* being persecuted, but not by hexed swivel-chairs, colour-coded yoghurts, KGB hypnotists evil-eyeing him from the stalls. Karpov, the 'model Soviet', sat through it all, glazed and devout, like a Futurist poster. And after his victory he obediently

Anatoly Karpov, right, the world champion, in a demonstration game at the XVII Congress of Komsomol, USSR, 1978.

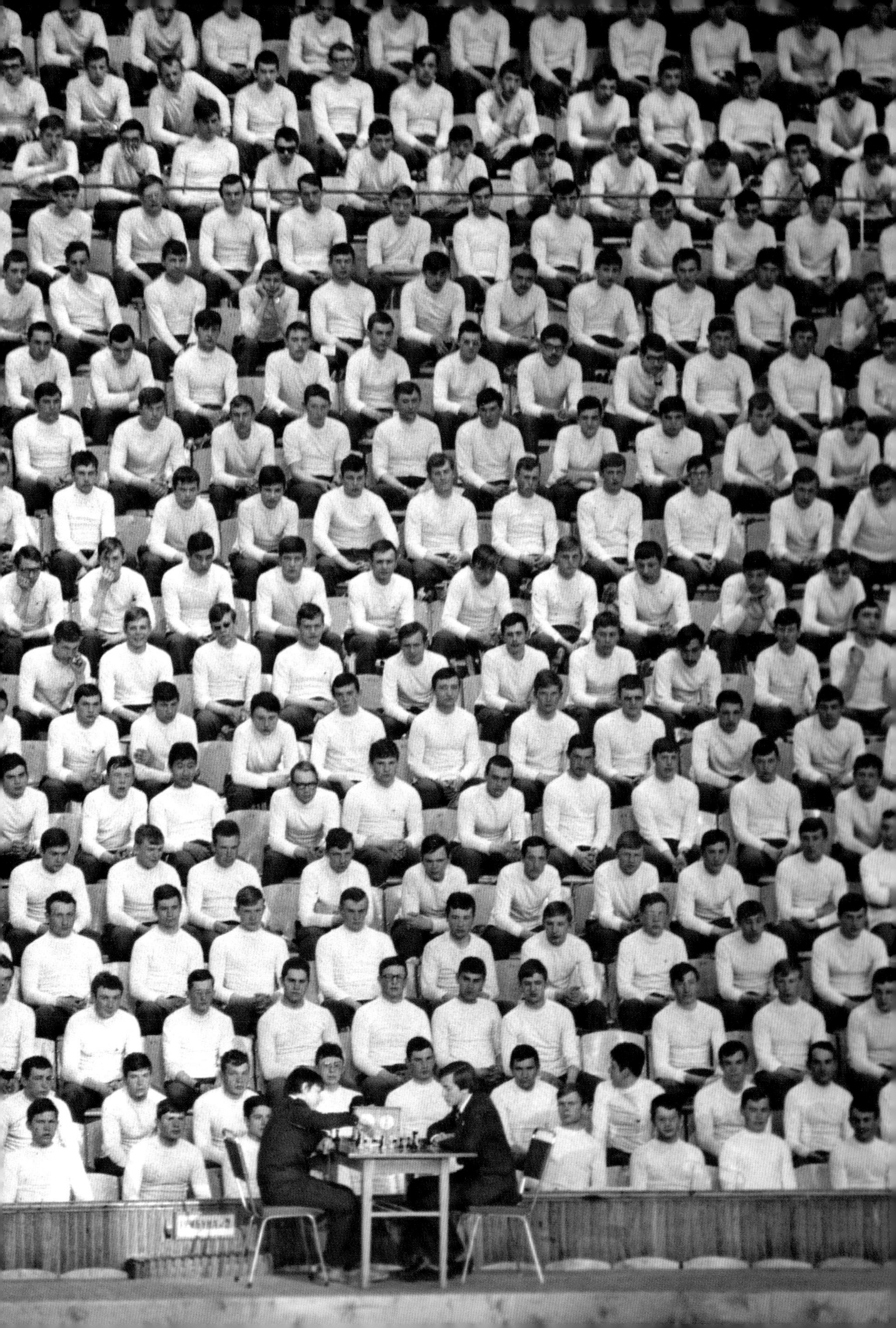

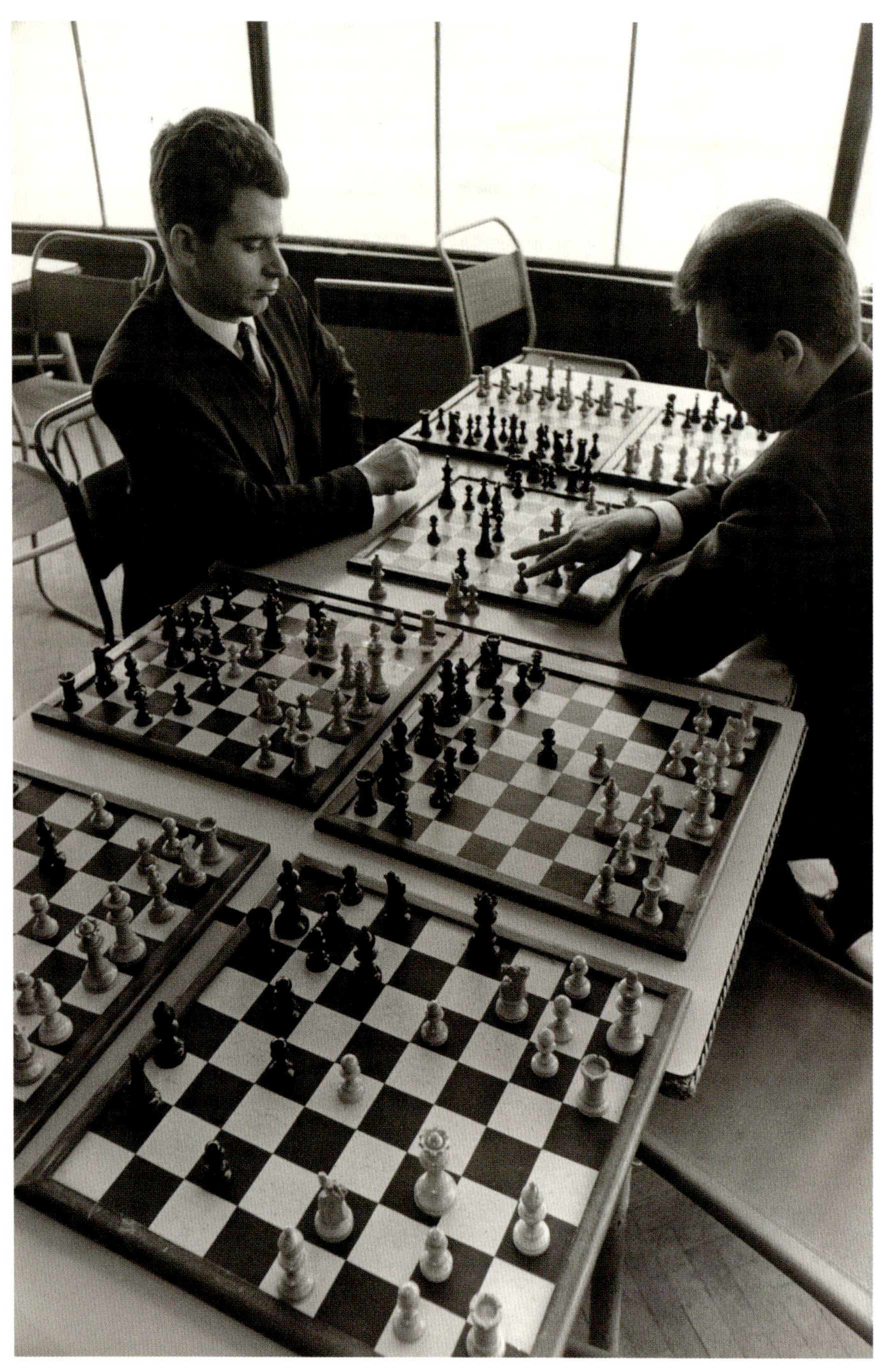

Boris Spassky and Svetozar Gligoric of
Yugoslavia, practising before the start
of the Hastings International Chess
Congress, England, 1965.

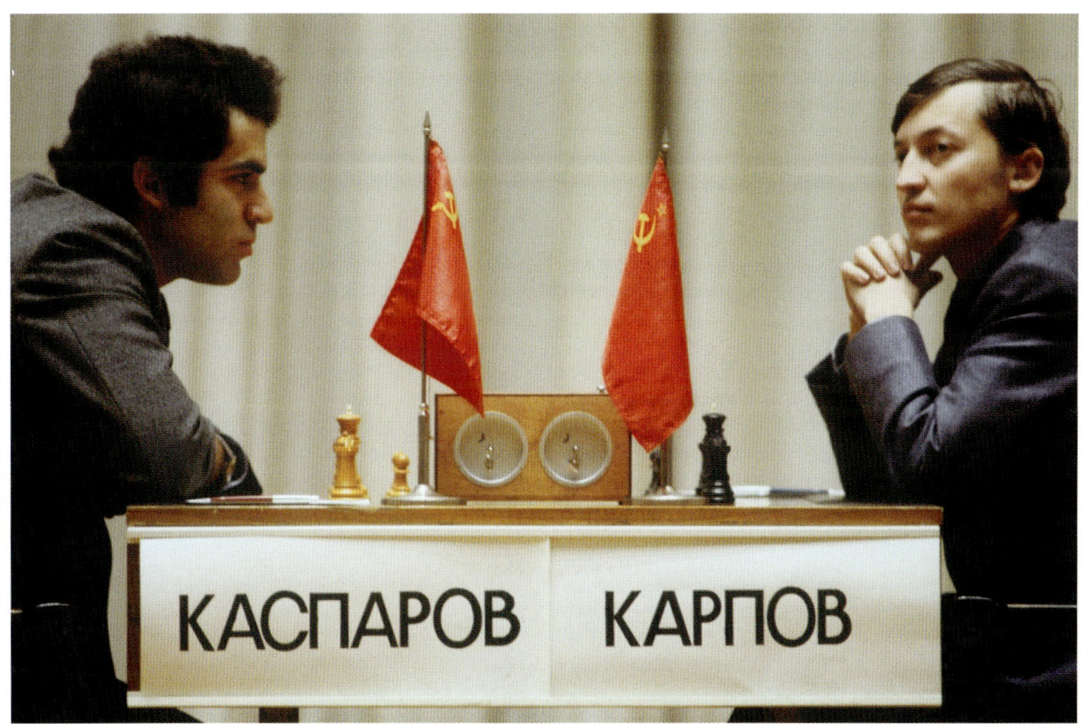

cabled Brezhnev, as Botvinnik had cabled Stalin in 1936 ('Dear beloved teacher and leader...').

Just before the 1978 Championship I interviewed Korchnoi in London, at the Savoy. At one point, twisting powerfully in his chair, he fell silent, and then grew dreamy. With some wistfulness he confessed that he despaired of ever bringing home, to people in the West, the crawling sliminess, the full squidgy horror, of Anatoly Karpov. 'You know, in Russia we have a fish', he said, 'called a *karp*. A disgusting fish. You wouldn't eat it. That's what Karpov *is*.' I said, 'We've got that fish too. Called a *carp*.' Korchnoi looked startled. 'You have? ... Good! Good!'

Already, and perhaps over-vividly, Korchnoi sensed that Karpov would not be allowed to lose. The 1978 match was painfully close. Karpov won 6–5; Korchnoi claimed illegal conditions (that hypnotist had returned for the last game) and started court proceedings in Amsterdam; by 1979 Korchnoi's son Igor was in a labour camp. When the players met again three years later, TASS was calling Korchnoi a 'calculating huckster', the deserter of his wife and child, whom he hoped never to see again. Korchnoi felt these vast animosities *at the table* – and saw Karpov as their instrument ('Stop squirming in your damn seat, you little worm'). Korchnoi was deflected, tipped over; and in the end he spooked himself.

Garry Kasparov, left, and Anatoly Karpov in Moscow in 1985 during their second world title match. Kasparov won, 13–11, to become champion, ending Karpov's 10-year reign.

Karpov wasn't taken to the edge in 1981. But he was taken there in 1984, by Garry Kasparov; and the outcome was the most drastic scandal in the history of the game. Fallout from that 'accident' still poisons the current encounter.

Stressful tales of venue-fixing, spy-planting, rule-bending – or cheating, if you prefer. The outsider, who thinks that chess is pure and cerebral, tends to be shocked by such suggestions. But the insider is not shocked, because he knows that chess, like the human brain, is partly reptilian. This is the game of pins and pincers, of forks and skewers; this is the game of the *spite check* and the *shame mate*. Clearly these psychodramas wouldn't keep happening unless something about the game encouraged them. If, tomorrow afternoon, the World Champion were playing his twin brother, his mirror image, the air between them would still be crackling.

How do you cheat at chess? It strikes one as a contradiction, like cheating at the violin. One of the excruciations of chess is its autonomy; there are no variables; there is no one and nothing to *blame*. Snooker is whisperingly called 'chess with balls' but in chess there is no run of the green ('Dear oh dear, things just aren't going Anatoly Yevgenyevich's way out there'). In tennis you can blame the bounce, the tape, the wind, the glare, the racket, the shoelaces. Even the lumpen simplicity of darts features the loathed 'bounce-outs'. An Argy fullback may break your legs, help you up by tugging on the hairs of your arms, and then, as you start to protest, hawk in your mouth. Now that's cheating. But how do you cheat at chess?

'Sit your opponent with the sun in his eyes,' said Ruy Lopez, who flourished in the sixteenth century. It would seem that cheating at chess is as old as the game; no doubt the languid nawabs and caliphs of sixth-century Asia were kicking each other's shins beneath the table. Alekhine used to cosset his Siamese cats on the board before big games, on the off-chance that his opponent might harbour an allergy. During lightning play, 'chessers' who find themselves a rook down have been known to castle with a piece from the neighbouring board. Nimzowitsch used to smoke an especially noxious cigar. There are further stories of squashed tomatoes, doctor's bleep-gadgets, and eye-contact techniques in the sexual-harassment line.

In his 1977 qualifying match with Korchnoi, Boris Spassky arranged for his 'box' – a curtained booth on the stage, to which the player occasionally retreats – to be positioned *behind* his opponent's chair; and there he lurked, emerging only to make his moves. When he did appear he sported a dazzling sun-visor. It doesn't sound particularly outrageous, but it worked. Korchnoi was on the verge of emotional collapse and threw away four games in a row. He recovered, and won. The intriguing fact is that Spassky, the white knight of Reykjavik, Fischer's courtly and long-suffering victim, had switched colours. Integrity, it appeared, was an anachronism, or an aberration. Fischer was an innovator on the board, but perhaps his main gift to the game was the institution-alising of bad behaviour. This was 'professionalism'. From then on, everyone was playing black.

The Moscow fiasco of 1984 was of a new order of irregularity. Probably domestic Soviet chess has seen greater and more humourless injustices (the reversal of results because of 'faulty' clocks, and so on); but you can't do this sort of thing when the world is watching. Chess insiders were shocked by Moscow. Even Bobby Fischer must have raised a hand to check that his wallet was still in place.

During the early games Kasparov showed his only temperamental weakness as a player: hunger. He played with arrogant greed and was soon trailing 0–4 (the winner being the first man to six, with draws not counting). A little later he was trailing 0–5: an abysmal margin. No breather or pep-talk, no pint of lager is going to bring a chess-player back from that kind of deficit, that kind of demonstration. But now Kasparov formulated a remarkable and ruthless strategy. He started to draw, game after game, dull, spoiling, inexorable. His first idea was, simply, to exhaust Karpov, to break Karpov's health. His second idea was to learn how to play him. This was a task that he had skimped in preparation; he was now doing his revision on the board. At twenty-one Kasparov was already a great player. But he was becoming a greater one, in front of Karpov's eyes. And Kasparov had something else. 'Playing a game against Kasparov is like playing three games against anybody else,' said the British GM Tony Miles, fresh from a 5½–½ drubbing by Kasparov in Basel. 'It's *very* hard to put into words. There are no quiet moves, no simple positions. Everything is *sharp*. But mainly it's his presence. You're constantly aware of his strength, his impatience. He drains you.' Playing a game of high-level chess has been compared to sitting a two-day exam. For Karpov in Moscow, it was five months of Finals.

After 46 games the score was 5–1 to Karpov, with 40 draws. Karpov had had no victory for 21 games. And he had lost 22 pounds. Then Kasparov won game 47; and game 48. 'It was extraordinary,' said a chess writer, and International Master, who covered the match. 'We began in September with great drama as Karpov took his lead. On November 24 he stopped winning. Then – a winter of draws. The band of analysts was dwindling. The press room was like a bunker. Suddenly there were rumours about Karpov's health, and you could feel the political pressures. There were "technical" time-outs – for instance, eight days to change venues. There were meetings with contacts on street corners. Journalists wondered whether they were being followed. Everybody knew that Karpov was in a de luxe private clinic, suffering from exhaustion.' After Kasparov's second straight victory the President of FIDE flew from Dubai to Moscow and ended the match. A new word entered the language: FIDEgate.

It is illuminating to recast the Moscow Championship as a set of tennis, the final set of an imaginary Super-grandslam. The Champion is serving for the title at 5–0. After a game involving 100 deuces, his serve is broken. The next game goes to 300 deuces. By this time the Champion is limping, wincing, howling with fatigue. The Challenger wins the seventh game, and wins the eighth with ease. The umpire now decides that everyone has had enough. 'I wouldn't like to be 3–5 down to Karpov *on his death bed*,' said Nigel Short, the world No.9 'People say he looks weedy, but mentally he's very, very tough.' At this stage, however, Karpov was playing like a man with a nagging brain injury: and it is quite clear that Kasparov sensed victory. The decision still incenses him. For Kasparov it is as if, during an endless rally, with the crowd gasping and shrieking, the Champion's weak baseline lob has gone up, the Challenger ravenously awaits it at the net – and the umpire extends a long hand from his perch, snatching the ball from the air.

The umpire is, of course, Mr Florencio Campomanes, President of FIDE. There is almost something captivating, something blithely Chaucerian, about Campo, with his air of farcical unreliability. If there is no smoke without fire, then Campomanes is a veritable Vesuvius, fizzing and burping with partiality and bad faith. You feel that the world of chess is too small for his talents: he ought to be in arms dealing, or nuclear proliferation.

A Philippino, a one-time Garcia man and now a follower of Marcos (with whom he is said to have many interests in common), Campo was elected to the Presidency in 1982, on 'the Third World ticket'. The extent to which he dominates FIDE is made clear by its recent resolution 'thanking him for his initiative' in aborting the Moscow match, a decision so reviled by the world press that even the *Sun* joined the chorus (RED KING OF CHESS SET TO CRACK UP). 1986 is election year, and Campo has introduced a new 'tax on draws', by which every drawn game diverts 1 per cent of the purse to Campo's chess-development programme in the Third World. Kasparov cleverly preempted the ploy by donating his share of the winnings to the Chernobyl relief fund. Karpov was obliged to follow suit.

Without going too deeply into the intrigues, one can simply say that Campo disports himself like a Third World politician. 'When I ask President Marcos for two million dollars, at worst he wants to know whether he should bring the money straight away or whether I can wait for a cheque.' There are many stories of his intimidation of journalists (threats of denying visas, etc.) and his general admiration for Marcosian strong-arming. Ever since the Moscow row, Campo has cobbled together a defence of this 'unpopular decision' by directing counter-conspiracy charges at 'a small band of journalists' led by Raymond Keene ('skilful', 'cunning', 'forked tongue'). This is the tone of a recent FIDE newsletter, from the disinterested pen of Casto P. Abundo:

> It is no surprise that Keene lies in his book... in an obvious attempt to *wash his hands* of the affair. Now, in shameless *hypocrisy*, he charges 'incorrect decisions by the President'.

Campo's main adversary, however, is not Raymond Keene. Campo's main adversary is far more centrally placed. He is Garry Kasparov.

Why did Campo do it? Possibly he bowed to pressure from the Soviet Chess Federation, whose officials have a stake in Karpov. But then Campo has a stake in him too. All these careers and ascendancies are interlinked. 'You can't expect to please everybody, or even anybody,' said Campo, with astounding serenity, among the hoots and guffaws of the Moscow press conference. Campo didn't

please anybody. Karpov looked sick, up on the podium with the glozing Campo, he looked morally queasy. Soon afterwards he claimed that his 'sports and public reputation' had been 'blasted'. 'By his decision,' Spassky has said, 'Karpomanes' had 'actually destroyed Karpov'.

During the rematch in 1985 Karpov's image took a further tousling. *Der Spiegel* accused him of diverting $½ million through a German agent, who had absconded with the money and was now wanted by the police. It was further claimed that Campo was trying to retrieve the money on Karpov's behalf. The crisis was spectacularly unwelcome. But by this stage, anyway, Kasparov had the whole world behind him. To stamping feet, to cries of 'Garry! Garry!', he surged to victory on a crest of rectitude. Youth, aggression, justice! Only the Chess Federation Karpovites were left muttering in the press room. 'There is nothing we can do,' they said. 'There is nothing we can do.'

So things will stand when White pushes his first pawn tomorrow afternoon. And the question remains: what are they up to? What of the chess itself, the eerie engagement with the 32 pieces and the 64 squares?

'Their styles are so different,' says Tony Miles, 'you can't even compare them. Kasparov is the perfectionist: he analyses to infinity. He likes to establish a tree of complications, say a five-move line with six alternatives per move. He thrives on complexity. You can't out-analyse him. You'll get blasted out of sight. Karpov is more practical and classical, more of an artist in his way. He likes straightforward positions with no forcing continuations. He makes intuitive general assessments and consolidates small advantages. Then he makes them pinch.'

And if you raise your eyes from the board? 'When I played Karpov,' says Nigel Short, 'it took me about half an hour to get over my awe at playing the World Champion. Then it was business as usual, just another game. With Kasparov – it's hard to describe. I found his presence uniquely disturbing. I have never faced such an intense player, never felt such energy and concentration, such will and desire burning across the board at me.'

One can well imagine the exhaustion of playing Kasparov. Watching him do a ten-minute spot on a chat show is exhausting enough. The galvanic giggling, the agitation, the expressiveness: he doesn't sit on his chair – he hovers on it. Recently Kasparov beat ten computers simultaneously, blindfolded. How flattering for the species. There are over 288 billion possibilities through the fourth move (by White *and* Black). Yet the mark of a good chessplayer is not how many moves he considers but how few – as Karpov knows. Although the betting is on Kasparov, some of the emotional money is tending back towards Karpov, the saddened swat with the Baskerville eyes.

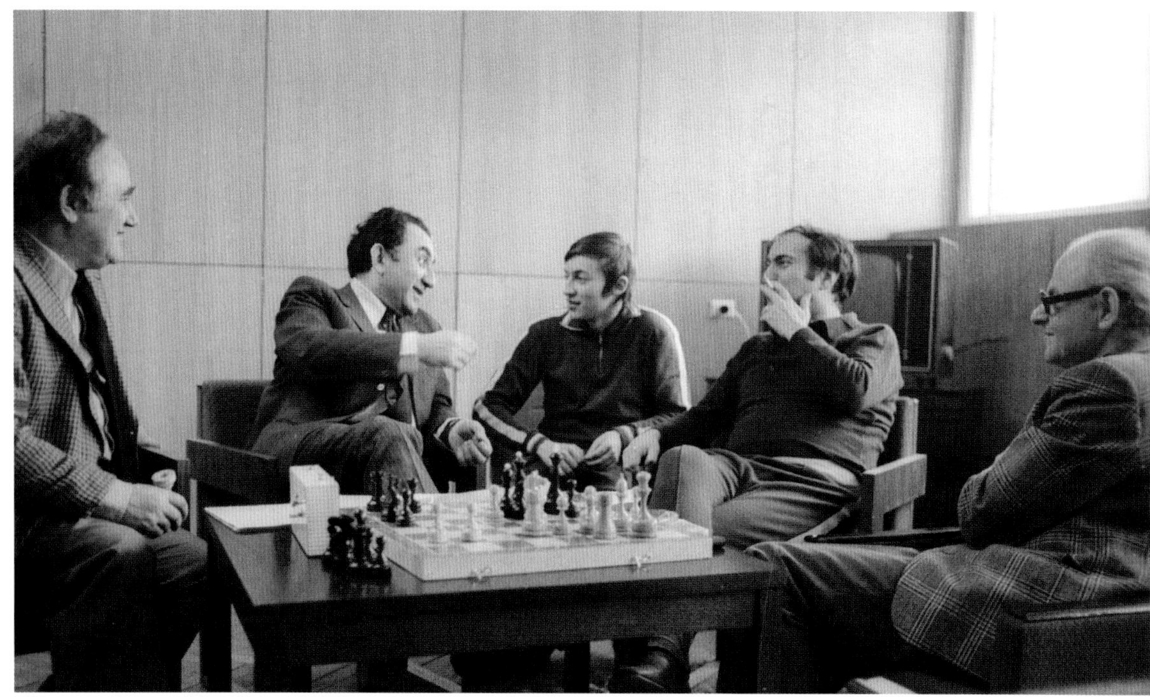

'Chess is like life,' said Spassky. 'Chess *is* life,' said
Fischer, who paid the penalty for his obvious mistake.
Chess has been called an art, a science and a sport. It
can't be an art, because every brilliancy depends on the
fuddled collusion of the opponent: even 'the Immortal
Game' would have died the death if Black had had his
wits about him. It can't be a science, because, simply, it
has no content: the singularity of chess is not its readiness
but its refusal to serve as a matrix for anything else. And
it can't be a sport, not quite, because it is both infinite
and precise; every game is recoverable; every game can
be re-experienced through the markings on a page. 'It's
definitely not an art,' said Nigel Short. 'If I have the choice
between a beautiful combination and a mundane way
of wrapping up the game, then I'll wrap up the game.
You must win. It's not an art. It's a fight. It's a fight.'

Martin Amis, *Observer*, 1986

Above, from left to right: Efim Geller,
Tigran Petrosian (world champion,
1963–69), Anatoly Karpov (world
champion, 1975–85), Mikhail Tal (world
champion, 1960–61) and Semyon
Furman, Moscow, 1975.

Right: Vasily Smyslov (seated left, world
champion, 1957–58), during a match.

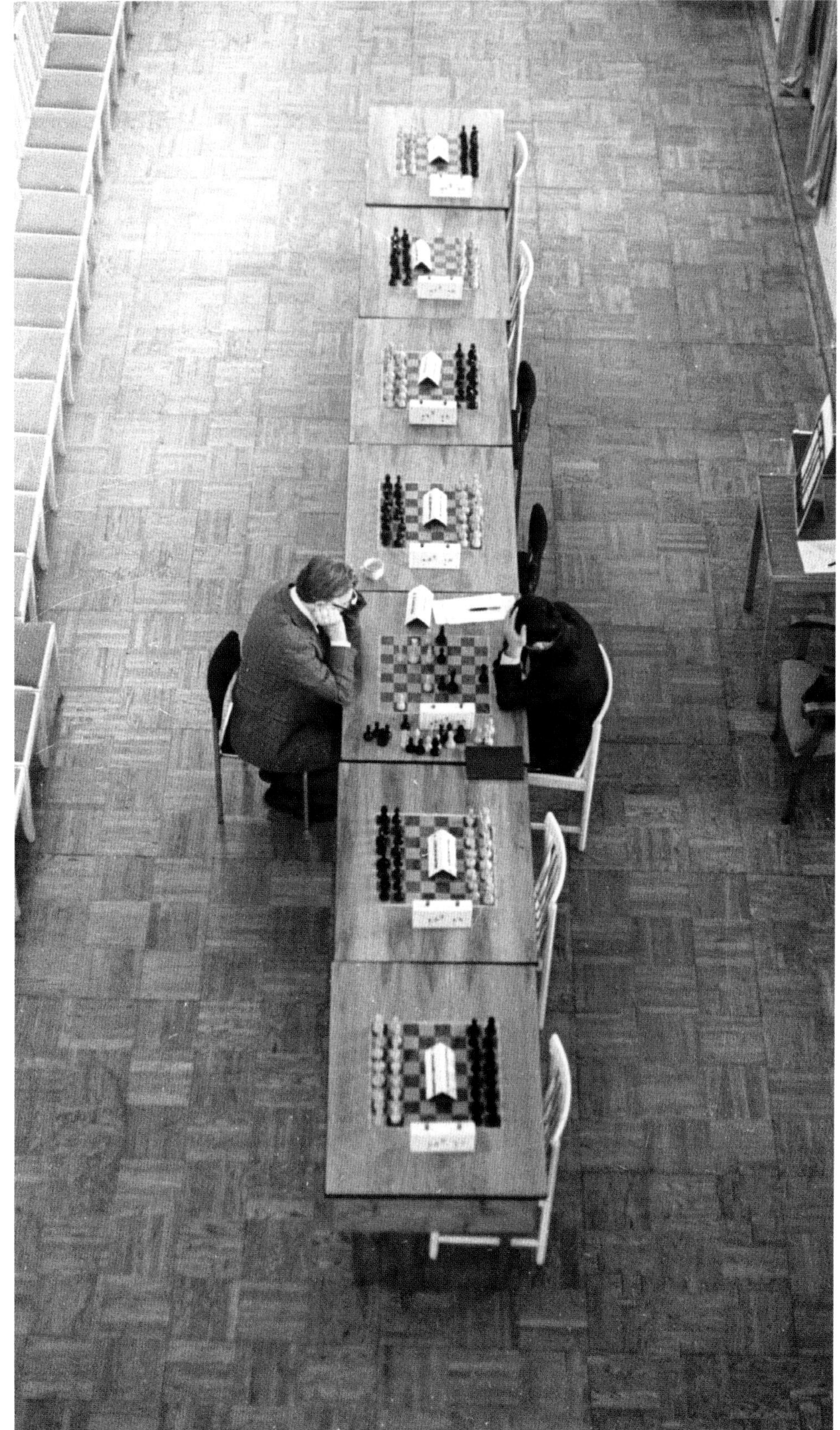

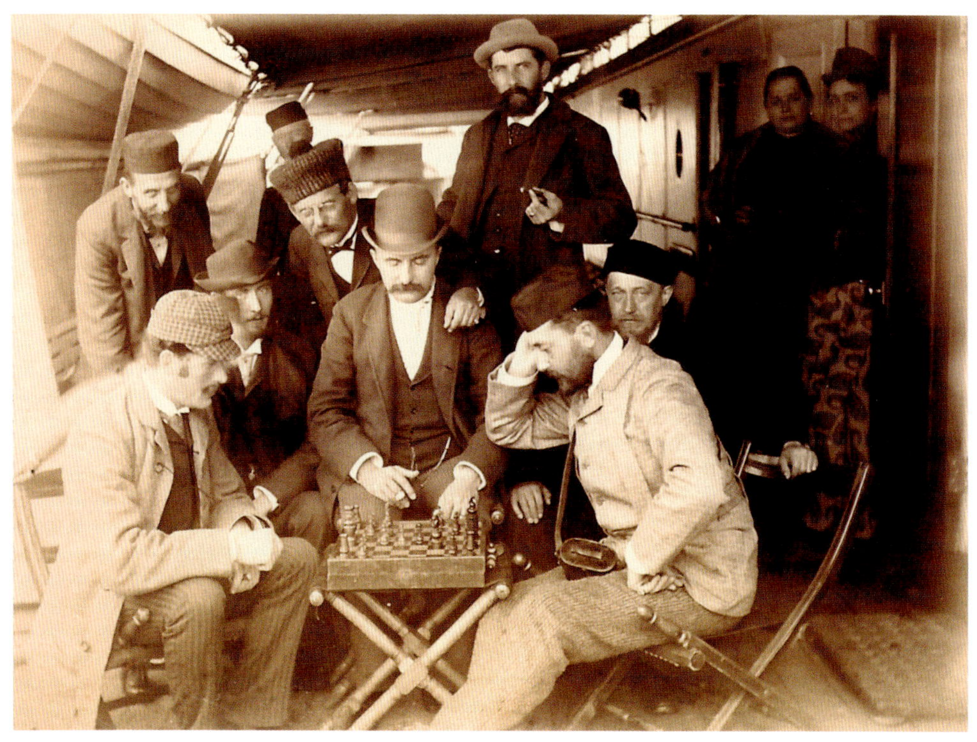

Baron H. von Blottnitz; George Kirchner; Herman Ohme; Friedrich Niewandt; and William Elliot Smith, among others, watching and participating in a chess game aboard the steamship SS *Fulda* during a transatlantic crossing in July 1888.

Right: A man plays chess against two women, 14 May 1894.

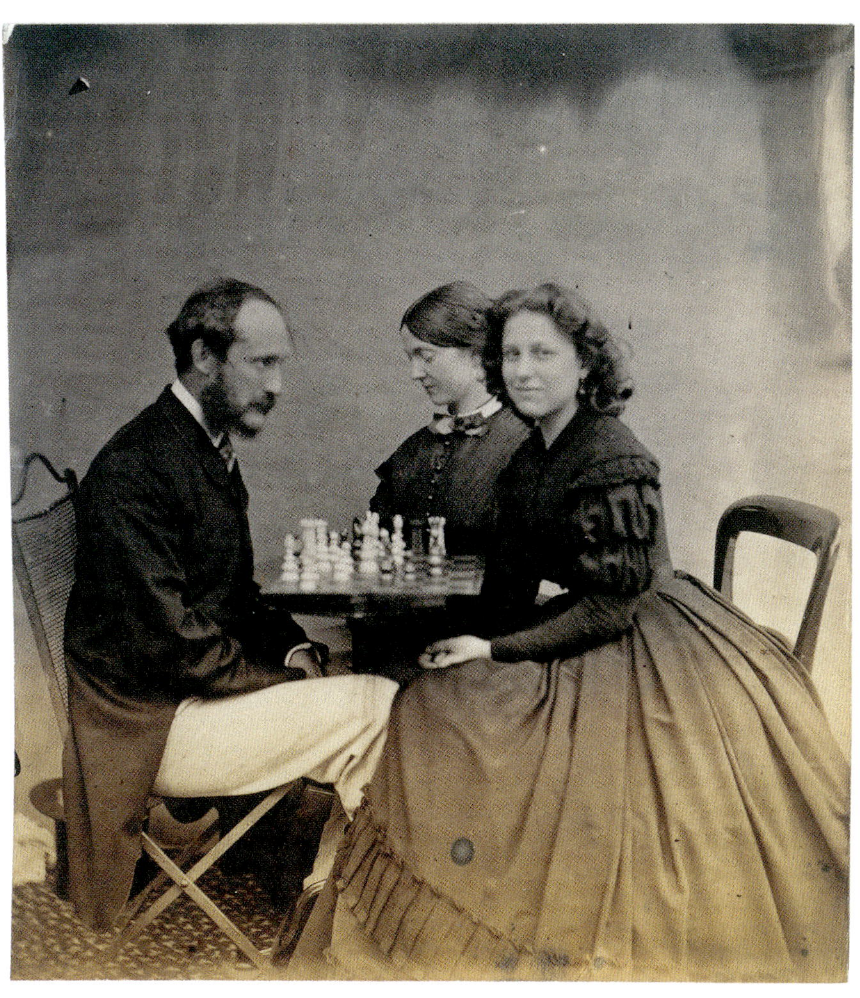

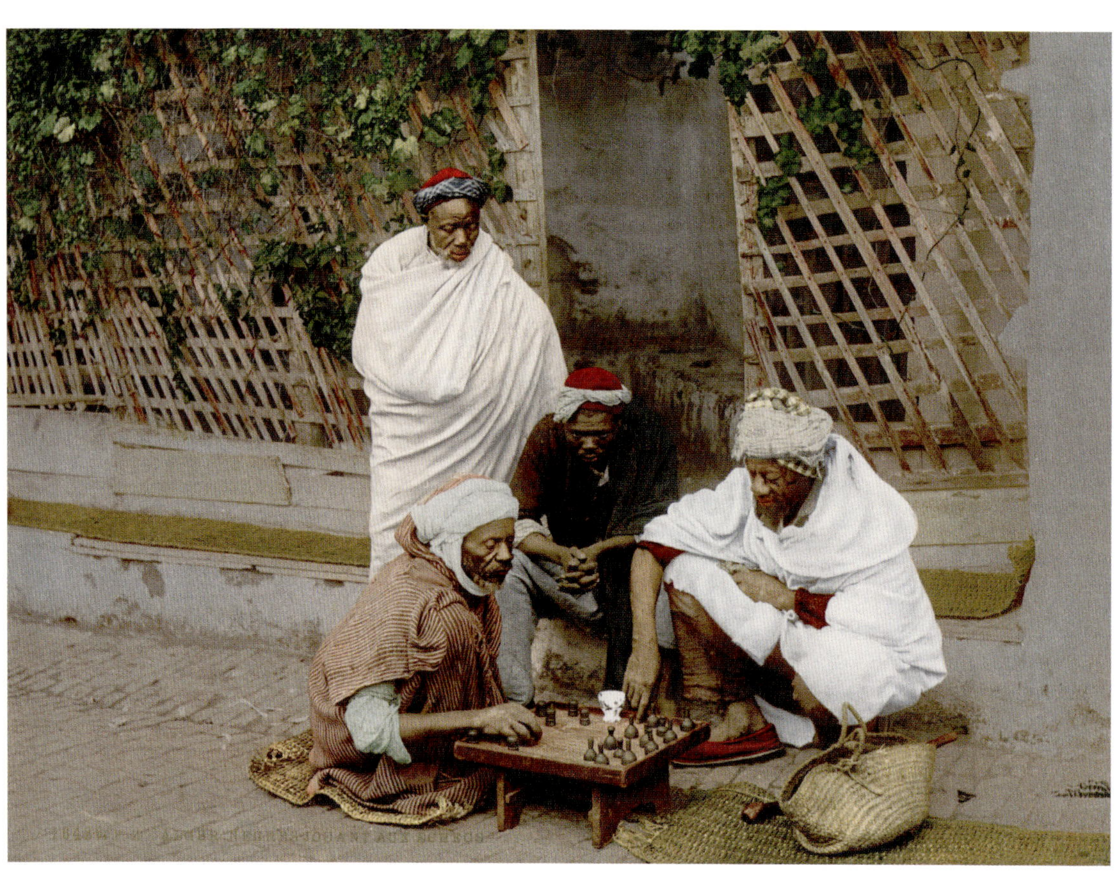

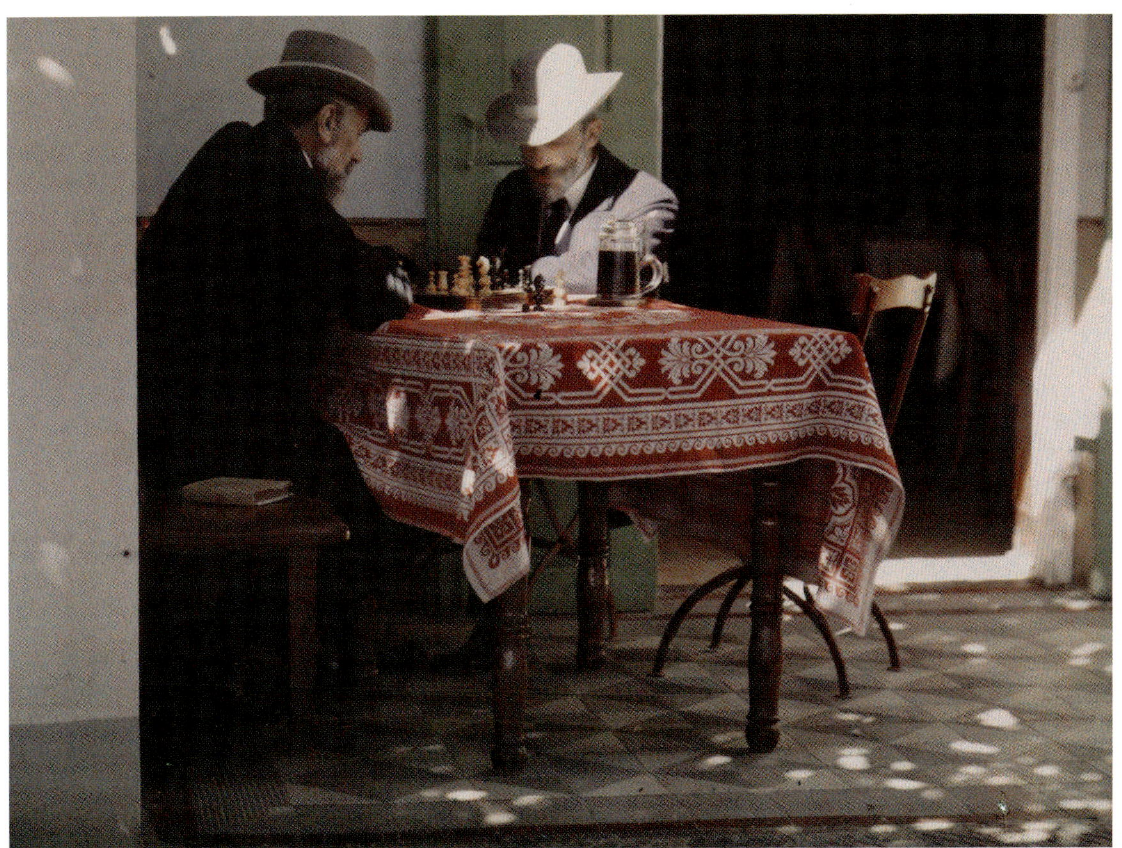

Dr Fritz Raab (right), a friend of
the photographer Alfred Stieglitz,
playing chess in Munich in 1907. It's
likely that his opponent is Herr Götz
of the Bruckmann printing firm – the
company was producing a book of
autochromes by the photographer
Edward Steichen at the time.

Left: Men playing chess on a street
in Algiers, 1899.

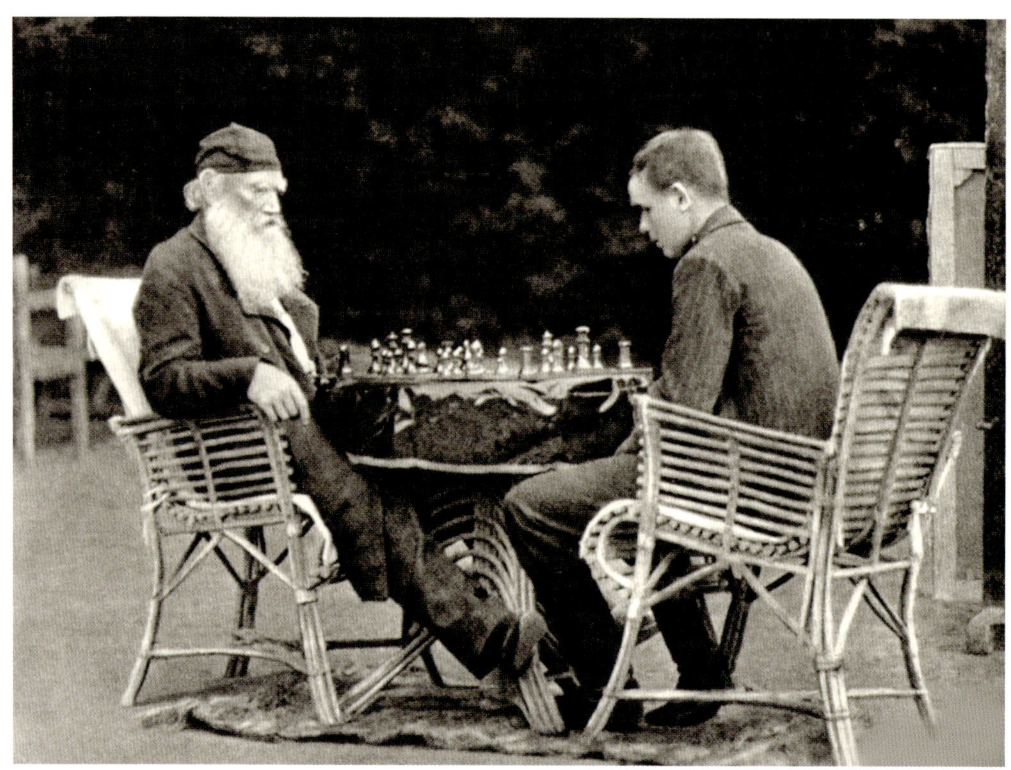

Leo Tolstoy (left) plays chess with Vladimir Vladimirovich Chertkov, the son of Vladimir Grigorievich Chertkov, Tolstoy's friend and publisher, who took this photograph at Yasnaya Polyana, Tolstoy's home. Russia, 1907.

Right: Leo Tolstoy plays chess with Mikhail Sukhotin, his son-in-law, at Yasnaya Polyana in 1908. Among those looking on are Tatyana Lvovna Tolstoya, Tolstoy's daughter and Sukhotin's wife, with her niece on her lap, and Sofia Andrejevna Tolstoy, or Countess Tolstoy, Tolstoy's wife, who is sitting next to a grandson.

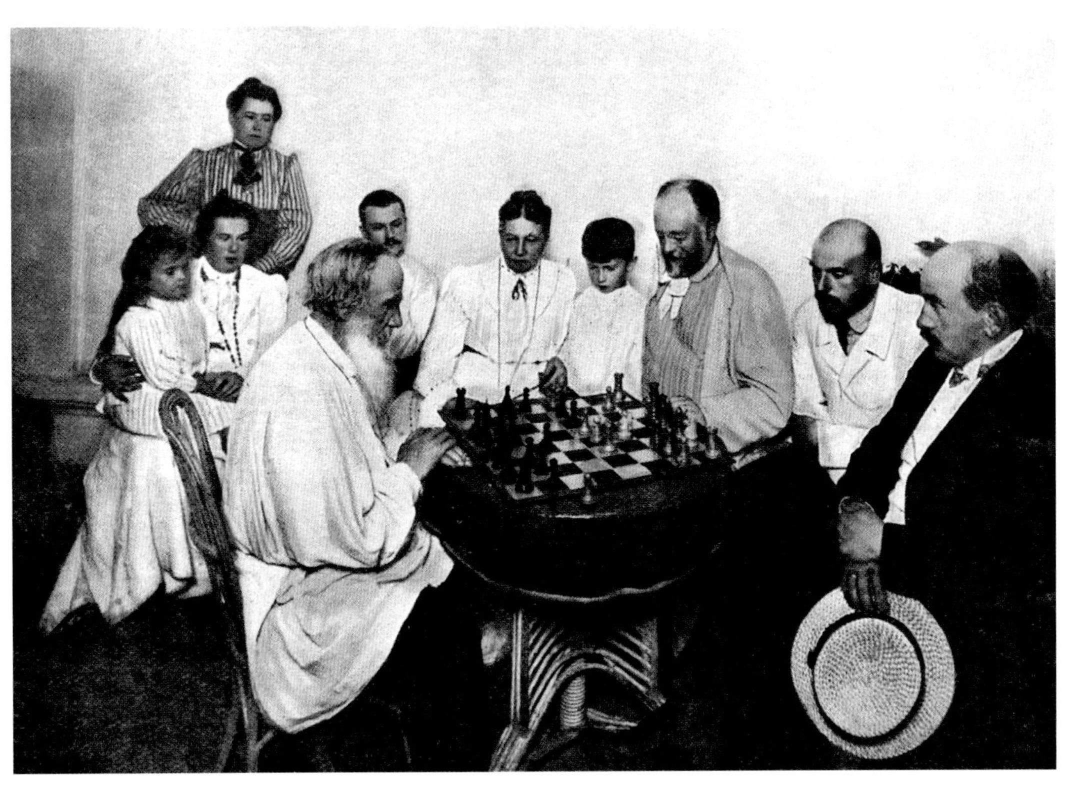

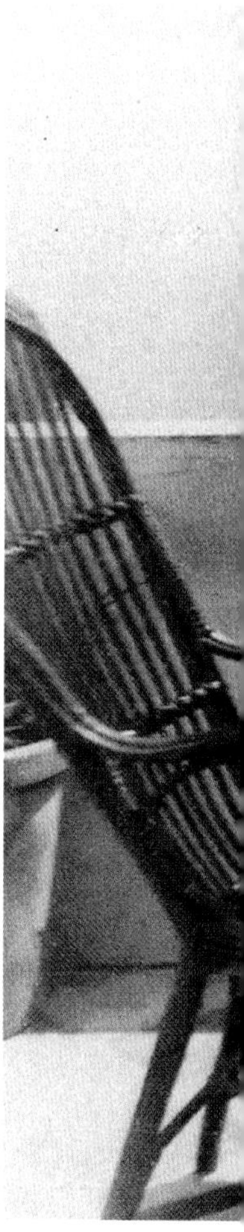

Alexander Bogdanov, a physician, philosopher and revolutionary, plays chess with Vladimir Lenin, the first leader of the Soviet Union, as writer Maxim Gorky watches, Capri, Italy, 1908. It is sometimes claimed that Lenin is yelling 'Checkmate!'

Overleaf: A human-sized chess game in Palace Square, Leningrad. The game was played on 20 July 1924, the day that the International Chess Federation, also known as FIDE, was founded in Paris. The white pieces were members of the Red Army, directed by Peter Romanovsky, who had won the second Soviet Championship the year before. The black pieces, controlled by Ilya Rabinovich, another strong master, were members of the Red Fleet. After five hours, the game, which was watched by 8,000 spectators, ended in a draw.

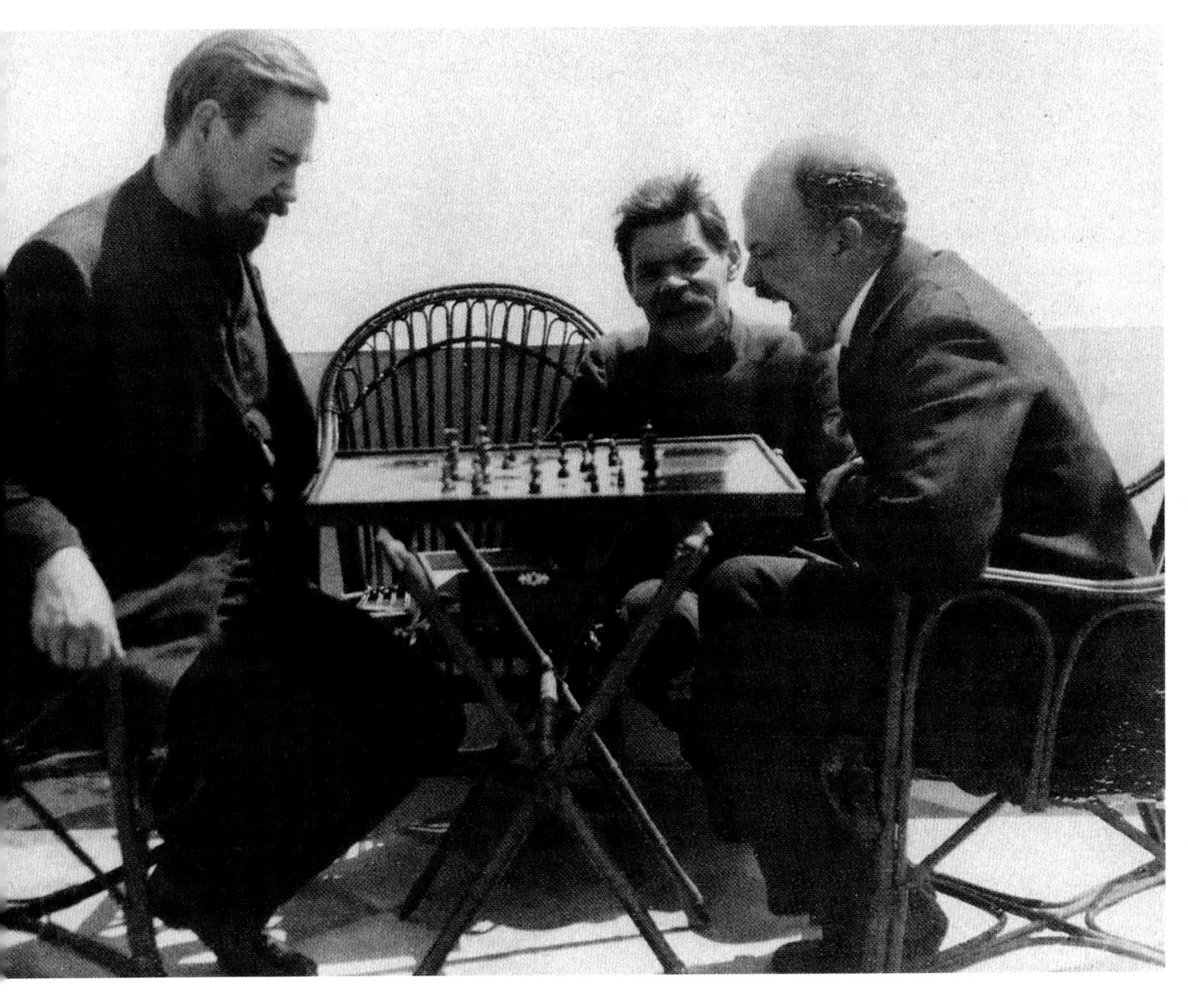

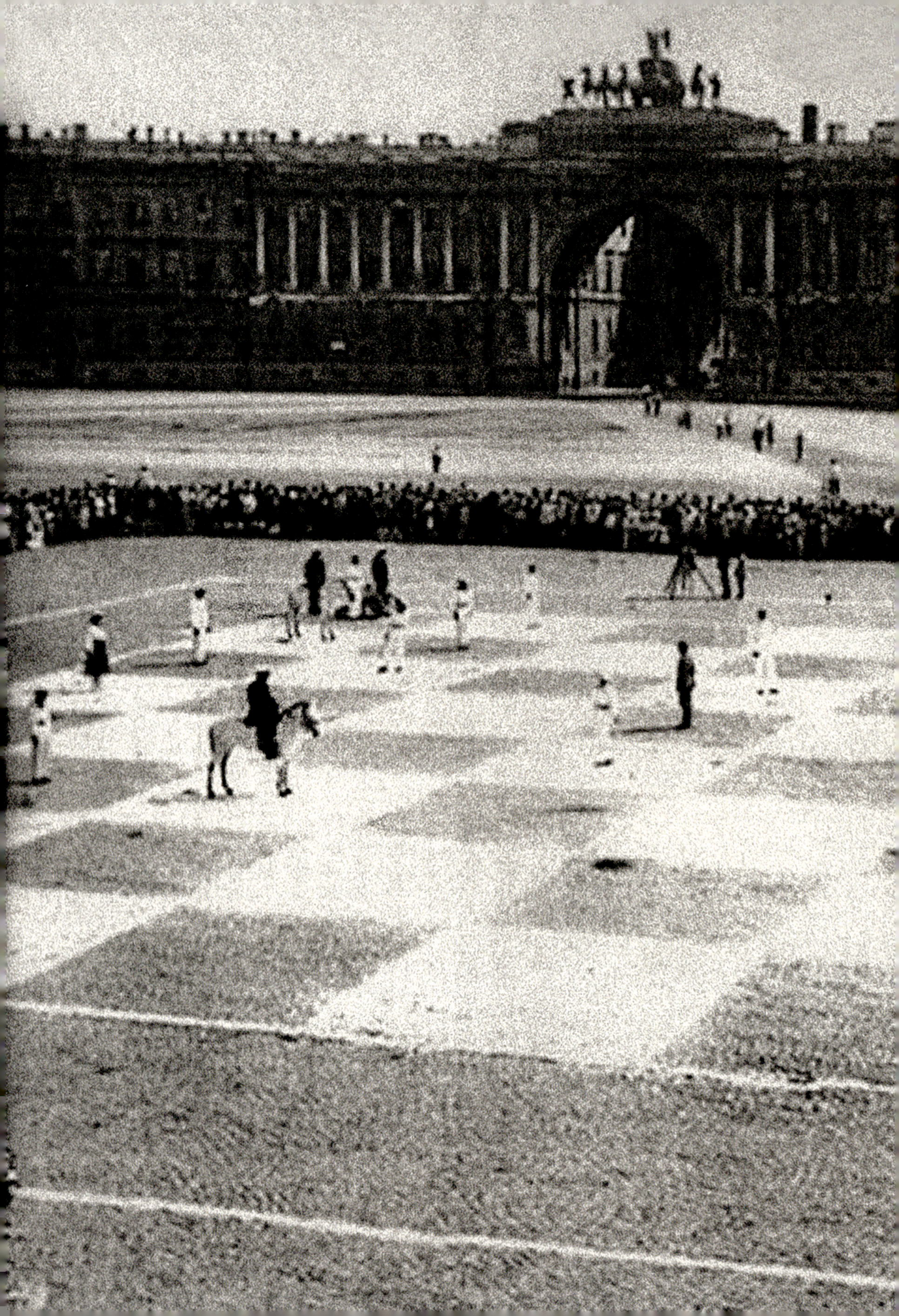

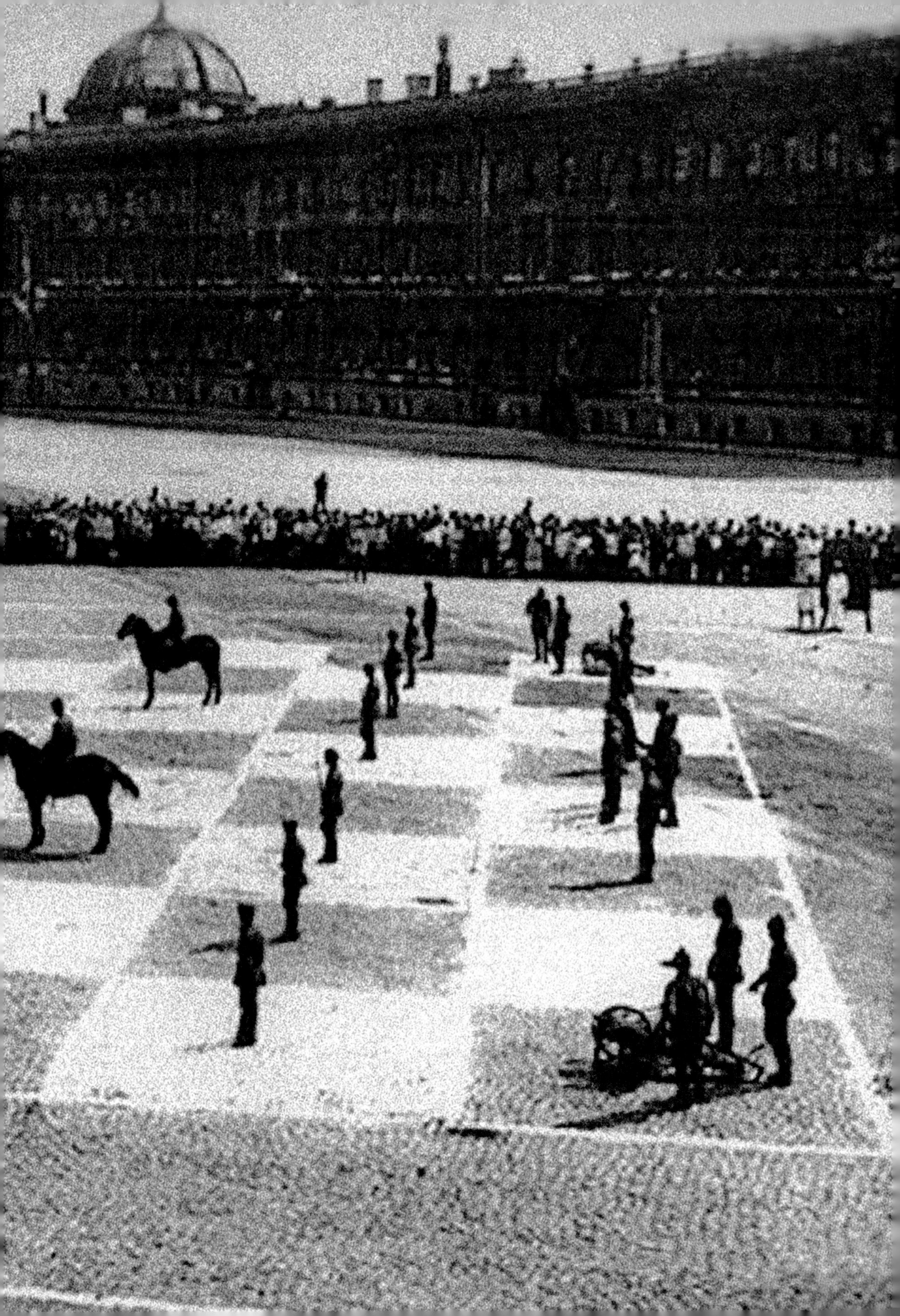

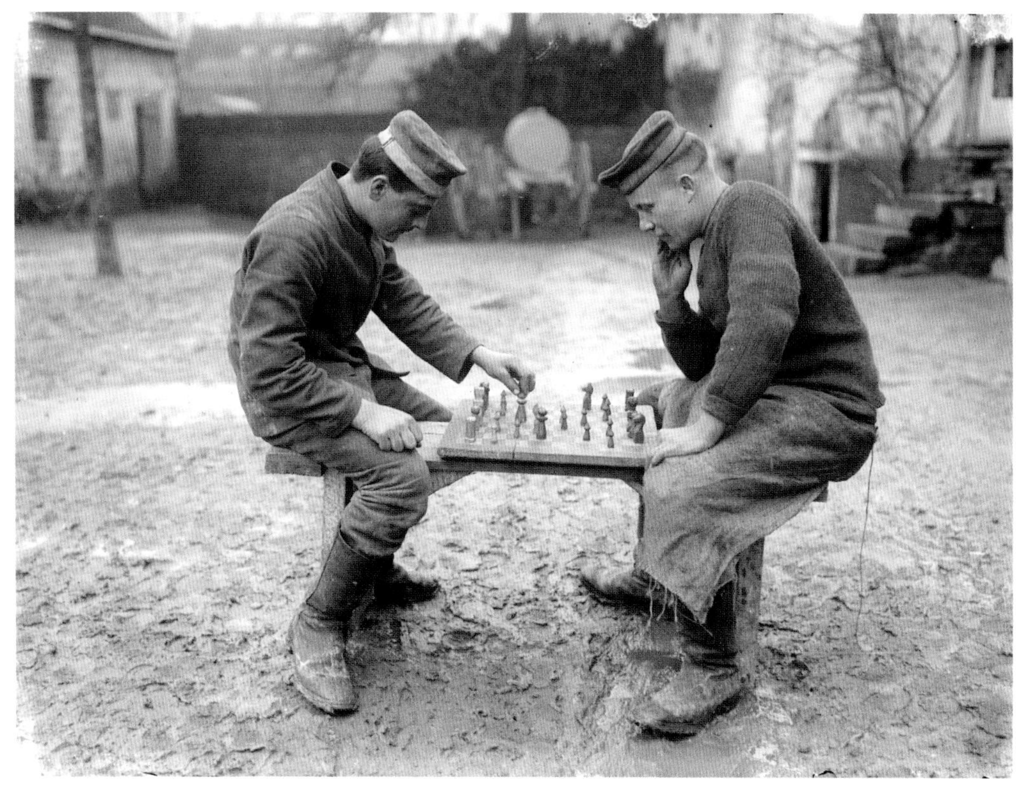

During lulls in the action in World War I, World War II and even during the more recent war in Ukraine, chess has always been a favourite pastime for those in combat. For prisoners-of-war, it can be a solace – a way to relieve the boredom and perhaps forget, at least temporarily, about their circumstances.

Military schools have also long looked to chess as a good metaphor for teaching strategy and tactics to officers.

Above: German prisoners from the Battle of the Somme, World War I, Querrieu, October 1916.

Right: German soldiers in the trenches during World War I, 1916.

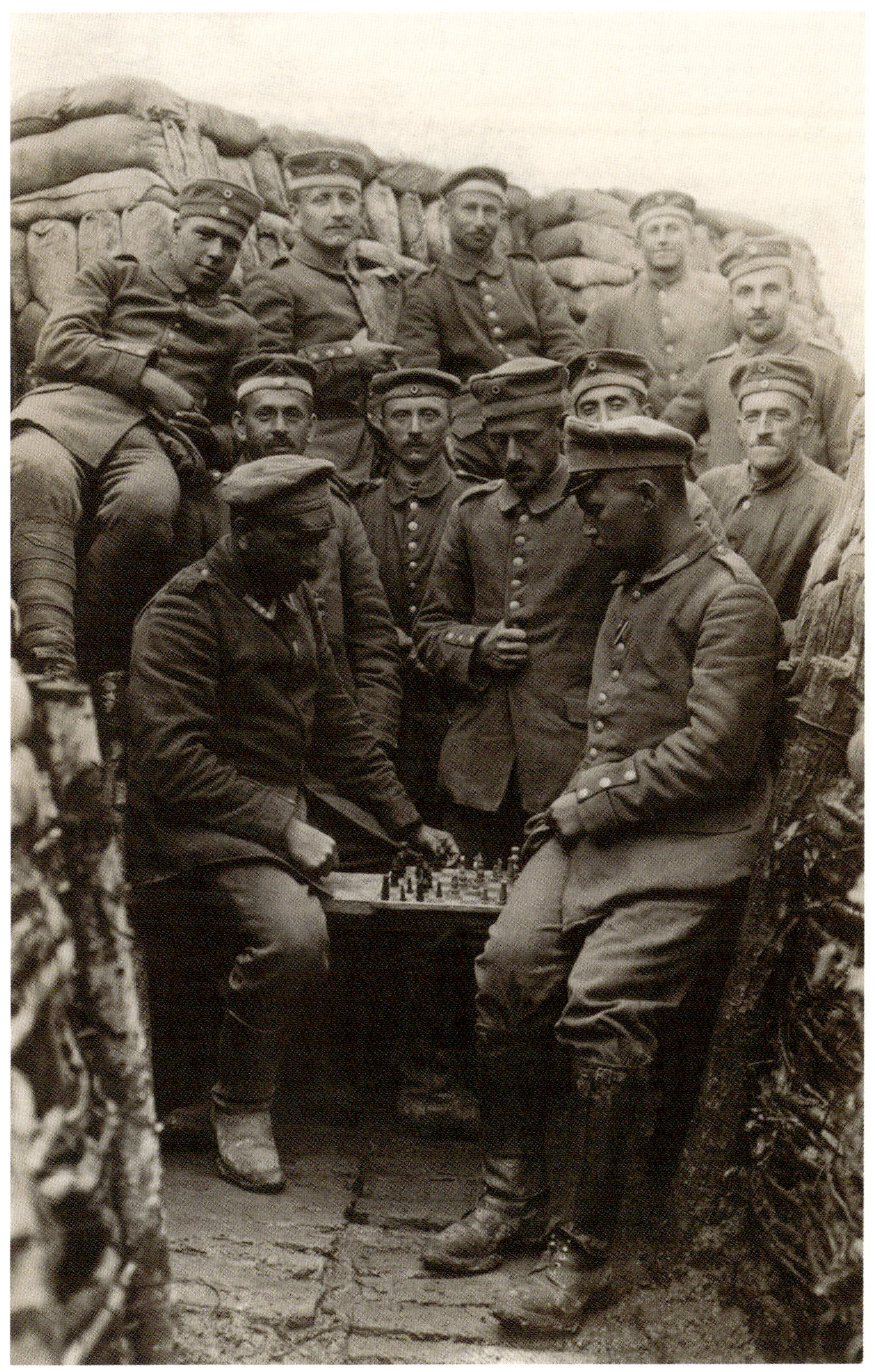

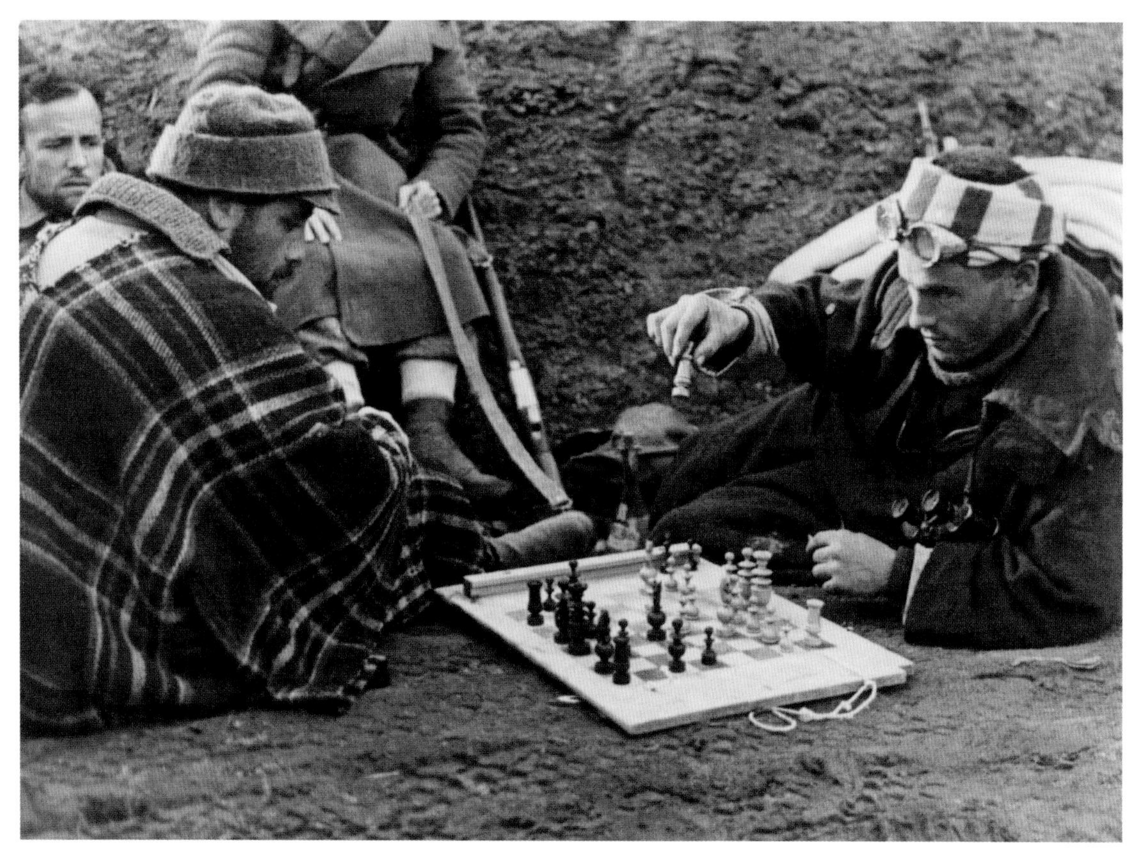

Republican soldiers during the Spanish
Civil War, Madrid, c.1938.

Right: Soldiers of the 162nd Turkistan
Division, France, 1943.

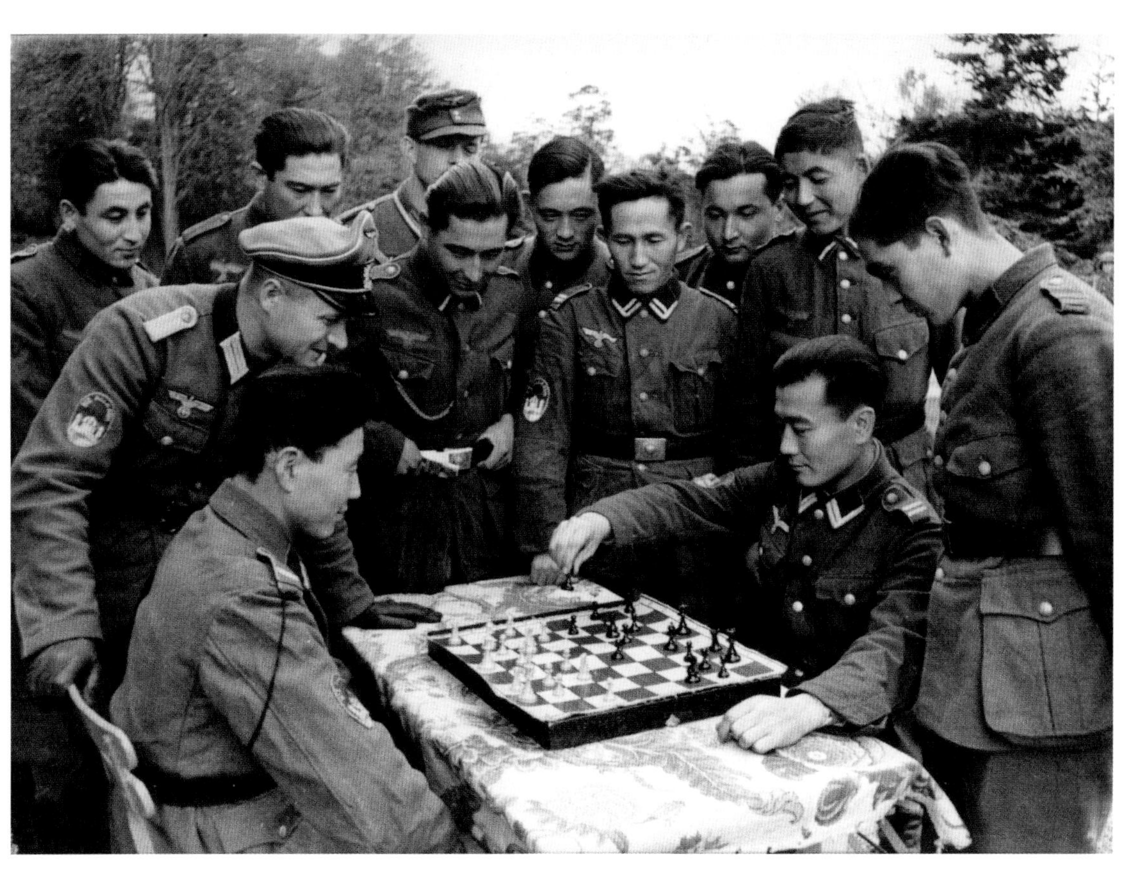

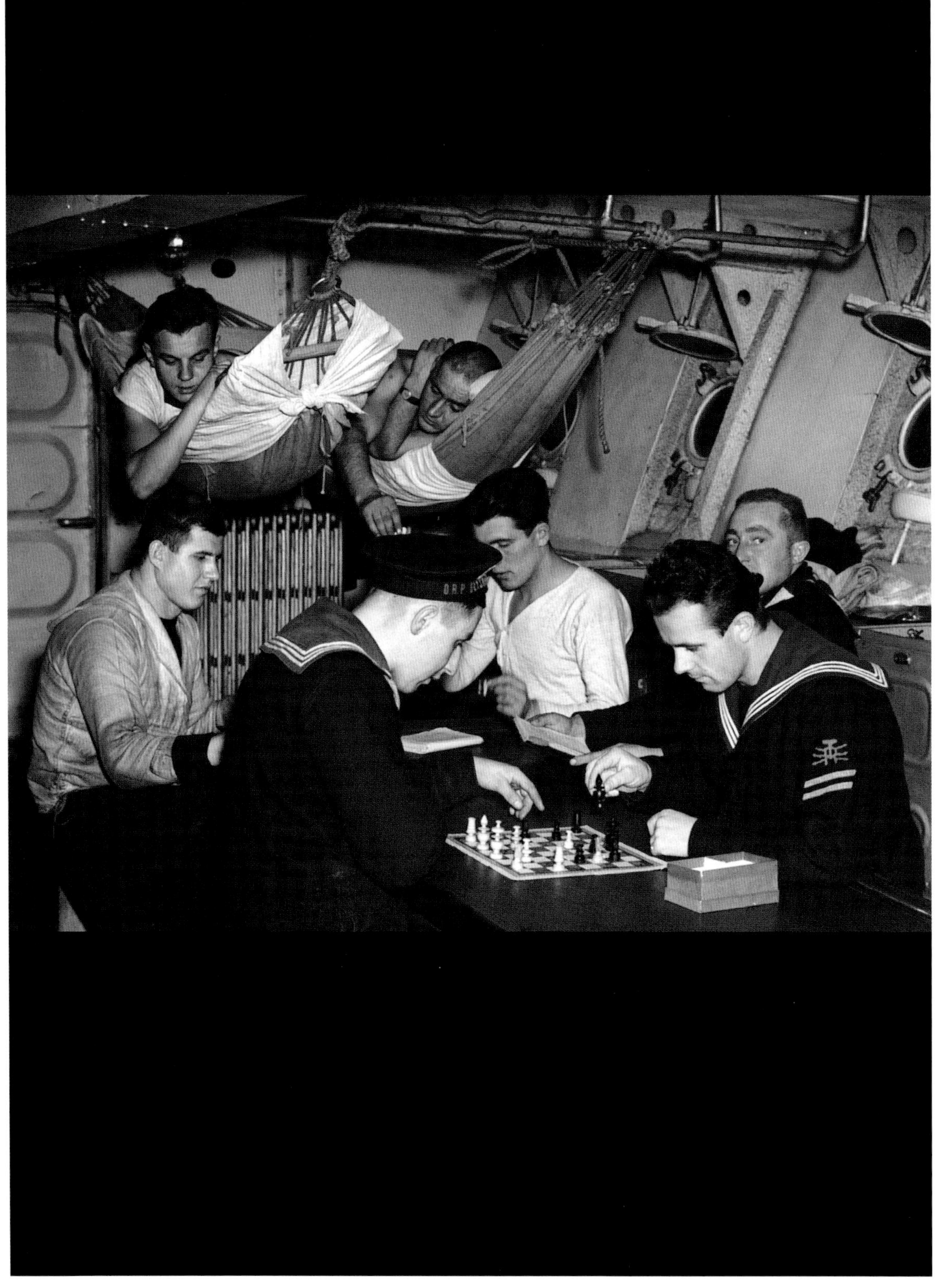

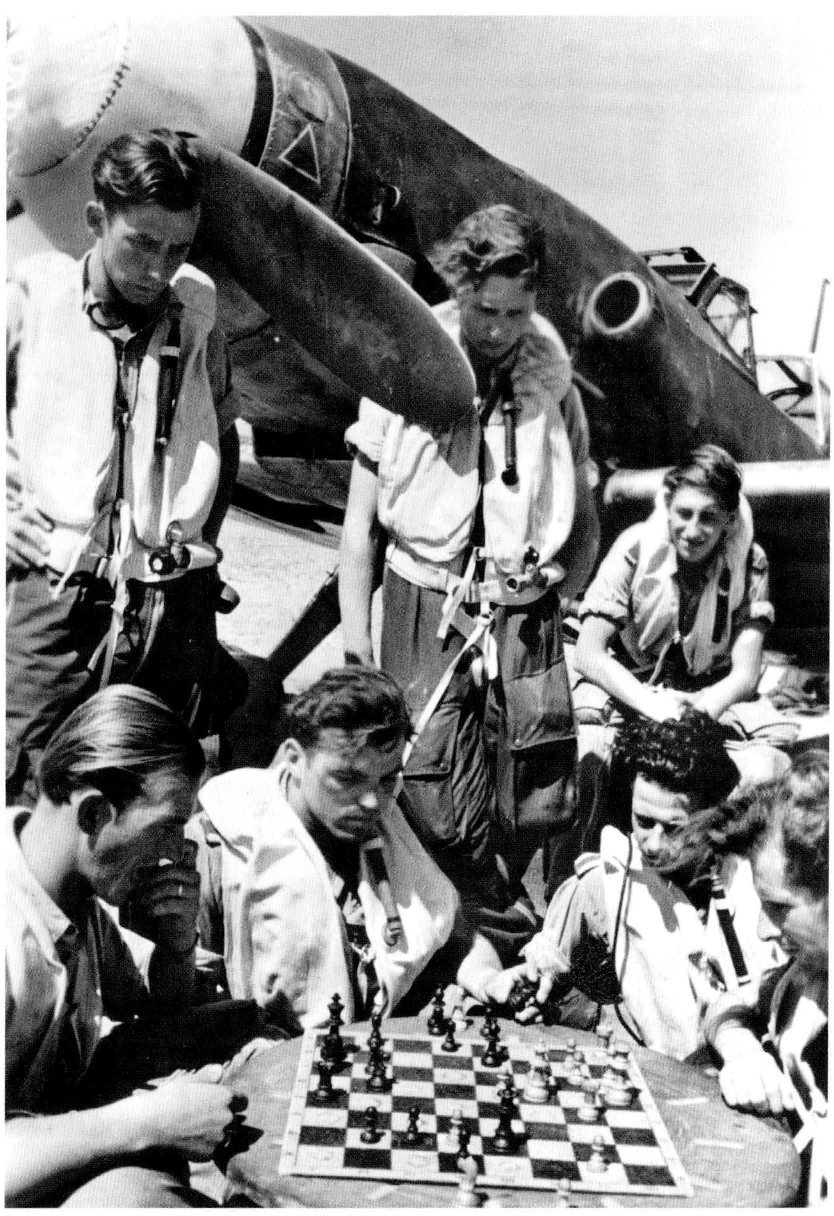

Above: German Luftwaffe pilots on
stand-by, 1944.

Left: Polish sailors playing chess in
their cabin, 1939.

Right: A 1941 photograph of Josip Broz Tito, who
ruled Yugoslavia from 1944 to his death in 1980,
playing chess in a bunker during World War II.

Overleaf: Palestinian fighters in Damour, a city
20 kilometres south of Beirut, which had just
been attacked by Israeli forces during the
Lebanon War, April 1982.

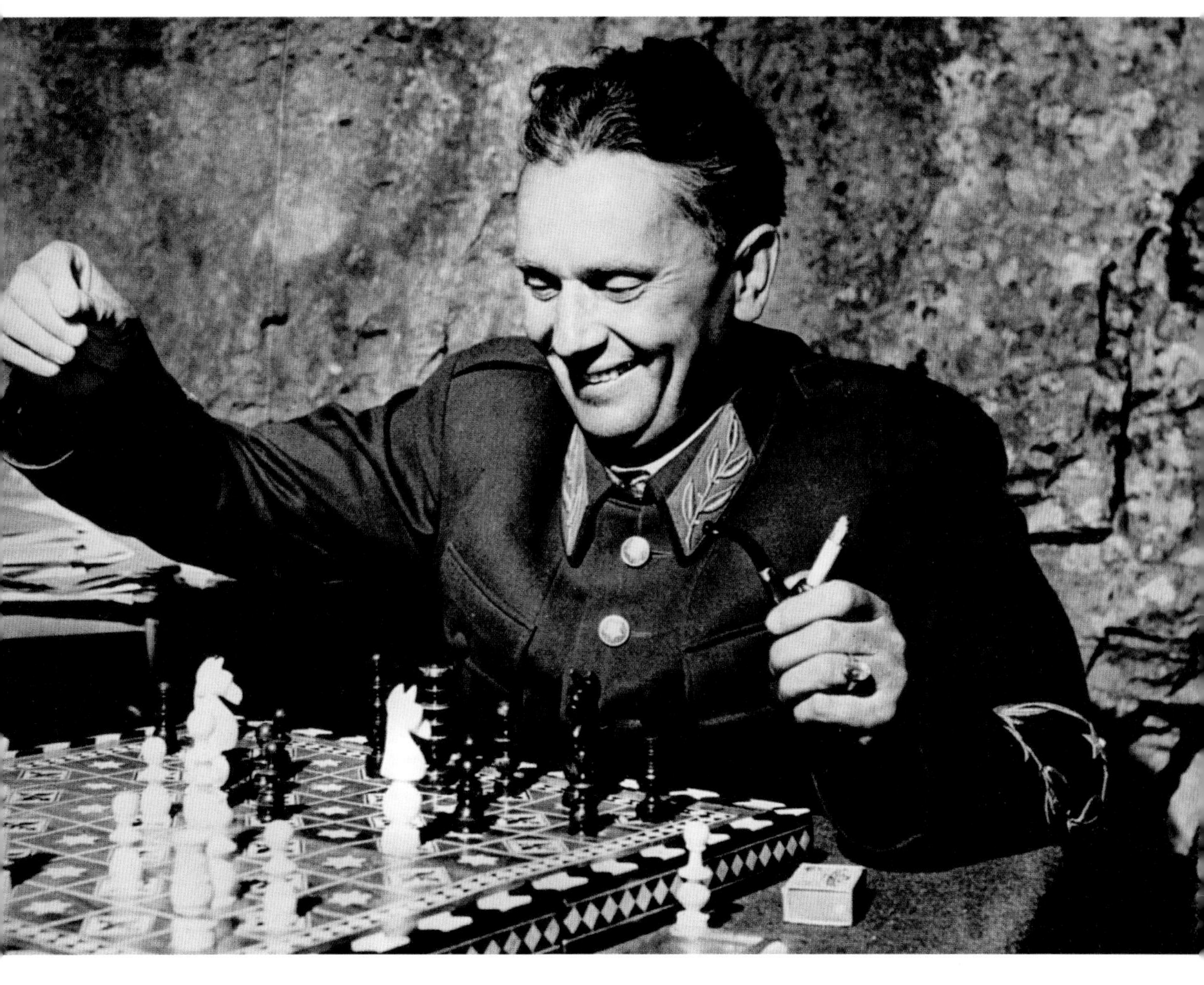

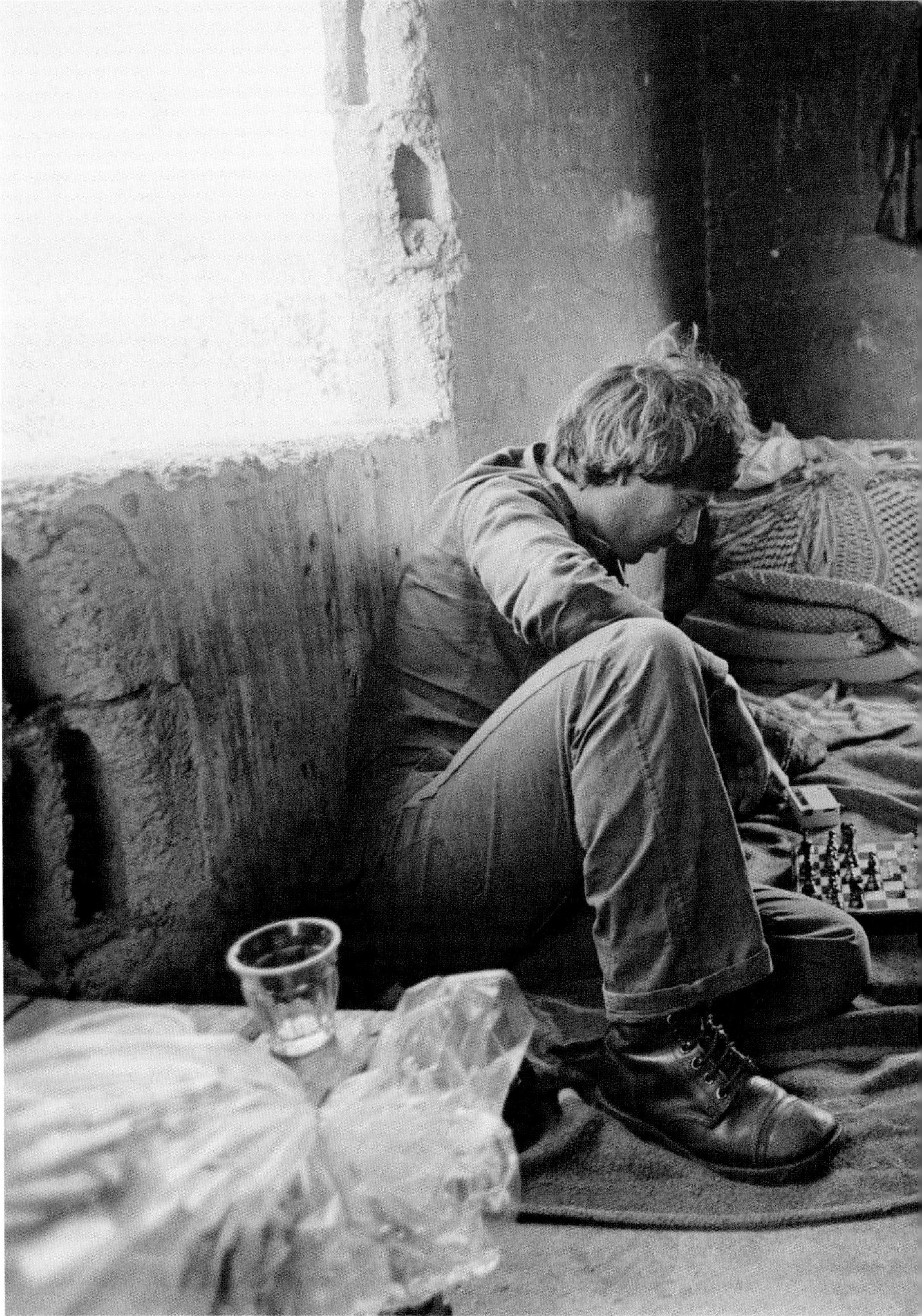

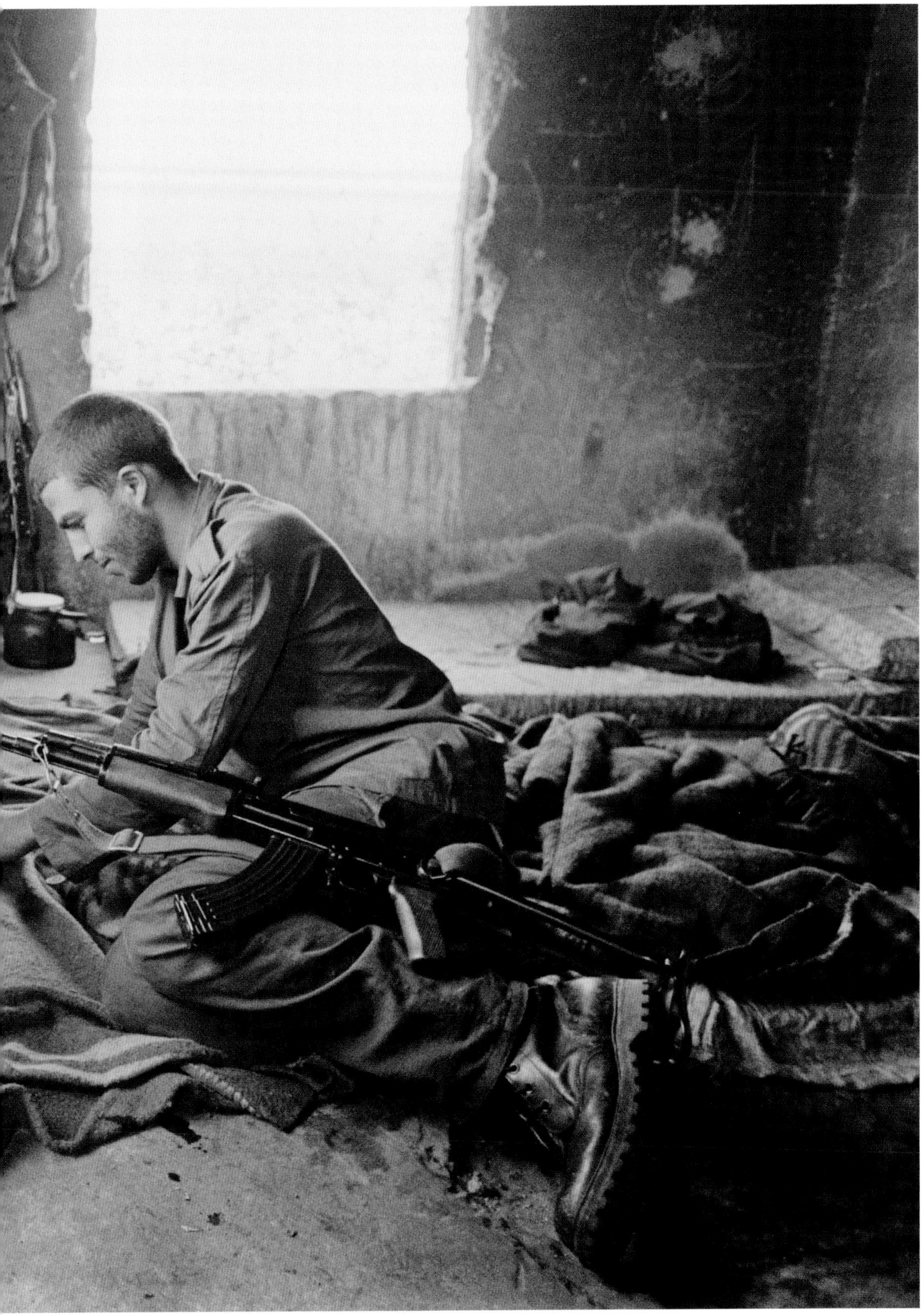

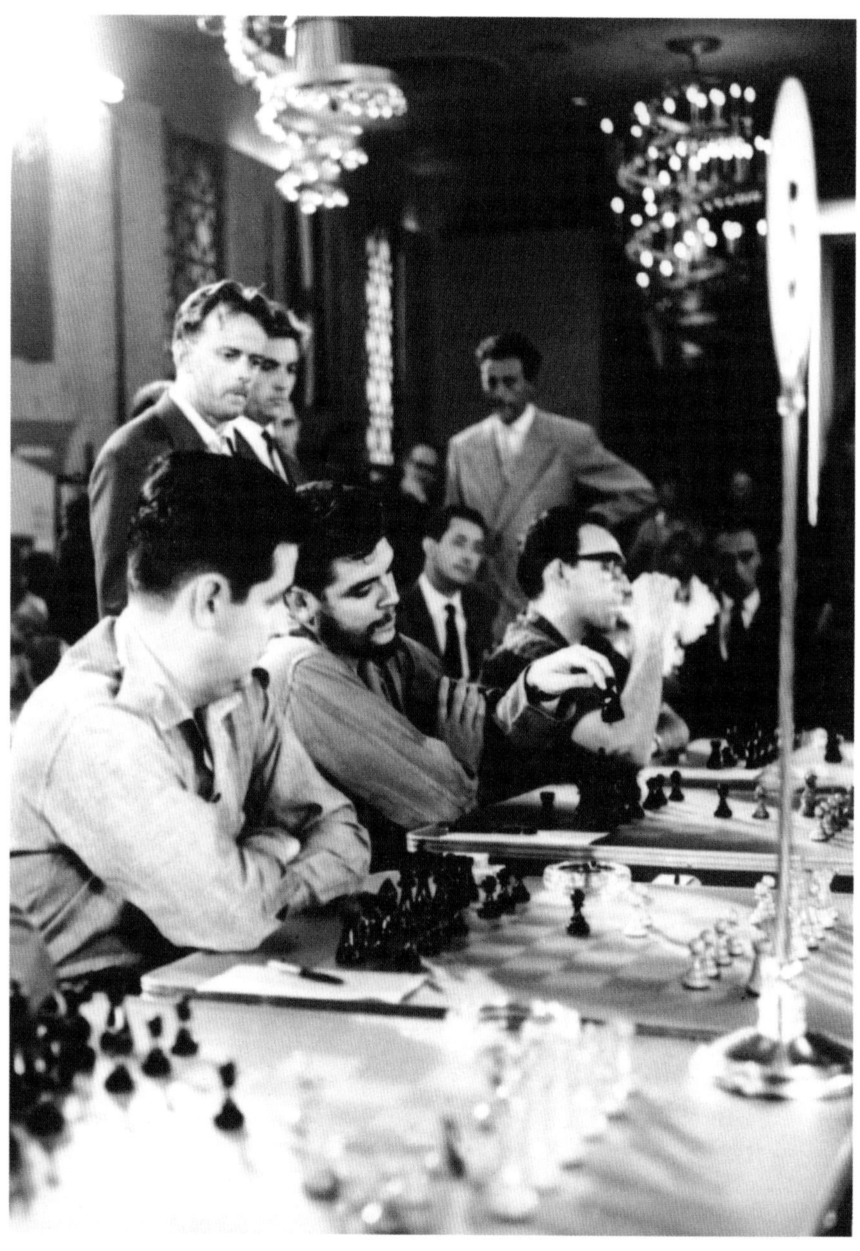

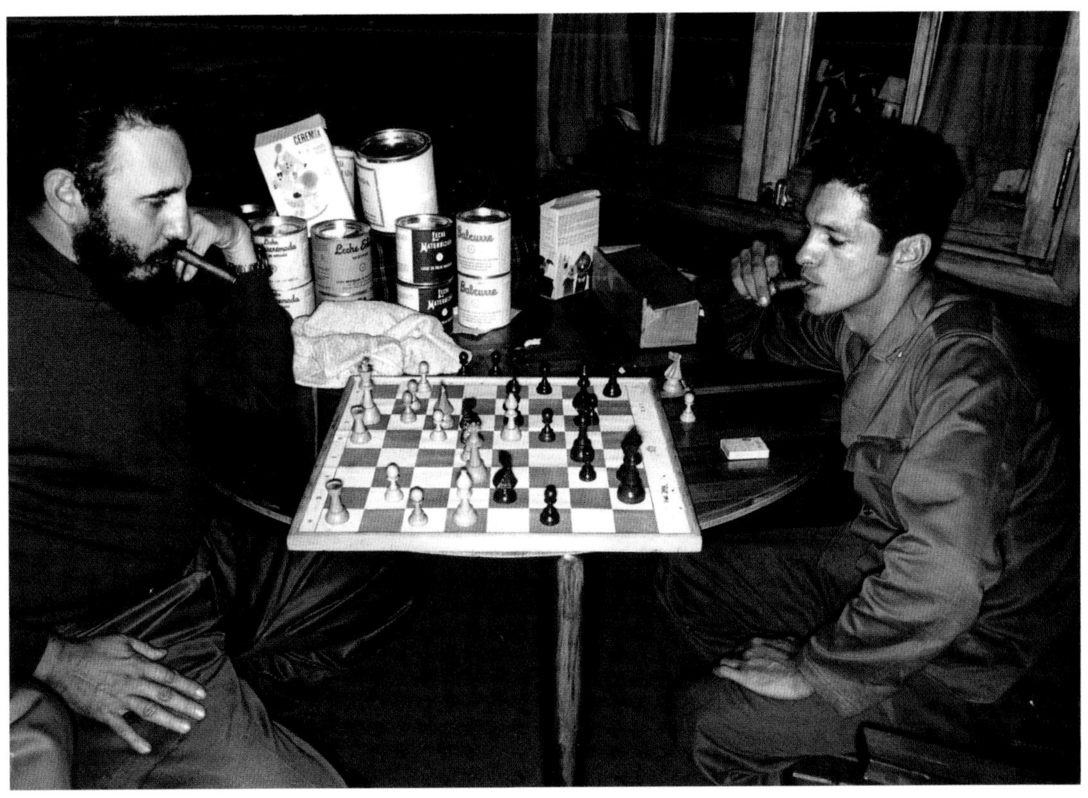

After he had overthrown Fulgencio Batista, Fidel Castro (left) led Cuba from 1959 until 2008. He was a huge chess fan, helping organise and bring the Chess Olympiad to Cuba in 1966. Here he plays an unidentified soldier in 1967.

Left: Ernesto 'Che' Guevara (with beard), who helped Castro lead the Cuban revolution in 1959, served as his second-in-command and later held important roles in the new government. Like Castro, he was a passionate chess fan. In the early 1960s, Guevara played in simultaneous exhibition matches with several prominent players, including Miguel Najdorf, Viktor Korchnoi and Mikhail Tal, the former world champion.

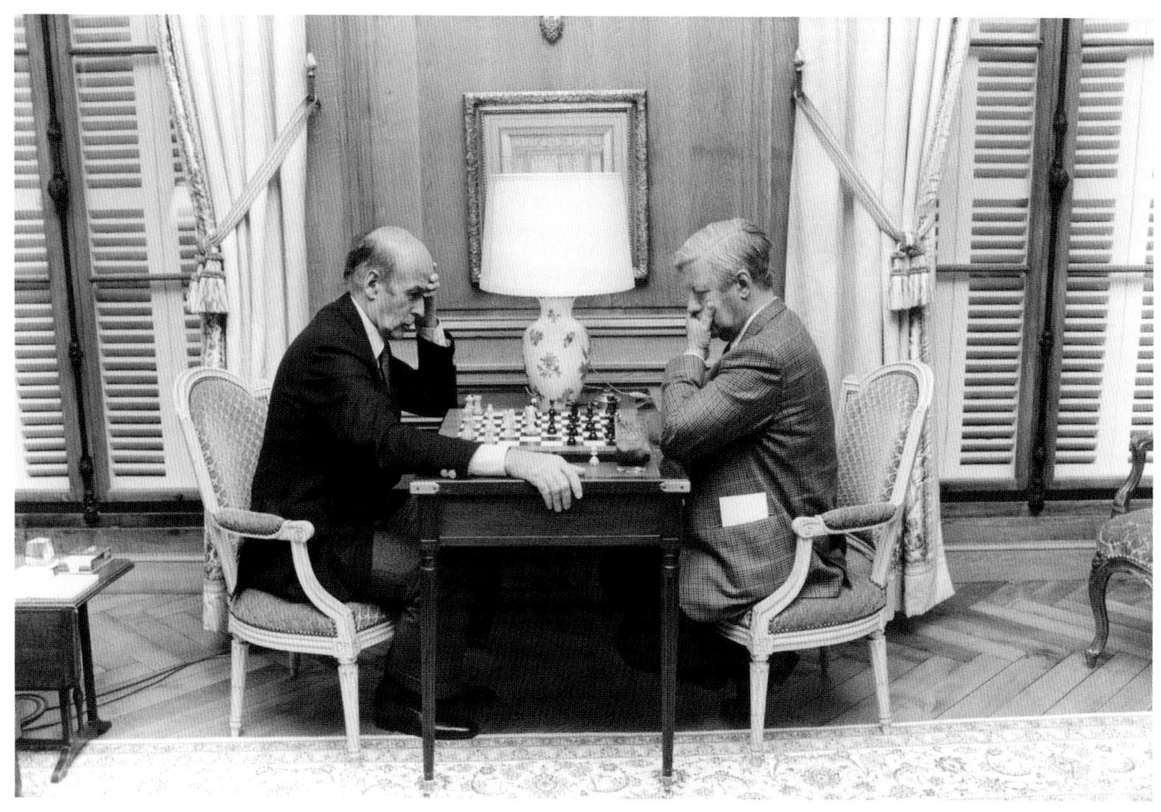

Valéry Giscard d'Estaing (left), the former French President, plays against Helmut Schmidt, the former West German Chancellor, shortly after each had left office. The game took place in the library at Château de l'Etoile, the property of the former French President in Loir-et-Cher, France, 20 May 1983.

Right: Nicolae Ceaușescu (wearing a white cap), was the head of state of Romania from 1967 until 1989. This photograph, taken in Bucharest on 30 May 1982, shows him playing chess with Stefan Andrei, Romania's Minister of Foreign Affairs. Elena Ceaușescu, Nicolae's wife, who was First Deputy Prime Minister of the country, is standing next to them holding a grandson, while Valentin Ceaușescu, the couple's oldest child, is in the background. Nicolae and Elena Ceaușescu were overthrown in a revolution and executed on Christmas Day 1989.

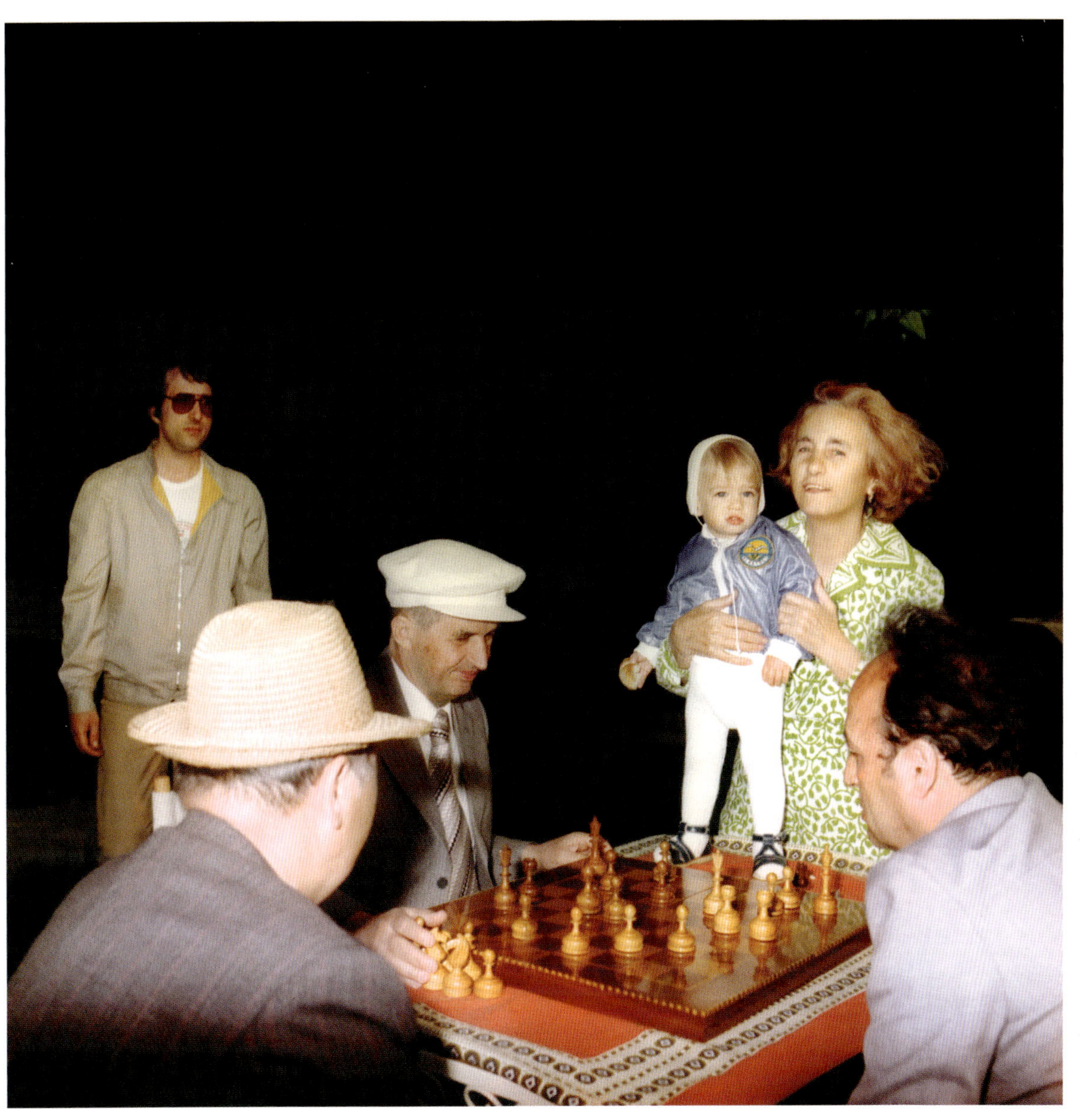

On 14 June 1970, a game was played between
two cosmonauts orbiting the earth and ground
control. The cosmonauts were Vitaly Ivanovich
Sevastyanov (right) and Andriyan Grigoryevich
Nikolaev, while ground control was represented
by Nikolai Petrovich Kamanin, a Soviet air force
general, and Viktor Vasilevich Gorbatko, another
cosmonaut. The board used by the cosmonauts
was made from plastic with special notches for
the pieces, so that they could slide around or
be moved to the side when they were captured
without floating away. The game ended in a
draw after four orbits and 35 moves.

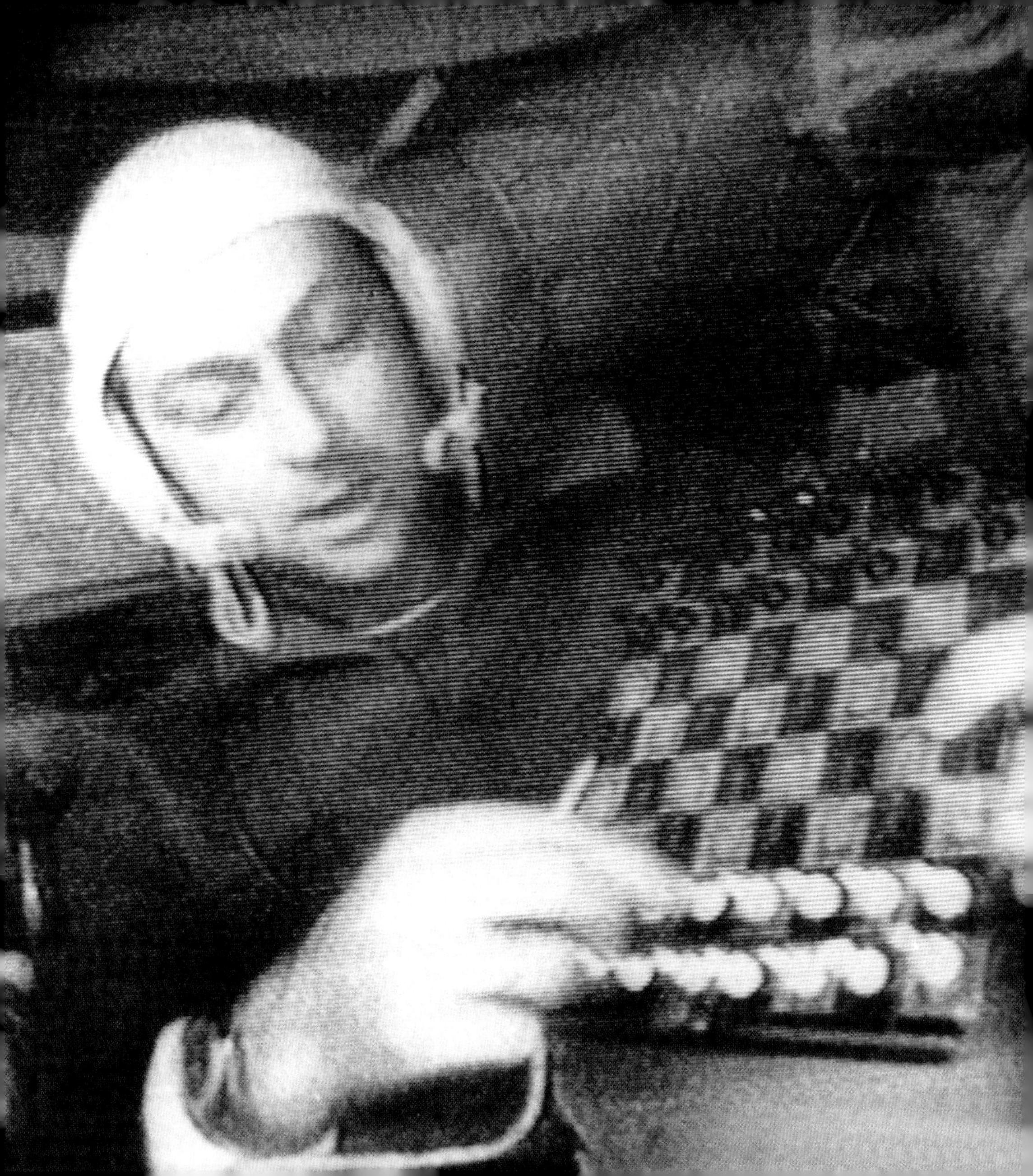

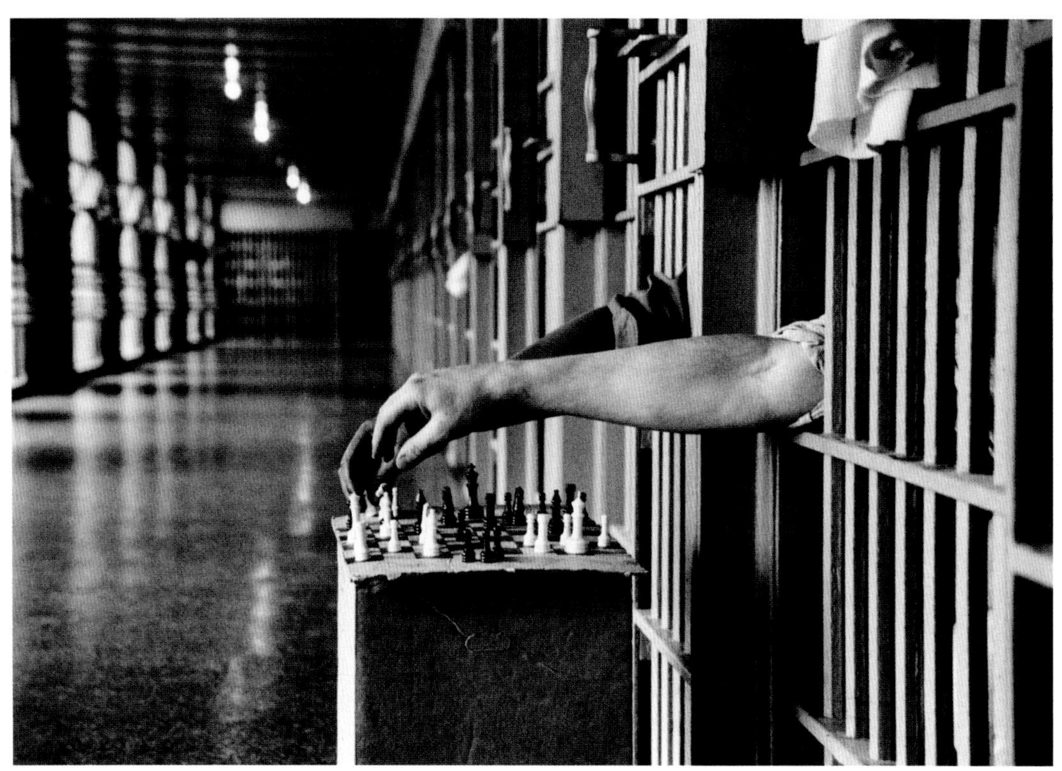

Chess has long been a popular diversion in prisons, but in recent years, the game has also increasingly been seen as a tool to aid rehabilitation, because the skills that make someone good at chess, such as being patient and thinking about the consequences of your moves, are the same skills required to make good decisions.

In 2022, the International Chess Federation, the game's governing body, organised a global online championship for teams of players in prisons. Each team consisted of four players and over 85 teams from 46 countries participated. A team from the Philippines won the men's division and a team from Mongolia triumphed in the women's.

Above: Attica Correctional Facility, New York, 1972.

Right: Death Row, Texas, 1979.

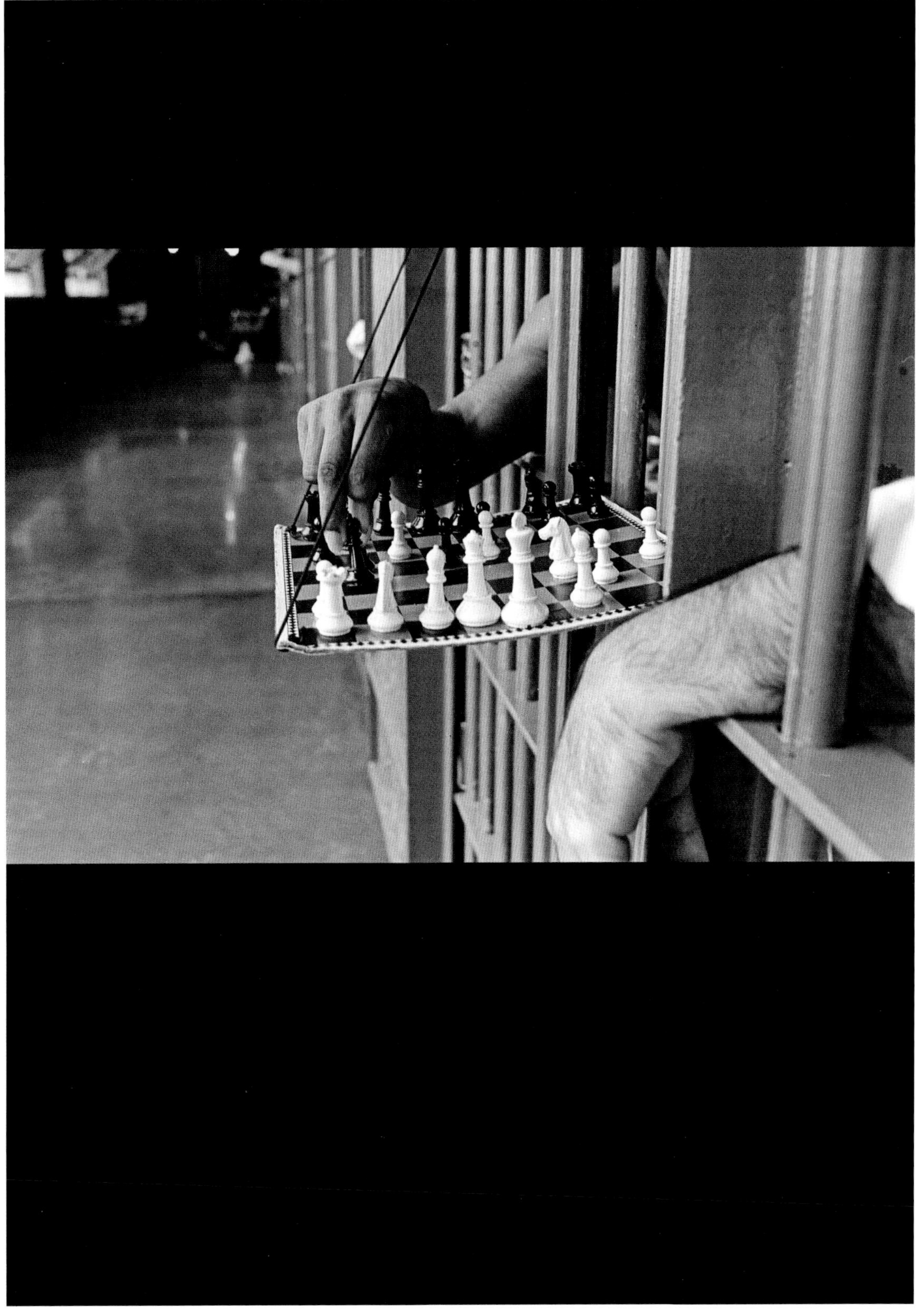

From Moscow to London to New York City and points in between, playing chess in parks, and sometimes in the streets, is always popular.

One of the meccas for street chess has long been the southwest corner of Washington Square Park in New York, where chess tables were installed decades ago. Rich, famous, poor and unknown – all have congregated there to play and watch. It has also been the setting for films, such as *Searching for Bobby Fischer* (1993).

Right: Children playing chess in Moscow, 1947.

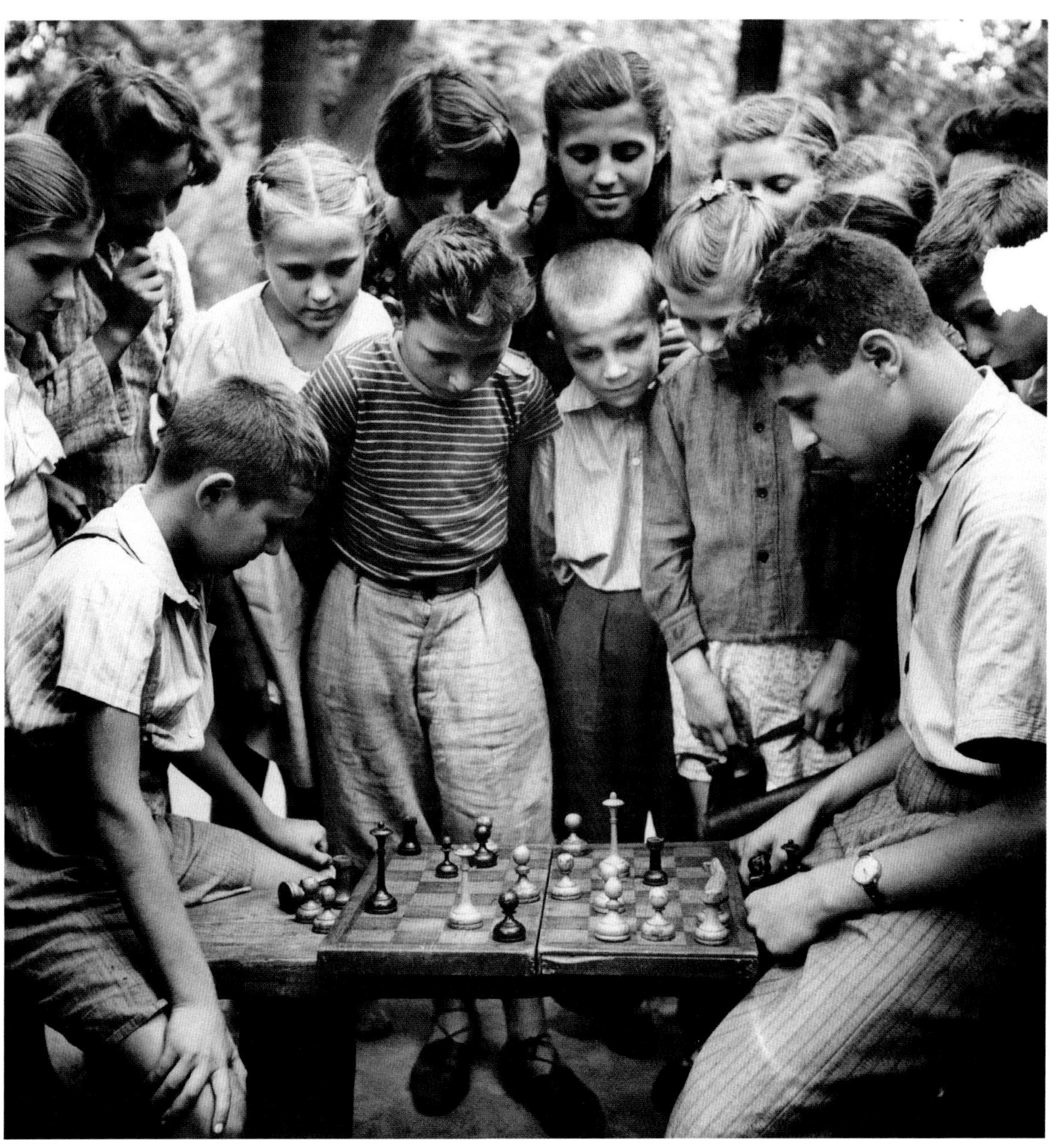

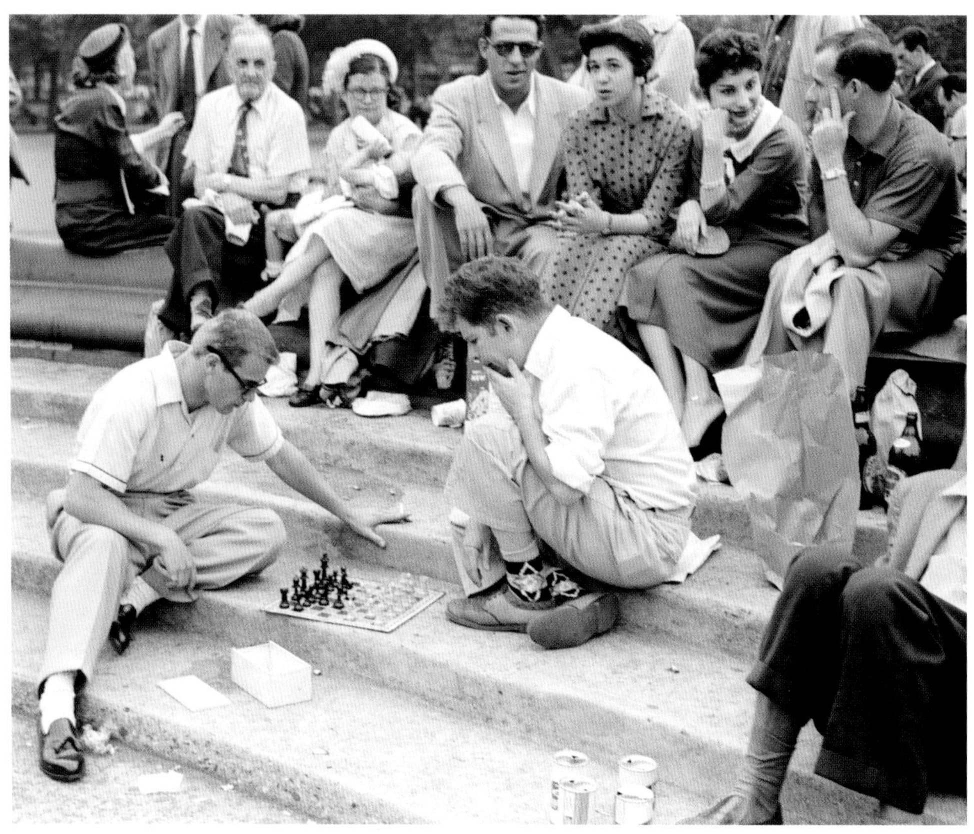

Three snapshots of Washington Square Park, New York. Above: Chess is on the menu for a lunch break, c.1942. Right: Playing during a concert in 1956. Overleaf: A crowd at the tables in 1962.

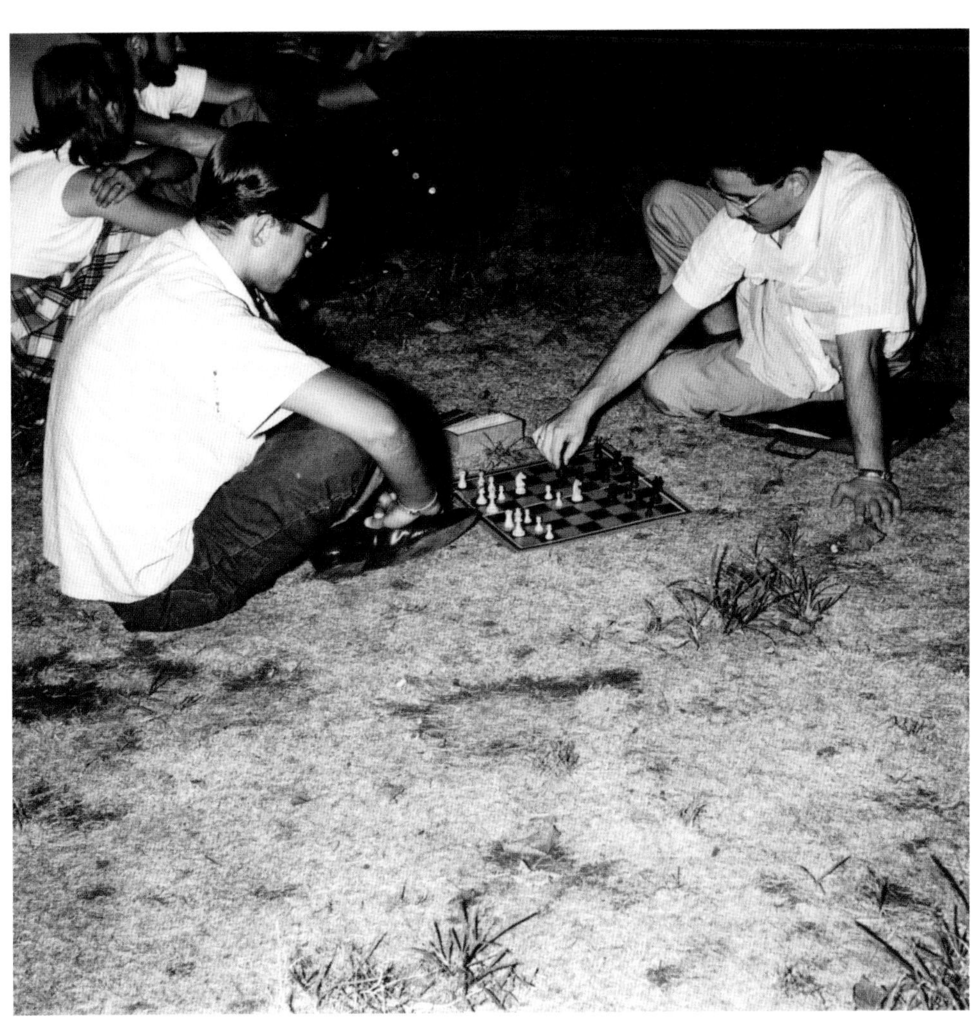

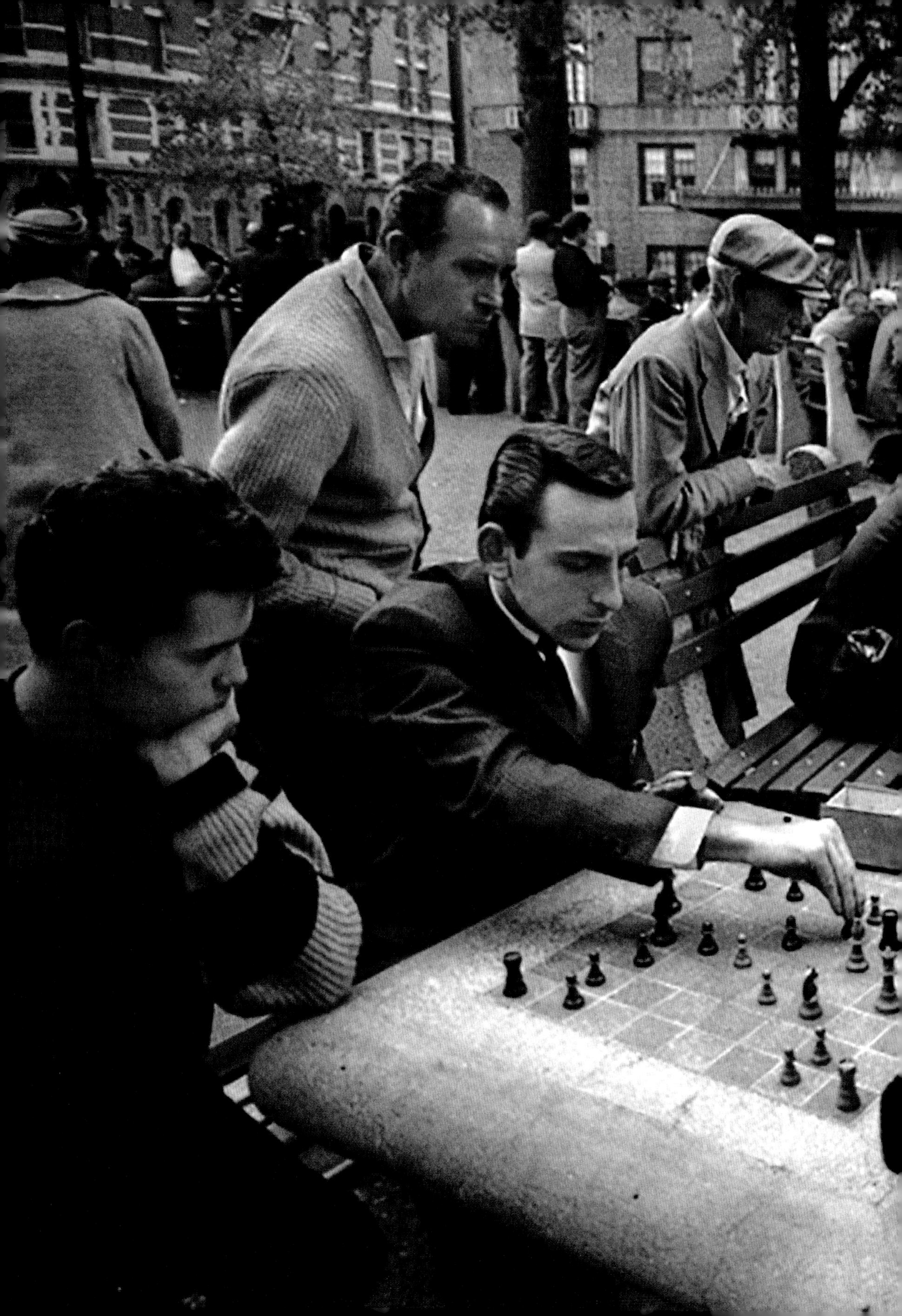

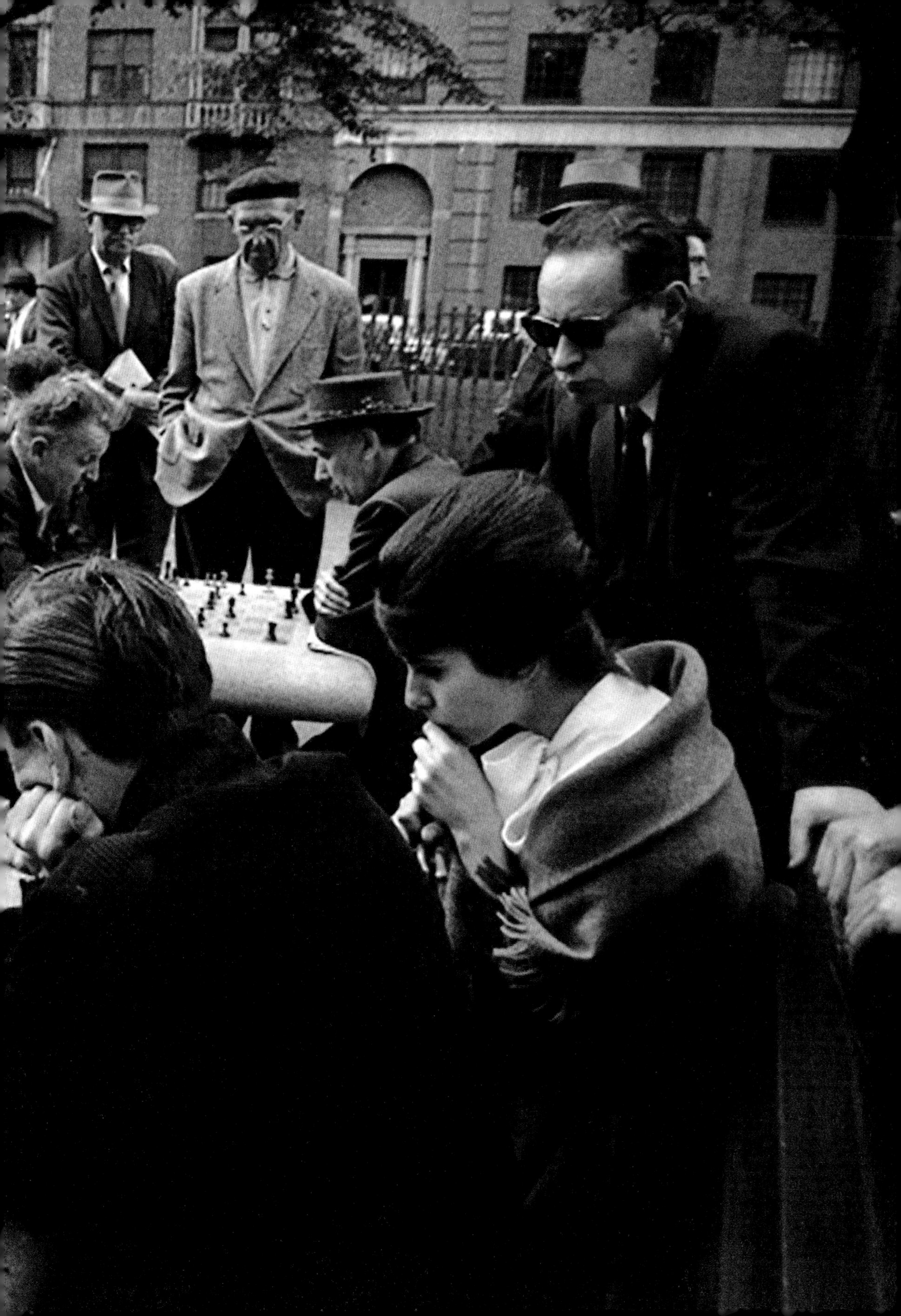

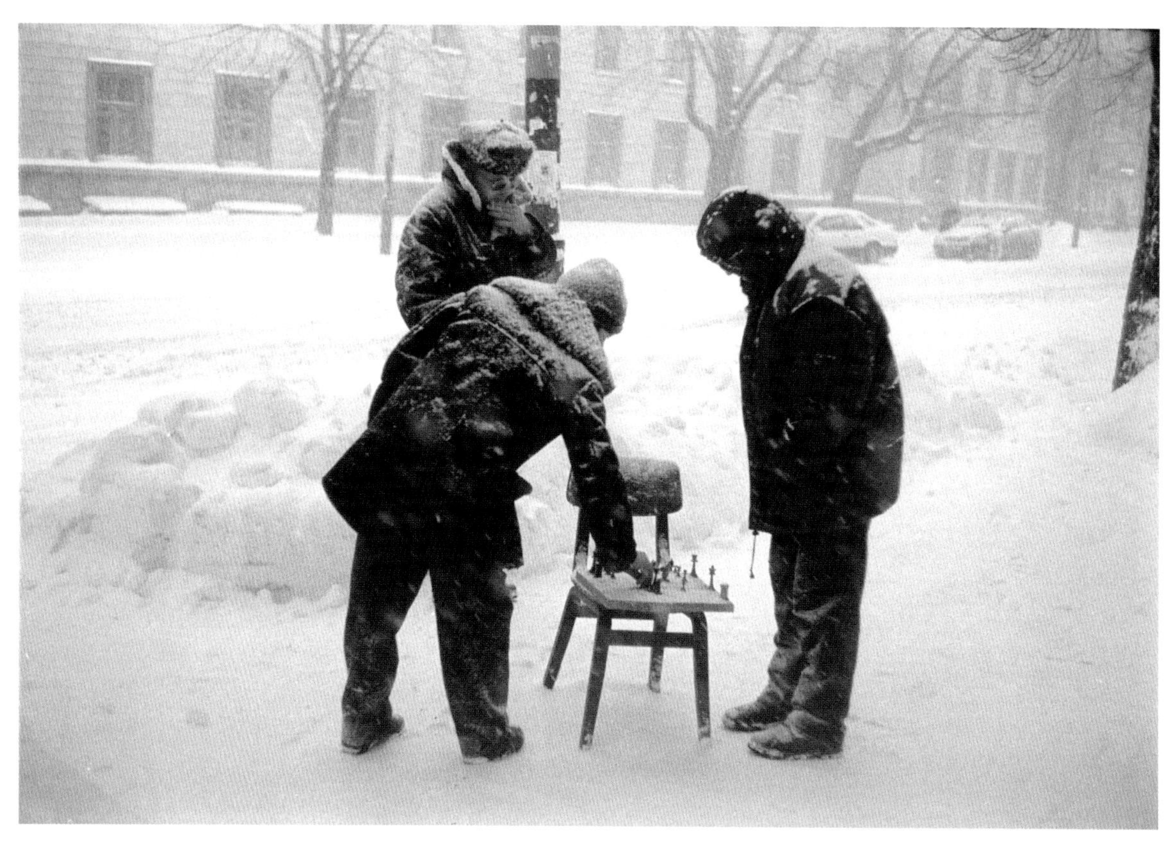

What's a little snow? The games
must go on! Above: An undated
photo from Odessa, Ukraine.
Right: Moscow, c.1950s.

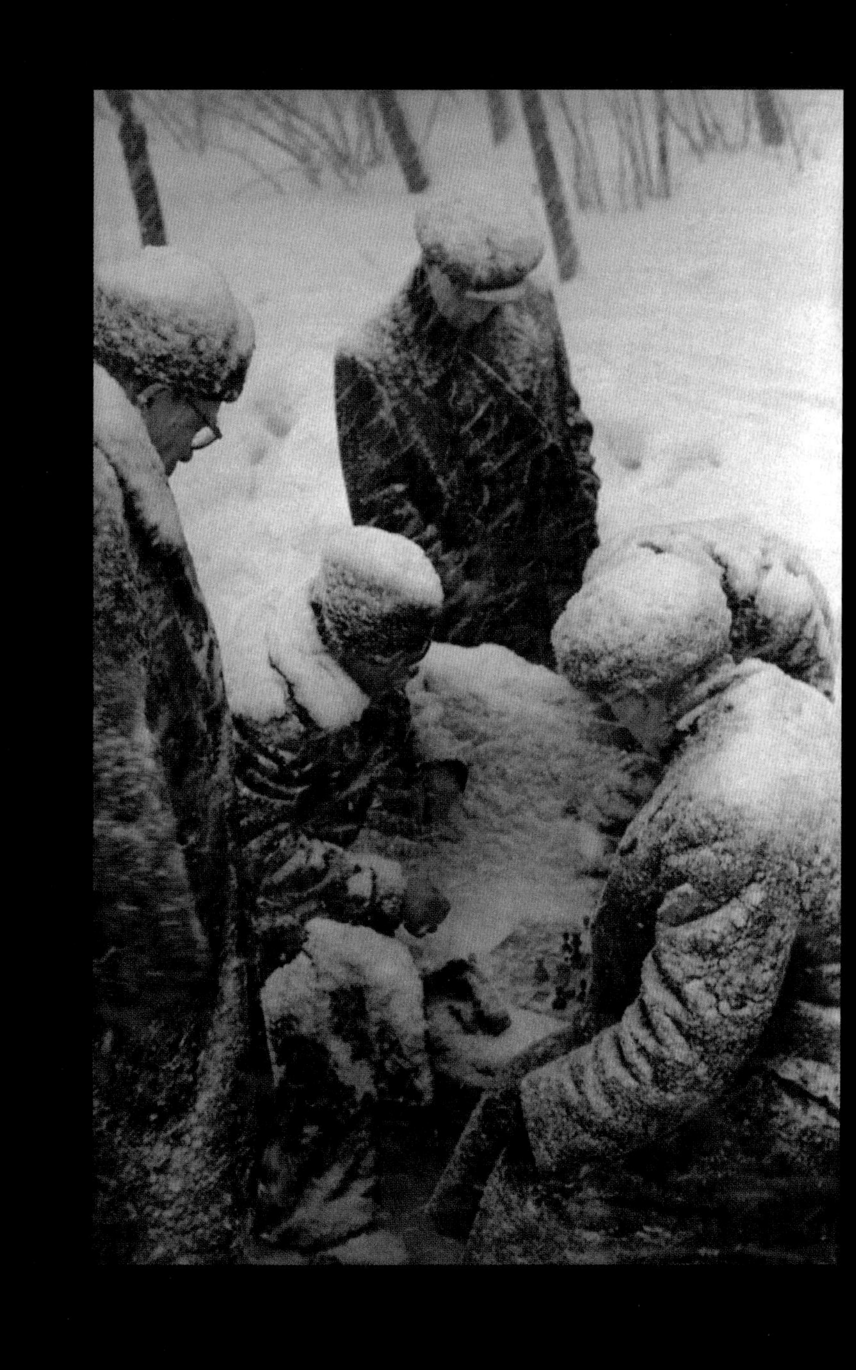

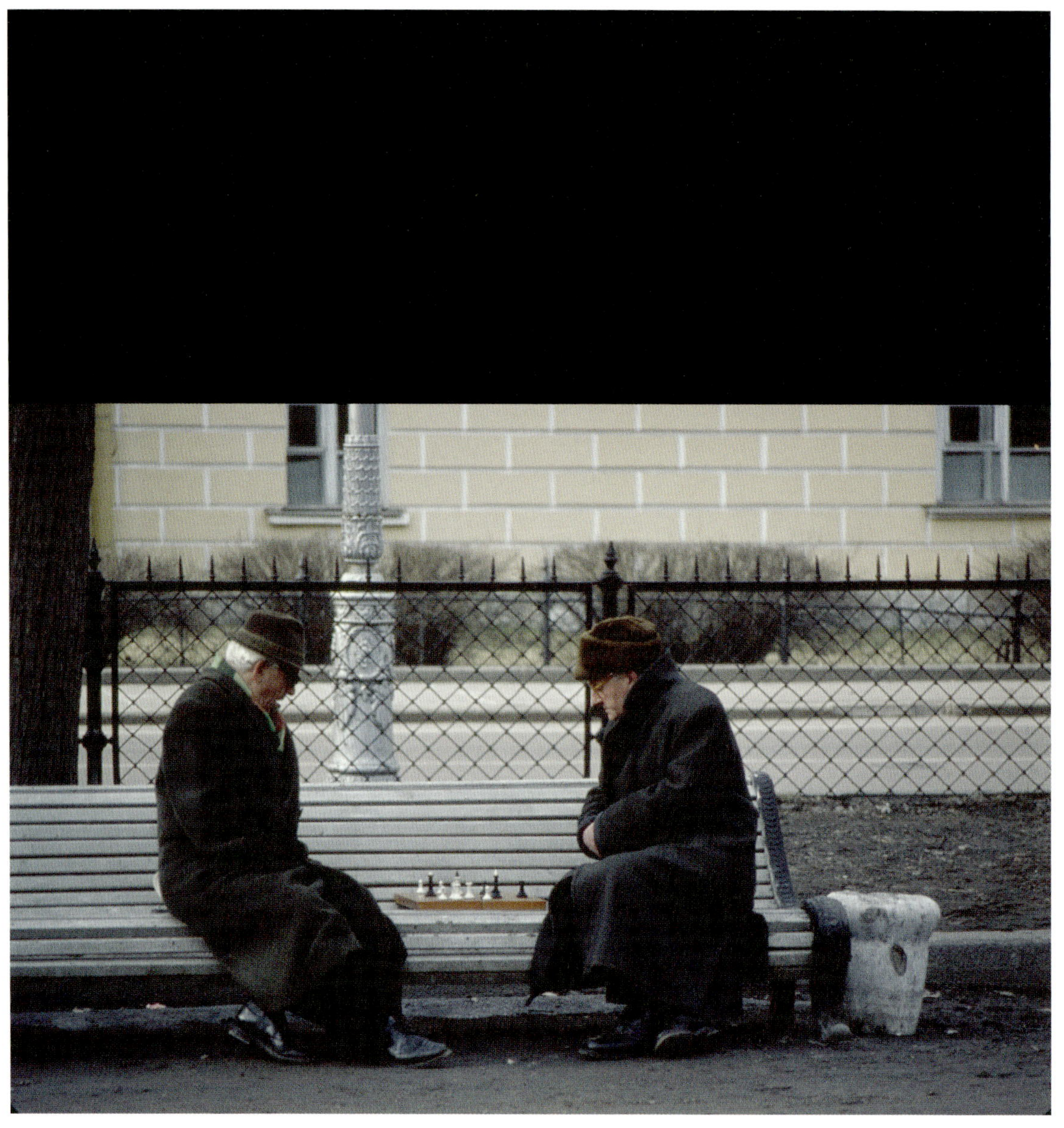

It's cold outside, but not too cold for chess.
Leningrad (now St Petersburg), 1958.

Right: Central Park, New York, 1948.

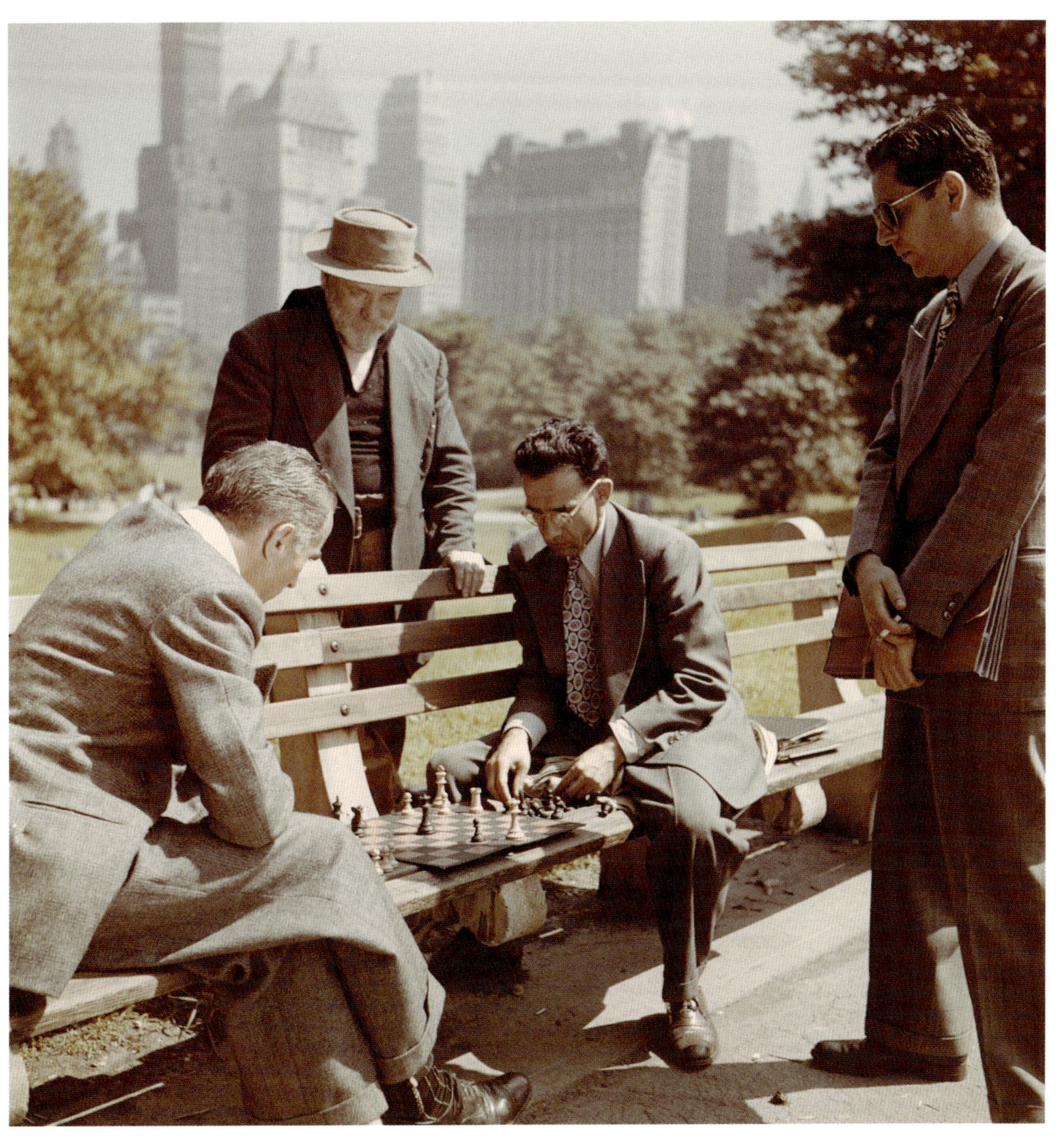

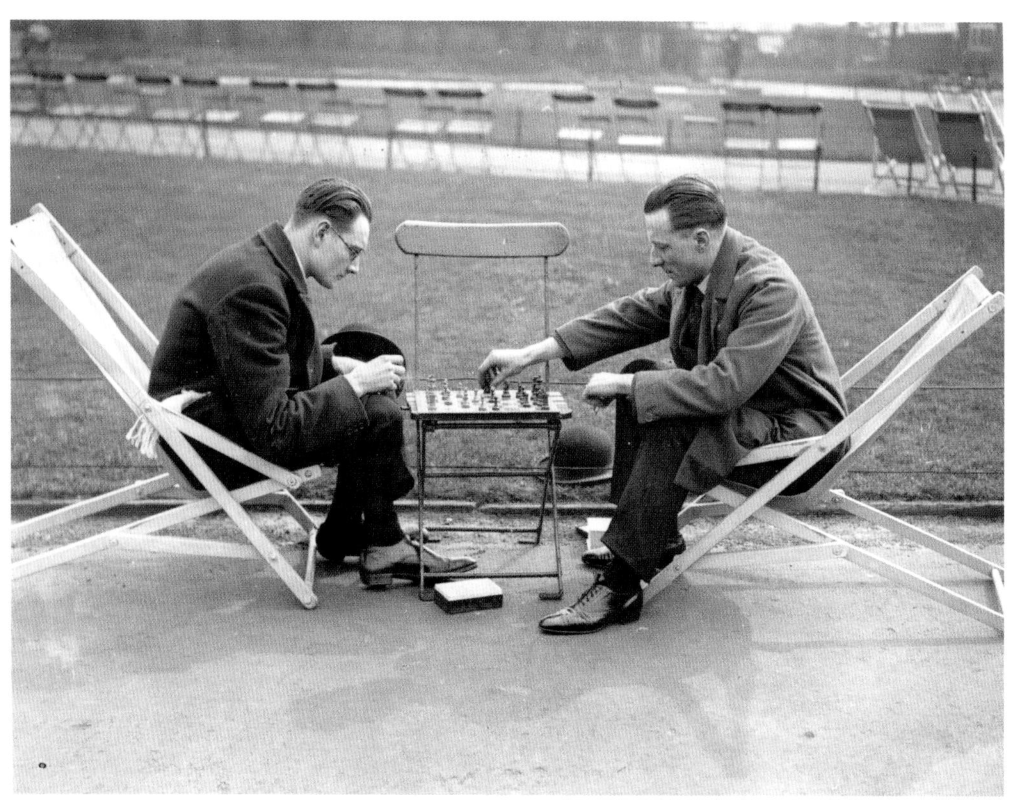

Playing chess in a central London
park, c.1930.

Right: Two women play chess
during their lunch break. Trafalgar
Square, London, 1936.

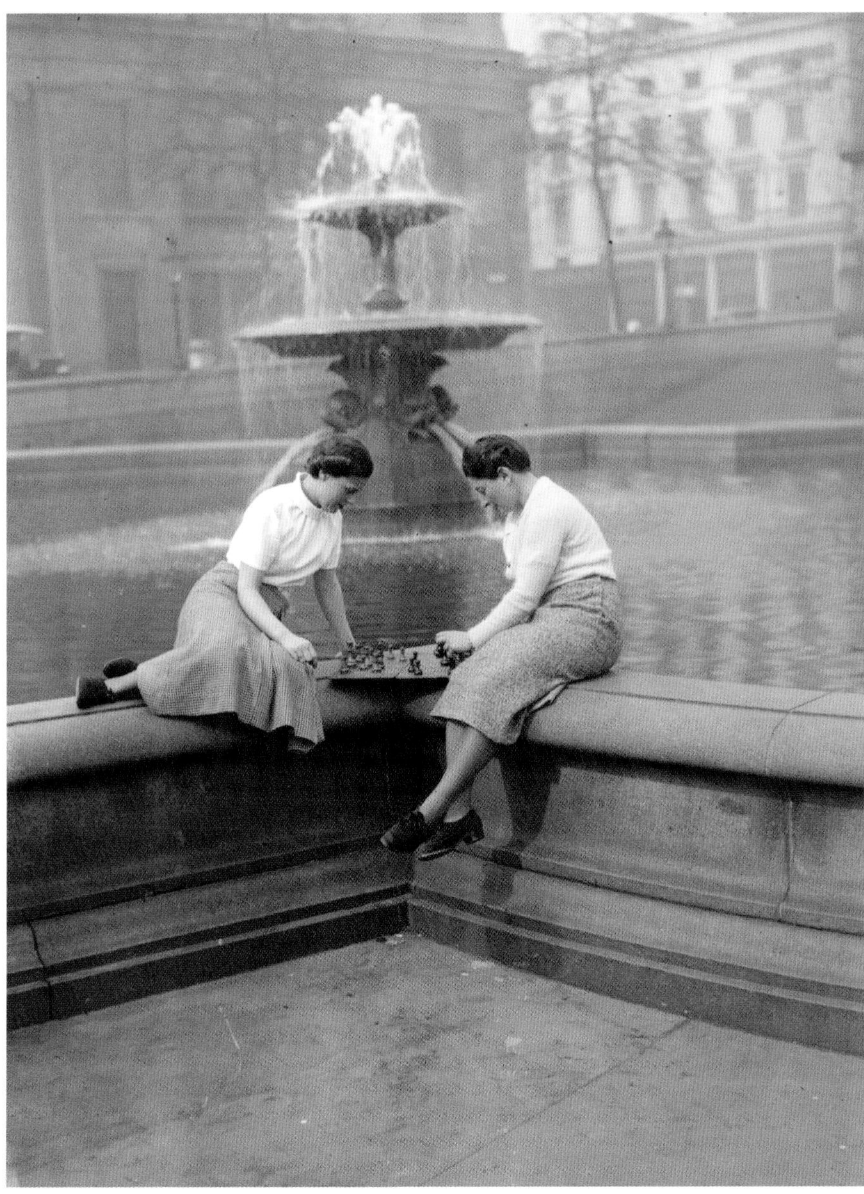

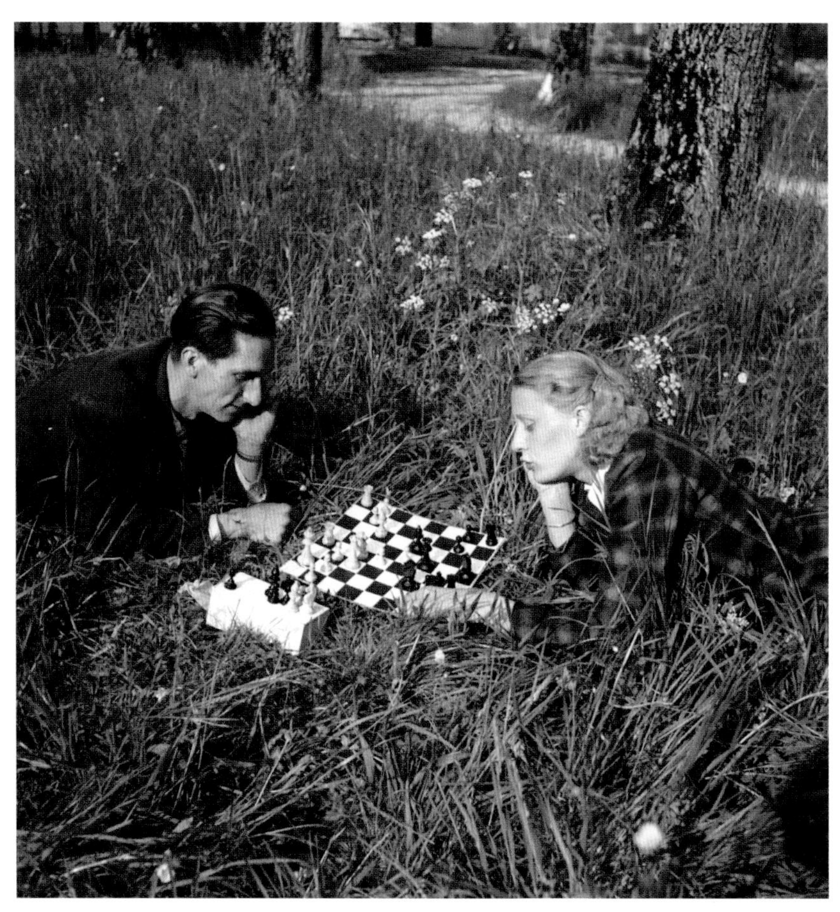

Unknown, France.

Right: Monique Lefevre and an
unidentified man, in Central
Park, New York, 1958.

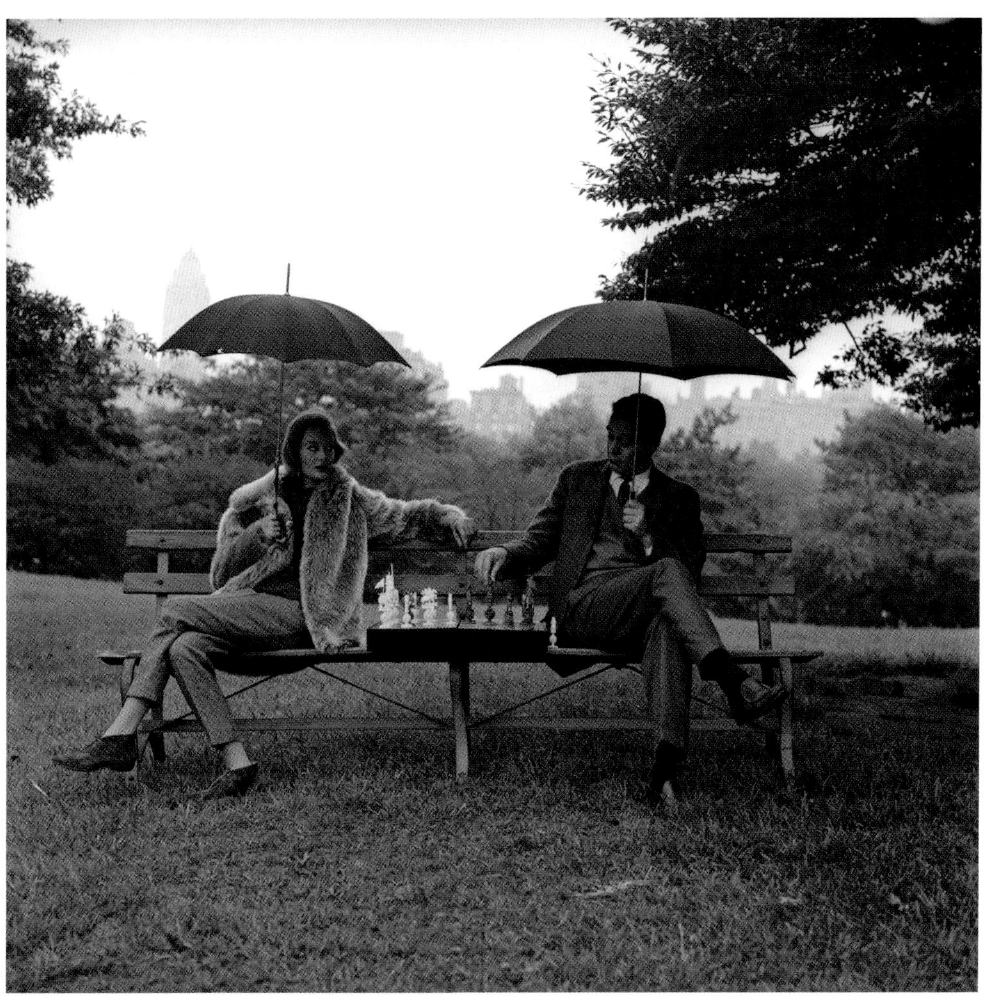

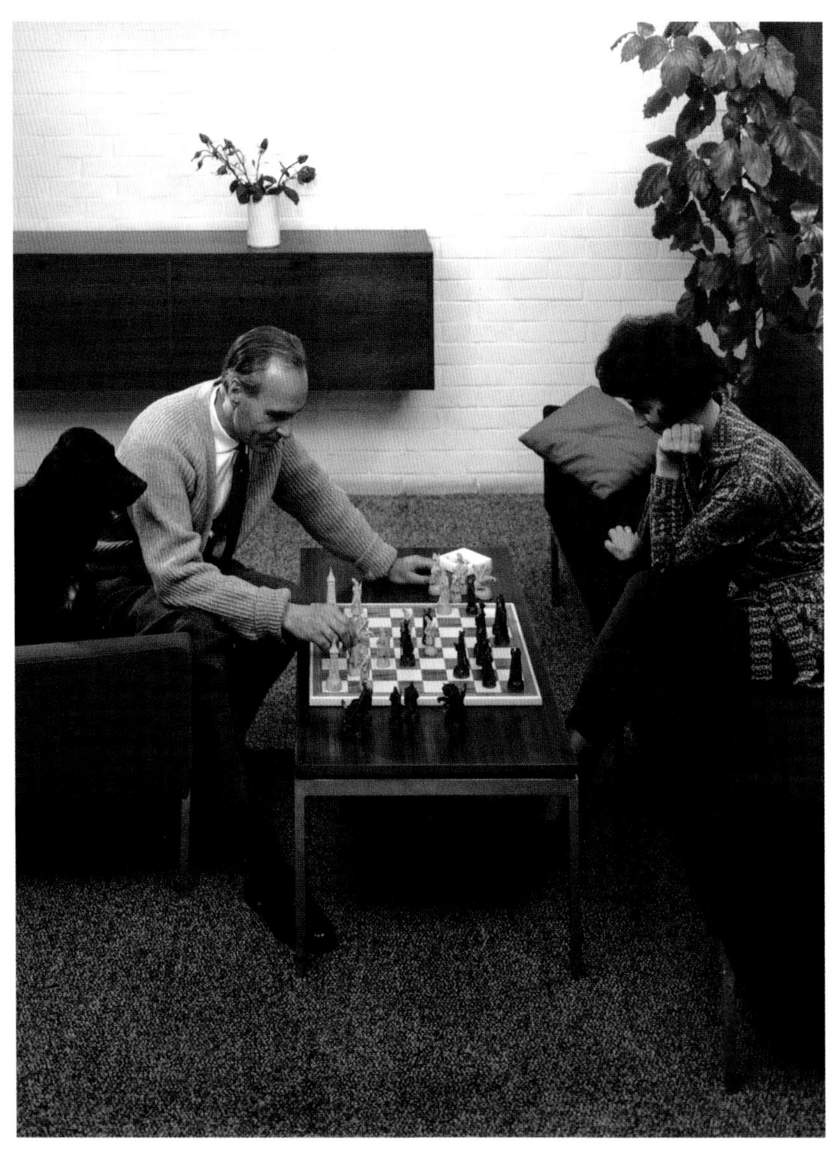

A married couple play chess at home,
Germany, 1958.

Right: Playing chess in the park, location
unknown, 1960s.

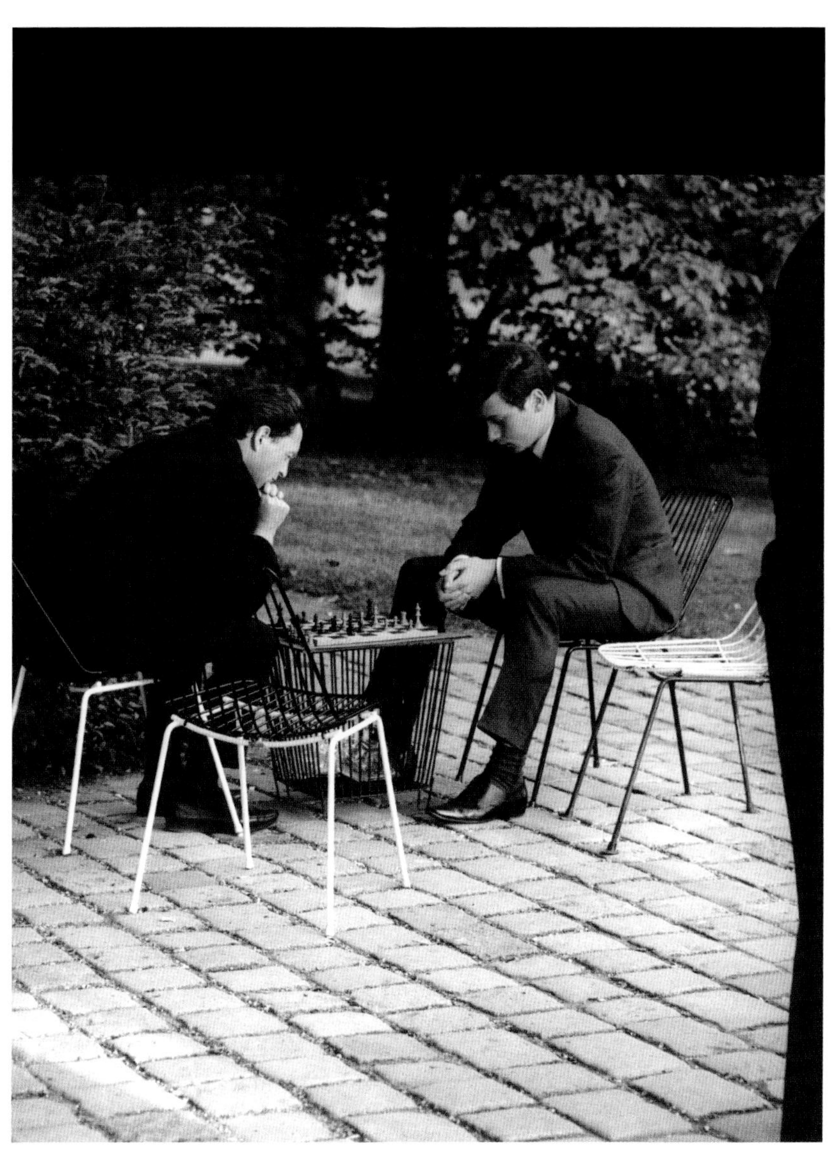

There are many variants of chess and quite a few
of them are in three dimensions. One of the best
known is Total Chess, invented by Charles Beatty,
shown here playing the game with his wife, Joan,
in Montgomeryshire, Wales, in 1946. Total Chess
is played on a 8x8x4 board (i.e. a typical chess
board, but with three more 8x8 boards in the
third dimension). The game has the same number
of pieces as in regular chess, with many of the
same rules, except that the movement of pieces
is 'extruded' vertically. One oddity is that pawns
'cast shadows' that no piece can cross through,
except for knights, which can jump through them
as in ordinary chess. Like regular chess, games
end when a king is checkmated.

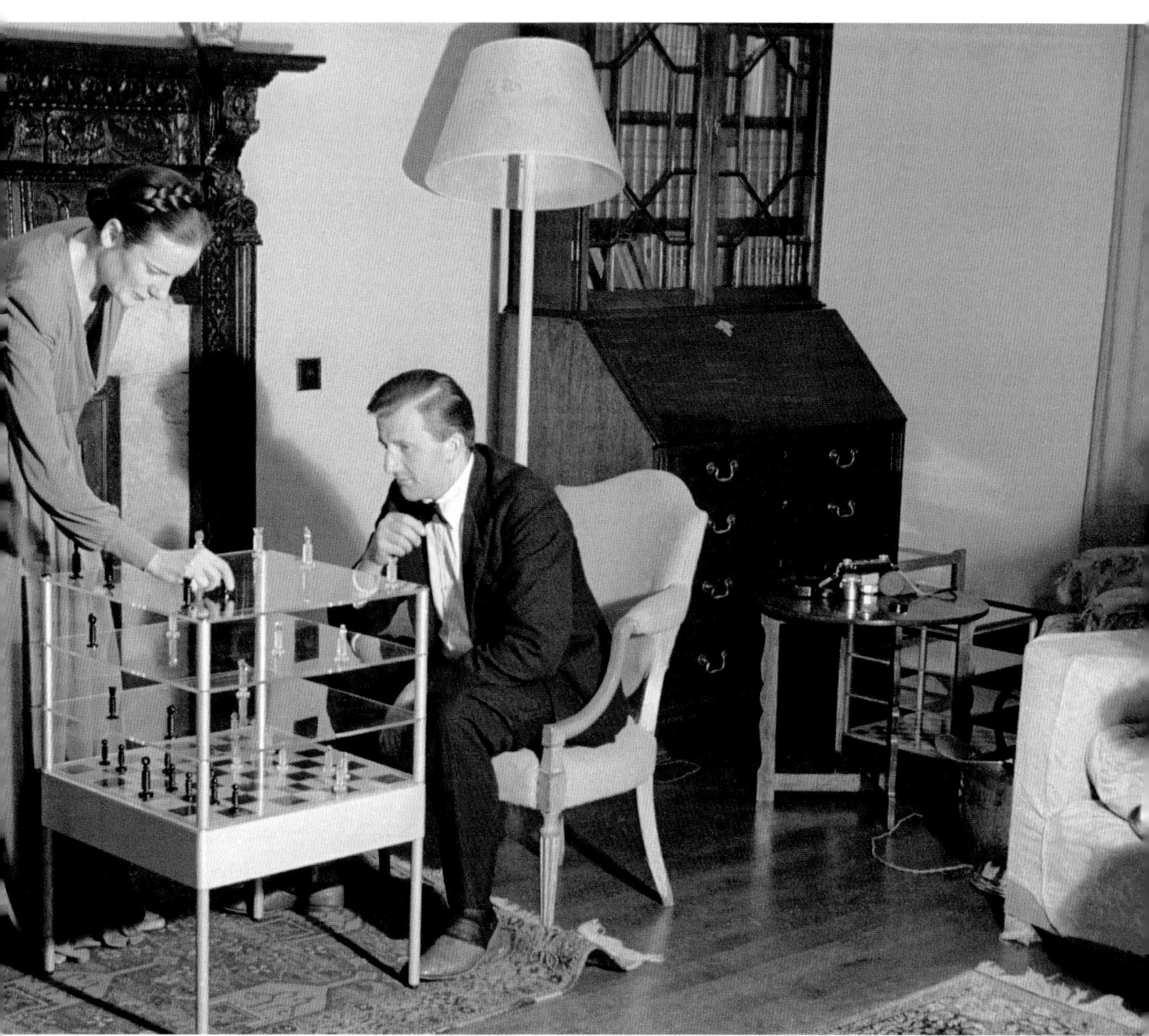

Since the dawn of the computer age in the 1940s, the ability to play chess was seen as a measure of a computer's ability to approximate artificial intelligence. Early machines tried to replicate how people think, without much success. Then engineers began to design chess computers that made best use of their strongest capacity: the ability to calculate quickly, also known as brute force. By the 1970s, computers had made real progress. One early pioneer was the IBM 360/195, pictured here, running Master (Minimax Algorithm Tester) during the 1974 World Computer Championship in Stockholm, with programmers Alex Bell, Geoff Lambert (partly hidden), Peter Kent and John Birmingham, alongside chess expert John Waldron.

Chess computers finally conquered humans in 1997 when Deep Blue, designed and built by IBM, beat Garry Kasparov, the world champion, in a six-game match. Today, anyone can buy relatively inexpensive software that plays chess far better than any person. Though playing chess well is no longer a challenge for computers, the game continues to be useful for researchers studying, testing and developing artificial intelligence.

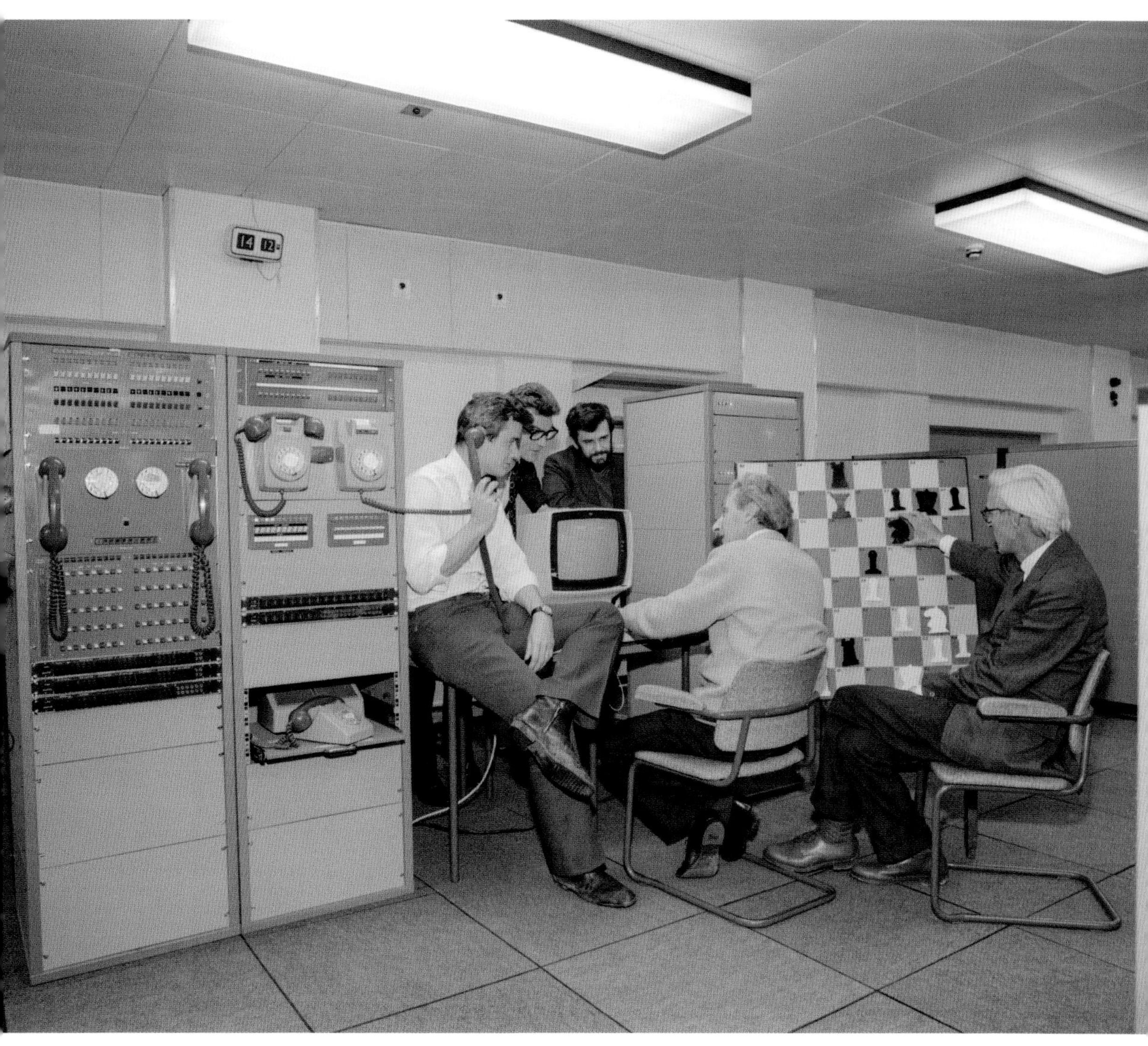

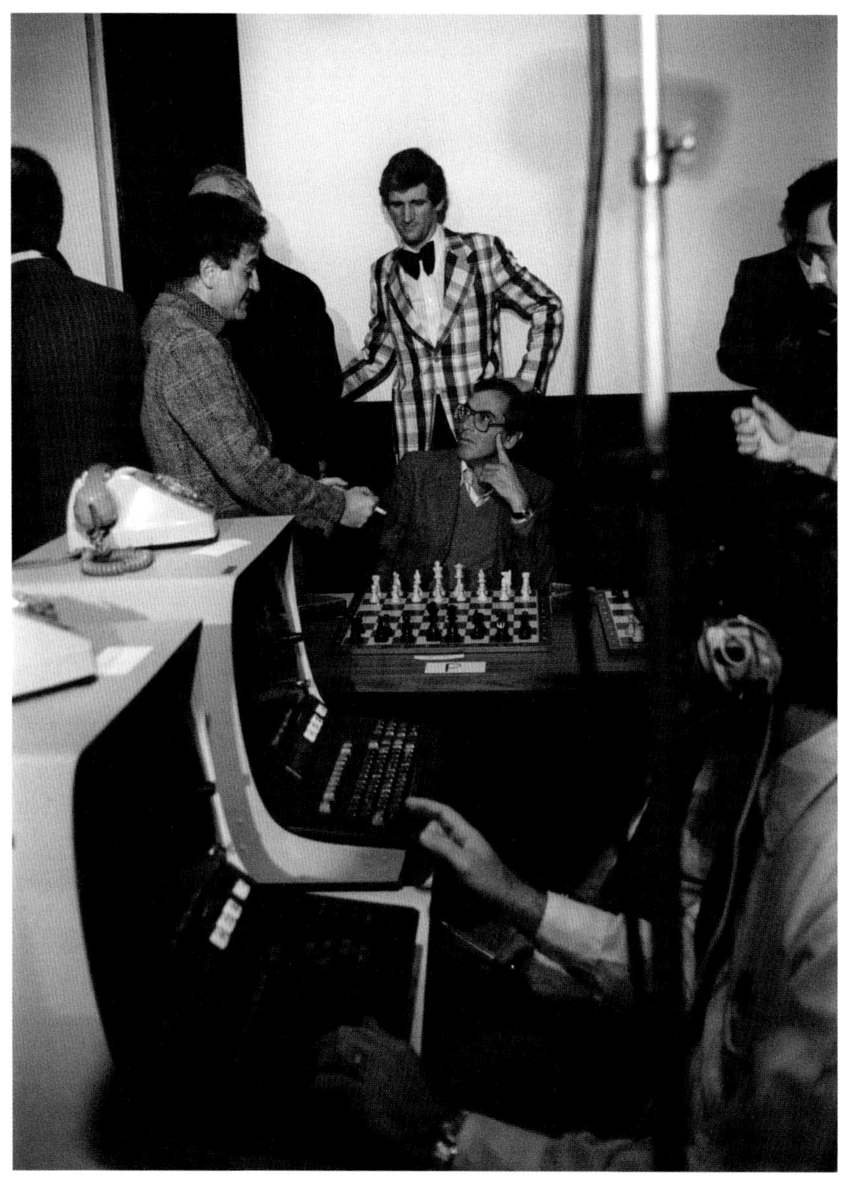

Chess players playing against the computer,
Paris, 1977.

Right: 'Groper' the chess robot, developed
at Lanchester Polytechnic, England, 1979.

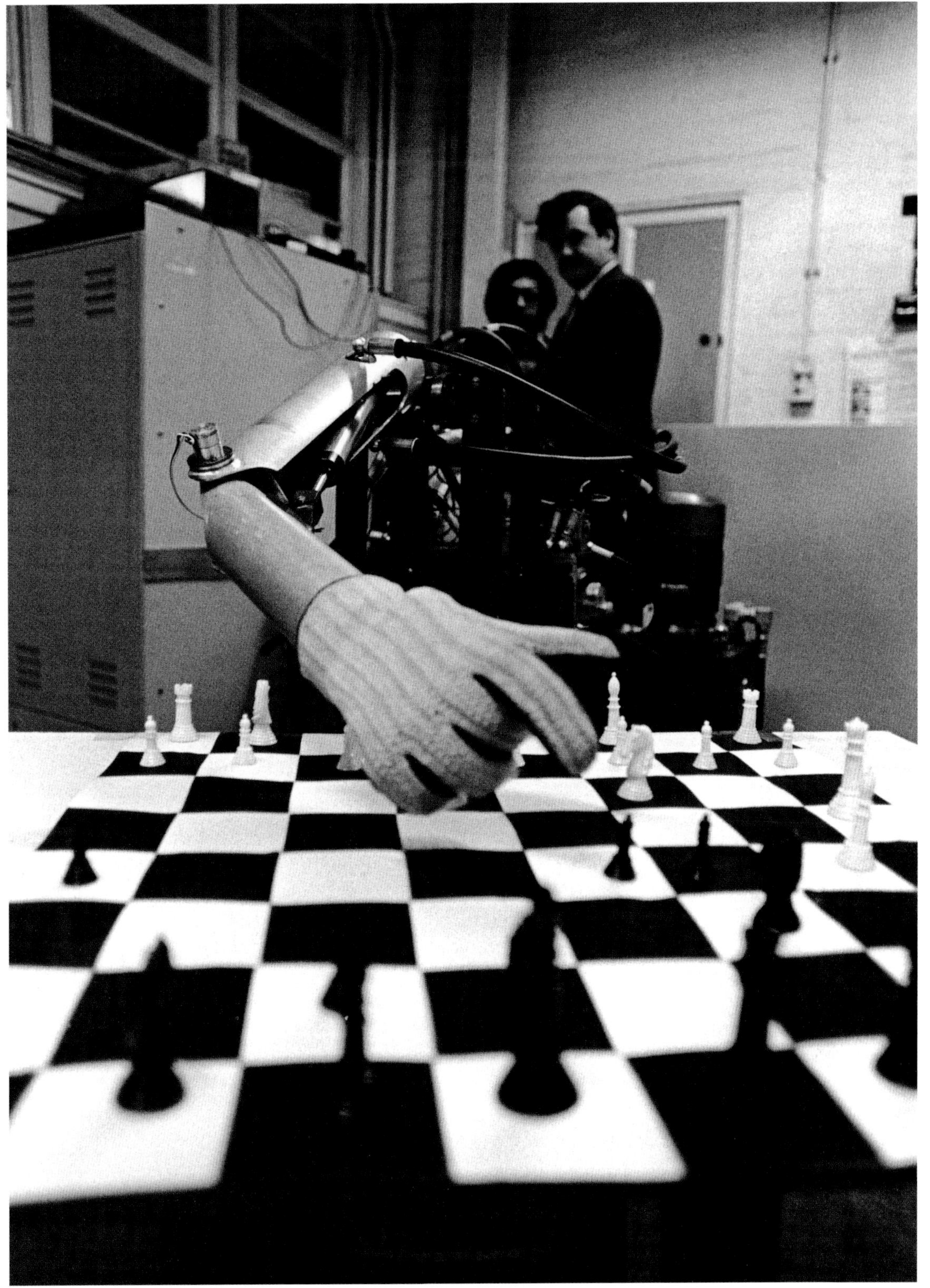

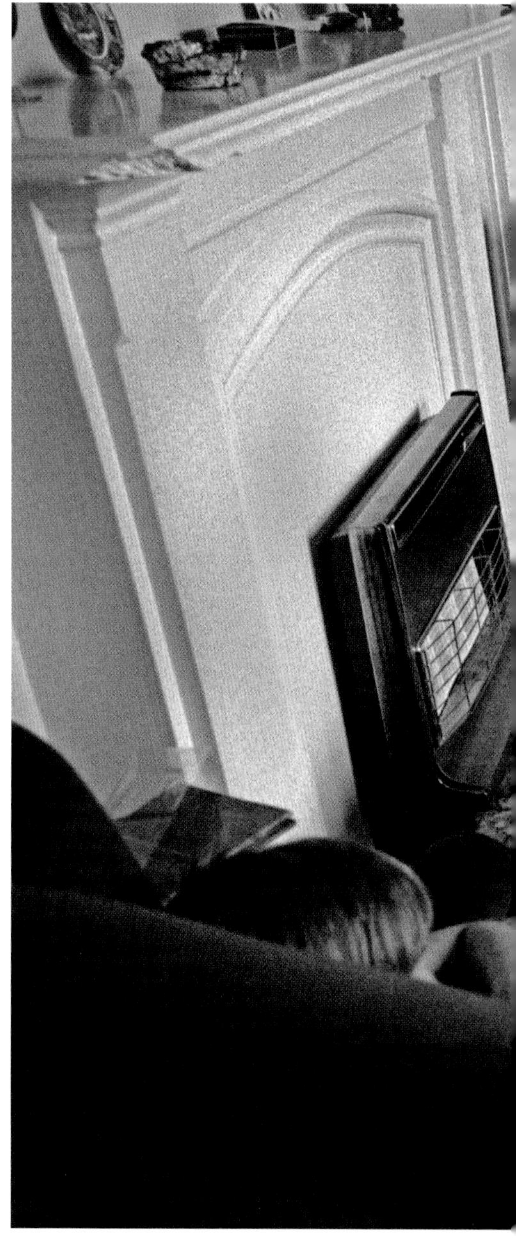

Stephen Hawking, the theoretical physicist, playing chess with his son, Tim, while his daughter, Lucy, reads on the sofa, at their home in Cambridge in 1977. In 2016, Dr Hawking made a video with Paul Rudd, the actor who played the Marvel character Ant Man, promoting quantum chess, a variant in which the pieces, adhering to the rules of quantum mechanics, are on at least two possible squares, making it extremely difficult to checkmate the king.

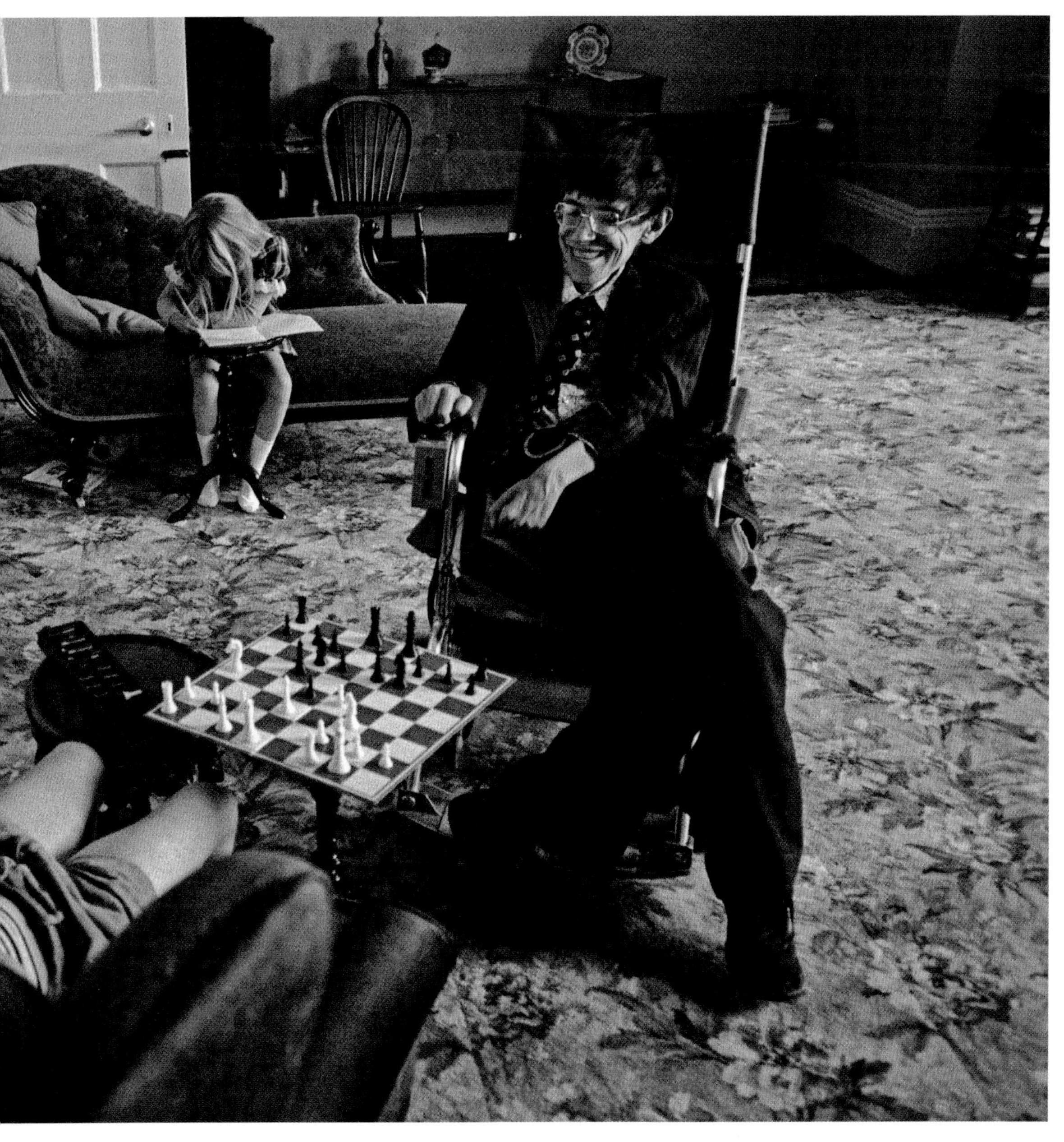

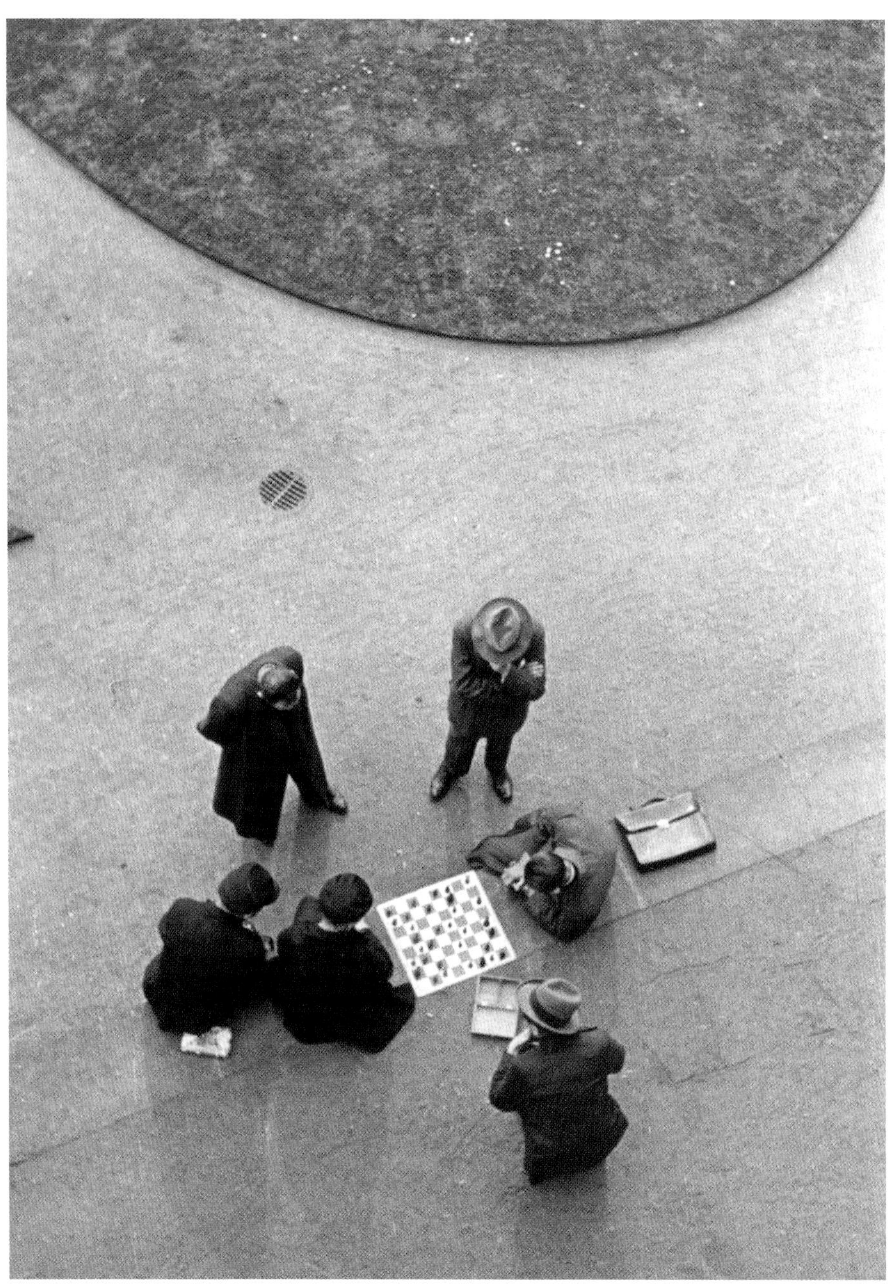

Above: People playing chess in Zwinger Garde, Dresden, Germany, c.1930.

Overleaf: Serebryany Bor, or Silver Forest, a large resort park in northwest Moscow, 1954.

Right: Gorky Park, Moscow, 1931. Gorky Park, named after Maxim Gorky, the writer and socialist, was a centre of chess activity before World War II. Among the players who got their start there were Vasily Smyslov, the world champion from 1957–58, and Yuri Averbakh, a world championship contender.

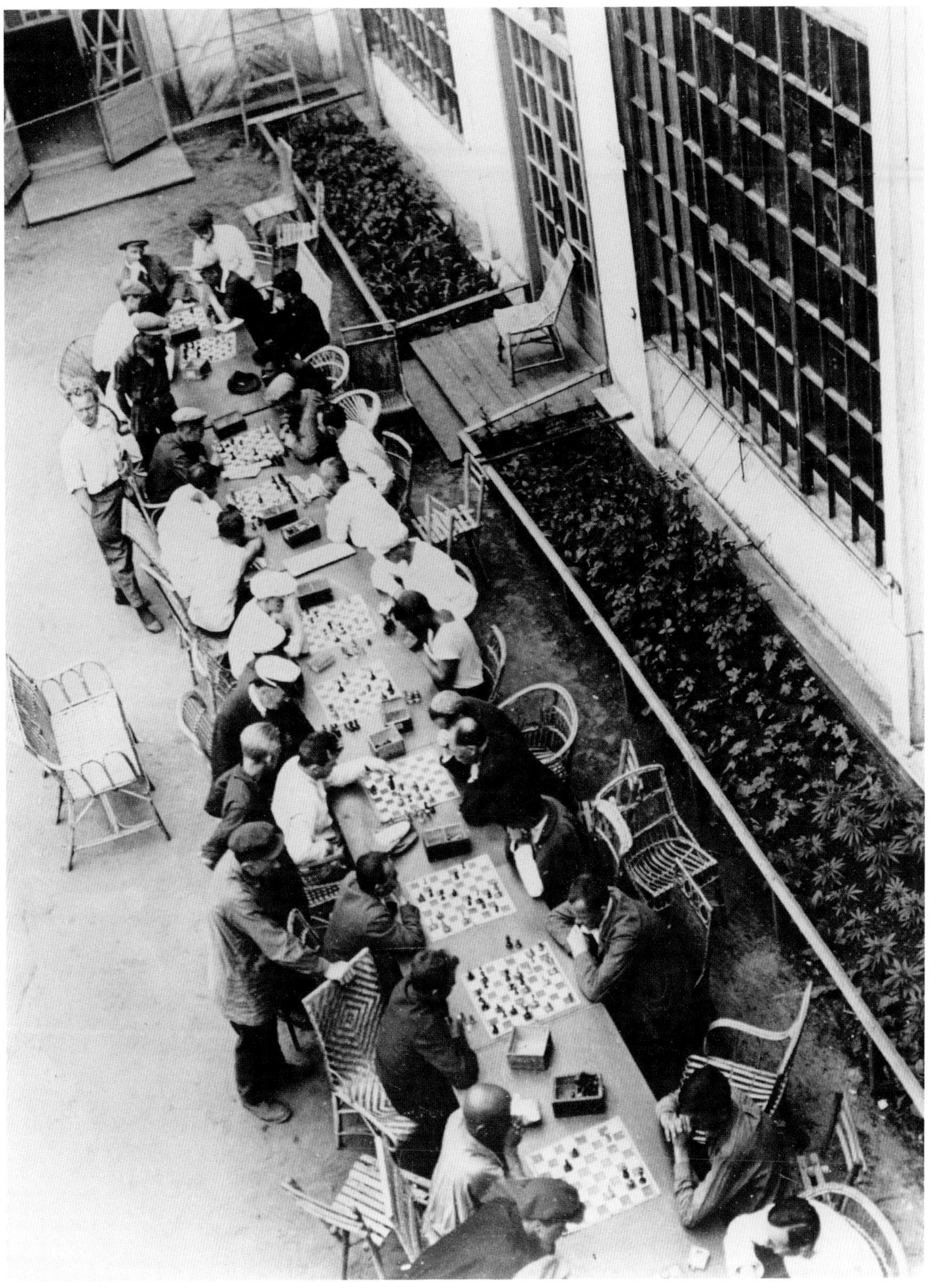

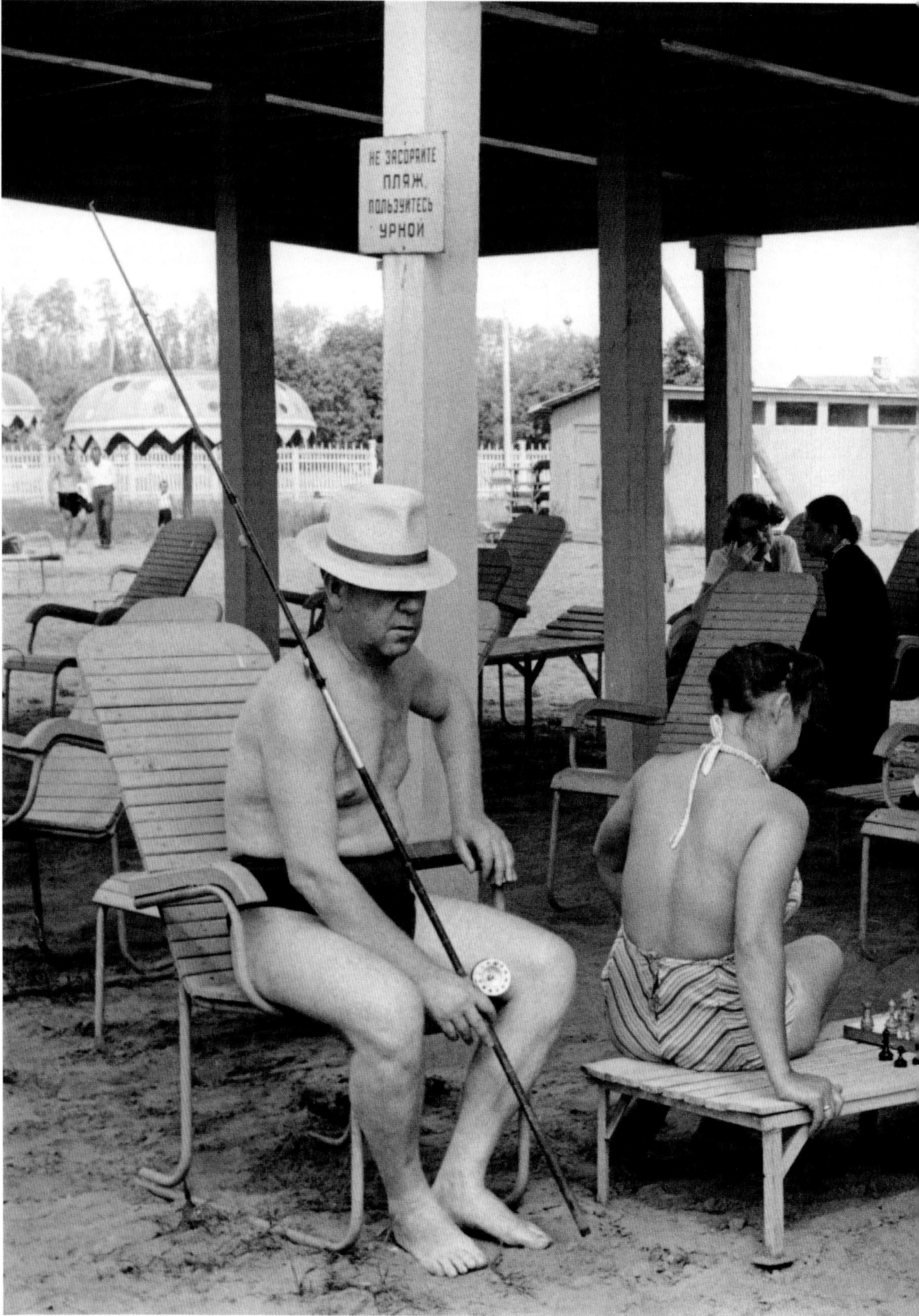

НЕ ЗАСОРЯЙТЕ
ПЛЯЖ,
ПОЛЬЗУЙТЕСЬ
УРНОЙ

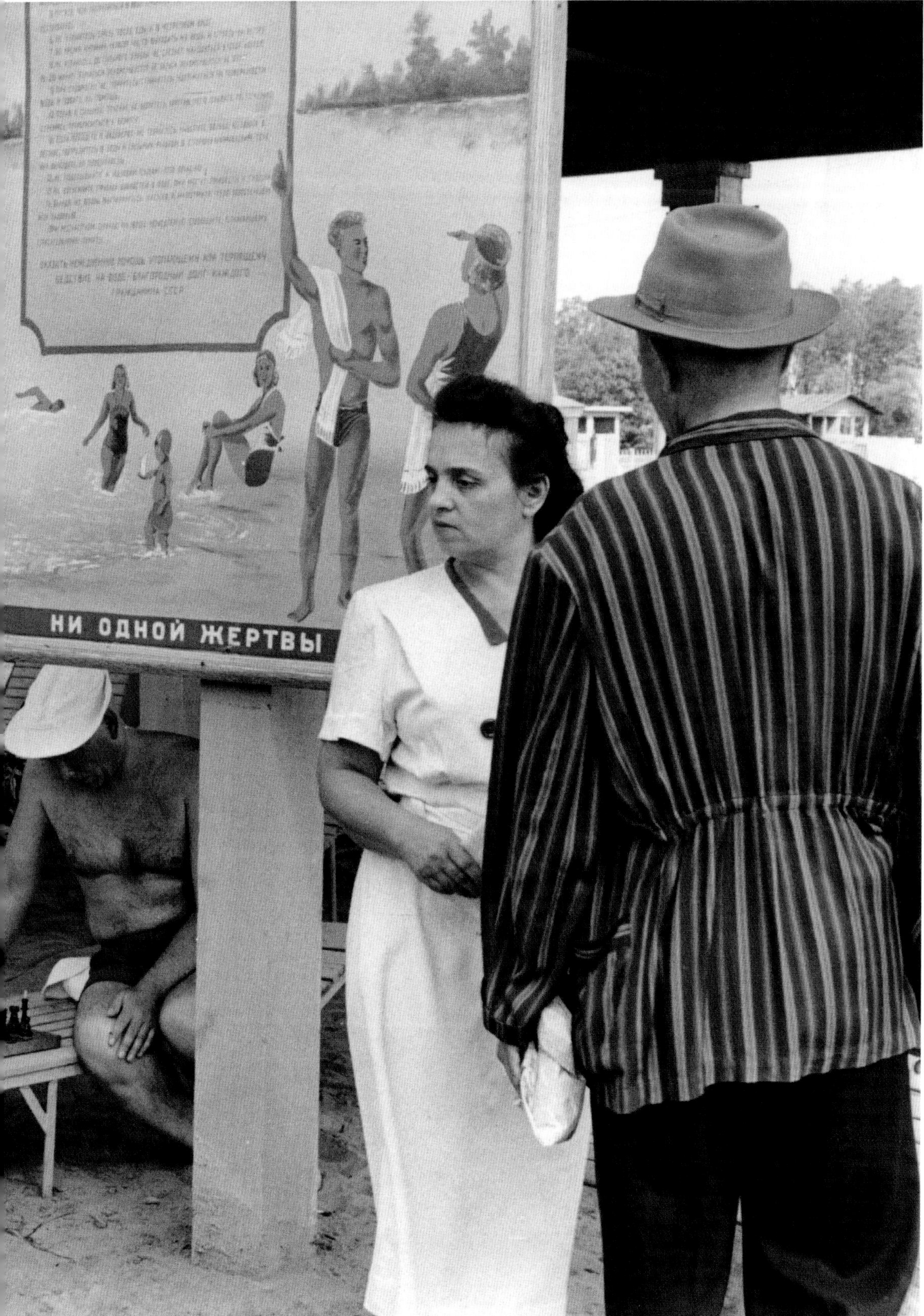
НИ ОДНОЙ ЖЕРТВЫ

No one knows exactly when people started setting up chess tables and playing in the streets of New York. The practice certainly dates back to the 1960s. Right: Tables on 7th Avenue, 1990.

Overleaf: Playing chess on the beach, Los Angeles, 1964.

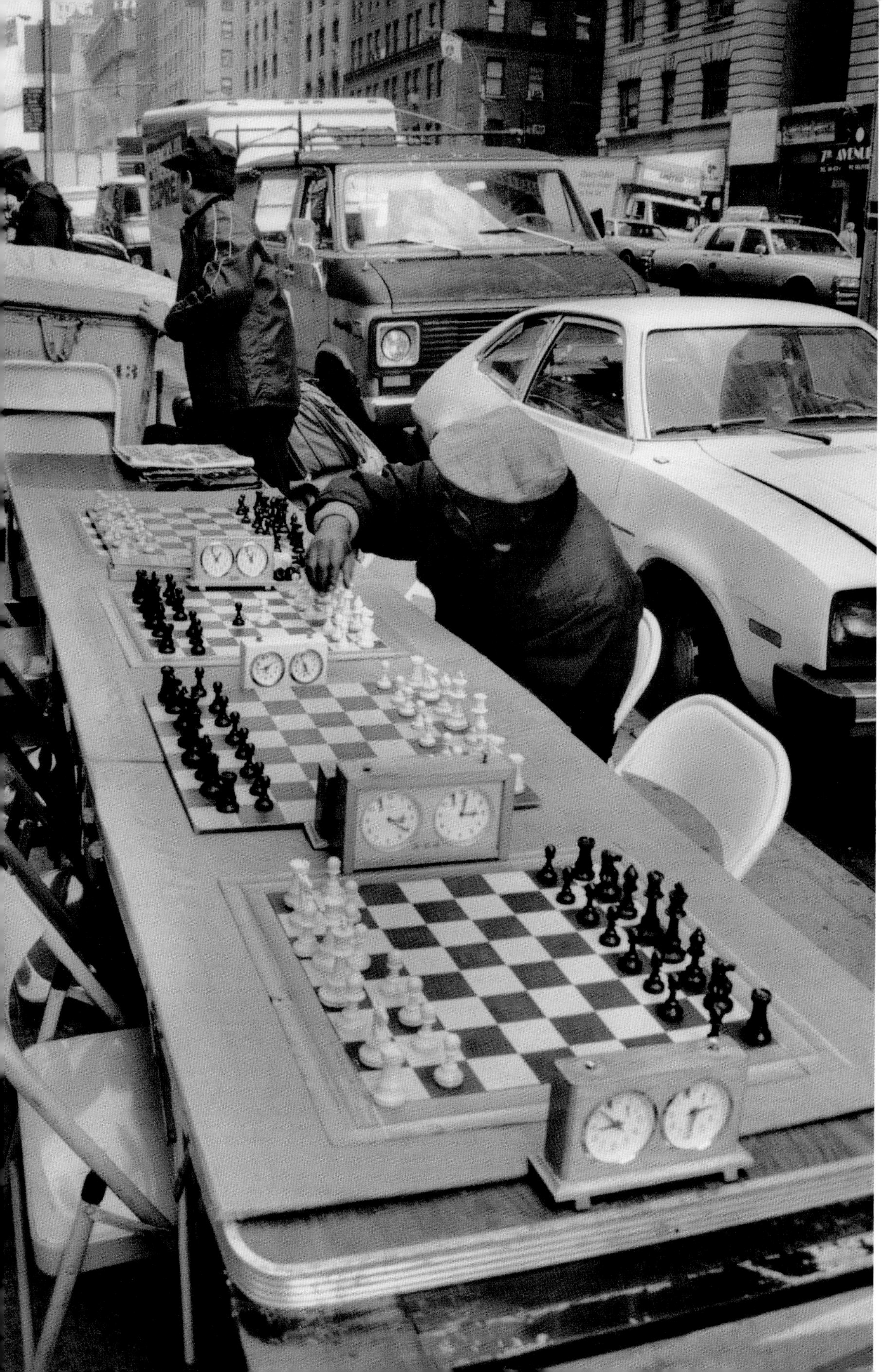

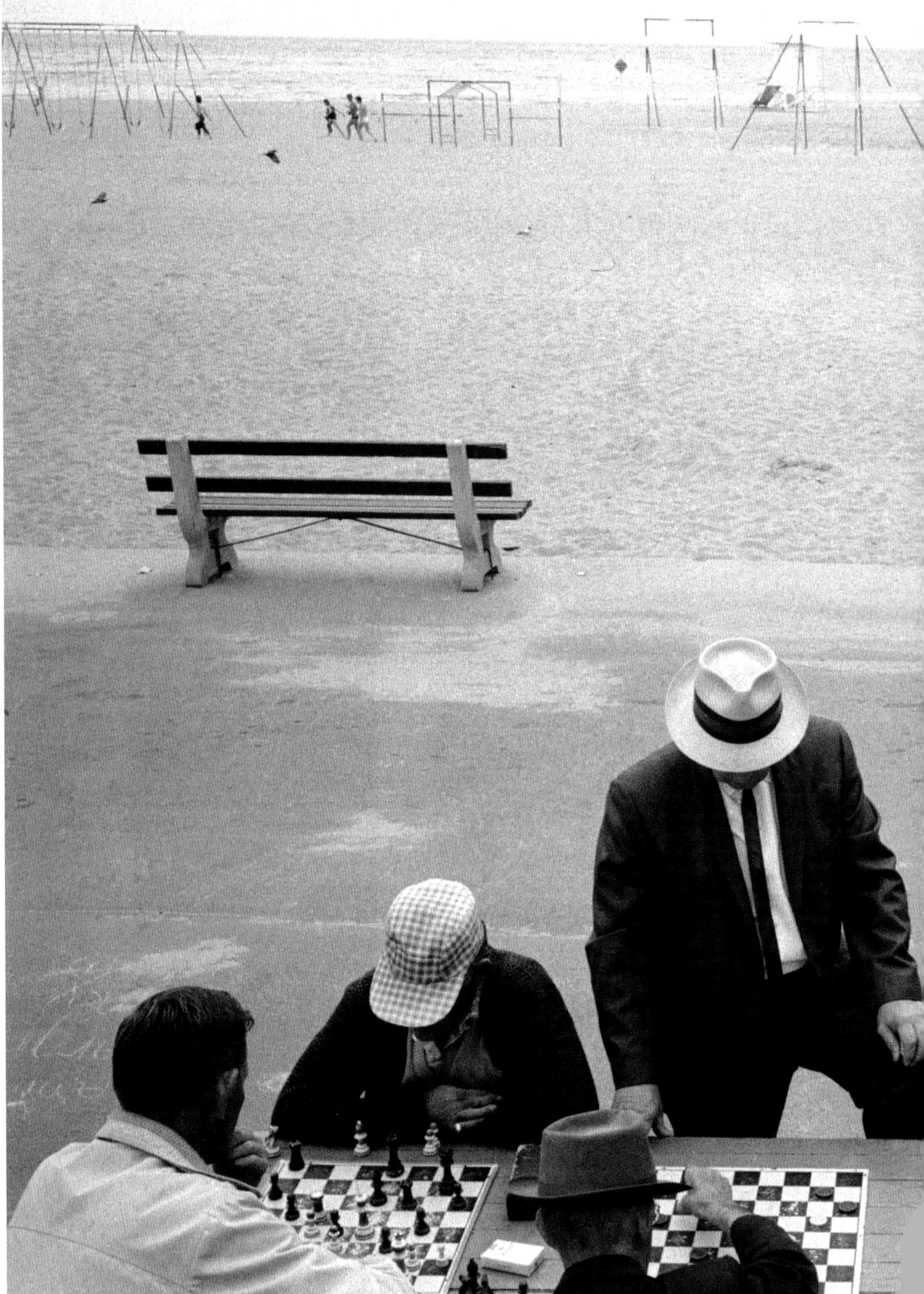

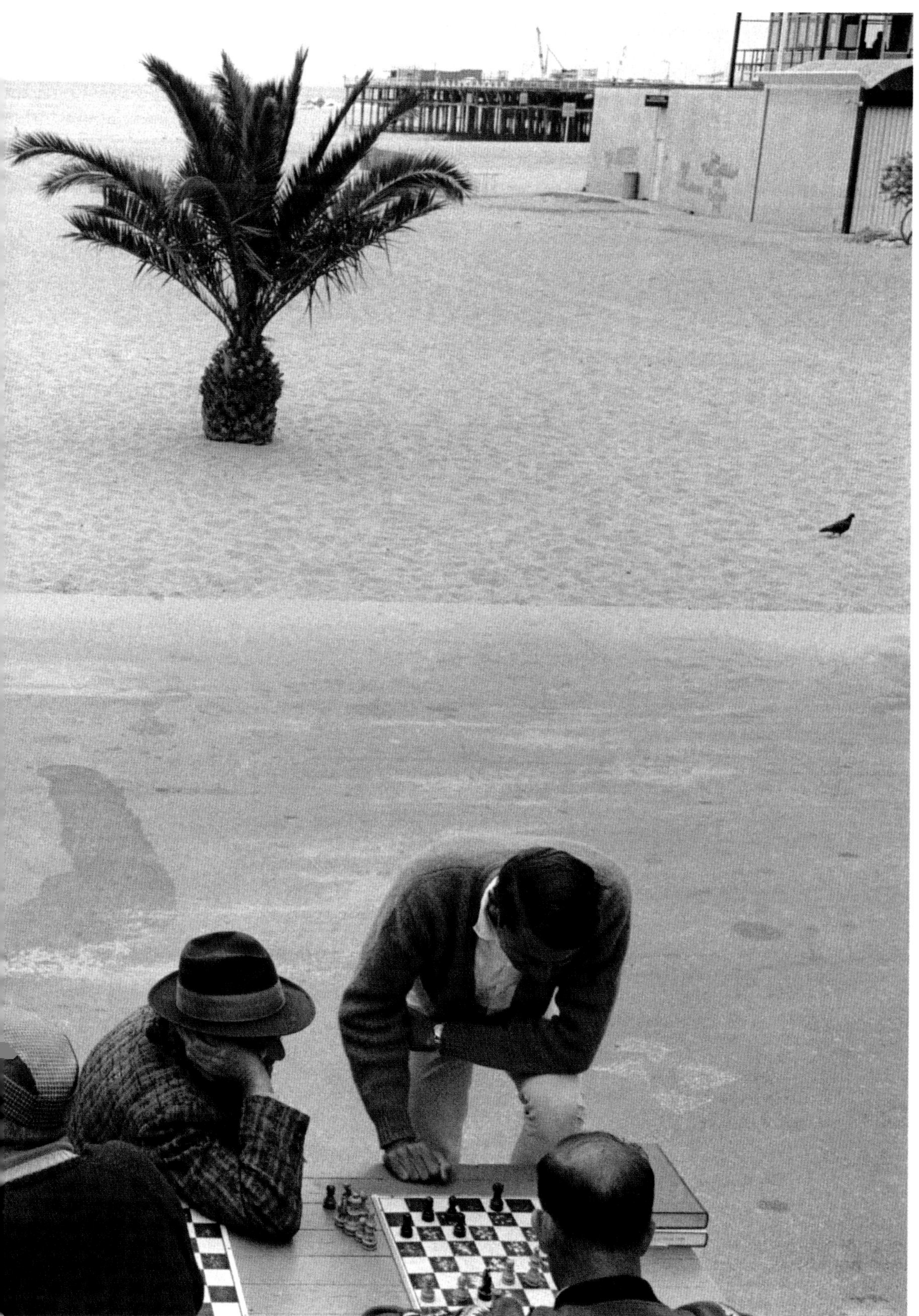

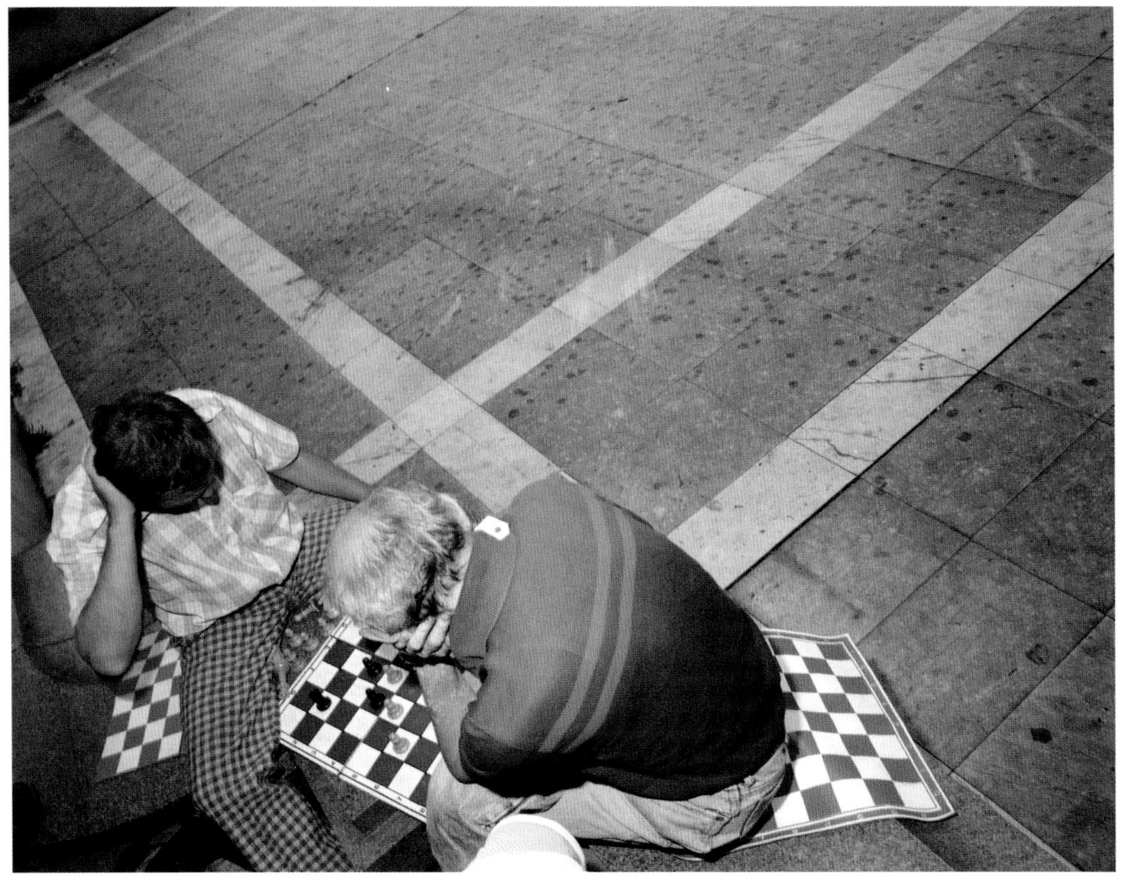

Above: Chess on the streets of Sofia, Bulgaria, date unknown.

Opposite: This photograph and those on the following pages show how chess can be played almost anywhere, including at the beach or in a sauna. It is particularly popular in the Szechenyi outdoor thermal baths of Budapest, Hungary, where there is a strong chess tradition.

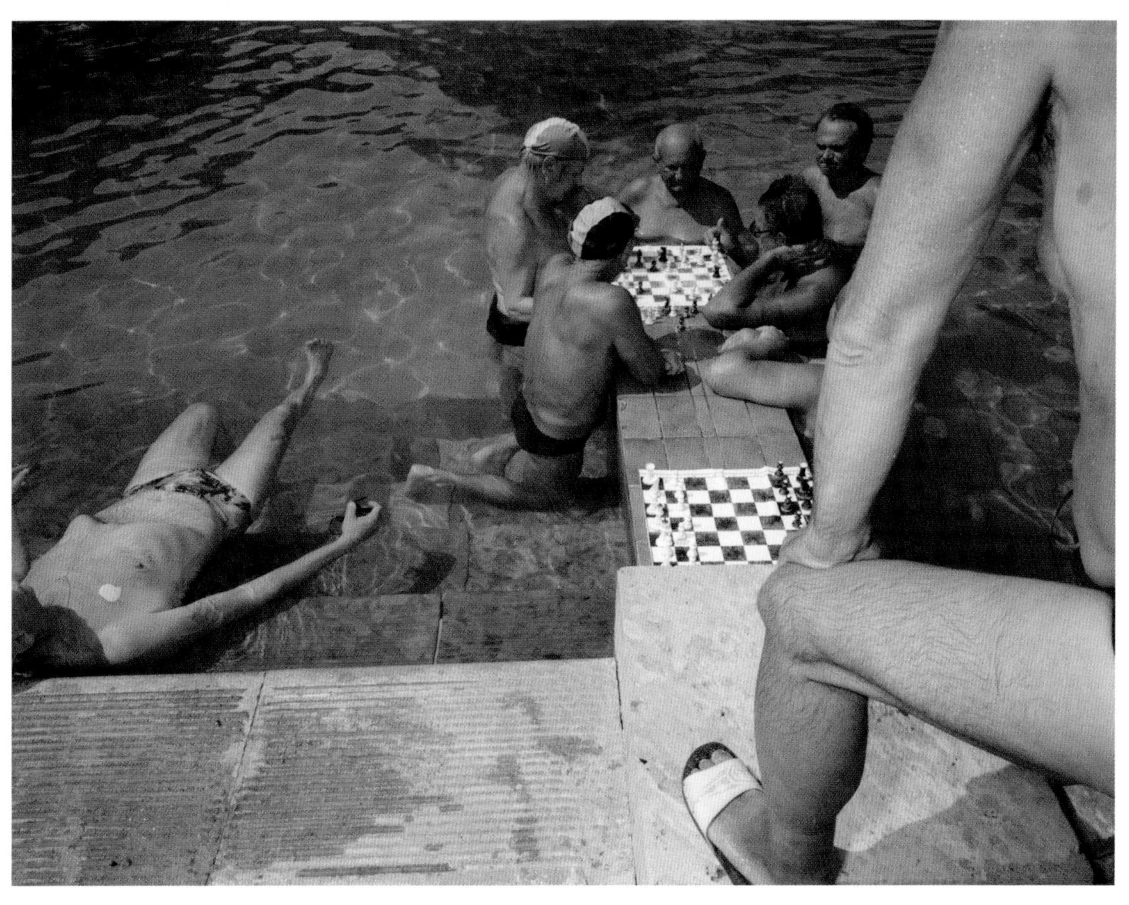

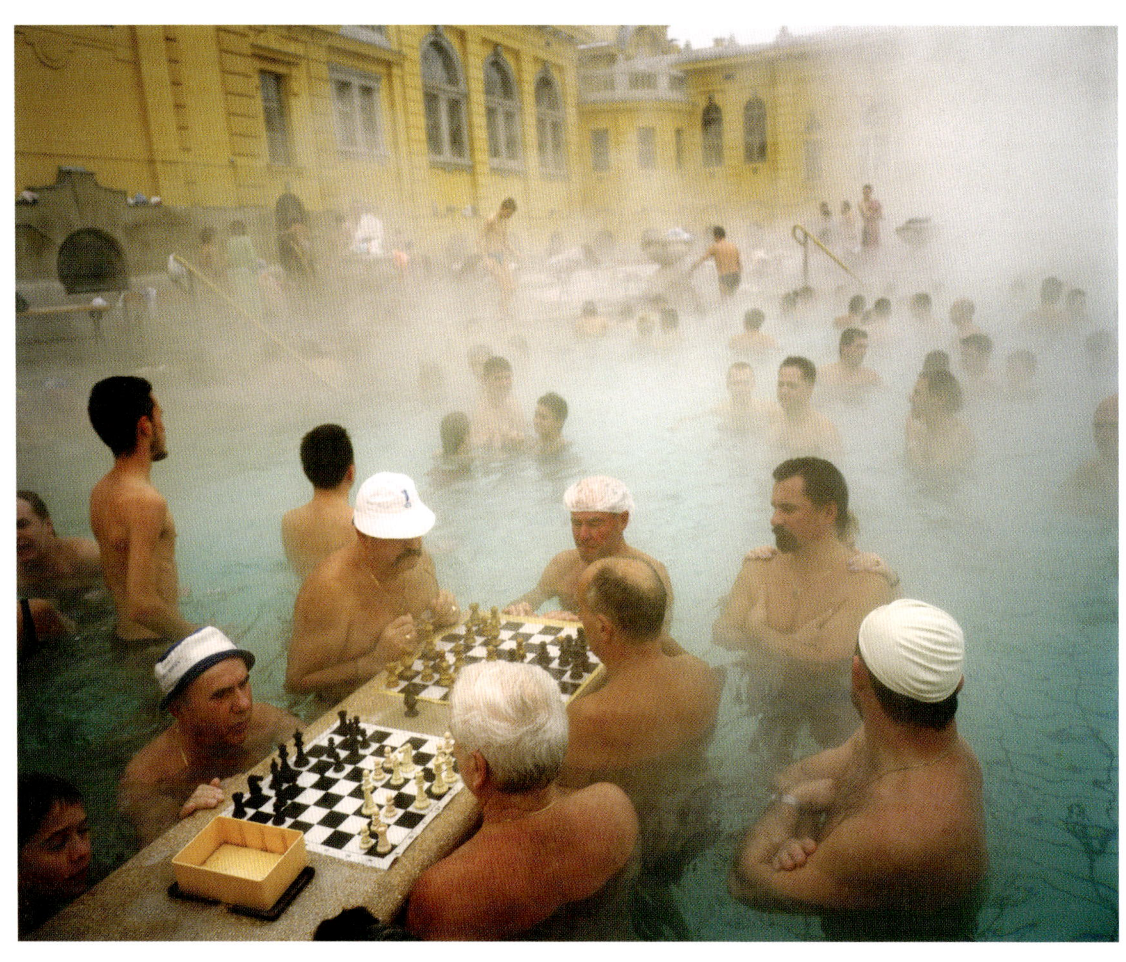

The regular crowd of chess players at
the Szechenyi thermal baths, 2000.

Right: On holiday on the Black Sea
coast, Gudauta, Georgia, 1967.

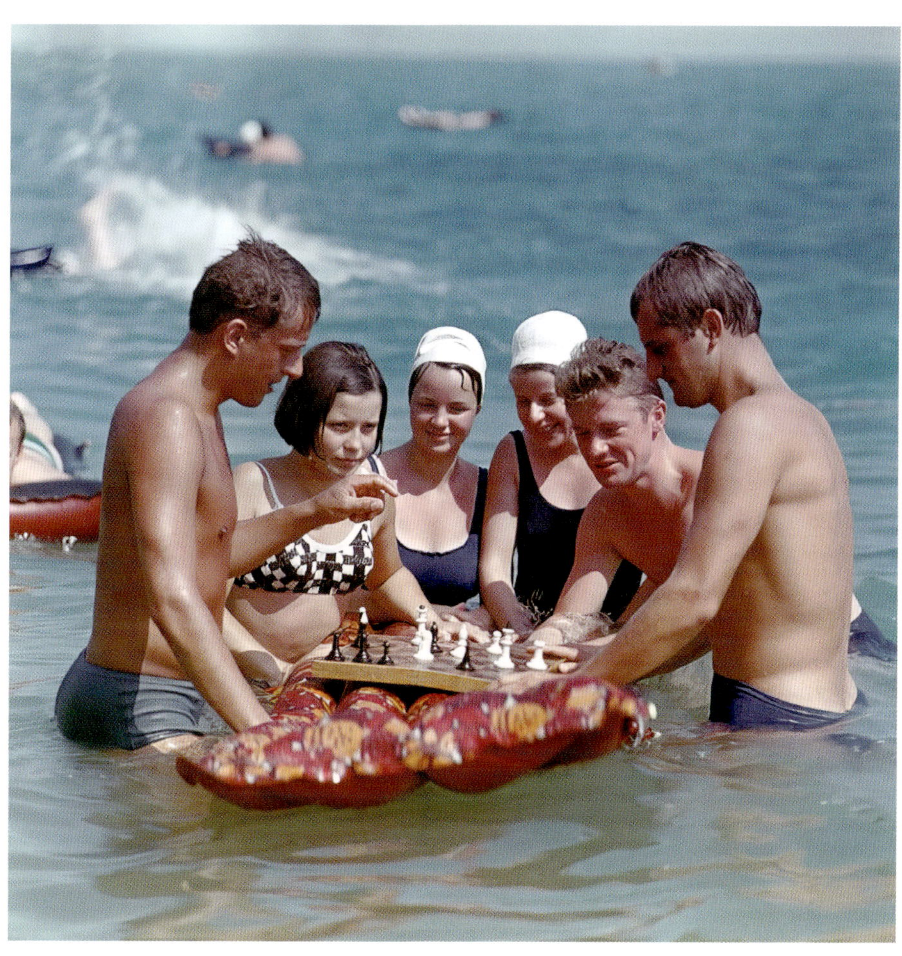

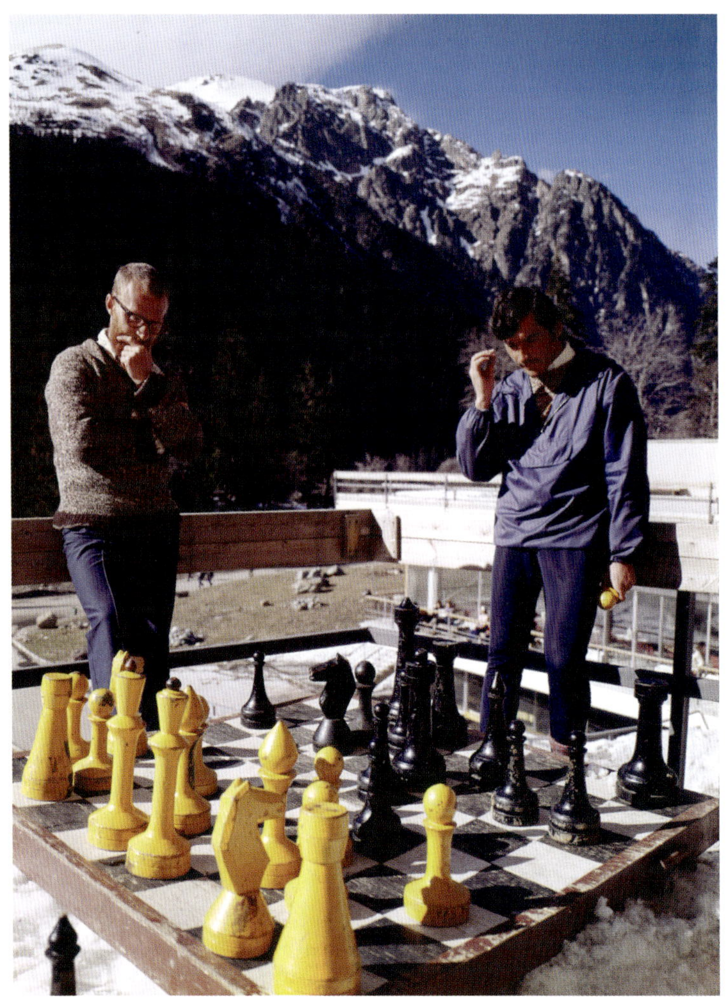

Outdoor chess in Dombay, Caucasus
Mountains, 1974.

Right: Children play chess on a beach
in Yevpatoria, Crimea, 1979.

Overleaf: A game of chess in the sun,
Sochi, Russia, 1981.

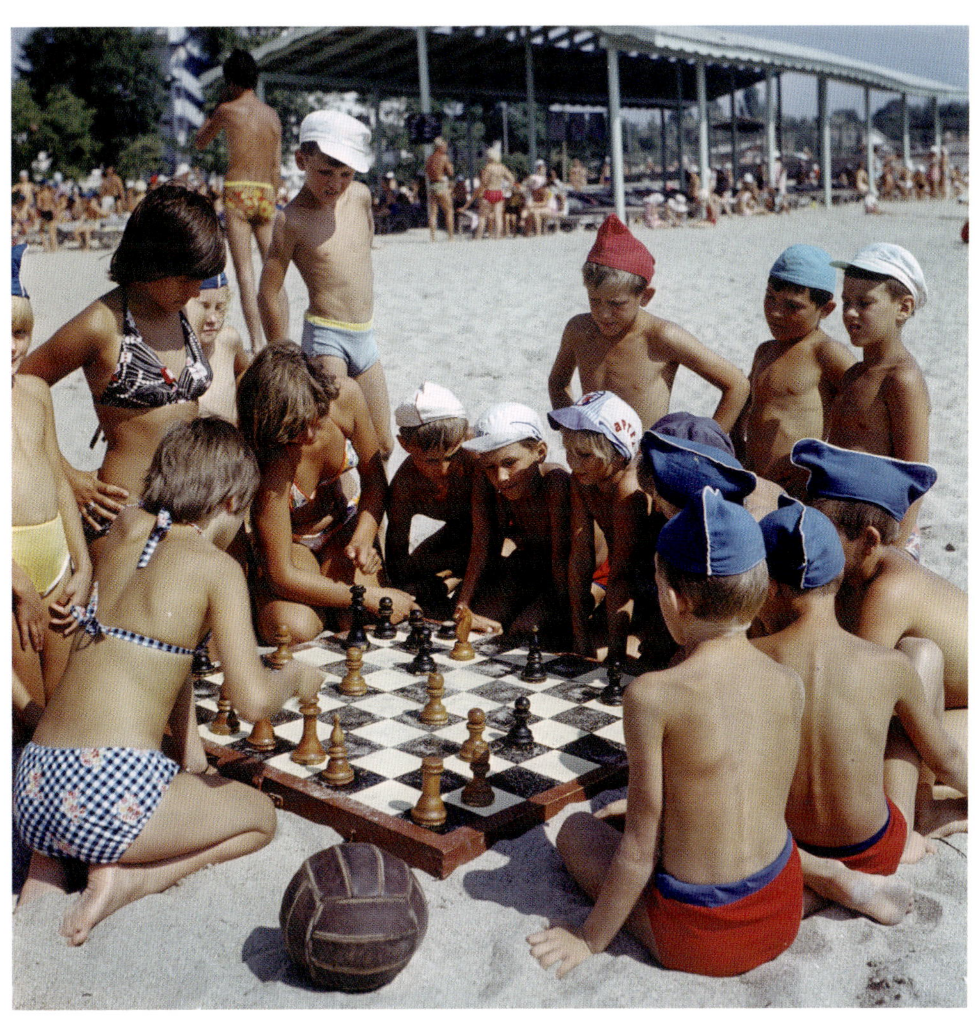

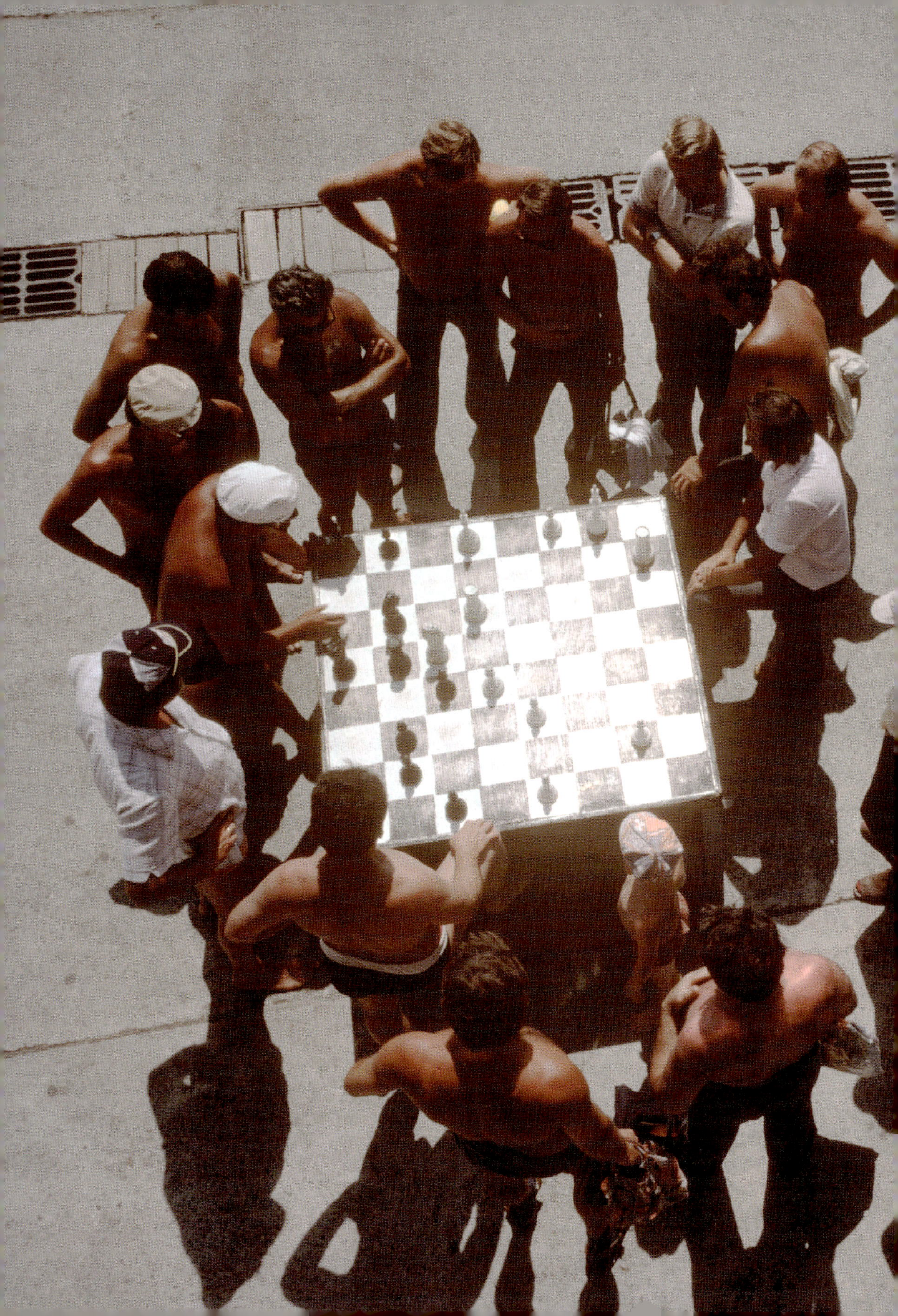

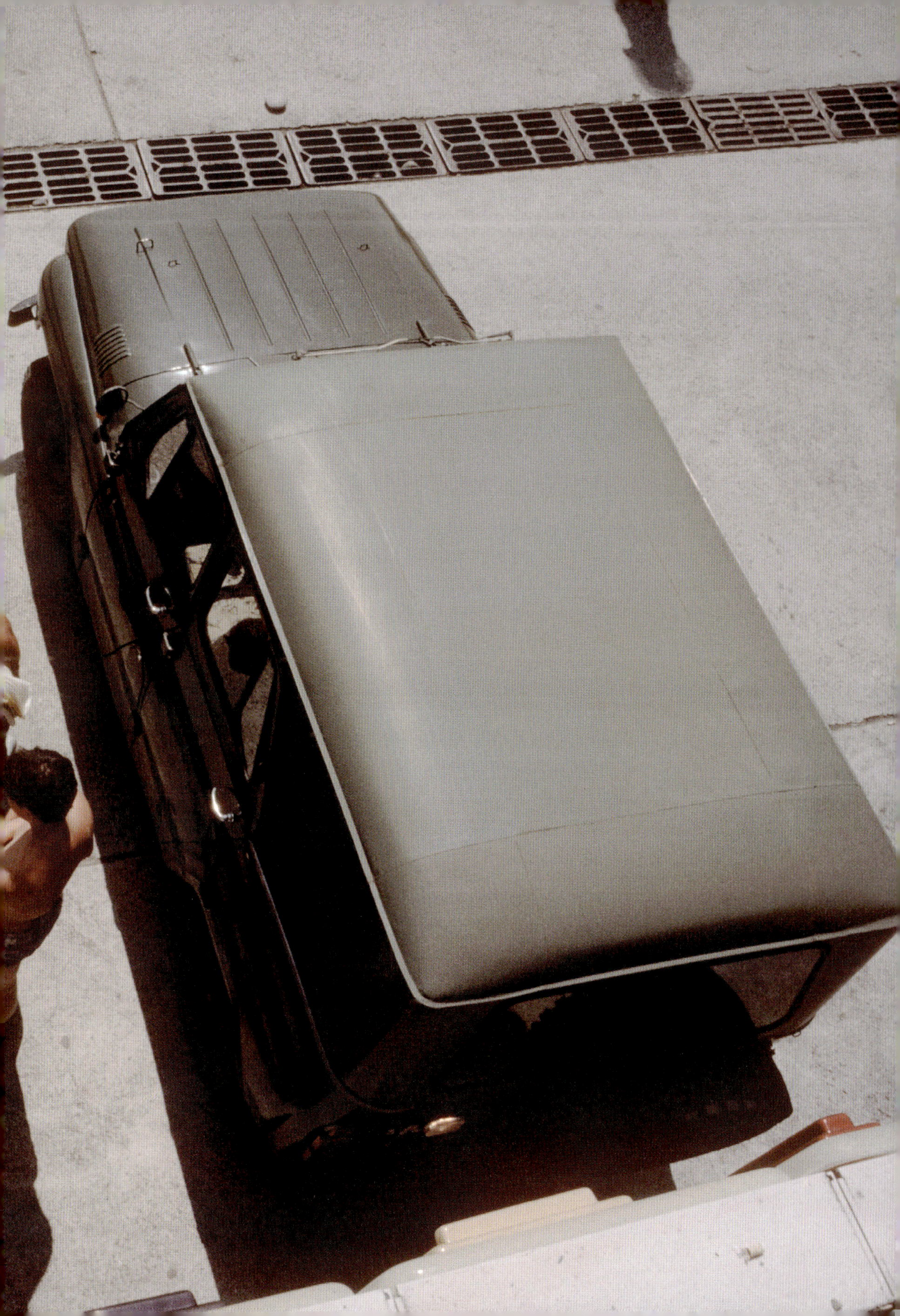

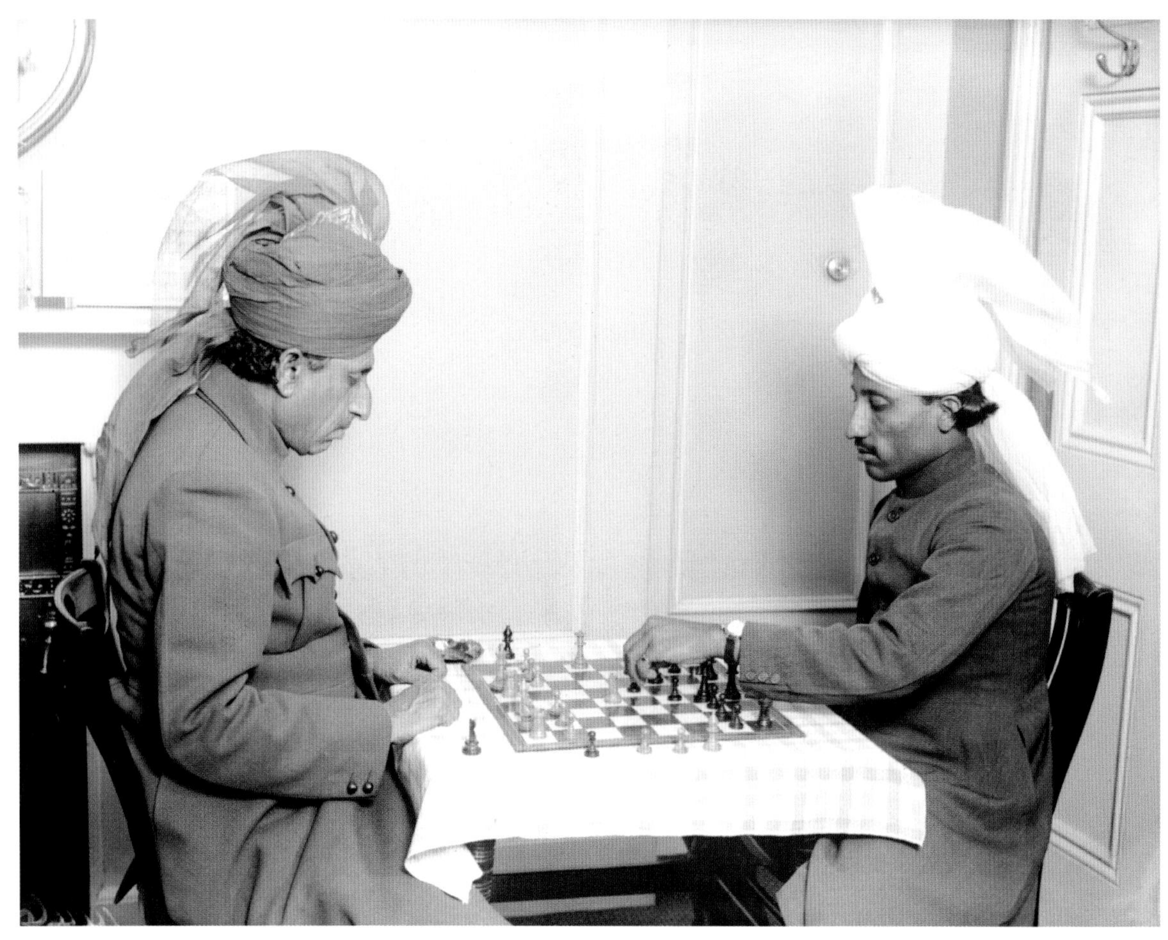

Sultan Khan (right) and Sir Umar Hayat Khan Tiwana, Khan's benefactor, in 1929. In a meteoric four-year career, Khan, who was from the Punjabi region of what is today Pakistan, won the British Championship three times and beat many of the world's best players, despite having little formal chess training. In 1933, Khan and Sir Umar returned home, after which Khan barely played any further chess tournaments. José Raúl Capablanca, the world champion from 1921–27, who lost to Khan in a tournament game on 31 December 1930, called him a 'genius'.

Right: Playing chess during the monsoon floods in Varanasi (also known as Benares), Uttar Pradesh, northern India, 1967.

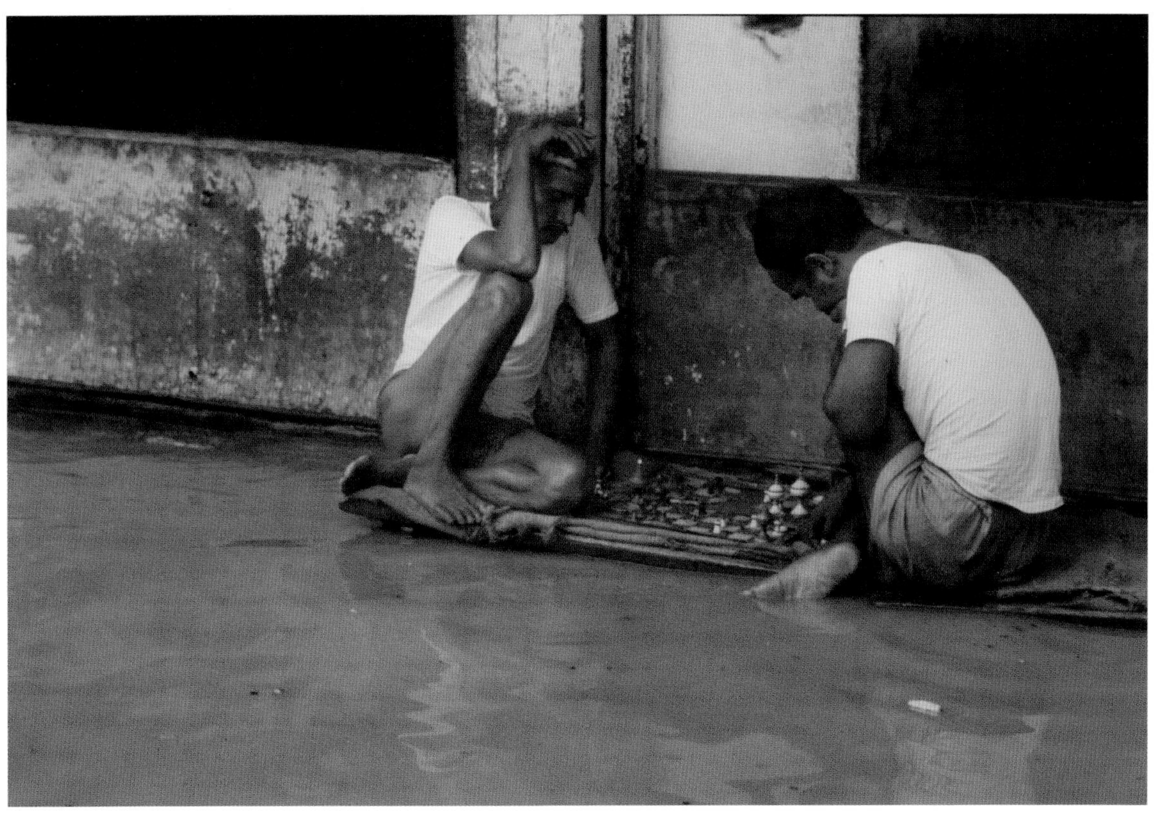

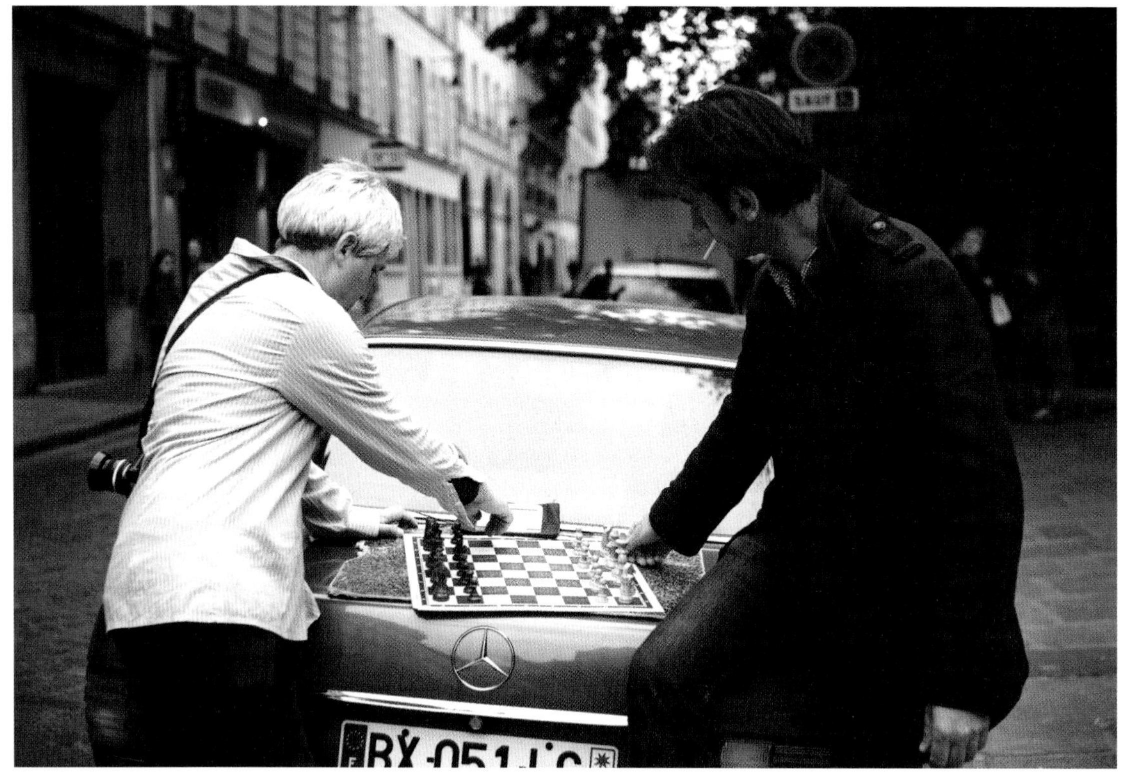

Preparing to play a game of
speed chess on the back of a
Mercedes-Benz, Paris, 2014.

Right: This photograph, taken on 25 November
1969, shows Donna Gaines, who later rose to
international super stardom as Donna Summer
('Queen of Disco'), playing chess with her
colleague and companion at the time, Ron
Williams. She had just been offered a recording
contract after finishing a stint in the German
production of the musical *Hair*. She achieved
global success almost exactly seven years
later with the release of the single 'Love to
Love You Baby' (1975).

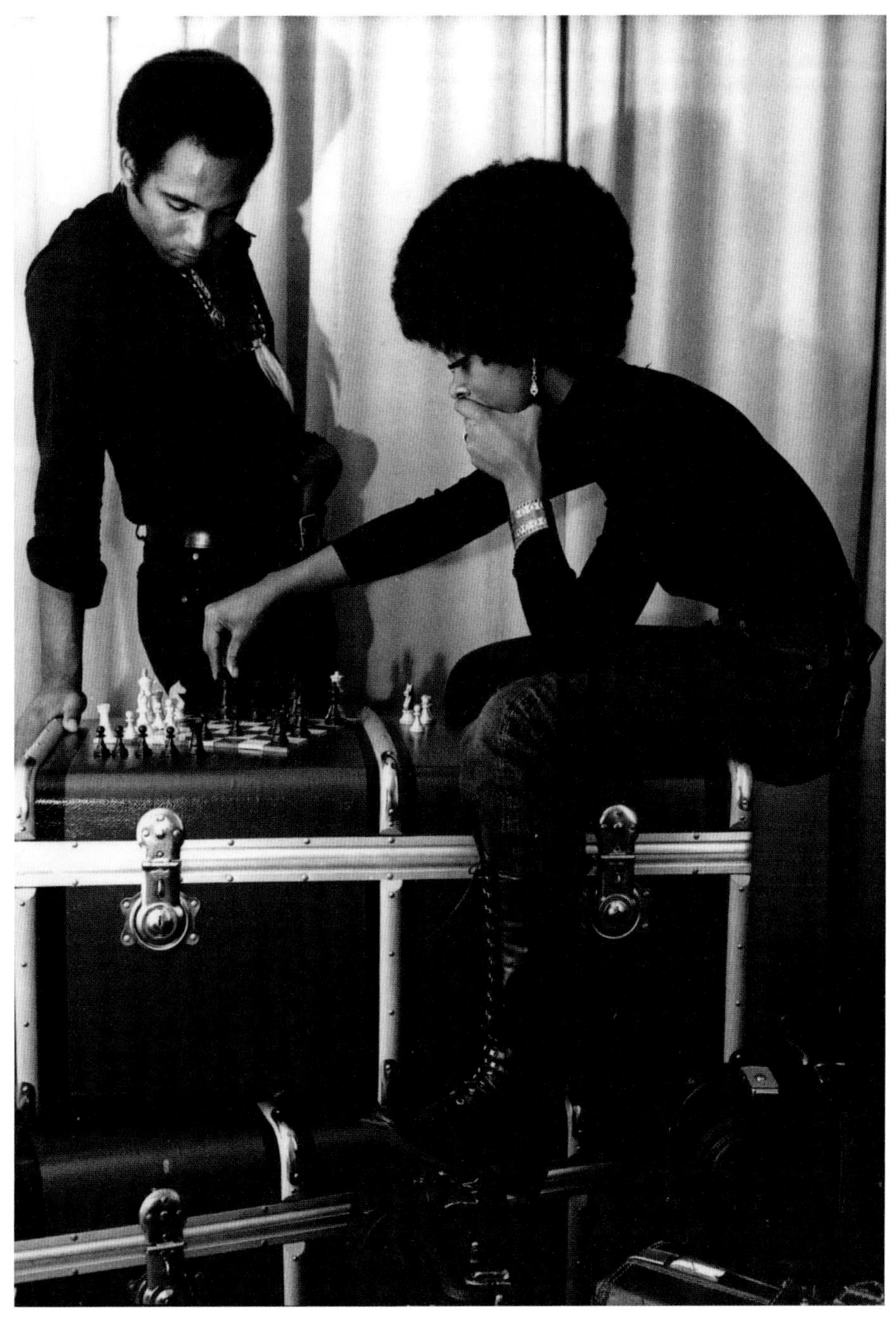

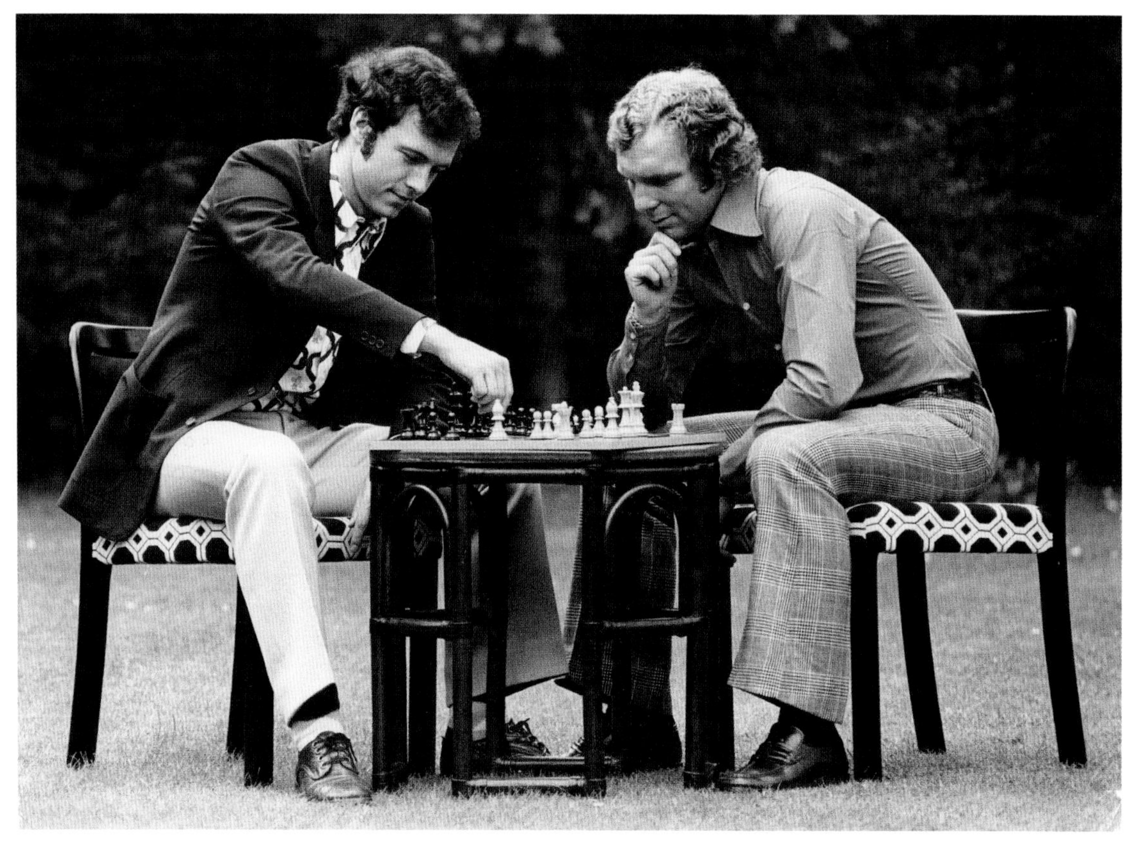

Franz Beckenbauer (left) and Bobby Moore,
in the mid-1970s. Friends and rivals, they were
two of the greatest defenders in the history
of professional football.

Right: Neil Diamond playing chess with Joy
Anderson, a member of his British fan club,
in Kensington Gardens, London, May 1972.
The chess set was a gift from the fan club.

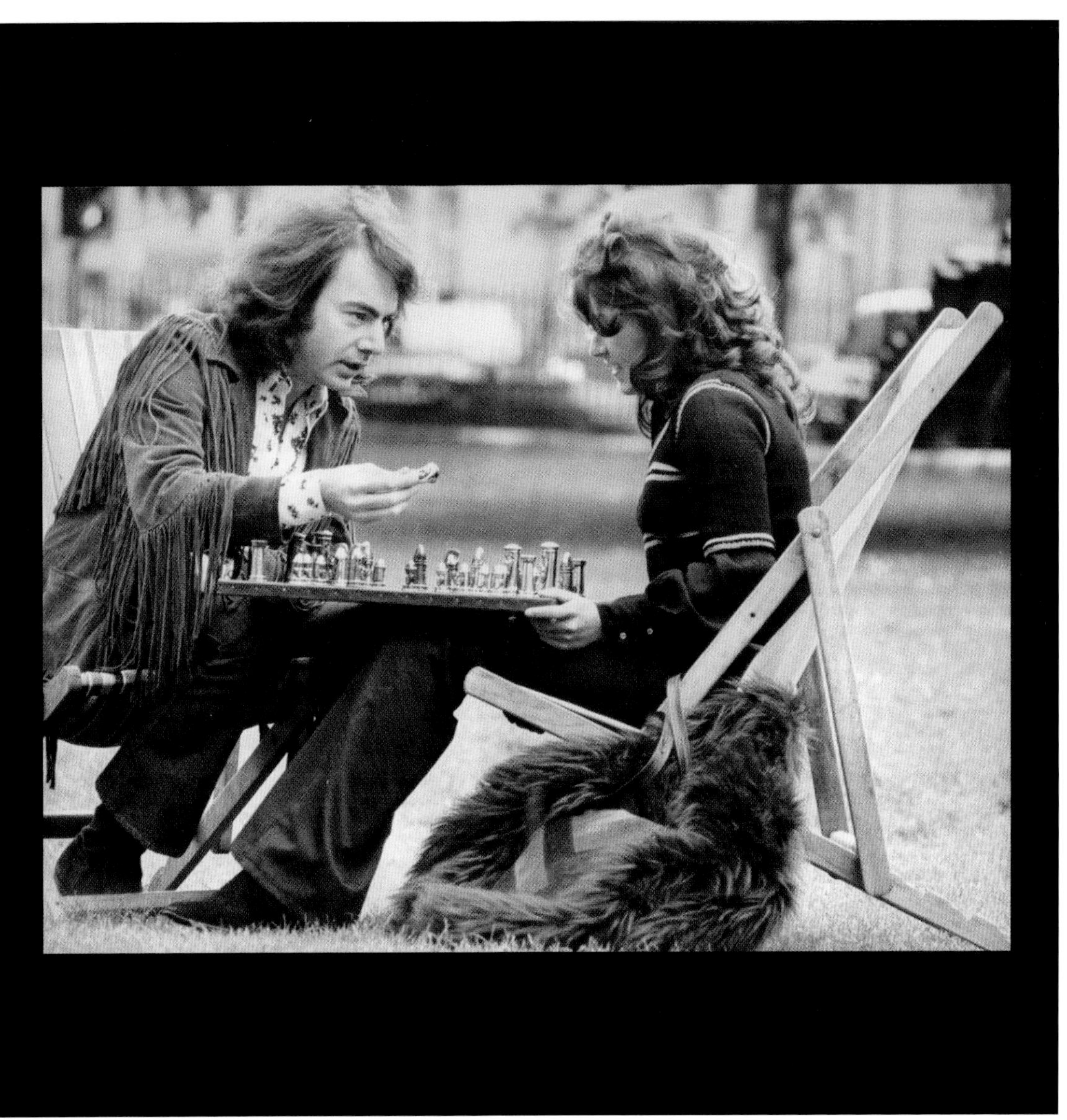

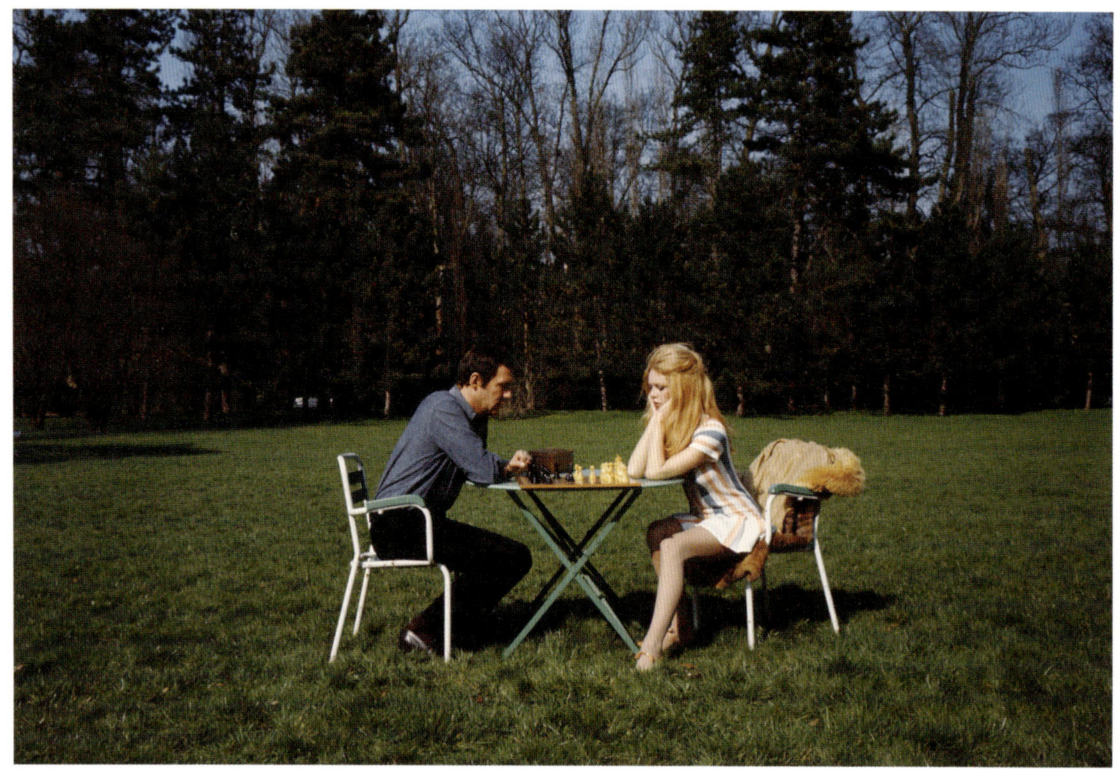

Above: Co-stars Maurice Ronet
and Brigitte Bardot on the set of
The Women (1969).

Right: Chess has often appeared
in advertising, often for unrelated
products, such as in this 1963
advertisement for a Buick Special
Coupe, 1963.

Overleaf: In the film *Imagine* (1972), by John
Lennon and Yoko Ono (as well as in the music
video for Ono's song 'Don't Count the
Waves'), the couple play chess using her
1966 work *Play It By Trust, aka White Chess
Set*. The idea is that the players will lose track
of whose pieces are whose, forcing them to
talk to each other, and – as the title suggests
– trust each other, if they want to continue
playing. The concept turns what is nominally
a game of competition or war on its head,
transforming it into a game that actually
encourages cooperation.

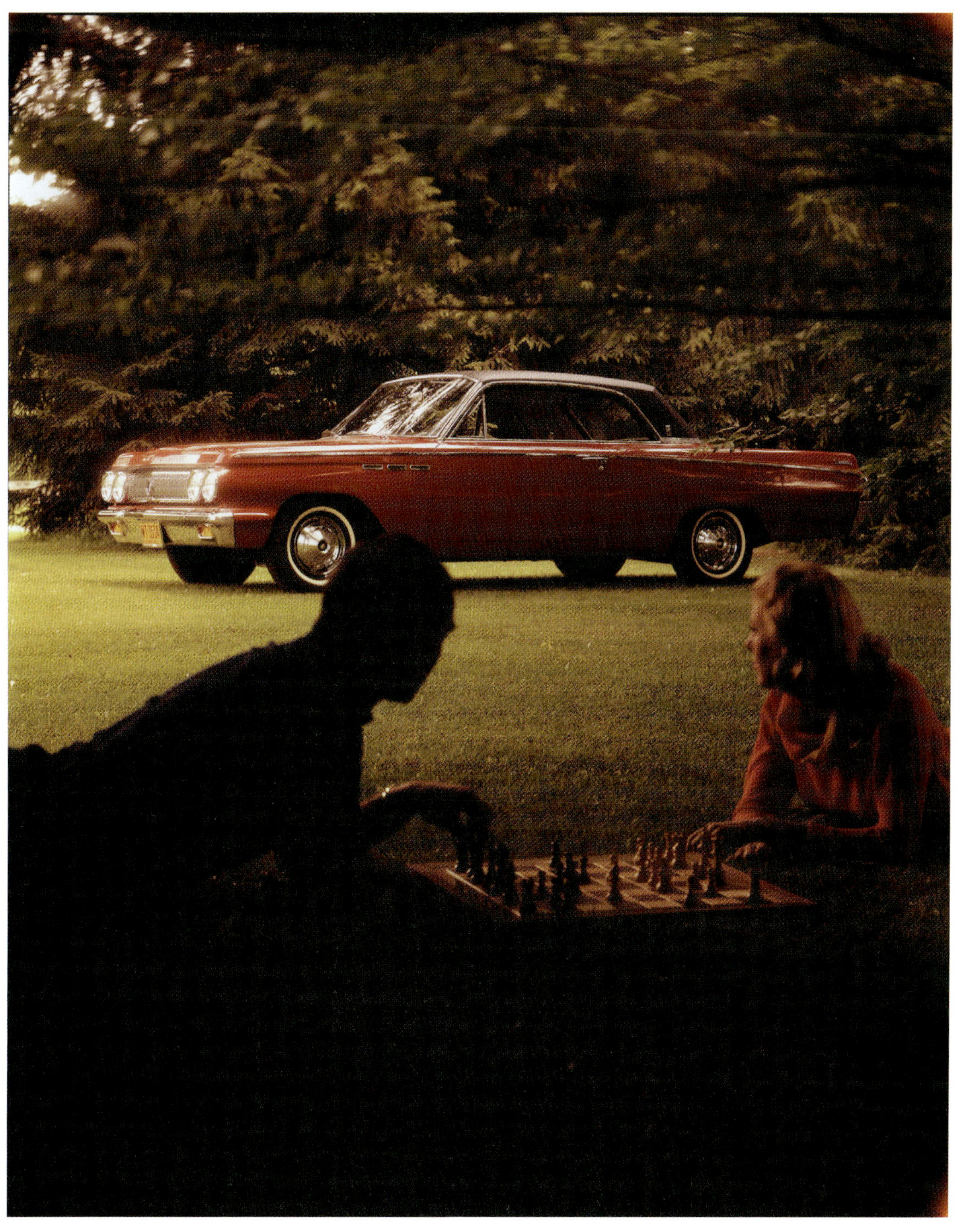

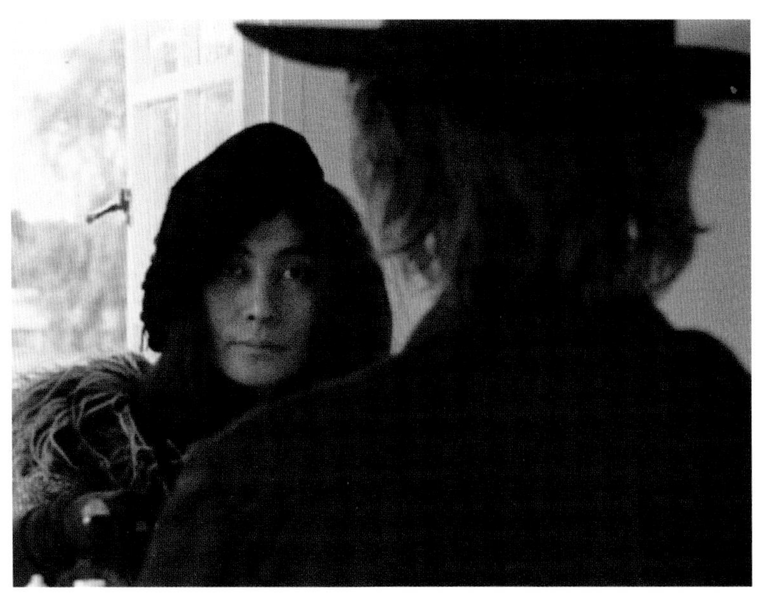

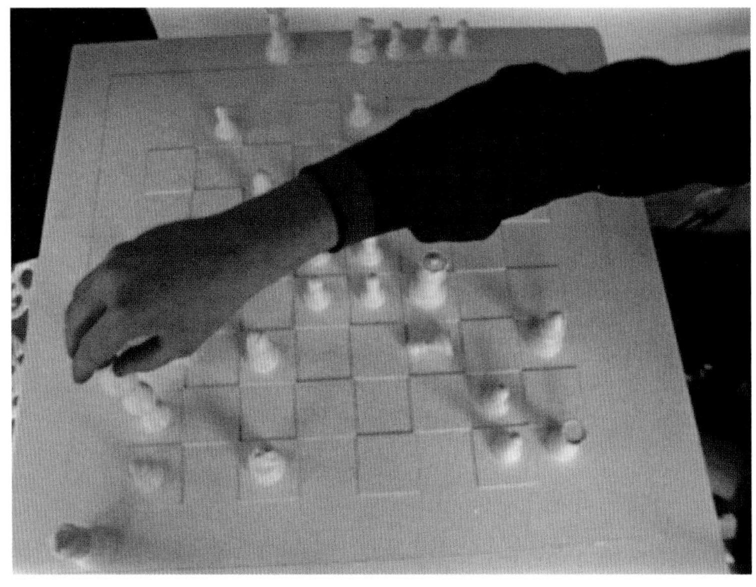

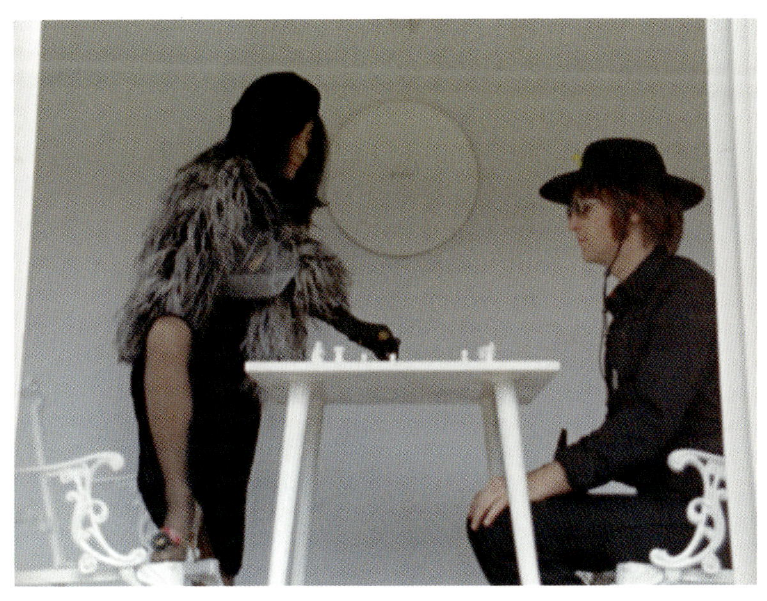

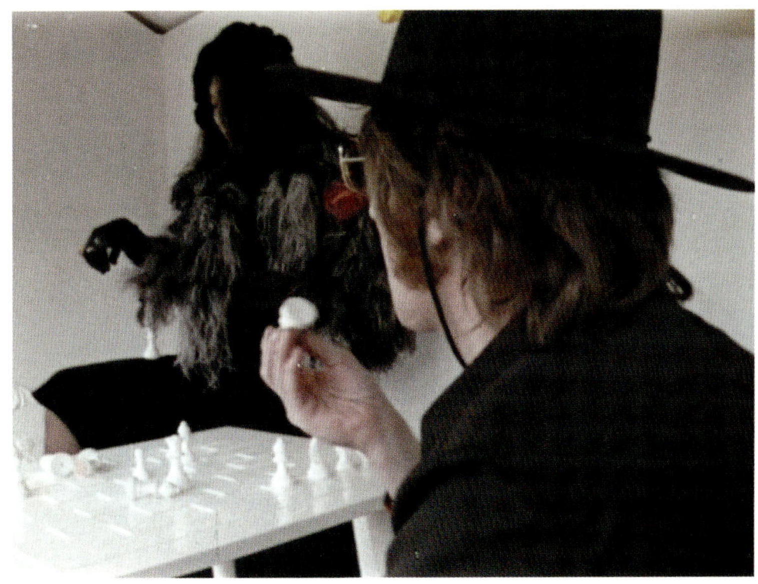

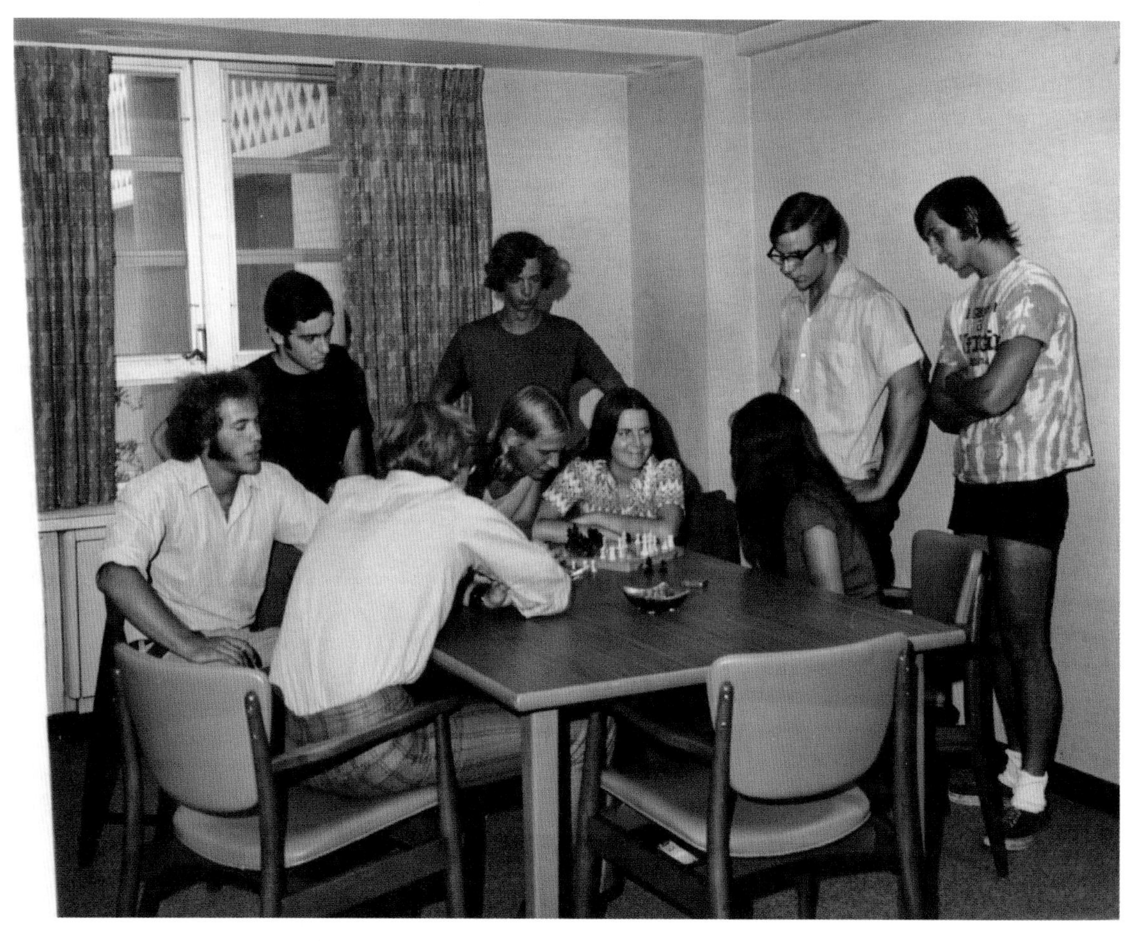

A group of students playing
chess, Marymount College,
Virginia, 1972.

Right: Zagreb University, 1974.

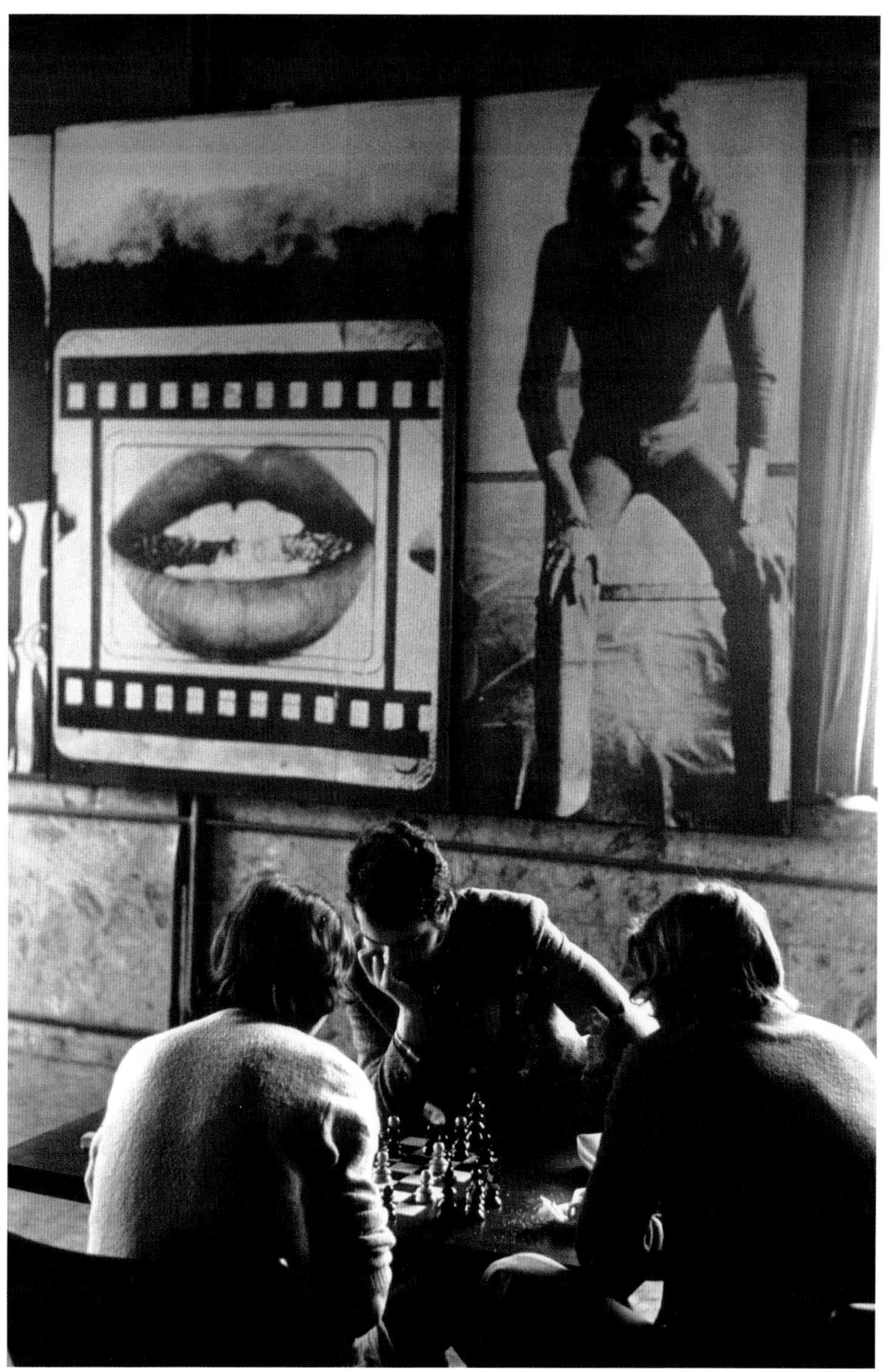

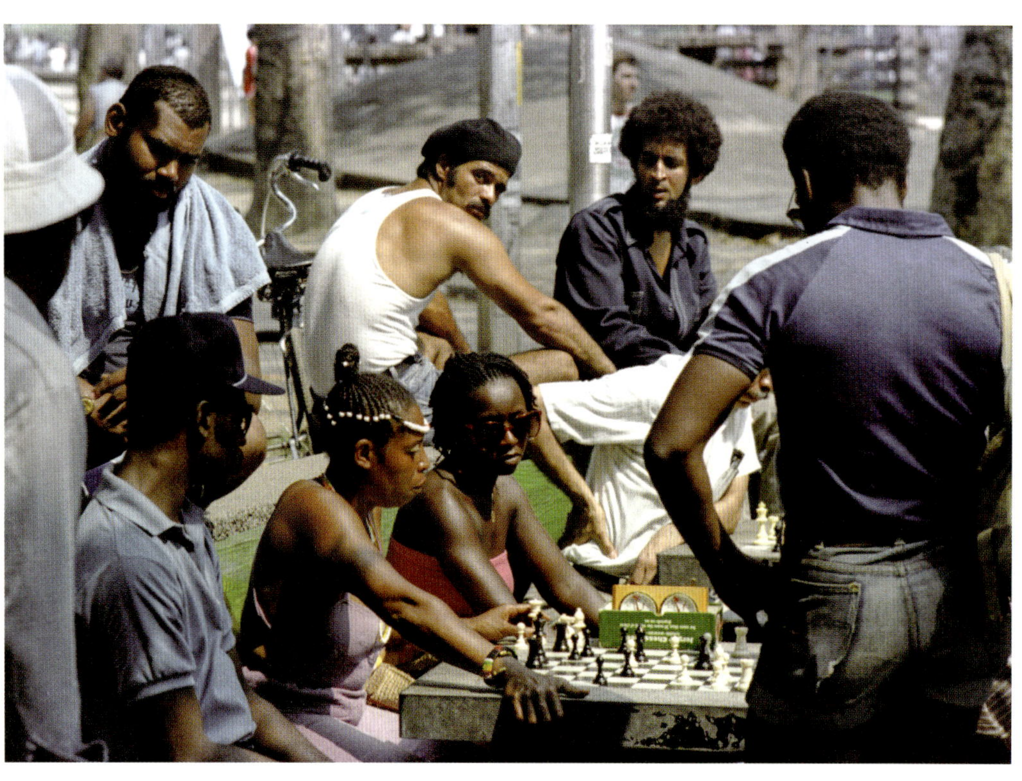

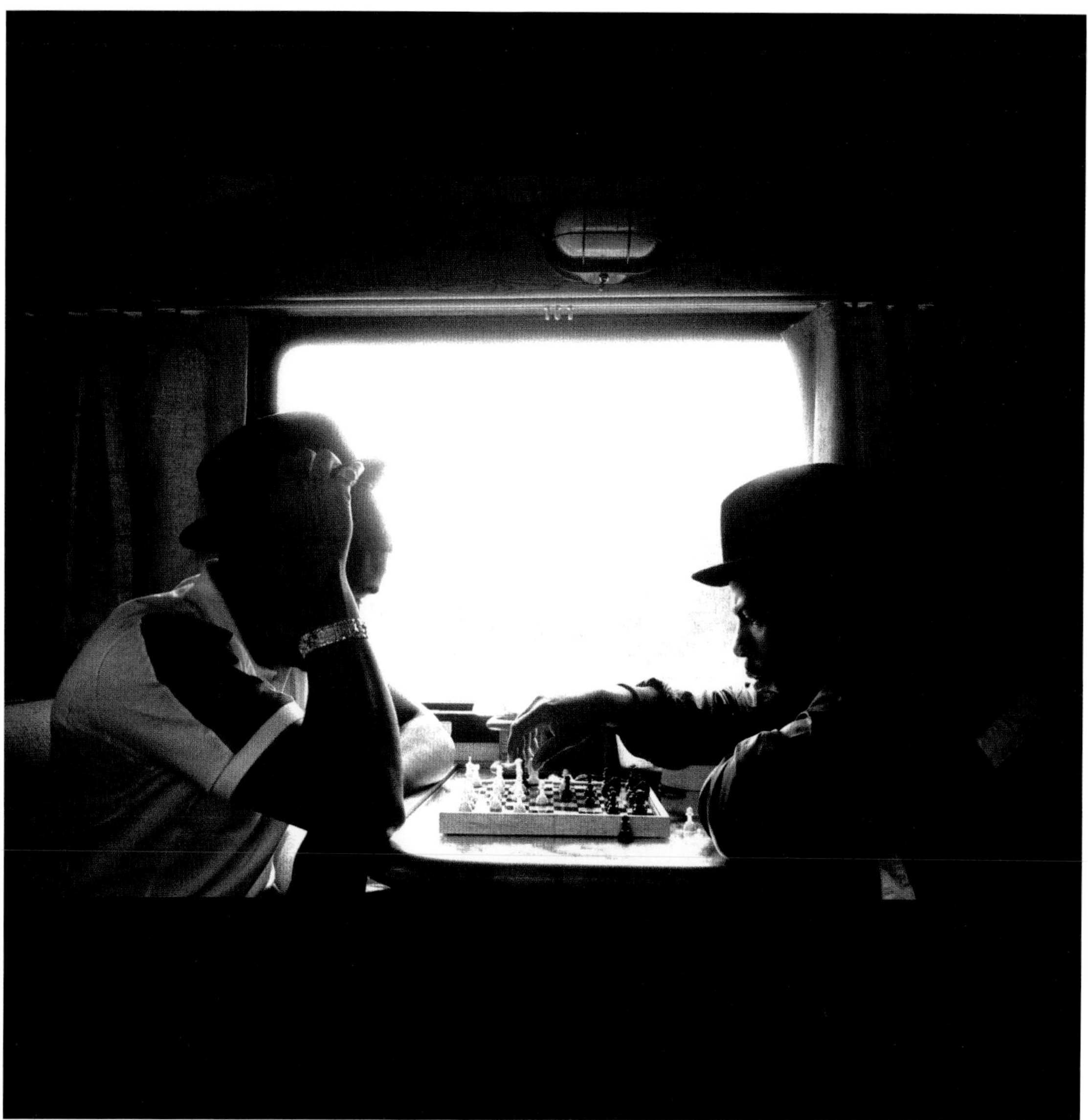

Members of the rap group Run
DMC on the road between
Virginia and New York, 1986.

Left: Gathering around the
chess tables in Washington
Square Park, 1980s.

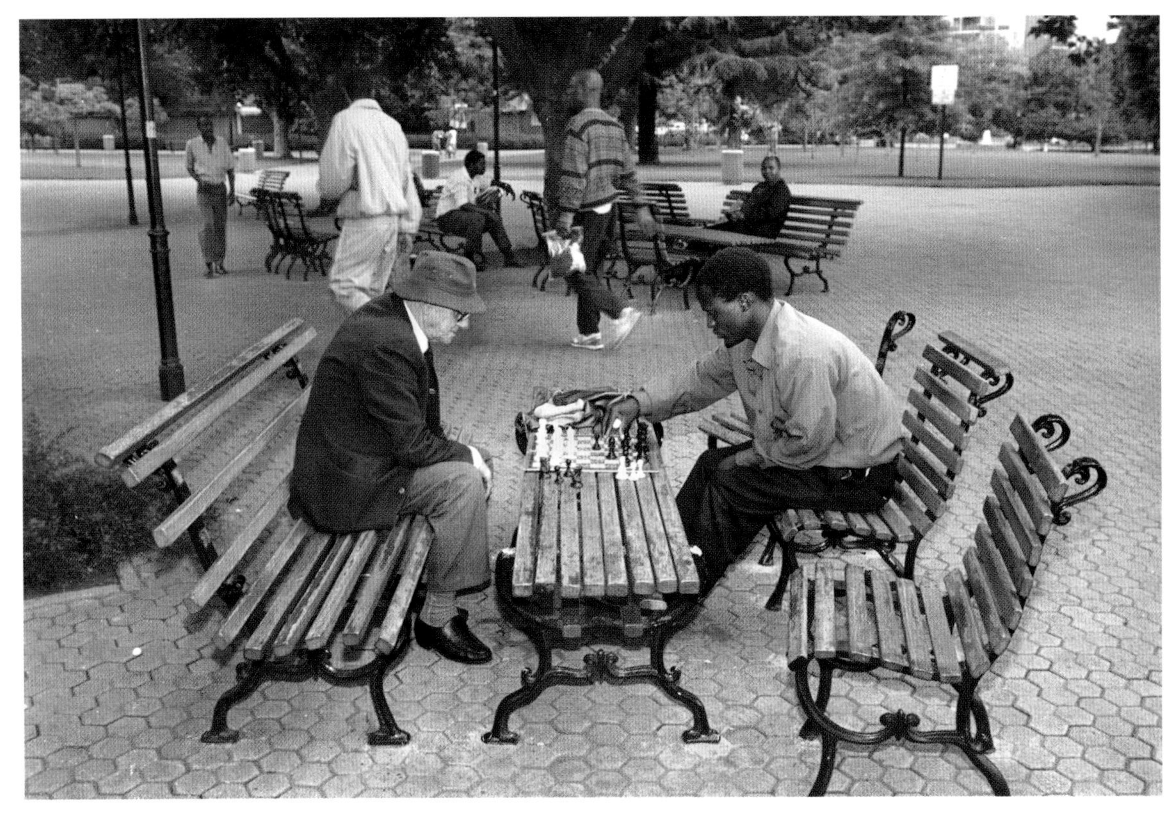

Joubert Park in Johannesburg, South Africa, 1989. This park has been a popular place to play chess for decades – the racial segregation of apartheid was not enforced here, as evidenced by this photograph.

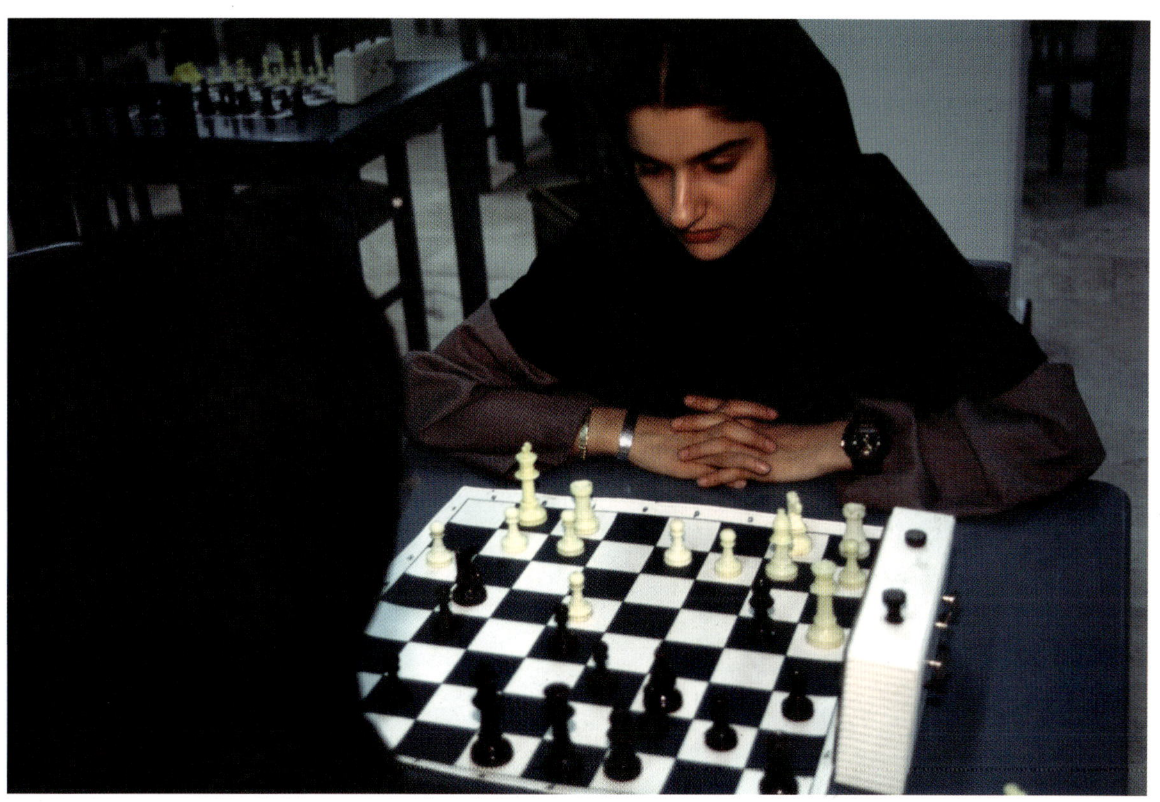

Two young women wearing hijabs play chess in north
Tehran, Iran, 1995. Under the rule of Supreme Leader
Ayatollah Khomeini, chess was banned as 'un-Islamic'
from the end of the Iranian Revolution in 1979 until
the late 1980s. After the ban was lifted, Iran, one of
the ancient centres of the game, began developing
many talented players, becoming a world power in
chess. However, in recent years, the law that women
must wear hijabs in public has not been followed by
some female players when competing internationally.
Facing punishment, including the possibility of
imprisonment if they return to Iran, many have chosen
to defect to the West, causing the country to lose
some of its top players.

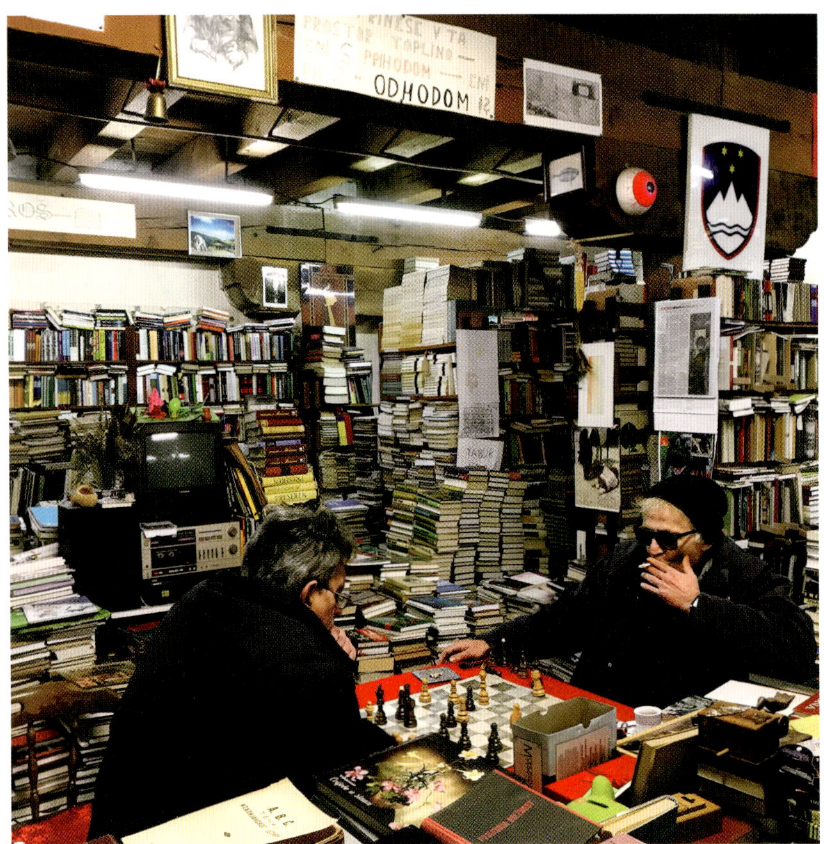

Playing in a used bookstore in Maribor,
Slovenia, January 2018.

Right: This photograph, taken in June 1993,
during the Bosnian War of 1992–95, shows
two residents of the suburb of Hrasno,
Sarajevo. To test a cease fire that had come
into effect a few days earlier, they played
a game of chess 50 yards from what was
one of the most dangerous frontlines in the
Bosnian capital.

Overleaf: Chess has been part of the ethos of the
Wu-Tang Clan, the hip-hop supergroup, since its
formation in the early 1990s. RZA, the group's
principal founder, said he got hooked on chess at
the age of 11. He later taught the game to GZA
and Ghostface Killah, seen playing here in the
documentary series *Wu-Tang Clan: Of Mics and
Men* (2019). The debut album of the group, *Enter
the Wu-Tang (36 Chambers)* (1993), which many
rank as the greatest hip-hop album ever, included
the track 'Da Mystery of Chessboxing'. GZA later
released an album called *Grandmasters* (2005),
with DJ Muggs (also featuring members of Wu-
Tang Clan), entirely devoted to chess.

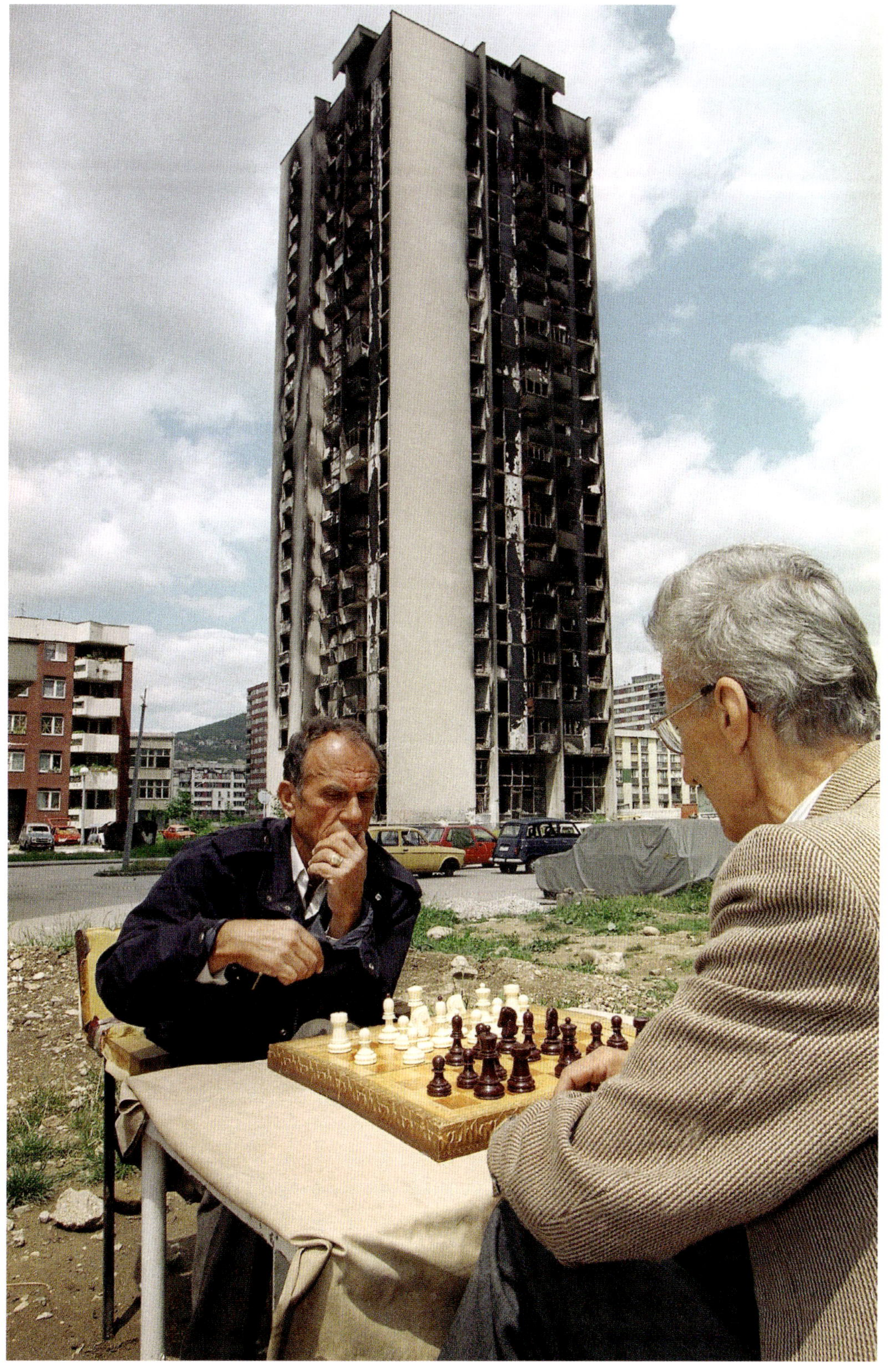

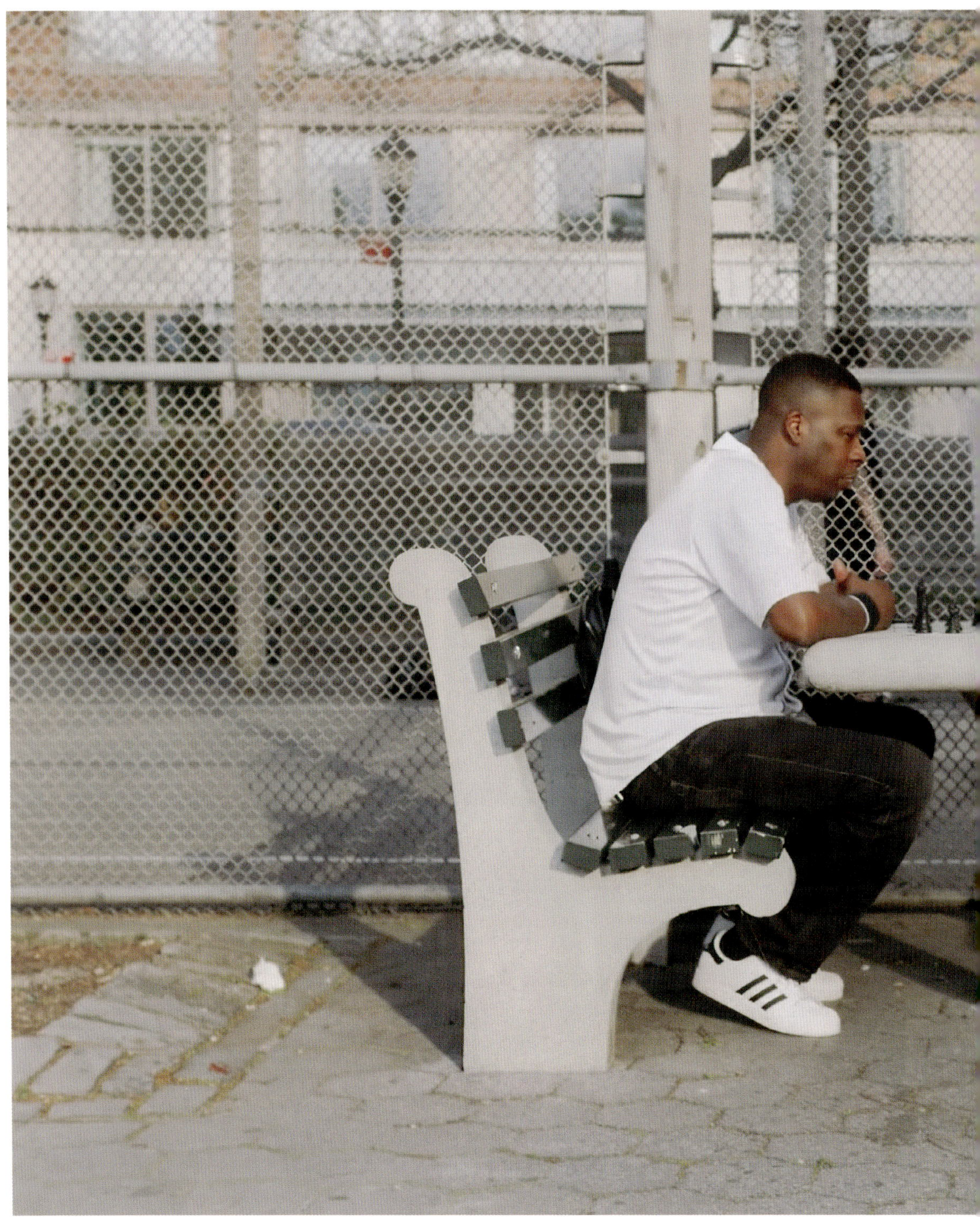

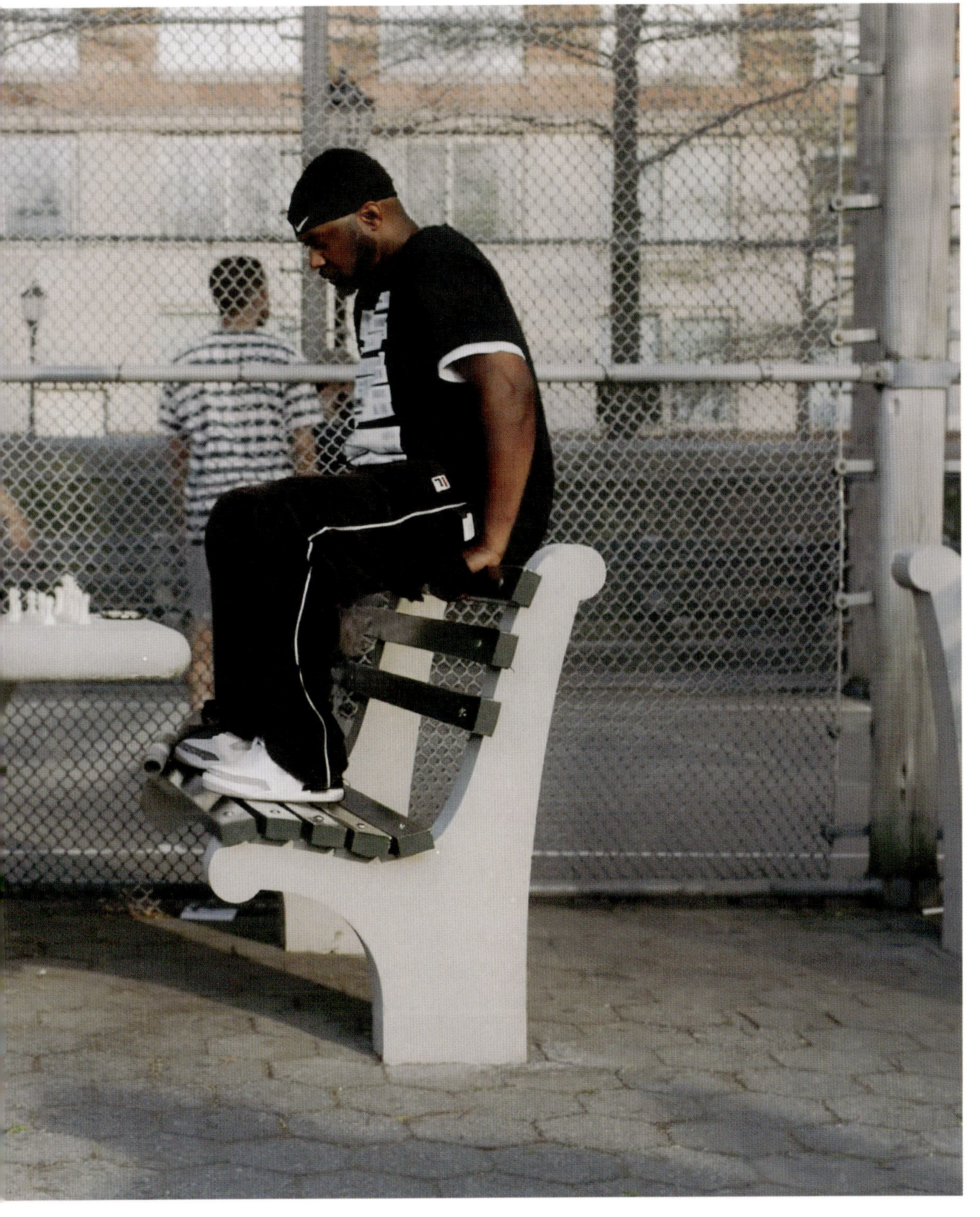

Viswanathan Anand is unarguably one of the greatest chess players in history. Five times winner of the classical world championship as well as the rapid and blitz world championships, he was ranked no. 1 in the world for 21 months, remaining among the world's top-10 players for more than 30 years – an almost unmatched feat. These achievements have earned him some of India's highest honours, including the Khel Ratna and the Padma Vibhushan awards. In a sports-mad nation of 1.4 billion people, he is among the country's best-known figures.

As remarkable as his individual accomplishments are, his impact on the game has been far larger. He has singlehandedly inspired a renaissance of the game in the country where chess was born, but where its traditions had been largely forgotten. Today, there are millions of people studying chess in India and the country's top players have taken their places among the best in the world. This transformation is almost all due to Anand.

How and when did you discover chess?
I was six years old. My older brother and sister were playing around with the chess set which happened to be in the house – they are both more than 10 years older, so I was the little guy – and I said to my mother, 'Why don't you teach me to play chess. I want to play chess.' Probably at that point, it was only sibling rivalry. She taught me and then, the story goes, I kept at it for a couple of months and my parents thought, 'Well if he is interested in chess, why not put him in a chess club?'

Luckily, there was a chess club not too far away. This was in the then Soviet Cultural Centre, the consulate of the Soviet Union in Madras [now Chennai]. It was a very well-stocked chess club, one of the strongest around in those days. It had fantastic old wooden Soviet sets with good clocks and a lovely outdoor space. I started going to the club quite often.

Do you recall what attracted you to chess, aside from sibling rivalry, was there something that engaged you and made you passionate about it almost immediately? Or did it take time?
I never really thought about why I played chess. It just seemed very natural. There was the joy of beating someone. I liked the idea that I could follow a strategy and win. When that approach started to run out, my sister bought me a chess book: *Chess Openings* by I.A. Horowitz. Then everybody started showing me newspaper chess columns, and I would try this and that.

So chess was an outlet for competition?
Yes, very much. I think that at the age of six, if you had

told me about the beauty of chess, it would have been meaningless to me. For me, I liked the idea that I could play the game and that there were these hacks, there were little things that you could learn from a book and maybe try to catch an opponent.

I started to go regularly to these club gaming sessions where we would all sit around a chessboard and play winner-stays-on. The joy of staying there a bit longer, beating your opponents, was what I liked.

At what point did you start to get good? Was it immediately or did it take a little while?
I was one of the top juniors when I was in my schooldays. I would finish second and third in the school championship, sometimes even win it. I would do decently at the club against players much older than me. In those days, age mattered. You didn't catch up quite as fast as you do these days. I started winning tournaments and I became a national figure about four or five years after I got really involved.

At 10 or 11?
At 12. In 1983 was my breakthrough year. By 1982, I was already playing the junior nationals; I had won my state competitions. By the way, Chennai was the strongest state in India at that point; I didn't come from some backwater. You can always compare it to Moscow, yes, but Chennai was very much a chess centre. We had international masters, we had people who had gone to Europe and brought back *Informants* [issues of *Chess Informant*, a regular publication chronicling the recent games of the world's top players] and who would pass them around the chess club. There was also the year that I was in the Philippines in 1979.

How and why did you go to the Philippines?
My father was working in the Indian railways, and he got an assignment with the Asian Development Bank project to help the Philippines railways. We went there just after the [1978] Karpov–Korchnoi world championship match finished and the Philippines was in kind of a chess boom.

First thing after we landed, my mother picked up the phone and called around to see if anyone knew if there was a chess club. She decided, let's go for the top, let's go for Eugene Torre [in 1974, Torre had become the first non-Soviet Asian to become a grandmaster and was a friend and associate of Bobby Fischer]. Unfortunately, Torre is a common name in the Philippines, so she called a number and said, 'Mr Torre, my son is a fan of yours.' The man on the other end of the line said, 'Okay, I think you want my brother, but I can help you find a club.'

You became an incredible blitz player when you were very young, correct?
Pretty much. There were not too many blitz tournaments, but we played blitz all the time in the club, so these winner-take-all sessions were always blitz and I played a lot of them. Pretty soon, I had this habit of moving instantly – I would not think about my moves.

At some point, my father told me, 'By the way, if people tell you to slow down, don't. Do what feels natural.' That was very good advice because already people were telling me, 'You have to slow down, and you have to think.' I eventually came around to it, but when I was young, I just continued playing incredibly fast.

Most of the legends are true: finishing games having used five minutes on my clock while my opponent had used two-and-a-half hours, while I walked around bored. I would see the move that I wanted to make instantly, and I couldn't wait. Invariably, thinking for me involved sitting on my hands and wondering, 'When will it be okay for me to make a move now?' But most of the time I was not actually thinking about the move itself.

Anatoly Karpov said, 'Chess is art, science and sport.' Do you agree?
I would say that the art and the science are completely at the service of sport in the sense that my attitude to the game is: of course I would rather win a lousy game because of an opponent's blunder than play a masterpiece and not win. Karpov's statement felt like something you might say at a cocktail party, rather than something you meant.

But at the same time, I love the beautiful games of Mikhail Tal or Bobby Fischer, where everything goes like clockwork. I can admire that kind of game.
You become aware of the beauty in chess very fast, but people tell you, 'If you see a beautiful combination or a simple pawn ending that is a winning move, then go for the pawn ending.' You are supposed to bring in the point, not increase the odds of failing.

The science part comes naturally: you do have to study the game. And you enjoy the beauty while you are at. The first time you see Kasparyan's studies [Genrikh Kasparyan was a Soviet chess player considered one of the greatest endgame composers in history], you think, 'My God, this is unbelievable.'

I understand where Karpov was coming from. But for me, sport was always the most important element. Whatever I studied or learned, it was always, 'What can I do with this?'

Bobby Fischer said, 'Chess is life.' That is too much, isn't it?

Not at all. I think there are chess players whose lives and thoughts are swallowed by chess. Fischer himself was one. I think that Fischer was being very honest in that sense.

There were people who were bon vivants as well, famously José Raúl Capablanca [1921–1927 world champion]. For him, the statement would have rung false. But for Bobby it was true. For Viktor Korchnoi as well, probably.

The people who are lost in chess are the socially awkward ones. I fancy myself as someone who can switch chess on and off, for whom chess is not life.

How does chess fit into your life?
For me, it is something that I did, something that dominates my life, but over time, I realised that I could be a better chess player if I could get away from it once in a while. After some of the difficult moments, I would run away for a month. When I came back, the hunger for the game would return. I always felt that was part of the rhythm. But in my 20s, I wasn't interested in too many other things, I learned to be interested in other things slowly.

Did you finish your education?
It was never stated, but I felt that I should go through university simply so that I could tell people that I went to university. On top of that, it didn't seem to me that I would spend all of my free time thinking of chess anyway. I did a commerce degree, so it has some economics in it, some accountancy, and some mathematics. Not a full bachelor's degree in economics, but a full bachelor's degree in commerce.

I was world junior champion and grandmaster when I started my courses, and by the time I'd finished my exams, I was in the world top 10. That was the point I decided to stop, in 1991. I played the candidates match [to determine the challenger for the world chess championship] with Karpov in Brussels, then came back to finish the two exams I'd postponed and that was it. After that, I became a full-time player.

Somehow it would have been very embarrassing for me if the answer to a question about my education would have been, 'Well, I skipped the last year of school.' That was the reason that I finished.

These days, I'm less rigid in my thinking. If you have an interesting career, quite often that career will open doors in the way a university career would have done previously. You will meet people from other walks of life, you will get to travel. Certainly, as a chess player, you get to travel and have very interesting life experiences. There are people who are lost in chess, but there are many chess players who are great fun to talk to and can converse on many subjects. Some of them even switch careers years later.

What are the moments in your career that really stand out for you?
When I became a strong grandmaster and I started to be invited to the best tournaments. Probably 1991 more than anything else. In 1992, 1993 and 1994, things got a lot better, but these experiences began in 1991 because they were just fantastic events.

Some of my fondest memories are from 1991 – the Brussels candidates, the Linares tournament, the Munich tournament, the Interpolis Tilburg tournament, and winning Reggio Emilia at the end of the year. It is like you stopped being a college student and you get your first job and it pays well and you are able to live nicely and you really enjoy that first year.

Then, when I challenged for the world title in 1995, my status in India went up one notch. I was already pretty famous because I had been India's first grandmaster and the first Asian world junior champion, but a lot of people watched me in 1995.

Five years later, I became world champion and I was getting all the country's top awards, I was being invited to the presidential palace, I was on the top TV shows. There are moments when you feel, 'This is just amazing'; it is harder to get excited now, after you've done something a few times. The first time it happens, you always go through it in a blur.

Was becoming world champion in 2000 by winning a knockout tournament, when the world titles were split, any different from winning the title in Mexico in 2007, when the world title had been reunited?
Only the chess part of me felt the difference; this was because the chess journalists and a few other players and fans would come up to me and say, 'How nice, but it is the other title.' I found that very irritating.

My reaction was first, 'You're an idiot. I didn't ask your opinion and I don't know why you gave it to me.' But it sits inside you, because you know it's what they're thinking, even if the polite ones have the brains not to say it.

Winning in Mexico eliminated 70 per cent of that, because no one was denying that this was a unified title – for me, that was great. But there was that last bit left to be done. Some people would still say, 'Yes, Mexico, but it wasn't a match like Wilhelm Steinitz won.' [Steinitz became the first widely acknowledged world champion in 1886.]

And then Bonn [where Anand soundly defeated Vladimir Kramnik, the previous unified titleholder, in

the 2008 world championship] closed the thing. Within three or four months after my win in 2000, I started to forget the irritating questions, but you also stop appreciating how special it is. But after 2008 it was very special, because nobody questioned the legitimacy of the title.

The thing about these knockout tournaments [as in 2000], I get the arguments for and against them, but viewed from today's perspective, which format is legitimate? Magnus Carlsen doesn't want to play classical anymore. People's preferences change, even fans' opinions change.

But there was a time when it really got under my skin, because a part of you ... it really matters what your peers think – even if everyone else thinks you are wonderful, a part of you wants to know that your peers are not over there biting their tongues.

Any other highlights?
Yes, the emergence of rapid chess tournaments, especially the ones in Monaco, which started in 1992, the Amber tournaments [1992–2011], and the Frankfurt/ Mainz tournaments, which started in 1994.

Then very briefly there were the Paris Immopar Rapid tournaments [1992]. They didn't last, but it was the first time we had played in a theatre with an audience buying tickets to watch ... For a while, we thought we'd already arrived at the future. Nowadays, a lot of youngsters think, 'Oh finally, chess has made it.' But it has made it in the past, too.

Definitely for me, these rapid tournaments were very special. I looked forward to them every year and I had the best records in them. In Amber, I was the biggest winner – I think I won it five times outright and five times I was second [Anand actually won it outright seven times and tied for first on four other occasions]. In Frankfurt/ Mainz, I won the most titles for sure – 11 or 12. In Corsica, I won seven titles, in León, I won 9 out of 13 or 14. These were tournaments I was really dominating. Alexander Grischuk [a Russian ranked among the world's best for 20 years] once mentioned that it was a pity that those were not official world titles, because then my record would look huge.

The classical titles and tournaments were very enjoyable as well. But the rapid events, every once in a while, you felt, 'This might be the future of chess.' It turned out that we were probably right.

Your famous game against Aronian at Tata Steel in 2013, which included a double piece sacrifice, is one of the most beautiful games ever.
Yes, with some of my games, especially that one, people come to me and say, that game is just magical – even

more than the games in Bonn, which I like a lot, for sporting reasons as well.

The game against Aronian has this feeling of inspiration.
Yes, particularly because I had completely forgotten my preparation: I couldn't remember a single move and it looked to me that I was lost. The only preparation I remembered was that I was not lost, but why? I had to figure it out.

Chess is a difficult sport to get good at, to master. And even when you understand something, to remember it under pressure is the challenge.

Chess is a cruel sport and when I say that, I am not using the term flippantly. You can spend hours doing everything right and spoil it in one instant and there is no one to pat you on the back, there is nothing for you then. There are times when I think, 'I really hate this thing.' Of course, when the opposite happens, you feel very blessed. And that is why chess fans genuinely appreciate you because you are doing something that they can't do very easily and they respect it, they look up to it.

Are there some surreal memories in your career, like when you played Kasparov for the world championship in 1995 on top of the World Trade Center?
Yes, there are many memories like that, playing in the heart of big cities like New York. But equally on some small island, when someone recognises you: that also feels special.

Chess is a global sport. I agree that it is not popular in the same way everywhere, but it has dedicated fans everywhere and it is a language and a community that you are part of, and I have benefitted from that. The chess world is a lovely community to belong to.

I am recognised most in India and the fact that a chess player can have that status is special, but it is a global sport and it is nice to be recognised in many places, to have someone come and say, 'I want to take a photo with you.' Those are the most touching moments. It is clear that someone really put themselves out and that is the moment when you stop thinking of chess as only a sport and you think, 'Maybe it is the beauty – they are not able to play at my level and that is what they appreciate.' It could be that they saw my flag next to me and they want me to win and it means a lot to them.

Sport gives you these moments and it is often the fans who are more excited than the players themselves. For them, it can very easily fall into the category of a job, but for fans, they will enjoy and cherish it for a long time. Time and again I find that something I did years ago will have more meaning for someone else than it has for me.

What would you say to people about your career?
I do acknowledge that Sultan Khan and Manual Aaron were there before me [Khan was a brilliant player from the Punjab region of what is today Pakistan, who won three British championships in four years and beat some of the world's best players during his brief career before going back home and ostensibly giving up competitive chess; Aaron was the strongest player in India for decades, winning the national title nine times between 1959 and 1981], but more than anyone I revived the game of chess in its ancestral homeland and, to be honest, it was single-handed. From 1987 or 1990, when I broke into the top 10, until [Dommaraju] Gukesh overtook me and became no. 8 in the world in 2023, there was not a single other Indian in the top 10.

I am a five-time world champion and I was also the main reason for the resurgence of chess in India – that is enough.

How does it feel to see chess coming alive in the country where it was born and to realise that you are the inspiration for that?
I actually realise that in the same way that Bobby Fischer inspired a lot of people to pick up the chessboard and find out about chess. There are probably more Indian parents and youngsters than I can count who decided, 'We should try chess!'

It even goes deeper than that. I realised that I inspired the coaches who coached the coaches now coaching Praggnanandhaa [Rameshbabu Praggnanandhaa, a top-20 player aged only 18] and Gukesh – almost three generations of players who went on to coach others. There were people 10 years younger than me who learned chess in the late 1980s and early 1990s, who then went on to coach players, and after those players' careers finished, they started coaching players, and so on.

I kept chess in the newspapers for the last 30 years with my results. It could have dropped out of the public eye, but because I was there, it had some resonance; I am quite proud of that. So, I won't conjure up some false modesty. I acknowledge it – it would be silly not to.

I once read something about an album, it might have been Ray Charles or something, and some guy said, 'This album only sold 30,000 copies, but everyone who bought those 30,000 copies started a band.' I feel that in India, my role has been very similar.

I want to put it this way: I feel that I have left the game of chess in a better place than when I found it.

Interview by Dylan Loeb McClain

Acknowledgements and photo credits

Front cover: *The Thomas Crown Affair* © 1968
Metro-Goldwyn-Mayer Studios Inc. All Rights Reserved.
Courtesy of MGM Media, photo: UnitedArtists/Kobal
/Shutterstock
Steve McQueen's personality rights, publicity rights, and
trademarks containing his name are the property of
Chadwick McQueen and Molly McQueen. Licensed by
BENlabs.

pp8–9: Everett Collection Inc/Alamy Stock Photo
pp10–11: Archive Photos/Getty Images
pp12–13: mptv/eyevine
pp14–15: mptv/eyevine
p16: ullstein bild/Getty Images
p17: Everett Collection Inc/Alamy Stock Photo
p19: Pictorial Press Ltd/Alamy Stock Photo
p20: Photo 12/Alamy Stock Photo
p21: Trinity Mirror/Mirrorpix/Alamy Stock Photo
p22: Courtesy Jimmy Scalia Archives
p23: Allstar Picture Library Ltd/Alamy Stock
p24: Bill Waterson/Alamy Stock Photo
p25: Silver Screen Collection/Getty Images
p26: Interfoto/Alamy Stock Photo
p27: *What's New Pussycat* © 1965 Metro-Goldwyn-
Mayer Studios Inc. All Rights Reserved. Courtesy of MGM
Media Licensing, photo: United Artists/Kobal/
Shutterstock
p28: Everett Collection Inc/Alamy Stock Photo
p29: akg-images/Mondadori Portfolio
pp30–31: Gordon Parks/The LIFE Picture Collection/
Shutterstock
p32: Everett Collection Inc/Alamy Stock Photo
p33: *From Russia with Love* © 1963 Danjaq, LLC and
Metro-Goldwyn-Mayer Studios Inc. and related James
Bond Trademarks, TM Danjaq. All Rights Reserved.
Courtesy of Eon Productions and Metro-Goldwyn-Mayer
Studios
p34: *The Thomas Crown Affair* © 1968 Metro-Goldwyn-
Mayer Studios Inc. All Rights Reserved. Courtesy of MGM
Media Licensing, photo: Michael Ochs Archives/Getty
Images
p35: *The Thomas Crown Affair* © 1968 Metro-Goldwyn-
Mayer Studios Inc. All Rights Reserved. Courtesy of MGM
Media Licensing, photo: Everett Collection Inc/Alamy
Stock Photo
pp36–37: Everett Collection Inc/Alamy Stock Photo
p38: Universal/Kobal/Shutterstock
p39: Philippe Le Tellier/Paris Match/Getty Images
p40: *Dr. Strangelove Or: How I Learned To Stop Worrying
And Love The Bomb* © 1963, renewed 1991 Columbia
Pictures Industries, Inc. All Rights Reserved. Courtesy of
Columbia Pictures, photo with thanks to the SK Film
Archive LLC, Warner Bros. and University of the Arts
London
p41: Collection Christophel/Alamy Stock Photo
p42: Joe Shere/mptv/eyevine
p43: Bettmann/Getty Images

p44: Beatles Book Photo Library
p45: Photograph by Daniel Kramer, Camera Press
London
p46: © Iconic Images/Terry O'Neill
p47: Bill Ray/The LIFE Picture Collection/Shutterstock
p49: Charles 'Teenie' Harris/Carnegie Museum of
Art/Getty Images
pp50–51: Gerard Gery/Paris Match/Getty Images
pp52–53: Pictorial Press Ltd/Alamy Stock Photo
p55: © Estate Brassaï - RMN-Grand Palais, photo: RMN-
Grand Palais/Dist. Photo SCALA, Florence
p56: René Maltête/Gamma-Rapho/Getty Images
p57: René Magritte, *The Giant (Paul Nougé)*, 1937,
Gelatin silver print, 8.1 x 5.2 cm (3 ³⁄₁₆ x 2 ¹⁄₁₆ in.), The
J. Paul Getty Museum, Los Angeles, © ADAGP, Paris and
DACS, London 2023
p58: Philadelphia Musuem of Art, 125th Anniversary
Acquisition. The Lynne and Harold Honickman Gift of the
Julien Levy Collection, 2001, Accession number 2001-62-
150, © ADAGP, Paris and DACS, London 2023
p59: Courtesy Max Ernst Museum, Bruhl des LVR,
© ADAGP, Paris and DACS, London 2023
p60: Pat English/The LIFE Picture Collection/
Shutterstock
p61: Courtesy of the Robert Motherwell Papers, Dedalus
Foundation Archives
p62: Digital image, The Museum of Modern Art, New
York/Scala, Florence
p63: © Michel Sima/Bridgeman Images, chess set © Man
Ray 2015 Trust/DACS, London 2023
p64: Smithsonian's National Portrait Gallery, © Estate of
Arnold T. Rosenberg
p65: © Philippe Halsman/Magnum Photos
pp66–67: Copyright Estate of Julian Wasser, Courtesy of
Craig Krull Gallery
pp68–69: Photographs by Eldon Garnet
p70: Robert Doisneau/Gamma-Rapho/Getty Images,
© ADAGP, Paris and DACS, London 2023
p71: Photograph by J. Kasmin, Camera Press London
p72: Carl Mydans/The LIFE Picture Collection/
Shutterstock
p73: © Philippe Halsman/Magnum Photos
p74: Peter Stackpole/The LIFE Picture Collection/
Shutterstock
p75: Hulton-Deutsch Collection/Corbis/Getty Images
p76: Zip Lexing/ Alamy Stock Photo
p77: Karl Bulla/ullstein bild/Getty Images
p78: Pastpix/TopFoto
p79: H. F. Davis/Topical Press Agency/Getty Images
p80: ullstein bild/Getty Images
p81: © Velikzhanin Leonid/TASS/Mary Evans
p82: Photo: Europeana
p83t: Photo: Yuriy Somov, Sputnik
p83b: Photo: A. Ekekyan, Sputnik
p84: Wil Blanche/Sports Illustrated/Getty Images
p85: John G. Zimmerman/Sports Illustrated/Getty
Images

Published in 2024 by FUEL in association with World Chess

Murray & Sorrell FUEL Ltd
FUEL Design & Publishing
33 Fournier Street
London E1 6QE

fuel-design.com

Edited and designed by: FUEL

Picture research: Sophie Hartley

Text: Dylan Loeb McClain

From World Chess: Ilya Merenzon, Matvey Shekhovtsov,
Nadia Panteleeva

Special thanks to International Chess Federation:
Dana Reizniece-Ozola, Aleksandr Martynov

Kasparov v. Karpov by Martin Amis is published with kind
permission from Penguin Random House.

Distribution by Thames & Hudson / D. A. P.
ISBN: 978-1-7398878-6-5
Printed in China